Literacy, Power, and Democracy in Mozambique

Conflict and Social Change Series

Series Editors
Scott Whiteford and William Derman
Michigan State University

Literacy, Power, and Democracy in Mozambique: The Governance of Learning from Colonization to the Present, Judith Marshall

Computing Myths, Class Realities: An Ethnography of Technology and Working People in Sheffield, England, David Hakken with Barbara Andrews

The Culture of Protest: Religious Activism and the U.S. Sanctuary Movement, Susan Bibler Coutin

Gender, Sickness, and Healing in Rural Egypt: Ethnography in Historical Context, Soheir A. Morsy

Life Is a Little Better: Redistribution as a Development Strategy in Nadur Village, Kerala, Richard W. Franke

¡Óigame! ¡Óigame! Struggle and Social Change in a Nicaraguan Urban Community, Michael James Higgins and Tanya Leigh Coen

Manufacturing Against the Odds: Small-Scale Producers in an Andean City, Hans C. Buechler and Judith-Maria Buechler

The Bushman Myth: The Making of a Namibian Underclass, Robert J. Gordon

Surviving Drought and Development: Ariaal Pastoralists of Northern Kenya, Elliot Fratkin

Harvest of Want: Hunger and Food Security in Central America and Mexico, edited by Scott Whiteford and Anne E. Ferguson

Singing with Sai Baba: The Politics of Revitalization in Trinidad, Morton Klass

The Spiral Road: Change in a Chinese Village Through the Eyes of a Communist Party Leader, Huang Shu-min

FORTHCOMING

"I Am Destroying the Land!" The Political Ecology of Poverty and Environmental Destruction in Honduras, Susan C. Stonich

The Myth of the Male Breadwinner: Women and Industrialization in the Caribbean, Helen I. Safa

Literacy, Power, and Democracy in Mozambique

The Governance of Learning from Colonization to the Present

Judith Marshall

Westview Press
BOULDER • SAN FRANCISCO • OXFORD

Conflict and Social Change Series

Photographs courtesy of Sam Barnes.

Cover illustration by Jose Tangawizi.

This Westview softcover edition is printed on acid-free paper and bound in library-quality, coated covers that carry the highest rating of the National Association of State Textbook Administrators, in consultation with the Association of American Publishers and the Book Manufacturers' Institute.

Published in 1993 in the United States of America by Westview Press, Inc., 5500 Central Avenue, Boulder, Colorado 80301-2877, and in the United Kingdom by Westview Press, 36 Lonsdale Road, Summertown, Oxford OX2 7EW

Library of Congress Cataloging-in-Publication Data
Marshall, Judith, 1942–
Literacy, power and democracy in Mozambique : the governance of learning from colonization to the present / by Judith Marshall.
p. cm. — (Conflict and social change series)
Includes bibliographical references.
ISBN 0-8133-8140-1
1. Literacy—Social aspects—Mozambique—History—20th century.
2. Literacy—Political aspects—Mozambique—History—20th century.
3. Literacy programs—Mozambique—History—20th century.
I. Series.
LC158.M85M37 1993
302.2'244'09679—dc20 92-47018
CIP

Printed and bound in the United States of America

The paper used in this publication meets the requirements of the American National Standard for Permanence of Paper for Printed Library Materials Z39.48-1984.

10 9 8 7 6 5 4 3 2 1

To the women and men in Mozambique whose lives, struggles and dreams I shared -- working to build "people's power" and dismantle apartheid.

Contents

Tables and Figures

Tables

Figures

Acronyms

ABE	Adult Basic Education
AIM	Mozambique Information Agency
CEP	Popular Education Collectives
CFM	Mozambique Railway
CIM	Matola Industrial Company
DNAEA	National Directorate of Literacy and Adult Education
DNEA	National Directorate of Adult Education
DPSEM	Provincial Directorate of Statistical Services for Mozambique (colonial period)
FRELIMO	Mozambique Liberation Front
GD	Dynamizing Group
IMF	International Monetary Fund
INDE	National Institute for the Development of Education
KIEC	Kurasini International Education Centre
MONAP	Mozambique Nordic Agricultural Programme
NES	National Education System
NESAM	Nucleus of Mozambican Secondary Students
OMM	Mozambican Women's Organization
OTM	Mozambican Workers' Organization
OJM	Mozambican Youth Organization
ONP	Mozambican Teachers' Organization
PRE	Economic Recovery Programme
PRES	Social and Economic Recovery Programme
RENAMO	Mozambican National Resistance
SEE	External Education Service
SDA	Social Dimensions of Adjustment
UDRA	Food Branch Management Unit
UNEMO	Union of Mozambican Students
WENELA	Witwatersrand Native Labour Association

Preface

This study explores the relations between literacy and "people's power" in the context of Mozambique's project of socialist construction. It analyzes the meanings and practices of literacy for women and men in a factory setting through an ethnography of Matola Industrial Company (CIM). Literacy is understood not simply as language skills, but as the complex interplay of language meanings and practices based as much on class, race and gender as on grammar and syntax. Literacy is also understood as integrally related to state formation.

Three historical chapters explore how the CIM workers brought to the classroom social constructions of "schooling," of the power of literacy, and of themselves as "legitimate" -- or "illegitimate" -- users of language(s) and bearers of knowledge. These constructions were shaped under Portuguese colonialism, where schooling was signalled as the way to bridge the distance between "savage" and "civilized" but which worked to create "failure" instead. A radical recasting of what it meant to be "illiterate" emerged in the liberated areas and in the vibrant literacy movement at independence. National literacy campaigns after 1978 further broadened access to schooling but showed a growing tendency to formalization and bureaucratization. The illiterate again became an administrative category whose "deficiencies" needed remedying rather than the fundamental resources for socialist construction.

Chapters 5-8 analyze literacy at CIM, exploring the organization of time and space for particular kinds of social communication in the classroom and on the shop floor and the impact of interlocking factory hierarchies, organized through class, race/ethnicity and gender, on literacy. Chapter 9 reflects on these experiences of literacy as indicative of fundamental problems in the broader process of socialist reconstruction, and points to contemporary signs of a renewed pedagogy of empowerment.

Judith Marshall

Acknowledgments

This study of the relations between literacy, "people's power" and state formation in Mozambique emerges from an association with the Frelimo Party and the struggle of the Mozambican people over the past two decades. The contrast between the hope and promise of Mozambique during my first visit as Oxfam-Canada representative just after independence in 1976 and the devastation today would be hard to overstate. The apartheid regime has orchestrated a slow destruction extending to every rural district, every point of economic infrastructure, and every basic service. The shallow roots of the socialist culture in the making have not stood up well to the onslaught.

I would be the last to argue that the external factors are the definitive ones. Nonetheless, at many points during the study, as I focussed critically on the way internal social relations created or denied a space for "people's power," I felt the need for a more adequate device to signal the constant impact of this all-pervasive war. Certainly during the 1978-84 period when I lived in Mozambique and during the research carried out in 1985 and 1986 for this study, I was intensely aware of how much the systematic destructive power of the apartheid regime on Mozambique's doorstep defined the parameters of the possible in constructing socialism. It is not surprising that Graca Machel, the Minister of Education, could say during the 10th Anniversary celebrations in 1985 that the main thing to celebrate was Mozambique's survival -- as a republic, and as a people's republic. Now, as a result of the 1990 constitutional amendments, it is a "people's" republic no longer.

I am indebted to a great many people for making this study possible. The Mozambican friends and colleagues who contributed to the study are far too many to name individually, but they will recognize themes of our endless discussions woven throughout the chapters. Many of these discussions about what literacy was and could be came together in the Manga project. A special acknowledgment goes to those most closely linked to Manga -- Domingos Chigarire, Helena Francisco, Carlos Fumo,

Antonio Gonçalves, Leonardo Nhantumbo, Aldovanda Martins and Teresa Veloso. The revitalization of literacy emerging from that project, and its very critical assessment of how literacy had come to be done in Mozambique, gave me encouragement not to soften the negative aspects encountered in the CIM literacy center where I did my research.

To the Ministry of Education and to the CIM staff and workers who facilitated that research, I owe a debt of enormous gratitude. Particular thanks go to the CIM literacy students and teachers themselves, the Director of Human Resources and Economy, Abdul Carimo, and the staff of the Training Department, Samuel Zita, Aurélio Tembe and Lopes Chigoiane.

One of the richest aspects of my many years of association with Mozambique and southern Africa was the community of solidarity activists who came and went, carrying on throughout an extended conversation about fundamental questions of socialist transition and people's power. I owe particular debts of gratitude to Angélica Aguilera, Sam Barnes, Julie Cliff, Lucia Echecopar, Polly Gaster, Ole Gjersted, Joe Hanlon, Kenneth Hermele, Anton Johnston, Sheila Katz, Dot Keet, Don Kossick, Denise Kouri, Jo Lee, Agneta Lind, Susan McCord, Barry Pinsky, Otto Roesch, Chris Rosene, Albie Sachs, John Saul, Pat Saul, Teresa Smart, and Stephanie Urdang.

The trip to Nicaragua and Brazil during the course of the research served to draw me once again into the center of debate and discussion about popular education. Of the old and new friends who emerged in the context of the trip and whose influence can be felt on this study, special thanks are due to Carlos Alberto Afonso, Cleyde Fernandes Afonso, Rick Arnold, Marcos Arruda, Eduardo Baez, Bev Burke, Deb Barndt, D'Arcy Martin, Malena de Montis, Maria Nakano, Herbet de Souza, Joao Francisco de Souza and Rosa Maria Torres.

I wish to acknowledge the extraordinary support, encouragement and stimulation from many colleagues, both students and staff, in the Department of Sociology in Education in OISE. Their commitment to critical social science as a useful tool in social change and their own involvement in multiple issues and struggles made it a congenial working environment, encouraging rigorous scholarship and activism simultaneously. Special thanks go to Pramela Aggarwal, Kari Dehli, Jenny Horsman, Nancy Jackson, Linzi Manicom, Judith Millen, and Alice de Wolff, with whom I met on an ongoing basis for mutual sharing of our work.

An enormous debt of gratitude, respect and affection is owed to Philip Corrigan for his extraordinary contribution to my stay at OISE. The reflections on the Mozambican experiences would have been cast in a much narrower frame without his steady flow of commentary and documentation to push back boundaries and his phenomenal capacity and availability to engage with other people's texts and lives.

Encouragement to make the study more accessible came from many sources, one being educators in South Africa, anxious to learn the lessons of their neighbours. A special thanks is due to Shirley Walters and the staff at CACE at the University of the Western Cape for including the study in their thesis series and for stimulating seminar discussions and links with literacy groups. Another special thanks is due to Naomi Reimer for her work in formatting.

Finally, I wish to thank my immediate family for their strong support and encouragement for my sustained contact with Africa over the years, and the many ways they have facilitated and shared in my maintaining a life rooted in two realities.

J.M.

1

Literacy: People's Power/ Assimilation of a Social Order

> When we consider the first use to which writing was put, it would seem quite clear that it was first and foremost connected with power; it was used for inventories, catalogues, censuses and instructions; in all instances, whether the aim was to keep a check on material possessions or human beings, it was the evidence of the power exercised by some men over other men and over worldly possessions.
>
> (Conversations with Levi--Strauss Quoted in Carbonnier 1969)

> Houses are houses and the more of them the better; but education is never just "education" -- it is the assimilation of a social order.
>
> (Quentin Hoare: Quoted in Hoyles 1977:35)

> . . . the collective skills and energies of workers and peasants are the major productive forces of socialist construction. What socialist construction should also make possible is the actualization of the dreams . . . the aspirations and hopes of the masses. These too are real resources for socialism.
>
> (Corrigan and Sayer 1984:48)

"Literacy," whether in scholarly texts, policy documents or as "common sense" knowledge, tends often to be taken as an unqualified good, a mark of individual advancement and broader social progress. There are common day-to-day assumptions at work about what it means to be literate -- employable, integrated into society, able to cope with work and family, having access to books and therefore knowledge. There are equally strong assumptions at work about the "pathology" of being illiterate -- marginality, incompetence, deprivation, being a ward of society. Economic backwardness, unemployment and technological redundancy are laid at the feet of illiteracy. Conversely literacy skills are signalled as the key to higher productivity, stable family life, competence in consumer society and informed political action at the ballot box. Literacy rates are also taken to be meaningful indicators for measuring a Third World nation's readiness for "development."

Built into this conceptualization of literacy is a positivist vision of human evolution, unfolding through the centuries, catching up "backward" nations into an inexorable process of "modernization." There is a "developmentalist" logic built in, an implicit assumption that the growth of mass literacy that took place in the northern hemisphere will now inexorably reach the mainly southern countries making up the "Third World." This concept of literacy has also tended to be adopted uncritically by Third World leaders themselves over the post several decades. Third World policy makers, whatever path for development they have espoused, have placed an exaggerated amount of faith in the power of mass schooling. They have seen in literacy the promise of an end to backwardness and marginalization, a pathway to modernity and economic development.

As Quentin Hoare has pointed out, however, education must be distinguished from other social services, such as housing or health care. While these can be treated as "goods" to be shared more equally and increased in purely quantitative ways, there is a very special ambiguity attached to education:

> For on the one hand, it represents a vital human *need* -- common to all societies and all people in some form, and as basic as subsistence or shelter. On the other hand, it is a fundamental component of the power structure in any society -- the means whereby assent is secured to the values and privileges of the dominant class. Education, in fact, is the point at which vital needs and power structure immediately intersect. It is thus never neutral or "innocent," as the other social services can sometimes be.
>
> (Quoted in Hoyles 1977:35)

A more critical investigation of the path of mass literacy in western social development, while it in no way denies the liberating power of literacy, shows literacy also to have been a powerful force for broader processes of social control in the emerging capitalist nation states. Mass literacy, the imposition of a language, a way of speaking it, a privileging of certain kinds of experience into knowledge, a regulation of texts, certification for mastery of those texts and not others within a hierarchical system of state-sponsored schooling -- all these have been integral to new ways of containment and subordination. Behind the social construction of literacy which posits literacy as an unqualified good, and the more of it the better, lies a history of state-sponsored public schooling that has more to do with large-scale projects of moral regulation and social control than with individual or collective liberation.

Tracing the path in European and later North American social development from the oral culture of the medieval era to the restricted literacy of the early modern era to the mass literacy that emerged from about 1930 onwards, one finds a gradual, uneven, and at times contradictory process. The shift from oral to literate modes took place over a lengthy period during which the two modes interpenetrated so deeply that any idea of one flourishing without the other was unthinkable. They were also interconnected as differentiation. Twelfth century charters were addressed to "all those seeing and hearing these letters" and often ended with "good-bye." By the thirteenth century they were already more impersonally cast with such phrases as "Let all persons present and future know." A similar change took place with regard to wills which, until the thirteenth century, had been basically oral acts, even when recorded, depending on spoken wishes heard by witnesses. By the end of the thirteenth century, the validity of the will depended on its being in the correct documentary form and not on verbal assurances of witnesses. Thus the shift from memory to written records proceeded gradually. (Clanchy 1979)

If in the middle ages in Europe, there was a period when the powers of the oral and the written were intermingled so that the binding power of texts and signatures was doubly guaranteed by the reverence shown to the physical form of the text, this could also be found in early missionary accounts of their activities. Studies of the first contacts between missionaries and Africans in southern Africa by Jean Comaroff point to this appropriation of the power of the word through actions involving the actual texts.

> Like the power to transform the world through ritual, literacy seems to have been understood less as an acquired skill than an internal mystical power: the treatment of the body with the written word and newsprint was later to become a regular part of Tswana healing, especially among the illiterate poor.
>
> (Comaroff 1985:203)

There are innumerable problems in giving precise accounts of literacy in the middle ages, as Michael Clanchy's very illuminating work makes clear. One is that the very accounts of the period use the terms of "litteratus-illiteratus" and "clericus-laicus" in very particular ways. These cannot be translated into their modern equivalents as a basis for determining whether knights listed as "litteratus" or various groupings listed as "clericus" were literate in the twentieth century sense of that word. (Clanchy 1979)

Another difficulty is the imposition of contemporary assumptions about coupling reading and writing, and about a close association between literacy and spoken languages. Writing was a skill quite distinct from reading and reading was more often linked with speaking aloud than with eyeing script. The variety of written and spoken languages added their own complexities.

> The variety also obstructed the rapid spread of literacy, in the modern sense of the majority of people acquiring a minimal capacity to read and write the language they spoke. Elementary instruction in reading and writing started in Latin because that was the traditional language of literacy and sacred Scripture. Those who wrote in vernaculars, whether in Middle English or French, were building novel and complex structures on a foundation of Latin. Neither Middle English nor French was sufficiently standardized . . . to become the basis of elementary instruction in reading and writing until well after 1380. If a person in Edward I's reign had learned to read in English or French but not in Latin, he could never become litteratus nor could he have understood the majority of writings circulating in his own life-time because these were in Latin. English and French had to have become common business and literary languages before it was practical or desirable to initiate literate skills with them.
> (Clanchy 1979:22,23)

The powerful institutions of the church and the legal professions had tended to maintain literacy as their preserve during the middle ages. During the mercantile era that preceded the emergence of capitalism, however, literacy was already a vital tool for merchants and navigators. (Hoyles 1977:17) The invention of the printing press at the end of the fifteenth century clearly brought about further dramatic changes.

The Printing Press -- and a World Mediated by Texts

The pioneering work of Elizabeth Eisenstein in *The Printing Press as an Agent of Change* (Eisenstein 1979) begins to document this little acknowledged revolution in communications and the relationships between the communications shift and other developments associated with the transition from medieval to early modern times. While Eisenstein admits readily to printing's role in spurring the spread of literacy, her main project is to trace not the shift from oral to literate culture, but from one kind of literate culture to another. The transition from scribal culture to print culture created a literate environment of a totally different nature.

Eisenstein makes a set of thought-provoking conjectures on the impact of printing on western society and thought. (Eisenstein 1981) She singles out four major areas: dissemination, standardization, editing and preservation. First, the mere fact of dissemination and access provided by printed texts ended the traditions of wandering scholars travelling to consult texts or commentators spending a life-time on single texts. Suddenly texts were available. The first century of printing was characterized by intellectual ferment as new combinations of old ideas suddenly made accessible resulted in entirely new systems of thought.

The impact of standardization was profound. Textually mediated representations of experience were available for the first time. Some of the most important were the pictorial statements -- maps, charts, diagrams, the uniform reference guides such as calendars, thesauruses, dictionaries, the regular systems of notation -- grammatical, mathematical, musical. All of these prefigured major developments in science and bureaucracy, whole ways of viewing day-to-day experience and mediating that experience through texts.

Similarly, the printing conventions having to do with editing and reorganizing texts led to procedures of codifying, clarifying, cataloguing. Built-in aids to the reader appeared -- title pages, graduated type, running heads, footnotes, tables of contents -- all of which gave new access and new ways of viewing reality. From this came rational systems, new ways of bureaucratic organization, ranging from law books offering legal precedents and the beginnings of a codified legal system to new views of history, science and literature.

The very fact of preservation had radical implications for patterns of cultural and institutional change. The energies devoted by scribal culture to seeking out and re-copying documents gave way to fixed bodies of literature widely disseminated, a textually mediated sense of self and world beginning to emerge, the beginning of the modern knowledge industry. All of this had huge ramifications for state formation.

> Studies of dynastic consolidation and/or of nationalism might well devote more space to the advent of printing. Typography arrested linguistic drift, enriched as well as standardized vernaculars, and paved the way for the more deliberate purification and codification of all European languages. Randomly patterned, sixteenth-century type-casting largely determined the subsequent elaboration of national mythologies on the part of certain separate groups with multilingual dynastic states. The duplication of vernacular primers and translations contributed in other ways to nationalism. A "mother's" tongue learned "naturally" at home would be

> reinforced by inculcation of a homogenized print-made language mastered while still young when learning to read. During the most impressionable years of childhood, the eye would first see a more standardized version of what the ear heard. Particularly after grammar schools gave primary instruction on reading by using vernacular instead of Latin readers, linguistic "roots" and rootedness in one's homeland would be entangled.
> (Eisenstein 1979:61/62)

Ivan Illich puts forward the same line of argument in the examination of "vernacular values" in his provocative study, *Shadow Work.* (Illich 1981) Illich explores the moment in fifteenth century Europe when women and men were taken from their immediate world which included ready communicative competence in multiple local languages to a standardization of language and text. He argues that whatever power for domination was gained by Queen Isabella of Spain in authorizing the famed voyage of Christopher Columbus in 1492 pales into insignificance against the power for domination gained through another project which gained royal support at the time. This was Elio Antonio de Nibrija's first Spanish grammar.

Literacy and Protestantism

Mass literacy proceeded, then, through a slow process of putting down roots, a trajectory not to be confused with the history of schooling, for in fact the two did not proceed at the same rate nor were they subject to the same gravitational pulls. Of these, there were many -- the printing press, Protestantism and the emergence of capitalism all being fundamental ones.

The restricted literacy of the middle ages religion in which the clergy were sole depositees and interpreters and preached to the ignorant masses gave way to Protestantism. This meant not only mass access to the "book" but differing interpretations of it -- and entry to a whole new age. In some countries state and church combined to regulate literacy. In Sweden, for example, literacy and religion were integrally linked with successful certification in literacy necessary by the local priest as a prerequisite for marriage. Nor was this evangelical zeal nationally bounded. The Protestant missionary societies that formed in the nineteenth century took their preoccupation with individual, direct access to scripture to the far corners of the earth, and encouraged a vast enterprise of codifying local languages and providing translations of scripture into multiple tongues.

> The great religions of the Book, Protestantism, soon to be joined by the Counter Reformation, could probably have made do with a modicum of reading ability on the part of the faithful. . . . But the market economy, backed by and relying upon the machinery of the centralized state, expanded the role of writing as a necessary condition of modernization.
>
> (Furet & Ozouf 1977 in Graff 1981:216/217)

Literacy and Economic Development: Which Comes First?

The detailed history of literacy in Europe and North America from the fifteenth to nineteenth centuries has only begun to be reconstructed.[1] An important theme of these studies is a re-examination of the link between literacy and economic development. While there is a good deal of debate about ways of measuring literacy and its actual incidence (Stone 1969; Sanderson 1972; Cressy 1980), none of the detailed case studies of literacy bears out the widely held notion of a direct, causal link between literacy and economic growth. Yet this argument continues to be held dear by the human capital school of education (Blaug 1970) and those espousing theories for Third World development based on minimum literacy levels for economic take-off (Anderson and Bowman 1965), "modernization" (Almond 1960; Apter 1965), "stages of economic growth" (Rostow 1960), or the 1990 World Bank rediscovery of the social dimensions of adjustment.

In England in the late eighteenth and nineteenth centuries, schools were specialized institutions for instruction in literacy skills. Few attended regularly or stayed longer than a year or two. Practical skills were learned through households and work groups as part of a broad pattern of socialization of which apprenticeship is a well-known but formalized example.

> Thus insofar as economic growth in this period entailed the acquisition of a large number of practical skills by a growing proportion of the population, developments in literacy and education were probably irrelevant to it. And, insofar as economic growth resulted from the increased productivity of labor brought about by the shift from domestic to factory production, literacy and education were also probably irrelevant, for many of the new industrial occupations recruited a largely illiterate work force, so much so that many industrial communities were markedly more illiterate than their neighbours.
>
> (Schofield 1973:213)

There is little basis historically, then, for positing universal relationships between literacy and economic growth. In fact, for England, at least, the usual causal relationships between literacy and economic growth might profitably be reversed. The reduction in illiteracy in nineteenth century England would appear more as a cultural change brought about by economic growth than as one of the causes of growth. (Graff 1981:213)

What is clear from these studies of literacy in western social development is the multiplicity of experiences of mass literacy and the complexity of the inter-relationships between literacy and other social processes. These include language codification, the printing press, the Protestant reformation, industrialization and urbanization, to name but a few. We can anticipate equally complex and inter-related factors shaping the process of literacy for the societies of Africa, Asia and Latin America, drawn into the vortex of western social development in subordinate roles through colonialism and expansion of the capitalist system.

Literacy as State Formation

Current debates on the conceptualization of "state" and "state formation" are highly suggestive for new ways to think about mass literacy. Current conceptualizations of the state move away from seeing the state as the long arm of the ruling class, a straightforward reflex of whatever social class holds economic power. They also reject the crude base-superstructure interpretation of society so prevalent within the Marxist tradition, with a neat division into an "economic base," with its reality derived from the material, over against another order of reality or "superstructure," the realm of the state, along with religion, education, the media and culture.[2]

The state can perhaps better be understood as neither instrumental nor superstructural but as relational. State formation understood in this way becomes the shifting constellation of forms and institutions and practices that work together to organize a particular social order. While instruments of naked control and coercion form part of that repertoire, the more interesting state forms are those less often identified. Production in a given society is organized through a set of economic *and social* relations. The social relations of production are formed by the seemingly neutral sets of institutions for ordering the day to day running of society, shaping subjectivities and constructing a social and moral order such as bureaucracies, legislation, the media and education systems. They include the "official" accounts of events and history, the working up of representations of past experience in ways that organize time and space, creating political subjects with a particular sense of identity as community or nation.[3]

The state, then, is best understood as an ideological project. (Abrams 1988) Its extensive bases of power are located not just in the organization of production but in the richly variegated texture of moral, cultural and habitual forms and institutions. There is an ongoing process of structuring at any given historical moment to legitimize, de-legitimize and re-legitimize a given social order.

In tracing out the development of state forms under capitalism, the questions of language, literacy and textually mediated forms of governance are fundamental. From a social world characterized by face to face contact with oral accounts of direct experience in multiple mother tongues came a movement towards forms of textually mediated experience in standardized language forms. The role of printing was central to this process of creating or breaking down a sense of "national" consciousness.

> Printing "preserved and codified, sometimes even created" certain vernaculars. Its absence during the sixteenth century among small linguistic groups "demonstrably led" to the disappearance or exclusion of their vernaculars from the realm of literature. Its presence among similar groups in the same century ensured the possibility of intermittent revivals or continued expansion. Having fortified language walls between one group and another, printers homogenized what was within them, breaking down minor differences, standardizing idioms for millions of writers and readers, assigning a peripheral role to provincial dialects. The preservation of a given literary language often depended on whether or not a few vernacular primers, catechisms or Bibles happened to get printed (under foreign as well as domestic auspices) in the sixteenth century. When this was the case, the subsequent expansion of a separate "national" literary culture ensued. When this did not happen, a prerequisite for budding "national" consciousness disappeared; a spoken provincial dialect was left instead.
>
> (Eisenstein 1969 quoted in Graff 1981:178)

Furet and Ozouf make the point that it is writing that truly marks the break with orality and the power of oral tradition. A new way of relating to the social and natural world is created, through an individualized, silent, internal exercise. Oral culture was public and collective; written culture was private, and personal. Such a transformation of the dominant mode of communication modified the whole social fabric, individualizing its members.

> Face to face discussions presupposes close neighbourliness, whereas the written word multiplies and standardizes information, for an intellectually individualized, geographically scattered, world. . . . What now

> underwrites inter-individual relations is no longer the immemorial utterances of old men, acting as guardians of local jurisprudence, but the dual authority of the market and the state, sealed in writing and embodied in contract and law.
>
> (Furet & Ozouf. Quoted in Graff 1981:223)

Fears of Mass Literacy

Within the emergence of capitalist society and the forms of state that create a sense of identity within it, mass literacy was clearly an important dimension. This is by no means to suggest that there were not voices pressing for a continued restriction of access to literacy to an elite. The fears against extending literacy to the masses are clearly articulated. Voices raised loudly for and against literacy raged loudly, in fact, until the first third of the nineteenth century.

There were many conservatives who feared education for the masses. Their assumption -- never actually put to the test -- was that education would make the masses resistant to back-breaking manual labour. There was fear that education would create expectations for people of going "beyond their stations," that they would come to lack respect for their betters. An end to the kind of deference reinforced by ignorance of print and communication could result in indiscipline, and even social protest along with an unwillingness to labour at subsistence levels and to remain powerless. Literacy was seen as a force that could heighten the dangers of civil strife, and even revolution, which so many feared in that Age of Revolution. Indeed in many places, literacy continued to be restricted and even systematically denied to certain sectors of the population such as slaves in the southern states of the U.S.

> This reactionary tendency, which feared schooling for the poor and working class, succumbed to the triumph of liberal progressive school promotion in the first half of the nineteenth century. Conservatives were out-argued and beaten down by sheer numbers, as well as by the facts and forces of rapid social change, the accompanying problems, and the urgent need for solutions. . . . As we can see now, the systematic and institutional provision of literacy and education for the masses formed a central element in strategies for establishing control in society. As control by traditional rank deference and the 'moral economy' were replaced by emergent class divisions, education was seen as the new social cement.
>
> (Graff 1978/9:2)

Literacy and Public Schooling

The centrality of mass literacy disseminated through state-sponsored schooling systems for creating social order and a social identity of "citizenship" is clear. Literacy seen in this way is integral to the whole process of state formation. Certainly the history of the rise of public schooling through which mass literacy became established shows clearly that literacy and increasing integration and social control have gone hand in hand, all in the context of a larger moral project.

At the point in the nineteenth century when mass education was introduced through public schooling systems, this ideological project of building a political subject was paramount in many countries of North America and Europe. Corrigan, Curtis and Lanning make this point forcefully in their article "The Political Space of Schooling:"

> Schooling was never intended to educate -- in the sense of skilling and making more knowledgeable -- more than a tiny proportion of the schooled population. The mass of the schooled population was rather to be *informed* and *transformed*. Public schooling in particular, in North America as in Europe, established itself only at the expense of well-established popular educational institutions. These "inadequate," "wretched," "miserable," "imitation," "sham" schools and the community controlled learning that went on in them were marginalized, stigmatized and destroyed by state schools. In their place states and governments sought to install "humanizing," "moralizing," and "civilizing" schools, where the "lower orders" and the "poorer sections" of the population could be "elevated." Seen more generally, schooling was situated in a far more extensive project of *civilizing* which was oriented towards "education in general" rather than to schooling as we commonly understand the latter term. "Education" and "civilization" involved, in the famous phrase, catching up and regulating "the hearts and minds" of all the lower orders (children and adults, men and women) through the ensemble of *provided* institutions which constitute modern state formation. The school, the prison, the park, the playground, the settlement house, the asylum, and other institutions were conceived by the ruling class as having an "educative tendency" for the population. They were also forms of *police.*
>
> (Corrigan, Curtis, Lanning 1987)

The extension of mass literacy in western societies, then, must be seen in the broad sweep of historical transformation that created the capitalist system. The movement from social control through monarchies, the church and ascriptive social positions gradually shifted to social control through the functions of a seemingly neutral, impersonal state. What needs to be investigated more deeply is whether and how mass literacy was essential to the exercising of power of that state, and what role literacy plays in the type of social integration established under capitalism. How did -- and does -- the constellation of institutions, forms and practices by which the ruling apparatus carries out functions of organization, regulation, administration, coordination and communication use mass literacy? The question is posed in its full complexity by the practices of the ruling apparatus of contemporary capitalist societies in the west, based as they are on textually mediated forms of social organization. Rule mediated through textual discourse is inconceivable without mass literacy. (Smith 1975, 1984, 1987)

> Our knowledge of contemporary society is to a large extent mediated to us by documents of various kinds. Very little of our knowledge of people, events, social relations and powers arises directly in our immediate experience. Factual statements in documentary form, whether as news, data, information or the like, stand in for an actuality which is not accessible. Socially organized practices of reporting and recording work upon what actually happens or has happened to create a reality in documentary form, and though they are decisive to its characters, their traces are not visible in it. . . . The construction of social phenomena in their familiar and recognizable forms as they appear to us, is in large part a product of the reporting and accounting procedures of formal organizations which in various ways provide for how the society is governed.
>
> (Smith 1973:1)

Textually mediated discourse, then, is a contemporary form of rule under capitalism.

Literacy and "Civil Society"

With the reconstruction of the history of literacy in western social formation comes a much clearer understanding of the contradictory tendencies within literacy. There is always a tension between the emancipating power of literacy and literacy as an instrument for greater social control, between literacy as a liberating tool of the popular classes and literacy as a control mechanism for preservation by an elite.

An important theme emerging from the detailed studies of the history of mass literacy is how often the forms of literacy and schooling that were established were, in fact, imposed to suppress already existent forms. At popular level there was a recognition of the power of literacy and a desire amongst the working class to become literate as a way of having a voice and greater control over their own lives.

Popular histories of England after the 1790s show ordinary people struggling to maintain grassroots organizations and desiring information, news, knowledge. There were efforts to put out working class publications. The pubs served as centres for literacy; newspapers, magazines and books were available not only for individual perusal but for public reading and discussion. Working men paid subscriptions to literary organizations and created libraries for themselves. References to discussion groups, reading groups, libraries, reading rooms and public halls abound. Reading circles were prominent aspects, then, of nineteenth century taverns, pubs and ports of call -- all part of collective forms organized by workers in a movement of "social literacy."[4] The establishment of public libraries in Britain in the middle of the nineteenth century is best understood precisely as a means of suppressing pre-existing alternatives devised by workers themselves as a means of self-education in their efforts for "social literacy." (Corrigan & Gillespie 1978; Thompson 1963, 1968; Graff 1979)

Central to the traditions of socialist construction is a vision of this kind of "social literacy," of "people's power" in a new society where women and men regain the local control and decision-making power about their own lives and communities which has been systematically taken away from them within capitalist society as it has evolved. Tracing the development of the capitalist state, it is possible to identify the moment in the eighteenth century when property relations in ancient and medieval forms were transformed and when the "state" began to appear as a distinct polity, apparently separated from the realm of the private and personal, distanced from "civil society." "Civil society," collectivities of women and men interacting directly to reproduce the things and ideas and people that made up their social world, was at this point dissolved. These face-to-face groupings of producers were individualized, their relatedness to one another now expressed as political and legal relations through "the state."[5]

State and Civil Society

This seeming distance between "state" and "civil society" is both distinctive of and crucial to the functioning of capitalism. The modern state emerged in struggles first against feudalism and later against the working class and constitutes a distinctive form of organization of class power. Its historical specificity lies precisely in its separation from "civil society." What is new is the exercise of the collective class power of the emerging bourgeoisie through a distinct policy or public arena of general interests over against which is posed a depoliticized "civil society," realm of the personal and the individual. It is these boundaries between the political and the personal, the national and the local, the general and the particular, the collective and the individual which are articulated through the modern state and which are a *sine qua non* for the reproduction of commodity production under capitalism.

The state, then, is not independent of society, but an essential form of its organization, creating political subjects through a complex repertoire of institutions, forms and agencies which serve to regulate not only class relations but all of the other social relations of production, including class, race/ethnicity, gender, age and location.[6]

> . . . State-forms are related to the social relations and conditions of specific modes of production *in their historical development*. State-forms are not related contingently and accidentally, nor are they externally related -- as when the State is considered as a coercive set of relations (e.g. 'bodies of armed men, prisons') but, rather, internally. The forms of State are facets of a given mode of producing things, as essential to reproduction as particular kinds of property or technology – to be thought of, indeed, in the same terms as cultural *eidos* and moral *ethos*. . . . In class societies, State-forms will be both involved in the coercion of the majority *and* appear (phenomenally, i.e. in immediate experience) as separate from day-to-day production. . . .
>
> (Corrigan [ed.]1980:5/6: emphasis in original)

Mass literacy is integrally linked to this ongoing process of state formation. It is a means through which the set of organizational forms, practices, agencies, institutions and documents that make up "the state" act in concert to gain purchase on women's and men's lives, creating an identification as "citizens" of a determinate time and space, political subjects with knowledge of how to decode the state's regulatory signals of acceptable parameters of how to "be" and "do."

Access to literacy is, of course, differentially experienced. Literacy can by no means be reduced to a set of language skills, with no account taken of the social relations in which these skills are embedded and embodied as prevailing discursive practices. By discursive practices I refer to social relationships characterized by a common domain of language, symbolic representations and practices through which social existence is organized, and through which are mediated both an internal sense of belonging and an outward sense of being "other."

Social life is opened up to regulatory practices through the establishment of textually mediated discourse. People are worked up as social categories such as "battered women," "single parents," "illiterate" and treated as administrative categories, their differences homogenized into one common client identity by bureaucracies and ruling institutions. This opening up of social life to regulatory practices is accomplished through working up the features of a society in such a way that major areas of social life -- sexuality, activities of work and leisure, family -- become objects of socially organized discursive practices. Ruling institutions regulate women's and men's lives in this way. (Smith 1987)

The social construction of subjectivities organized through class, gender, race/ethnicity, age and location, then, include differentiated senses of self as bearers of knowledge, and legitimate participants in particular discursive practices. The very language chosen (or imposed) and the illiterates' perception of access to -- or marginalization from -- particular discursive practices as either desirable or threatening is experienced from a determinate position within a set of knowledge and power relations.[7]

Voice in Socialist Construction

"People's power," the experience of genuine popular democracy allowing women and men new forms of controlling their lives in workplace, community and family has been a persistent hope and intermittent practice of socialist construction. Building socialism implies building new forms of "state" that dismantle the separation between "civil society" and "state" as it emerged to organize commodity production within capitalist society. A socialist project presupposes an end to the state forms prevalent under capitalism which systematically reflect back a misrepresentation of the subordinated sectors and their lives and use this misrepresentation as a central mechanism of social control. A socialist project implies a new capacity for the multiplicity of groupings in civil society to voice their lives, a democratic space defined by equality and participation, but also, very importantly, by diversity.

A socialist project also presupposes the creation of alternative forms of state. The new forms of state go beyond signalling ideas and images how to "be" and "do" through a party and bureaucracy, even if couched in revolutionary language of the "New Man" -- or even the "New Woman!" In other words, socialism does not mean substituting repressive patriarchal state forms with paternalistic patriarchal state forms. The paternalistic forms of the state, with styles of governance which assume the right of the powerful to speak on behalf of other subordinate groups, still rob ordinary people of their own roles as agents of social change, using their own voices, energies and creativity.

Many recent projects of socialist construction have floundered on this very point, locating the democratic subject in some kind of amorphous group concept.[8] Commitment to action on behalf of "the people," or "workers and peasants" becomes a substitute for a more resolute commitment to political pluralism, a broad bill of human rights and a radical decentralization of power. When the espousal of "collective" definitions of democracy like "leadership of workers and peasants" or even "majority rule" does not include a simultaneous commitment to local expressions of popular democracy, including individual rights of freedom of expression, association and political choice, there is a strong tendency to erode any genuine popular participation in public policy. Without the promotion of a strong civil society in which the local, with all its diversity, is richly present, even the most promising processes of social transformation tend to become vertical, routinized, substituting paternalism for a genuine practice of democracy.

Building "people's power," then, is central to socialist construction, and has power as a historic resonance even when existing practices deny it. "People's power" presupposes new forms of "social literacy" in which collective groups of women and men name and validate their day to day experiences. It presupposes a process of empowerment for these groups enabling them to claim the specificity of their diverse locations of class, race/ethnicity and gender, rather than accepting a vertical naming of a collective subject. Whatever the politics of the party actually in power, groups in civil society defend their autonomy from party and state and their claim to space to articulate their own demands on public policy.

With the establishment of genuine participatory democracy a new kind of "civil society" begins to be created, in which people know their own way round and recognize their own ways of seeing and saying as valid and communicable. Literacy becomes a process of creating rather than transmitting knowledge, in which people develop a capacity to locate themselves in their own times and spaces, and legitimate their own activities and inter-relatedness. In turn, a new kind of popular state emerges, less concerned to regulate and control, to define policies and programmes centrally, more concerned to support and coordinate expressions of democratic practice at the grassroots and guarantee spaces at local level for input into shaping public policy. The link between literacy and democratic practice, then, is fundamental.

Governance, Schooling and People's Power in Mozambique

The critical reconstruction of literacy in western social development reveals a set of broad and complex issues related to voice, power, governance and civil society. When we trace the concept of literacy in the social development of Asia, Africa and Latin America, in societies historically integrated into the orbit of the capitalist world order in subordinate roles, what continuities or discontinuities with these issues do we encounter?

Have the "illiterate" emerged as an important social category in the social regulation carried out under traditional rule? colonial rule? under post-colonial regimes? As what point(s) has literacy taken on importance as a tool for popular forces to challenge their subordinate status? To what ends? With what degree of success?

There is a need for detailed historical reconstructions of the experiences of literacy in particular societies and much more searching questions about schooling and governance in order to address these questions. In this volume, I will endeavour to reconstruct the experience of literacy in one African country, Mozambique. Mozambique was historically subjected to the "ultra-colonialism" of a particularly backward imperial power, Portugal, and to a day to day "civilizing mission" binding it inextricably into the economy and society of richer neighbouring white settler regimes of South Africa and Rhodesia, now Zimbabwe.

What is the history of interaction between oral and literate cultures in Mozambique? At what point were the illiterate identified as a distinct social category and why? How did social regulation of the "illiterate take place under the rule of a backward European colonial power like Portugal? How did it change within the socialist project of FRELIMO, the liberation movement that fought a decade-long war to win national independence in 1975? At what points was literacy an important tool for institutions of "people's power" at local level? How was literacy organized nationally? What did the national literacy programmes replace?

My own connection with literacy in Mozambique began in 1976, when I travelled to the, then, newly independent country and visited local institutions of "people's power," including literacy centres. The connection was consolidated during the 1978-86 period when I worked in the literacy department of the Ministry of Education.

The women and men doing literacy classes after Mozambique became independent in 1975 made sense of what illiteracy meant in particular ways. They brought to literacy a social knowledge of how to "do school." They also had a socially constructed notion of what the classification of "illiterate" meant. Most of them were in the 25-45 age range and had grown up in rural districts of southern Mozambique. Not even the most remote village social system was immune from the impact of colonial institutions that worked to shape identity as "indigenous." The repertoire of the colonial state's forms to control social life included an ongoing and constantly changing process of regulating class, race/ethnicity, gender, age and location. The schooling system set up by colonialism was on of the key institutions in this process.

In Chapter 2, I will locate the world of literacy learners and teachers in a workplace literacy centre, Companhia Industrial de Matola, CIM. To understand what meanings the women and men at CIM attached to literacy and what feelings they brought to the classroom about themselves as illiterates or potential learners, I will trace out the social construction of illiteracy under colonialism in Chapter 3. I will look at how the concept of "illiterate" was worked up as an administrative category, embedded within a larger discourse turning on the moral project of civilizing the "indigenous." I will analyze how this project of formalizing the distance between the "civilized" and the "savage" relates to the need to regulate flows of cheap labour for the expanding mining economy of South Africa. In Chapter 4, I will look at the role of the colonial schooling system in that moral project, exploring it as an instrument to create failure rather than success in schooling. In Chapter 5, I will look at the radical recasting at independence of what it meant to be illiterate, and the spontaneous movement of self-education that emerged. This will include examination of the state-sponsored literacy campaigns introduced in 1978 and their impact on the popular forms of literacy in existence. I will also examine the way literacy tended to be formalized, reducing the illiterate to an administrative category rather than the human resources for socialist construction.

In Chapters 6-8, I will study the micro-world of literacy for the women and men CIM. This will included how the women and men in that factory made sense of their own experience of literacy and illiteracy, and made choices about what they could hope to accomplish through the factory literacy programme.

In Chapter 6, I will focus on the organization of "time" for doing literacy in a factory setting, and for researching it. I will explore the fundamental tensions between time for schooling and time for production in workplace literacy. I will also explore how finding "time" for literacy became even more complex with the war and deep economic crisis which forced urban wage earners to improvise "informal" economic activities in order to survive.

In Chapter 7, I will look at the literacy centre as a "space" for particular kinds of social communication that include the imposition of a language, a way to speak it, and a set of texts defining the contents of what was to be read, written and said. I will show how all of these were locked into a particular process of evaluation based on an annual national exam that served to validate transmission of knowledge and rote learning rather than social communication and creation of knowledge.

In Chapter 8, I will look at the interlocking hierarchies organized through class, race/ethnicity, and gender in which the literacy students and teachers lives were located, and how those subordinated positions impacted on the literacy centre.

In Chapter 9, I will analyze these experiences of literacy as indicative of fundamental problems in the broader process of socialist construction. I will look at the emergence of new spaces for popular education, from the movement for revitalization of state-sponsored literacy through the Manga project to contemporary forms of community education seeking to work at popular level. To conclude, I will explore whether, in the current context of war, debt, structural adjustment and a shift to a market economy, there are openings for new practices of democracy and literacy.

From Micro to Macro

A critical examination of language, voice, people's power and state regulation within the specificity of the Mozambican experience poses issues that have relevance far beyond the borders of Mozambique. Central to the issues of literacy, whether as a tool for "people's power" or a form of social control, are the social relations of power and knowledge. There is a continuing thread of challenge to vertical relations of power and knowledge to be found, a politics of democratic participation and forms of governance that liberate grassroots groupings to name their own issues, to validate their own local experience and to make demands for resource on their own terms and in their own voices.

Looking at Africa within the global economy emerging in the 1990s, these remain the central issues. The African continent has become a marginal area in relations to a carving up of the world by the major trading blocs of a Japan-led Asia, a Germany-led Europe and a U.S.-led hemisphere of the Americas. The failure of post-colonial regimes in Africa, whether taking up capitalist or socialist alternatives, to build strong economies and societies leave the entire continent considerably weakened. If the failures of Africa's few socialist alternatives, Mozambique included, are highly touted, it is perhaps the failure of its capitalist alternatives which is even more dramatic and all-pervasive throughout the continent.

Basil Davidson, noted African historian, poses the central question for the continent as one of popular participation.

> To find a pathway round the twin alternatives of failure, the politics of success has to be a politics arising from the arenas of mass debate. Which means, in practice and result, arising from local decision.
>
> Thirty years ago and less, this was what thinkers in the mould of Amilcar Cabral and the few others like him argued in their time and place. They argued for "people's participation" in the process of politics, for "participação popular," as the high road to state legitimacy. But few listened, few took them seriously: the guiding voice from outside, then,

> was either Marxism-Leninism-Stalinism, or else it sang the charms of bountiful Free Enterprise; and one or another form of non-participation followed. but today it begins to be different. In one way or another and a variety of languages, the case for "people's participation" (however defined) is what today's really interesting African thinkers argue among themselves and to whomever else will listen.
>
> (Davidson 1992:222)

The specificity of the micro-experience of Mozambique is undeniable, from the day-to-day dramas of literacy learners and teachers in the CIM factory classrooms to Mozambique's ill-fated socialist project amidst the regional complexities of southern Africa. Equally undeniable, however, is the macro relevance of the issues emerging from this experience for other struggles for democratic practices of participation, equity and diversity.

Notes

1. A number of excellent studies have emerged in recent years. For overviews see Graff 1978/1979, 1979, 1981, 1987b; Cipolla 1969. There are also a growing number of richly detailed case studies of England (Cressy 1980; Schofield 1968, 1973; Sanderson 1972; Stone 1969), France (Judt 1979), Sweden (Johanssen 1977), the USA (Lockridge 1974) and Canada (Graff 1979).

2. The crude base-superstructure argument used by many claiming the Marxist tradition is not necessarily Marx's own way of dealing with these concepts. For Marx, the economic and social relations of production are central, the social relations already pushing for inclusion of family forms and "ideas" from the social world as fundamental factors in the shaping the relations of production. For an important re-examination of Marx's own use of these concepts see Derek Sayer's *The Violence of Abstraction: Analytic Foundation of Historical Materialism*. London: Blackwell, 1987. Other important contributions to this debate to reconceptualize the state include Corrigan(ed.) 1980; Jessop 1980, Poulantzas 1978; Corrigan, Ramsay and Sayer 1978, Corrigan & Sayer 1985, Draper 1977,78; and Sayer 1987.

3. For a fascinating account of this process in contemporary Mexico see Ana Maria Alonso. 1988. The effects of truth: re-presentations of the past and the imagining of community. *Journal of Historical Sociology* I (1) March: 33-57.

4. The concept of social literacy is taken from P. Corrigan and V. Gillespie's *Class Struggle, Social Literacy and Idle Time.* Brighton: Noyce, 1978. Corrigan and Gillespie make a fascinating study of the context into which public libraries were inserted in England, arguing that they are best understood as a means to control and contain existent collective cultural practices of the working class, namely forms of self-education through public reading in pub settings, through working class publication and distributions networks, etc. Social literacy thus has a double sense, referring on the one hand to a specificity of content and purpose according to the class circumstances within which it flourishes but also to literacy

engendering social information/formation/reformation linked to more profound social changes.

5. This is one of the important themes of Marx in his writings in the 1840s, to which, significantly, he returns in the later writings. "Civil society embraces the whole material intercourse of individuals within a definite stage of development of productive forces. It embraces the whole commercial and industrial life of a given stage, and, insofar, transcends the state and the nation, though, on the other hand again, it must assert itself in its external relations as nationality and *internally must organise itself as state*." (1846, . . . , our italics) (Quoted in Corrigan & Sayer 1981:27)

6. I am drawing heavily for this discussion of state and civil society on the work of Derek Sayer and Philip Corrigan, particularly "Revolution Against the State: the context and significance of Marx's later writings" (1987) and Corrigan (ed.) 1980.

7. Shirley Brice Heath has done a series of fascinating comparative studies of pre-literacy in middle class and immigrant families in the United States. She documents that contrast between the language usage in these settings. Young children of immigrant families tend to be shown things which they then copy, while the middle class child tends to be shown something, followed up with a verbal display of knowledge. The middle class child learns to both copy *and* name the action. Heath gives accounts of middle class toddlers' language learning which is treated as of sufficient importance to warrant interruption of the conversation of any set of adults. The mothering characteristic of middle class households means that pre-school children learn language skills for naming objects, for ordering accounts ("Tell Daddy what we did today.") and for particular orderings of time and space well before they reach school. The middle class child entering the classroom already brings to schooling a sense of self as individual, a sense of self as bearer of knowledge, and a know-how about how to "display" knowledge. Such a child brings to schooling a self-identity as a legitimate participant in particular kinds of discursive practices, all of which facilitate schooling achievements markedly different from those of children from immigrant households who bring none of this capacity to display knowledge, none of this sense of self as legitimate participants in discursive practices etc. (Lecture given at the University of Toronto, 1985) Basil Bernstein's work on class differentiation and language acquisition in England brings forward a very similar argument. (Bernstein 1973-1977)

8. A very interesting debate around democracy and civil society, is currently under way in South Africa, where an opening for democracy has occurred at a historical conjuncture when there is great ideological fluidity. For an interesting account of this debate, see "Democracy and Civil Society in South Africa: A Response to Daryl Glaser" by Patrick Fitgerald in *Review of African Political Economy*, Winter 1990, No.49:94-110.

2

The World of Workplace Literacy

> With literacy, people don't earn more -- but everything they know is in their heads. They can go anywhere, do anything, ask for what they want, enter in. When people don't know reading and writing, they are afraid.
> (Interview with Cristina Mavale) [1]

I entered the world of Mozambican literacy first in 1976, one year after independence, and visited literacy classes organized by the Organization of Mozambican Women. "People's power" was very much on the agenda. The sense of empowerment of the women in the literacy classes was palpable. The provincial OMM activists were already high from the excitement of leaving rural capitals and families for the first time, not to mention the adventure of flying to Maputo. Their literacy programme introduced them not only to new language skills but to urban factories and museums and football stadiums, all within a highly supportive context affirming new roles for women in the new Mozambique.

I returned in 1978 to take up a position in the literacy directorate, which was poised to launch a first national literacy campaign. After four months of work on planning post-literacy programmes, I was transferred to the international cooperation department from where I accompanied literacy at a distance. On my return to work in literacy in 1982, I worked with other colleagues from the DNEA (National Directorate of Adult Education) on writing and testing new teaching materials for a new national literacy programme. The sub-system of adult basic education was part of a much larger project of educational reform. The new curriculum materials were introduced throughout the country in February 1983 and for the rest of the year, I worked with a team monitoring the introduction of these new materials into various workplace literacy centres.

We concentrated on six centres in Maputo city and province, following closely all aspects of the introduction of the new curriculum. The literacy centres included agricultural cooperatives at Ilha Josina Machel, most of whose members were women, a state farm at Boane, and a sugar estate at Maragra, where literacy was organized both for the industrial workers and cane cutters. The other centres were a major food complex, CIM, an oil and soap factory down the road from CIM called FASOL and the state railway, CFM.

The literacy activities monitored included the training courses for the voluntary teachers, the activities to launch the school year, the weekly functioning of classes including both organizational and pedagogical aspects, the system of evaluation, the incentives for both learners and teachers and the broader process of mobilization for literacy. The findings from these monitoring activities were fed into a broader research project on *The Problematic of Literacy in Mozambique* carried out by INDE, the National Institute for the Development of Education. (INDE: 1984)

During 1984, the work in literacy centres included more pedagogical support. This included experimentation with teaching methods in response to problems identified in the centres monitored during 1983. Much of my work during this period was concentrated on the literacy centre at CIM.

When I returned to do my dissertation research in 1985, my hope was to concentrate on the rural agricultural cooperatives on Ilha Josina Machel. This offered the possibility of concentrated work on rural women. Already in mid-1984, however, the war being carried out by Mozambique's "contras" and their South African backers had made access difficult.[2] On my return at the end of 1985, it was completely impossible to travel by road to Ilha Josina. Clearly I would have to work in Maputo. After some efforts to work out the logistics for studying both an agricultural cooperative in the Maputo Green Zones area and CIM, I readily opted to concentrate the study on CIM.

One of the staggering moments as I settled in to work as a participant observer at CIM was the recognition of how I had come to view the "illiterate." In other analysis and writing I had done on development in Africa over the years, I had built up a perception of African peasants and city dwellers as wily and stoic survivors of all that colonial oppressors and post-colonial "developers" could heap upon them. I came to realize that in my professional work in the DNEA I had been lured into "seeing" the women and men in the literacy centres as the "clients" whose literacy needs we were going to "service" through a state-sponsored schooling programme. In stark contrast to the community-controlled "People's Schools," of the pre- and post-independence period in which the learners had had some control in running the centres through vetting teachers and fund-raising, the illiterates by the mid-1980s had become an administrative category, whose "deficiency" we were there to remedy. The illiterates were an object of top-down planning, by national, provincial and district education staff, by administrators, by factory and farm managers. Their own self-definition, their own voices, were unheard.

The 1983/84 work in the cooperatives on Ilha Josina Machel had already alerted me to some of the forces working on us to shape our perceptions of the illiterate. In contrast to the other centres monitored where we met the learners only in the classroom setting, at Ilha Josina we always stayed overnight. This provided the opportunity to meet the cooperative members in their homes and in the community as well as in the classroom.

When we met them in the cooperatives, the women offered hospitality. As weary travellers we received it gratefully, very much needing the water or the chair in the shade on offer. They jokingly invited us to join them in their work, and gave us food -- corn or pieces of cassava. They were in control. We were the needy ones. Our conversations as peppers and carrots were being weighed brought revelations -- stories of how the cooperative members had been overcharged for tractor services at the agricultural station in nearby Palmeira, and vowed to learn Portuguese in order to manage their cooperative without being cheated. There were anecdotes about how a cooperative whose president spoke Portuguese was able to guarantee supplies for her cooperative and even snag more visitors. The contrast between the silence of these women in the classroom and their liveliness in their communities and cooperatives was dramatic.

I had written up this experience for the DNEA, and talked with colleagues about how our evaluation methodology tended to reduce what we looked for to what we could measure. The rich insights offered during a late afternoon stroll with the volunteer teacher or chatting with learners as they prepared their evening meal had no place in our report forms and were invisible as data. (Marshall:1984)

Even knowing all that, however, the contrast between the limited communications in the CIM literacy classroom and the complex reality of these urban workers' lives came as a shock. The interviews revealed women and men struggling desperately to survive a prolonged war and deepening economic crisis. They were passionately concerned about their children, resourceful, inventive, funny. They lived nightly traumas bedded down in darkness in Maputo's suburbs, desperately hoping bandit attacks in the area would pass them by. Their households were swollen with family members recovering from flight from brutal attacks in rural districts. The classroom made all that resilience and resourcefulness invisible. Classes by 1985 had become very formal, following a set routine. The CIM workers were completely silenced by the classroom process. They were made stupid by literacy!

A comment from a 33 year old worker in the Silos captured it. Augusto Bernardo Maibasse had worked for six years at CIM on the basic salary of 3,300 meticais.[3] He had given up his work as a market gardener when inputs like seeds and pumps for irrigation were no longer available with the post-independence breakdown of the commercial network for rural producers.

> You could think that people like me don't do things because we don't have the brains. We do have – we think of lots of schemes. But we don't have any money.
>
> (Interview with Augusto Maibasse, February 25, 1986)

Finding my way into the micro world of the CIM learners, and understanding how they put that world together and where literacy fit in was a daunting task. It was made the more so by the complex array of forces and power relations impacting on that micro world from the larger macro context of a socialist project under siege within the vortex of southern Africa.

Tapping into the Meanings of Literacy

The evaluation research to monitor the introduction of the new adult education system had left me both perplexed and dissatisfied. We had built up fairly extensive contacts with six centres over an 18 month period, and had a capacity to encapsulate in quantitative terms the realities of these centres. We were little the wiser, however, as to what the experience of literacy actually meant for those most intimately involved, the women and men actually studying and teaching.

The monitoring project had tried to go well beyond the national evaluation indicators. These were based solely on statistical control of attendance, punctuality, and a series of diagnostic tests leading up to the final exam. Our interview forms included questions about the teachers and their training, the frequency and nature of pedagogical support visits, whether books and supplies were actually in place, and how much of the programme of studies was actually completed before people were faced with the final exam. The classroom process itself was minutely monitored, keeping track of the exact time spent on each step of the lesson, noting patterns of response, who talked and how often, whether questions from the teachers were open or closed, etc.

None of this, however, gave opportunity to discover how the women and men coming to (or avoiding) the literacy centres put their worlds together. Literacy was still too narrowly cast as a set of technical skills without any appreciation of how language and schooling had to do with taking on a whole social order. What did it mean to the women and men coming to literacy to be labelled as "illiterates?" What desires and fears did literacy arouse in them? Did they really acquire new language and mathematics skills? If so, to what use did they put them? Did they have expectations that literacy would open up spaces for them to participate in language practices heretofore inaccessible? How was this different for men and for women, for blacks and whites, for urban and rural, for old and young?

My concern to learn how those doing literacy actually understood the experience prompted a study at CIM using qualitative research methods. Doing an ethnography[4] of a workplace literacy programme implied adoption on my part of an attitude of complete ignorance of the meanings attached to literacy by the participants themselves. This was not as artificial a starting position as it might seem, despite my lengthy involvement with literacy in Mozambique. The profound silencing of the illiterate in the literacy programme combined with limited opportunities for contact with learners outside the classroom meant that, in truth, there was little known about the meanings the illiterate themselves attached to literacy. Education officials and human resource department staff had ready enough answers about learner motivation. How illiterate women and men themselves made sense of being illiterate or working at post-literacy or choosing to drop out of literacy was almost entirely undocumented.

The basic stance, then, was one of seeking out the meanings attached to literacy by the women and men at CIM. What did the new speaking, reading and writing skills promised by literacy connote for them? What worlds were accessed by the choice of Portuguese as the language of literacy -- and what worlds denied? Had their expectations of what literacy could bring remained constant over the years? How did certification fit into their personal schemes for advancement or even holding on to their jobs?

> The essential core of ethnography is this concern with the meaning of actions and events to the people we seek to understand. Some of these meanings are directly expressed in language; many are taken for granted and communicated only indirectly through word and action. But in every society people make constant use of the complex meaning systems to organize their behaviour, to understand themselves and others, and to

> make sense of the world in which they live. These systems of meaning constitute their culture; ethnography always implies a theory of culture.
> (Spradley 1980:5)

The decision to do the ethnography at CIM was in part based on the fact that in CIM, literacy was well established and actually "worked." There seemed little point doing a detailed study of literacy in a setting where the organizational and pedagogical components were so precarious that they became the "obvious" explanatory tool. There were plenty of centres with no books, no teachers, no classroom facilities, and no management support. At CIM, all of these basic components were well in place and had been for a number of years. Ostensibly it was all to the workers' advantage to make use of the facilities created for study in the work place. Yet still there were major problems with absenteeism and failures. Few people continued on into post literacy. What was the cultural knowledge, the social construction of "self," of "schooling" or "survival" that people were drawing on to organize their behaviour vis-a-vis literacy?

One set of questions had to do with how the illiterate themselves understood literacy and organized their behaviour around it, questions heightened by the monitoring of the six centres during 1983. Another driving force shaping the research was the international debate around literacy, particularly the way literacy and power were coming to be understood in the context of popular education. The issues around literacy as a force for social and political change were sharpened by my participation in an extended conversation lasting four months between Mozambican literacy workers and their counterparts in Nicaragua and Brazil mid-way through my research at CIM.

Tentative efforts to revitalize literacy had emerged in 1984. A decision was taken to set up a pilot training programme at a centre in Sofala province called Manga. Planning meetings for this venture included early identification of a vital ingredient that was missing, the trainers themselves. How to train the trainers, to build a staff team that could bring a critical vision of literacy and a commitment to training that would empower others was the question. Giving existing trainers the opportunity for exposure to other experiences of literacy and a chance to get some critical distance in order to reflect on their own practices of literacy was seen as an approach worth trying.

Two groups of trainers were set up. I joined the four trainers going to Nicaragua and Brazil, consisting of three men and a woman, from 25-29 years of age. Three had worked for the preceding 4-7 years in the provincial literacy offices, meanwhile completing their general secondary schooling at night. The fourth had gone straight through secondary schooling and had been placed in the DNEA national office upon graduation in 1982.

It was a rich and tension-fraught four months, with intensive learning going on at both named and unnamed levels.[5] Important data and critical insights were gained as we shared group life and group travel over the two months in Nicaragua, six weeks in Brazil and two weeks in Argentina as guests at the World Assembly of Adult Education. Our time to Nicaragua took us from visits to literacy classes in the most remote rural Popular Education Collectives to exchanges of experiences with counterparts in the national and provincial adult education departments. It coincided with a probing analysis by the Nicaraguans of their five years of work in popular education under the Sandinista government.

The Nicaraguan educators were highly critical of their own vertical structures. They saw an increasing tendency to formalization, to top-down programmes and directives with little room for diversity and creativity in response to the differing realities of Nicaraguan learners. The analysis of vertical structures was analyzed both with respect to the actual literacy centres i.e. teacher-student and teacher-community relations, and with respect to relations between colleagues in the various levels of the Ministry of Education.

The Mozambican educators found this framework of analysis around vertical and horizontal structures and power relations extremely suggestive as a way of looking critically at their own experiences. In Mozambique, an even more formal hierarchy of power was very much in place. António Gonçalves, one of the provincial trainers, captured it succinctly and poignantly.

> I have the feeling at home that the education programmes don't come from me. My role is just to carry out what comes from above. My ideas and initiatives can only be put into practice after discussion higher up. People like me take their ideas home to dream about because they know that their ideas can be taken up only after a very slow process of authorization from above.
>
> (Marshall 1990a:102)

For the Mozambicans, the trip provided opportunity for exposure to other ways of thinking about and doing literacy. It was also the first time they had ever been called on to explain their own experience of literacy and act as spokespersons for Mozambique.

> The trip created a space and a legitimation for questions that was very novel for the Mozambican educators. Coming out of a phase of top-down methods with superiors always ready to supply "the answer," the four Mozambicans were suddenly confronted with a world turning more on

> questions than on answers. The contacts with Nicaraguan and Brazilian educators brought a lot of opportunity for reactions to what they had seen or been told in the form of questions. In turn, there were endless questions posed to them about Mozambique. Each day's visits, each drive from one place to the next, each meal offered by a host group blended into an extended conversation about literacy and life. . . . The questions came from fellow practitioners in the field who knew all too well the difficulties in sustain literacy programmes. . . . Struggling for the right question was part of discovering that literacy was a problematic undertaking in any context, one without easy answers or "correct" solutions.
>
> (Marshall 1990a:101,102)

Participation in this extended conversation throughout Latin America provided invaluable insights about how Mozambican staff trainers experienced literacy. One of the most powerful themes that emerged was the vertical structures and the impossible situation of being in the middle of the hierarchy. The Mozambicans spoke, at times with anger and disdain, of how senior level staff simply gave directives to be executed and never stopped talking long enough to hear what was really going on on the ground. So as subordinates caught in the middle, they lived with a mixture of outward deference to their superiors and internal disdain. They recounted with hilarity how they, the junior provincial staff, at times went on inspection visits to the districts and reproduced the whole hierarchy there. They were coached by the provincial senior staff about how to act towards the district staff. "When you go there, you *are* the province. You must demand that they report how they have carried out everything we have told them to do."

The issues and insights from this trip to Latin America, then, fed powerfully into the research process. They sharpened my own insights into the importance of vertical structures in silencing both literacy learners *and* staff. This, in turn, strengthened my convictions about the importance of a research methodology that could tap into those silences.

Approaching Research in a Factory Literacy Centre

The CIM food processing complex with its high walls and landscaped garden was located in the industrial suburb of Mozambique's capital, Maputo. Matola was built up in the 1960s in the final days of Portuguese colonialism, linked to Maputo by Mozambique's only stretch of a four lane freeway. Maputo itself is really two cities. There is the "cement city" built up by the Portuguese settlers with stately drives along the Indian Ocean, charming residential areas replete with frangipani and jacaranda trees, impressive banks and shops. It has the sidewalk cafes that in colonial days lured South African tourists for prawns and "vinho verde" and the ambience of "Europe in Africa" -- along, of course, with prostitutes of all hues. It also has a magnificent railway terminal alongside the port. Behind the splendour of Portuguese colonial architecture is a history of integration into the expanding regional economy, dominated, of course, by South Africa.

In stark contrast to the cement city, however faded and run down it had become in the 1980s, was the cane city, the "canicos." Historically these were the African townships, crowded with makeshift houses of a reed called "canico," with thatch or metal sheet roofs and little sanitation. In colonial days, legislative restriction on secure land tenure in urban areas for the black population, coupled with low salaries, kept families from building permanent structures. After independence urban housing departments encouraged various development programmes. Now swollen with refugees from the countryside fleeing the South African-backed-insurgents, the cane city is teeming with people of all ages, the ragged clothing and distended bellies of the children testifying to the ongoing crisis.[6] From a city of 600,000, Maputo's numbers have swollen to over a million.

As you drive the four lane stretch from Maputo, Matola's distinctive skyline of chimneys from the cement factory and oil tanks from the refinery is visible over the salt flats. In the mid-1980s when I travelled it daily, the occasional city bus that passed was filled to overflowing. More common were the impossibly overloaded trucks nicknamed "chapa 100" (license plate 100). These carried Matola passengers for 100 meticais (local currency) instead of the three and a half meticais fare of the now depleted city bus fleet. Landcruisers filled with foreign personnel and labelled with the insignia of various "development" and "relief" agencies crowded the roads -- UNICEF, FAO, MONAP, the Nordic agricultural programme and the more recent arrivals, CARE, World Vision and US AID.

The route to CIM passed a clover leaf junction leading to a light industry zone producing a range of products from glass and footwear, to textiles and batteries. There were also heavy industries in Matola including two steel rolling mills and a railway wagon and truck factory. CIM itself, the major food complex for the southern region of Mozambique, was nestled next to PETROMOC, the oil refinery, a natural gas complex, MOCACOR, and the cement factory.

All of the industries were producing under severe difficulties because of the destabilization programme linked to South Africa's low intensity warfare strategy. Production halts for lack of spare parts or fuel or raw materials were common. Many factory managements worked out barter arrangement to keep production going, invoicing goods back and forth from one factory to another without money actually changing hands. CIM's bread and pasta, for example was traded for fuel from Petromoc.

CIM was built with Portuguese capital as a major industrial project in the 1950s. It expanded during the 1960s when the Portuguese colonies were opened up to foreign investment. In its heyday, it was a thriving international operation with offices in Lisbon, Salisbury and Johannesburg. It included a milling complex, a biscuit factory, a sweets factory, a pasta plant and a shipping and handling agency. The photographic archives at CIM gave a dramatic depiction of colonial days. Rotund Portuguese cigars in hand, pointed proudly to their expanding operations or smiled benevolently at staff Christmas parties in which black faces were conspicuously absent. Female workers, Aunt Jemima-like with their white kerchiefs, handled conveyor belts loaded with biscuits. Male workers, dramatically whitened with grain-dust, dug through mountains of wheat and maize in the basement of the silos.

CIM's expansion was part of a more generalized boom from the early 1960s to the early 1970s. The enormous expenses of expanding wars in all three of the "overseas provinces," Angola, Mozambique and Guinea Bissau, forced Portugal to seek outside financing. By mid-1965, there was a virtual "open door" investment policy, offering tax holidays, free repatriation of capital and profits, simplified procedures, and no necessary association with Portuguese companies. Promises of capital from western countries were forthcoming. When Portugal announced its five-year development plan for 1968-1973, European and American corporations were expected to provide investments valued at $171.1 million while Portugal itself was to provide only $78.5 million. The years from 1968 to 1970 saw an actual increase of much more modest proportions, however, growing from $23 million to $28.5 million, although this was offset by other forms of assistance including a credit loan of $436 million to Portugal from the United States Import-Export Bank for use of the Azores military base and military aid channelled through NATO. (Munslow 1983:47)

The main beneficiaries of the "open door" policy, however, were Mozambique's richer neighbours, South Africa and Rhodesia. By 1973, South Africa replaced Portugal as the main exporter to Mozambique, with rapidly expanding exports of machinery, spare parts, fertilizer, iron and steel, wheat, potatoes and coal. Mozambique was more and more tightly integrated into the orbit of the South African economy. Both commercial enterprises and urban real-estate expanded considerably during these years. Local production of commodities for the expanding settler community also grew, all of it integrally linked into the regional economic system dominated by South Africa. In the period immediately prior to the coup in Portugal, Mozambique derived 42 percent of its gross national product and between 50 and 60 percent of its foreign exchange earnings from the rand. (Munslow 1983:48)

> Most of the factories were modern and well organized, and the industrial sector was substantial – easily outstripping that of neighbouring Tanzania, for instance. But "development" was mainly in end-of-the-line finishing operations rather than the exploitation of Mozambique's natural resources. Thus, the steel rolling-mill brought in rolled steel billets from South Africa and rolled them into reinforcing bars, even though Mozambique has its own iron ore. The oil refinery imported all of its crude oil. The railway wagon and truck factory actually had its buying department in Johannesburg, bringing in kits of material for assembly. The tire factory (built before independence from bank-raised capital but only commissioned after independence) imported all its raw materials. The bicycle factory imported kits for assembly. The huge cement industry imported 50 percent of its raw materials. And so on down to Companhia Vinicola – the Mozambican wine company – which imported its grape concentrate, and to the corrugated galvanized roofing sheet company, which imported flat galvanized sheet. In addition, the amount of wine that could be produced and the amount of cotton that could be ginned and woven were regulated and controlled by the Portuguese to prevent production in the colonies from competing with big capital in the metropole.
>
> (Sketchley 1985:259,160)

When it became clear that the colonial system was collapsing, Portuguese settlers began to flee, some even as early as 1973. The great majority of these settlers had arrived only in the 1950s, escaping the poverty of rural Portugal. Government-sponsored settlements in the rich agricultural areas of Mozambique were an attractive alternative. From a white population of under 50,000 in 1950, the settler community grew to well over 200,000 by 1973 within a total population of about 10.5 million. The settlers. were still first generation immigrants with strong ties to Portugal. In many cases, the agricultural settlement schemes had gone badly. With the impending FRELIMO government as a complete unknown, and with rumours rife, there was a general exodus in 1976-77. More than 90 percent of the settler population left.

After independence in 1975, the new FRELIMO government carried out a programme of nationalizations. These included schools, hospitals and rentable property. Factories and commercial enterprises were not nationalized, despite regular rumours to the contrary. With the general exodus of the settler community, however, many factories were abandoned. The new FRELIMO government was thus left with a de facto state industrial sector.

In some instances, the newly formed Dynamizing Groups took charge of abandoned factories. The Dynamizing Groups were groups of activists and FRELIMO sympathizers in workplace and community set up to create a FRELIMO presence at the base. Human resources were scarce for managerial and technical staff. The young and inexperienced appointees confronted delicate situations. These included sabotage by the departing settlers and the newly hostile climate of relations with South African suppliers.

The situation of the workers was no less difficult. During the chaotic period immediately prior to independence, there were a number of strike actions resulting in substantial pay increases. These included a four day strike at CIM. Some of these pay settlements were later recognized as destabilizing tactics by the departing colonizers, happy to leave behind enterprises where there was no hope of high enough production to cover the increased wage bill. One of the first tasks of the new Minister of Labour was to respond to expectations of continued salary increases across the boards.

Production Councils had been established by the post-independence government in 1976 to enable workers to play more active roles in planning and controlling production. Their mandate was to increase production and productivity, combat sabotage, fight labour indiscipline and generally promote the social conditions of the workers, including questions of worker health and safety. Alongside the Production Councils were state-appointed administrators, but the lines of accountability between the two bodies were very unclear, the more so when the Dynamizing Group also entered the picture.

More far-sighted foreign-owned companies such as MABOR, owned by the U.S. company General Tire continued to expand production during this period. They readily established a modus vivendi with the FRELIMO government and the new forms of workers power and state presence through Dynamizing Groups, Productions Councils, and later Frelimo Party cells and the workers' organization, OTM.

The Portuguese management that stayed on in CIM, headed by a Portuguese engineer, seems to have had neither the vision nor the means to operate in this way. After 1974, no new investments were made. From 1976, the accounts department ceased to do the books. Neither maintenance nor replacement parts were guaranteed. resulting in a general run-down of factory equipment. Many technicians fled. (CIM 1985a:2,3)

The CIM management basically refused to participate in the Production Council, leaving workers to discuss the running of the factory without inputs from the management. They were even more negative to the formation of the Frelimo Party cell after the III Congress in 1977. A period of open struggle ensued. There was a complete breakdown of communication. New administrators appeared, taking no responsibility for the decisions and errors of the old ones. In response to workers' demands, particularly for salary increases, but also for improved working conditions, promises were made and not kept.

CIM was by no means the only industry undergoing major struggles. The factories taken over by the state were also experiencing enormous difficulties. The situation at neighbouring CIFEL, a steel rolling mill, tells the tale.

> Six months after its formation, the twenty-seven man Production Council at CIFEL had de facto control of the factory. But "control" is the last word to use for a situation in which electric motors were burning out daily because of lack of routine maintenance; where stock records had fallen into disuse and storerooms became disorganized dumping grounds; where production had plummeted from 44,000 tons of steel bars in 1974 to just 6,000 tons; and where, even worse, the scrap rate (the percentage of spoiled and wasted raw material) had risen from 10 percent to over 30 percent. This last point meant that the material -- steel billets -- was being imported from South Africa in 10,000-ton lots, at US$250 per ton, and nearly a third of it converted into virtually worthless scrap metal after consuming huge amounts of imported energy. And this at a time when Mozambique did not have enough foreign currency to import food and medical supplies!
>
> (Sketchley 1985:263)

The situation at CIM became so complicated by the late 1970s that an initiative was taken by some of the workers to organize a group called the "Grupo de Madodas" (elders group). This group claimed that the Frelimo Party cell was not doing anything to resolve the problems of the workers, particularly in terms of salaries. They advocated direct confrontation with the administration in the form of a strike. (CIM 1985b:3)

Given CIM's importance as a major food processing complex guaranteeing basic supplies for the entire southern region of the country, government reaction was not slow in coming. The state intervened, taking over the factory on July 17, 1980, and appointing a new management team. The new general director, Antonio Almeida Matos, was highly qualified, with university training and previous experience as National Director of External Trade. He was also made director of UDRA, a management unit for the entire food and tobacco sector. He was backed by a strong team of senior and middle management to guarantee the technical, administrative and social areas.

The new Social Services department made CIM a model of social conditions for workers. Immediate improvements were made, starting with the meal service and daily tea breaks. A small bakery was set up to provide bread for the factory workers. Other services included improvements to the day care centre and first aid post, a social fund for workers to cover loans for marriages, deaths and illnesses, a pension plan, and a school offering adult basic education during work hours. By the mid-1980s, secondary schooling at night, a workers' housing cooperative and the right to buy factory produce, i.e. virtually a second set of monthly food rations, had been added.

While the benefits package improved greatly, the salaries at CIM changed very little over the years. Between 1974 and 1987, the only group to enjoy a salary increase was women. In 1982, CIM eradicated the discriminatory policy that paid women less than men. No woman could make less than the minimum wage of 3,300 meticais after this time.

By far the majority of the students doing adult education were in the least skilled jobs in the factory as assembly line workers, handlers, cleaners, etc., earning the minimum wage. In 1985/86, the minimum wage was still 3, 300 meticais. One post-literacy student was a machine operator and earned 4,000 meticais. The assistant to the shops head, doing fourth grade, earned 6,000 meticais. A few seasoned skilled workers who had risen to positions of responsibility with the exit of the Portuguese settlers earned salaries of 10-12,000 meticais. The senior managers earned salaries in the 16-20,000 meticais range.

With the rampant black market and soaring inflation of the 1980s, urban wages were far below the poverty line. All residents of Maputo with their residence cards and work cards in order had the right to monthly rations of oil, soap, sugar, and cereals for each member of their family. The total cost of rations per person at the subsidized prices was extremely low, compatible with the low salary levels. For months on end, however, soap and oil would be missing from the monthly food-basket. Meanwhile a bottle of oil on the black market sold at 1500 meticais, half the minimum wage. Clothing and footwear were also available on the black market at even more prohibitive prices. This meant that all salaried workers were forced to complement their wages with other economic activities at nights or on week-ends. No household was complete without multiple schemes -- some more legal than others -- for survival.[7]

While the salaries remained fixed, the benefits package increased considerably after the government intervention into CIM. CIM workers received daily food and uniforms. Most workers met their own daily nutrition needs through food provided by the factory. Morning tea consisted of bread, tea and sugar, followed by a substantial hot lunch and an afternoon tea break. Those workers with children in the CIM day care also depended on the factory for nutrition needs for toddlers and under fives. The weight loss for these children during workers vacations was dramatic! CIM workers also bought CIM products at controlled prices once a month, including maize meal, pasta, animal feed and sweets. In 1985, they began to buy bread from the factory several times a week.

In addition to CIM's own products, the CIM workers also had the opportunity to buy other products through the factory, including such items as "capulanas" (African cloth), batteries for radios, clothing and food items. To my knowledge no one ever calculated the cost of these items on the parallel market or thought about them as a wage supplement, but there is no doubt that the CIM workers had far better conditions than most workers. Added to the package outlined above was a loan scheme, a collective marriage plan and a pension plan. In this way the crippling expenses of births, deaths, illnesses, marriages and old age, faced by most workers alone, were confronted with relative equanimity by the CIM workers.

Leonor Benjamim, a party activist who did clerical work in the Workshops saw it this way.

> Not all workers have the power that we do here. For example, here your husband can die and CIM will do the funeral. For marriages and deaths, CIM is beside us. When a worker dies, his widow can count on support from the factory. She receives his wages for another six months, and in this way gets time to plan her next moves. When you have a son in trouble, you can bring him for CIM to take hold of. There is a ration system outside of the factory. We also have our internal system here inside. We receive everything that is produced here. That's why we have a very tough policy on robberies. When people rob, they have to leave CIM. There is no reason for robberies. We have the right to receive things every month - maize meal, pasta, sweets, chocolate. There is no necessity to rob and workers with a conscience don't do it. These are powers that are not enjoyed in other factories. Our factory is concerned about us. It's not the same in other places.
>
> (Interview with Leonor Benjamim, January 17, 1986)

As a Frelimo Party member and activist, Leonor saw CIM as a benefactor to be counted on by a widow needing to provide for her family or a father needing to find a way for his son to study or get a job. Most other workers seemed to see their relationship to CIM mediated purely through their wages. Many lamented vociferously that they could not get contracts to return to South Africa to work, where "you can actually buy something with what you earn." In truth, as the economic crisis worsened, even the generous benefits package provided by CIM was ludicrously small in relation to family needs. The package did guarantee a disciplined workforce. Jobs at CIM helped to resolve at least some survival questions.

Schooling at CIM

Building up a strong programme of adult basic education in the factory was a high priority for the new CIM management. Sketchy as the CIM archives were, it would seem that there had been some workplace schooling even in the colonial period. Despite the climate of contestation between management and workers in the period immediately after the coup, CIM records indicate a lot of education activities for workers. In 1976, there were 247 workers registered in literacy as well as the first four years of primary schooling.

A memo from the Dynamizing Group dated June 4, 1976, gives some indications of events. In the memo, the head of the school, Carlos Jossias Nhantumbo, indicates that since May 3 the school has had permanent staff teaching. The literacy teacher has had a training course and the other teachers all have at least 6th class. A report done at the beginning of 1977, however, speaks of the lack of support from the Dynamizing Group during 1976. "Last year we had no support from the GD. It never interested itself in the literacy sector. Only the person in charge has guaranteed the running of this sector." (Report January 2, 1977)

The period from 1978 to 1979, as the crisis between workers and management increased at CIM and as the new state sponsored literacy programme was put in place, is one for which there is little or no data in

TABLE 2.1 CIM Adult Education Results 1976/1977

	1976		*1977*	
	Attend	*Pass*	*Attend*	*Pass*
Literacy	110	49	108	22 (1)*
1st class	50	42	65	17 (1)
2nd class	40	30	39	18
3rd class	25	7	69	34 (2)
4th class	22	11	28	15
Total	247	139	309	106 (4)

* Bracketed number refers to women.

Source: CIM Social Services Archives.

the CIM archives. The First National Literacy Campaign was launched in July 1978, with evaluation done only towards the end of 1979. CIM archives give a figure of 377 registered, of whom 86 did the final test, 34 of whom passed. In 1980, the year of intervention by the state, no figures are given for literacy. In 1981, the data available suggest phenomenally high attendance and virtually nobody passing. The number attending literacy according to the archives was 331 with no passes, while 377 attended adult education with only six passing! Angélica Aguilera, the Chilean cooperant who directed the Social Affairs Department, explained the situation.

> During 1981, the school director was completely incompetent. He invented a documentary reality but in fact, there were few people attending classes. That's why the documents refer to 421 illiterates, 331 attending classes and nobody passing. In adult education (4th class) for the same year the documents refer to 377 attending classes of whom 6 passed. After he left, they found lost certificates in drawers and all kinds of other irregularities. A lot of people had to take the fourth class exam again to regularize their situation and actually receive their certificate.
>
> (Field Notes, January 16, 1986)

Quite significant efforts were put into organizing conditions for the adult education programme by the new management team and CIM could justifiably be proud of its accomplishment in significantly reducing the rate of illiteracy in the factory. A special intensive course for 15 workers in lower management positions was set up at the end of 1981, and from 1982 on, impressive results were made towards eradicating illiteracy.

First Impressions

My first impressions of literacy work at CIM, the Matola Industrial Company, were vivid ones.[8] Having spent many hours in literacy centres where one strongly suspected that learners had been hastily pulled together just for the occasion of the visit, I found the CIM a treat. Here was a fully functioning, well-organized workplace literacy programme.

> . . . I went to visit classes at CIM today. I had heard that CIM was impressive but I wasn't prepared for how good it actually was. They call their literacy centre a "school". It is in a section of the old biscuit factory. The office for AEA (Literacy and Adult Education) is small but tidy and includes a library with some instruction on how to borrow books. The person in charge of AEA was energetic -- and quick to take us off to the classes. A whole impression of efficiency predominates.

> The class itself was a revelation. The workers come in with a bit of bounce -- somehow the body language seems to indicate some fairly positive feelings about literacy in CIM. The lesson itself was tremendously impressive -- literally the first time I've seen a lesson properly taught, including all the steps done with care and a lot of participation. The teacher has a very good manner with them. When they acted out the mini-dialogue, they were very shy and the women giggled but they could do it.
>
> There was a chance for some chat with them at the end. I have the impression that spoken Portuguese is no problem for the students but will have to check this out more systematically. We also chatted with the teachers at the end. What a contrast with Fasol, where the teachers seem very mechanical and bored.[9] Here they were really quite open. There seemed to be an easy informality, with Aurélio, the school director. The first year teacher, Lopes, was fairly self-possessed but Carlos seemed very shy and a bit overwhelmed with our presence. Let's see how these impressions stand up over time.
>
> (Field Notes, May 15, 1984)

Lopes taught first year at CIM, and like many other teachers we had observed, he tended to jump over one of the fundamental steps in the lesson. This was the moment of "discovery" when students were asked to create new words by putting together different combinations of syllables. The manual suggested breaking the key word down into its component parts by writing each syllable separately, showing how each was part of a syllabic family with the five vowels, and then asking students to combine these syllabic families in different ways to create new words.

Normally when the students were asked to look at the syllables on the blackboard and find different ways to combine them into new words, there was a resounding silence. Often the teachers themselves then supplied one or two, almost always exactly those given as examples in the manual. They then jumped on to the next step, obviously feeling much more in control with rote drilling of the reading passage! I suggested to Lopes that we experiment with syllable cards at the next lesson. He assented readily and I brought some along.

The body language of the students in this activity was amazing -- a sense of energy and animation in stark contrast to the passive stance habitually adopted when the teacher was the authority figure at the front of the class and the students in rows. The camera caught the liveliness of the interaction. The words literally jumped at you from the table as the syllable cards were moved about. The words shifted from the high moral tones of the literacy books to the stuff of real life. One group formed the word, "lotaria" (lottery), their weekly hope to win reprieve from grinding poverty. Another group hesitated to show us one of their words. "pita." It was a slang expression roughly equivalent to "babe."

Lopes was so enthusiastic that he created another set on his own initiative for the next syllabic family. We had found that the quickest students rapidly tended to have all the syllable cards grouped around them with the slower ones again playing passive roles. When we did it for the second time, we selected stronger students and asked them to write down the words formed by their group on a list, thus challenging them to something slightly harder and giving a chance for discovery to the others.

We wanted to encourage teachers in other centres to try this method, so I asked a national staff colleague, Sam Barnes, to take photos of the students working with the syllable cards. She spent a day at CIM and took photos of the work with syllable cards plus more general shots of the classroom, the director's office, the students and the staff. The photos were left at CIM and when I returned the next week, I was happily surprised to hear that they had been put up in the entrance to the dining hall so that all of the workers could see them. Workers clustered around them as we entered for lunch. Literacy had become visible and identified as something valuable enough to photograph. The photos were also put to good use in the nearby literacy teacher training centre in Matola, illustrating how to work with syllable cards in small groups.

The dearth of simple reading materials and the need to link themes from the literacy programme with real life situations prompted another supplementary activity, a photo-story about the factory. Sam returned to take photos of the learners in their different sections, including the Pasta Factory, the Silos and the Day Care Centre. These photos were taken to class the next week and the students spent a session working on the photo story. The photos created enormous interest. After the students had had a chance to look them all over, they each chose a photo to present. This involved standing up with the photo, identifying what part of the factory it was, who was in it and what that person was doing. After all the photos were presented, the learners worked to place them in order, showing how pasta was produced, from the arrival of wheat as the raw material to departure from the Finished Products Warehouse as sacks of flour for the city's bakeries or boxes of macaroni for the city ration system and the army. Finally they created texts to go with each photo, all of which were joined together to form a story.

There were lots of moments of emotion. When it was almost completed, Marte Francisco, a normally completely silent worker from the Day Care, protested with vehemence, "The Day Care Centre is still missing." The photos taken while the story was being prepared captured

FIGURE 2.1 Literacy as "Transmission" or "Discovery"

the enormous interest and pleasure the activity generated. Aurélio and Lopes took the initiative to put the story up on display in the dining hall. I had a few copies photocopied and left them with CIM. Unfortunately, this project coincided with the end of my work in the national office and there was not time to follow it up.

Measuring Literacy

Spending a lengthy period at CIM in 1985/6 gave me an excellent opportunity to test the strongly positive impressions from the work at CIM in 1984. Once I entered more fully into the world of the learners and analyzed the work in literacy and adult basic education over a longer time span raised, I was faced with a much more complex picture.

Measured in terms of what could be quantified, many CIM workers over the years did pass the formal requirements of primary schooling for adults. In 1976, 57 percent of the workforce, then numbering 1400, was

TABLE 2.2 CIM Literacy Results 1982-1986

Year	*Level*	*Sat*	*Passed*
1982 *	Literacy	235	153
1982	Adult education	153	41
1983 **	1st year	140	47
1983	2nd year	150	26
1983	Adult education	88	42
1984	1st year	28	18
1984	2nd year	71	57
1984	Adult education	35	16
1985	1st year	No longer offered	
1985	2nd year	21	10
1985	3rd year	27	7
1986 ***	1st year	No longer offered	
1986	2nd year	10	8
1986	3rd year	27	12

* Adult education is the post-literacy programme, meant to give the equivalent of four years of primary schooling.

** Introduction of the first year and second year programmes of the Adult Education Sub-system of the NES (National Education System) with literacy divided over two years.

*** Introduction of the third year of the NES.

Source: CIM Archives.

illiterate. A decade later only nine percent of the much reduced workforce of 631 was illiterate. (See Table 2.2) There were 421 workers still illiterate in 1981; the major efforts to organize schooling made at this time reduced the number of illiterates to 234 in 1982, 140 illiterates in 1983 and 124 illiterates in 1984. At the same time, the hiring policy meant that new illiterates were not being admitted into the factory. By 1986, the work force had stabilized at 630 and the number of illiterates had been reduced to 56, or about 9 percent. The workers who were still illiterate were for the most part in the Mill, nine of them working in the maize section and 18 in the wheat section. They were all involved in shift work which made it extremely difficult to work out a time-table for them.

While undoubtedly the larger process of closing the Biscuit Factory and streamlining production included the relocation of less skilled and usually illiterate workers to other factories, still a significant number of workers got their literacy certificates over the years. This stands in marked contrast to national rates which were reduced from 95 percent in 1974 to about 70 percent in 1980, but have tended to remain at that level during subsequent years.

On the other hand, CIM was a major factory in the capital city with an enormous concentration of both human and material resources compared to other workplaces. In 1986, it still had about 245 workers who had not completed basic primary education. Only 55 workers were enrolled in the CIM school trying to do so.

Literacy and People's Power in Mozambique

On the face of it, CIM's accomplishments in literacy were impressive. The rate of illiteracy within the factory complex had been reduced from 57 percent in 1975 to less than 6 percent ten years later. From 1981 to 1986, 309 people had passed the literacy exam with another 113 people going on to complete basic primary schooling. In addition, many CIM workers had pursued general studies and specialized training courses at higher levels. Measured simply in terms of providing access to education and credentials for further training, the CIM experience was impressive.

Measured against the broader process of social transformation and the potential of literacy as a tool in constructing a vital civil society, including greater shop floor democracy, however, some different kinds of questions have to be asked. These include the broader meanings of literacy, the link between literacy and state formation and the role of literacy in building civil society.

At CIM, this means looking at the experience of participatory democracy within the classroom itself, and the extent to which the pedagogy of literacy was a vehicle for changing relations of power and knowledge. It means examining the tensions between vertical structures in which the teacher as authority figure regulated classroom discussion around prescribed contents, albeit now replete with socialist images, over against classrooms of empowerment. To what extent did literacy challenge old hierarchies of power and knowledge, organized through class, race and gender? To what extent did literacy encourage people to create new knowledge and communicative practices out of their own experiences? It is to these questions we will now turn.

Notes

1. The data collection involved extensive interviewing, In general the informants' names have been maintained, except for the very few instances where the information given was of a sufficiently sensitive nature that it could have had repercussions for the informants. In these cases, fictitious names were used.

2. See earlier footnote on MNR activities in Mozambique. By mid 1985, MNR activities had increased considerably. Documents found when the main MNR base in the central region at Gorongosa was captured by the Mozambican army in September 1985 showed clearly how, at the very moment the South African government was negotiating the Nkomati Accord of "good neighbourliness" and "peace," in 1984, the South African Defence Forces were making promises of continued support and stockpiling supplies to RENAMO. (Ministry of Information 1985).

3. The metical (plural – meticais) was introduced to replace the escudo in 1978. It was valued officially at 42 meticais to U.S. $1.00 until February 1987 although black market rates at that time were estimated at more like 4000 meticais to the dollar. In January 1987, a first devaluation occurred as part of an IMF World Bank agreement. The 420 per cent devaluation in January 1987 has been followed by a further large devaluations and, more recently, a series of smaller devaluations. The rate in July 1991 was just over 1000 meticais to the U.S. dollar.

4. For full discussions of ethnographic research, see Spradley 1980; Lofland 1971; Glaser & Strauss 1967; Becker 1970. It would seem that this approach to research is very useful for seeing more clearly forms of ruling through state bureaucracies. The sense-making of the client groups themselves -- the sick, the illiterate, battered wives, single parents -- is often lost to view in the top-down characterization of them as recipients of a particular social service. These services become an important part of social regulation.

5. For a fuller account of the South-South exchange as such, see "Gracias, Nicaragua! Obrigado, Brazil! South-South Exchanges as an Approach to Staff Training" in *Convergence*. Vol XXIII, No.1,1990:100-107. A report of the four-month trip was done in popular form in a hands-on kit of materials called "Training for Empowerment." The kit consists a User's Guide, 3 Background Papers, 9 Activities and Tools and a Resources section. Each of the activities or tools is

something that the group found Latin Americans using in their training that seemed particularly suggestive for getting at issues relevant for Africa. The tools include role plays, games, comic books and exercise, many of them probing at the basic question of education as transmission or creation of knowledge. The first game, for example, probes the questions of knowledge. What is it? Who has it? How did they get it? Why? The kit is available through DMI, 64 Charles St. E., Toronto, Canada M4Y 1T1.

6. RENAMO, also known as Mozambique National Resistance (MNR), is a surrogate force organized, trained, supplied and financed from abroad, principally from South Africa. It was initially formed by the Rhodesian secret service in 1976, but taken over and much expanded by the South African Defence Force, SADF, at Zimbabwe's independence in 1980. RENAMO terrorist actions throughout Mozambique are part of the broader low intensity warfare being waged against Mozambique, which includes occasional commando raids by SADF units directly, ongoing RENAMO activities, economic destabilization and sophisticated disinformation campaigns both within the region of southern Africa and abroad. (Fauvet 1984; Fauvet and Gomes 1982; Hanlon 1984; Hanlon 1986; Saul(ed.) 1985; Winter 1981; Ministry of Information, Mozambique 1985).

7. For an extremely insightful discussion of the politics of survival for the popular classes in the not dissimilar circumstances of present-day Nicaragua, see Coraggio 1986 and Vilas 1986. Coraggio argues that the fluidity of the working class, the tendency for it to disintegrate into an "informal" sector with multiple activities verging on the illegal must be understood in political terms. An over-ready characterization of such tendencies as creating an "idle" or "parasitic" sector, may threaten the survival schemes of the very social classes at the heart of the popular project.

8. My arrival to do research at CIM came after a long association with Mozambique, dating back to 1972. At that time I became actively involved in information and education work in Canada about the anti-colonial struggles in Portugal's African colonies. I had the opportunity to visit the FRELIMO secondary school in Tanzania during the final phase of the armed struggle in 1974. My first visits to independent Mozambique were made in 1976 and 1977, as programme development officer for Oxfam-Canada. These visits included contact with the then current literacy projects. From 1978 to 1984, I was employed on the staff of the National Directorate of Adult Education in Mozambique under the auspices of CUSO. My first contacts with CIM were in the context of work visits as part of the training department of the national literacy staff.

The active association with the DNEA continued when, in 1985, I coordinated a four month trip to Nicaragua and Brazil and accompanied the four Mozambican educators who made the trip. The exposure to experiences of literacy in Nicaragua and Brazil was part of their preparation to work in a new pilot project in staff training for literacy and adult education at Manga. I carried out the research in the period from May 1985 to April 1986.

9. Fasol is an oil and soap factory which, like CIM, had the resources to mount a well-organized literacy programme. The visits made to Fasol by the DNEA staff did not include sustained contact over a period of time or the in-

depth interviewing with students or teachers that would have allowed us to go beyond general observations. The broad impression, however, was one of little dynamism. The one strong moment of insight I had was a walk through the factory grounds after an incredibly boring and mechanical lesson in which the young worker who had been delegated to teach asked if I would like to see where he "worked." I acquiesced with great curiosity, since I thought he "worked" in the Fasol literacy centre, where lesson preparation and teaching accounted for more than half of each day. He showed me a warehouse full of cartons of oil where his job, when he was not preparing his lessons or teaching, was to do rudimentary stock control. As far as he was concerned, that was his "job" and, I suppose, his future, whereas literacy teaching was a kind of dead end.

3

The Colonial State as Educator

> We do not believe that a rapid passage from their African superstitions to our civilization is possible. For us to have arrived where we are presently, hundreds of generations before us fought, suffered and learned, minute by minute, the intimate secrets in the fountain of life. It is impossible for them to traverse this distance of centuries in a single jump.
>
> Armindo Monteiro, Portuguese Colonial Minister,1935
> (Quoted in Isaacman & Isaacman 1983:40)

> The colonized . . . is a person without a temporal dimension. He is a person unable to locate himself historically within his society and unable to locate his society historically. . . . The lack of historical dimension is the result of a deliberate and planned action of colonialism.
>
> (Address by FRELIMO leader Sérgio Vieira
> to the Second Conference of the Ministry
> of Education and Culture, 1977[1])

"Civilizing" the "Illiterate"

The classification of people as "illiterate" in Mozambique took on resonance only at the point when the newly established colonial government set out to consolidate its control and to open up social life to regulatory and controlling practices. The educational process of relocating African people in time and space, of situating them as a people without civilization whose time began when Vasco de Gama reached their shores, whose space was that of an "overseas" province of a distant metropole, was carried out at the beginning of the present century. It was in this period that women and men in Mozambique came to be categorized as "illiterate" with the provision of state sponsored schooling signalled as remedy for this "deficiency."

This phenomenon can best be understood as part of a larger process of establishing colonial modes of governance. The need for an ideological frame situating the African population as "other," and the mechanisms to create a distance between "us," safely within the boundaries of civilization, and "them," relegated to a position outside, emerged at a point where a centralizing body, the newly established colonial government, began to establish forms of ruling. Administrative categorization of people as "illiterates" within a larger discourse of civilizing and Christianizing became the control mechanism for moving from the status of "indigenous" to that of "citizen." This administrative categorization became an important instrument for establishing control, and, indeed, for the formation of the colonial state.

Portugal itself exhibited the classic features of underdevelopment, functioning on the periphery of Europe as an exporter of raw materials and labour and an importer of finished industrial goods. In consequence, its capacity to shape its colonial holding to serve the metropolitan economy was very limited. Capital accumulation even to set up the mechanisms for colonial exploitation had to be found elsewhere. In the colonial capital of Lourenço Marques, only 27 percent of the investments in 1900 depended on Portuguese capital. It was British capital that financed the city's electrical system, trolley system and first modern port facilities, a situation not dissimilar to that of Lisbon itself. (Penvenne 1979a:3,4) The nature of the link was succinctly characterized by Portuguese historian Oliveira Martins. "People think that England is bound to look after us; but what will happen when there are no more Africas with which to pay her?" (Munslow 1983:4)

From late in the nineteenth century, it was South Africa that exerted the main economic control over Mozambique. Mozambique was tightly integrated into the southern African economic sub-system and specifically shaped as a major supplier of vitally needed cheap labour to work South Africa's vast mineral resources. It also played a key role as provider of rail and port services to land-locked Rhodesia (now Zimbabwe), Nyasaland (now Malawi) and to the gold boom territory of the Rand for which Lourenço Marques was the closest link to the sea. Until 1909, English was the language of the port in Lourenço Marques, while Beira had an English language newspaper. By 1917, customs duties and trans-shipping charges constituted the single largest source of income for Mozambique. (Isaacman & Isaacman 1983; de Brito 1980; Munslow 1983)

Portugal Establishes Control

On the eve of the scramble for the partition of Africa in 1880, after three hundred years of nominal rule, Portugal could boast only a limited influence on a few coastal settlements. Often this amounted to a token force to establish a historic claim. Even important administrative centres such as Lourenço Marques, Quelimane and Inhambane had only a few military and civilian personnel, with poor training and a propensity for smuggling and bribery. (Isaacman & Isaacman 1983 19; Penvenne 1979a:5) The schemes for colonial settlement were singularly unsuccessful. Governor Noronha described the settlers in Lourenço Marques in the 1890s as deported soldiers, "degredados," (those in disgrace, being punished by exile) and " . . . a certain number of functionaries sufficiently unfit not to find placement in the metropole." (Penvenne 1979a:5)

The diverse African societies throughout the territory were adamantly opposed to any infringement on their autonomy, each having become skilled over the centuries in working out a "modus vivendi" with the shifting demands of the European presence in their midst. In the south relations were basically those of trade up to the last quarter of the nineteenth century, with active barter of ivory, horn, skins and oilseeds in exchange for cloth, beads, hoes, firearms and alcohol. In other areas of the country, slave trading was a major activity until well after mid-century, with coastal sultanates depending on the export of captives to maintain their political and economic power. Portugal's attempts to conquer these societies were largely unsuccessful. There were important defeats for the Portuguese colonial army in the north in the 1850s. The rich and densely populated Zambezi valley region saw five unsuccessful campaigns launched by the Portuguese between 1867 and 1875.

At the Congress of Berlin in 1884-85, the Great Powers rejected Portugal's claim to Mozambique, decreeing pacification and effective control as prerequisites for recognition as a colonial power. The next 25 years brought a new militancy from Portugal and shifting and conflicting claims for territory with Britain as the Lisbon dream of a Portuguese Central Africa linking Angola and Mozambique entered into conflict with the British dream of a Cape to Cairo route.

The wars of resistance from 1885-1913 were intense, as Africans throughout Mozambique sought to evade Portuguese control. Polities ranging from the Swahili sheikdoms of the north to the Ronga chieftaincies in the south fought bitterly, knowing that Portuguese control meant harsh taxes and expropriation of land and labour. The African polities, however, were unable to create the broad-based popular opposition necessary to withstand Portugal's military superiority. Weakened by competing with each other over the slave trade and by popular insurrections mounted by subject populations resenting the daily tyrannies of Afro-Portuguese or Afro-Goan leaders in the conquest states of the Zambezi valley, the African societies were defeated. By the beginning of the twentieth century, Portuguese had effective control over the southern half of Mozambique and within the next decade, the northern part as well.[2]

With successful establishment of a colonial empire came the need to consolidate forms of rule. Out of this came an elaborate exercise to try to legitimate what, if seen openly, was unacceptable, a persuasion of ruler and ruled that the super exploitation of black labour and privileged position of white settler were based on a natural order of inferiority and superiority. Integral to it was the idea of a civilizing and Christianizing mission belonging to the Portuguese and a position outside of "civilization" in some territory of savagery and childishness for the African. The whole ideological construct turned on forms and institutions regulating race and class.

There were three distinct periods in which the two sub-metropolitan powers negotiated and re-negotiated their interests through a shifting colonial state structure. In the early colonial period (1800-1926), southern Mozambique became a labour reserve for the South African mines while the centre and north were leased to foreign charter companies. In the absence of investment capital from Portugal itself, foreign companies, mainly British, were set up by the colonial state to exploit two thirds of the country. Working in close cooperation with South African, Rhodesian and English interests, they formed states within the state and exploited with extreme cruelty, turning their territories into tax farms and migrant labour reserves.

In the middle colonial period from 1926 to 1960, the Salazar regime attempted to use the colonies in a more classic manner as sources of raw materials for the nascent industrial capitalist class that had helped to bring Salazar to power. There was an attempt to limit foreign economic influence. At times direct contradictions emerged between the demands for labour to produce export crops such as cotton and later rice over against continuing needs for labour export to neighbouring countries. Both forced labour and forced crop cultivation were intensified, and a very substantial number of Mozambicans fled into neighbouring countries. There are estimates of as many as 380,000 Mozambicans in neighbouring British Nyasaland (Malawi) by the end of the Second World War and 476,300 by 1966. There were 123,316 Mozambicans in Tanzania by 1957 and many more Mozambican refugees in Southern Rhodesia (Zimbabwe) and South Africa. (Munslow 1983:70)

In the late colonial period from 1960 to 1974, Portugal found itself faced with an armed struggle for national liberation. Unwilling to decolonize because of its inability to neo-colonize, it finally opened its doors fully to foreign investment in 1965. This resulted in a period of even closer integration with South Africa, by then a growing industrial power.

Delineating briefly the texture of the colonial state as a set of forms, institutions and practices shaping the world of the Mozambican peasant producer, we see an all-pervasive regulating power that succeeded in totally disrupting socio-economic development of village communities. There was a much more brutal and crude use of coercive powers than was characteristic of colonialism in other parts of Africa. In large measure, the excessive brutality of Portuguese colonialism was linked to Portugal's extreme weakness as a colonial power. (Anderson 1961/2)

Local Texture of the Colonial State

Two central institutions emerged at the turn of the century to regulate peasant existence and, in so doing, establish the state. These were the system of forced labour known as "chibalo," and the system of migrant labour. The first native labour code was established in 1899, and the "chibalo" system of forced labour continued in various guises up until 1961. Even prior to 1899, the colonial state had introduced a number of measures designed to force African producers off their land and into a pool of cheap labour. This labour serviced European plantations, construction and operation of the ports and roads, domestic service and the like. These measures had proved ineffective, however. Some peasants simply paid the taxes through increased cash crop production. Others sought work in the mines and farms of the neighbouring British colonies.

A Government Commission was appointed in 1899 to make recommendations concerning the development of the colony. The question of mechanisms to tap the African labour force and channel it into wage labour was already the subject of much analysis, as testimony presented to an earlier government consultation in 1891 shows clearly.

> The European worker works in order to eat, and in nearly all countries there are more hands available than local industry requires, thus develops the enslavement of labor by capital -- of the proletariat by the bourgeoisie. In Lourenço Marques, as soon as the native has [earned] enough to marry one or more women, he then has his sustenance guaranteed by the labor of his wives and the product of his own labor then goes to buy more women, several head of cattle or to get drunk on alcohol. The result is that if in Europe the worker is in reality more dependent upon the capitalist than vice versa, (and this is very clear from the total lack of results workers have been able to realize by the majority of strikes), in Lourenço

> Marques, the Europeans, commerce, government projects, the railway and port works, etc. are dependent upon black [laborers] who in their turn barely depend or do not at all depend upon whites.
>
> Therefore, if in Europe as a result of the constant abuse of labor by the capitalist, the state finds it necessary to protect the workers, in Lourenço Marques, given the reverse situation, it is incumbent upon the government to *defend the interests of the European colony* [emphasis added] which more and more becomes identified with the interests of the state. Not only is this dependency felt by the employer with casual day laborers under the guidance of salaried [white] workers, but the same situation, or yet worse, attains with servants. No binding contract with blacks is possible under the actual laws now in effect.
>
> (Quoted in Penvenne 1979a:8)

The primary conclusion of the Government Commission in 1899 was the need to regulate the African labour force.

> We need native labor, we need it in order to better the conditions of these laborers, we need it for the economy of Europe and for the progress of Africa. Our tropical Africa will not grow without the Africans. The capital needed to exploit it, and it so needs to be exploited, lies in the procurement of labour for exploitation. Abundant, cheap, solid labor . . . and this labor, given the circumstances, will never be supplied by European immigrants.
>
> (Quoted in Isaacman & Isaacman 1983:32)

António Eanes, leader of one the victorious colonial armies in 1895 and a central figure in establishing early colonial policies worked with the Government Commission. The racist perceptions underlying his actions are a matter of public record.

> It is true that the generous soul of Wilberforce has not transmigrated into my body, but I don't believe I have in me the blood of a slaver; I even feel an inner fondness for the Negro, this big child, instinctively bad like all children -- may all mothers forgive me -- though docile and sincere. I do not consider him something to be exterminated because of the necessity of expansion of the white race, although *I may believe in natural inferiority.*
>
> (Quoted in Mondlane 1983:37, underlining in original)

The language of the commission's report touches on the same racist themes, interspersed with more elevated tones, purporting the lofty purpose of promoting Africa's advancement, and carrying out Europe's civilizing mission in Africa. The coercive side, however, readily justified by race, is never entirely absent.

> The State, not only as the sovereign of semi-barbaric populations, but also as a depository of social authority, should have no scruples in *obliging* and if necessary *forcing* [emphasis the committee's] these rude Negros in Africa, these ignorant Pariahs in Asia, these half-savages from Oceania, to work, that is, to better themselves by work, to acquire through work the happiest means of existence, to civilize themselves through work. . . .
>
> (Quoted in Duffy 1959:153)

Out of this royal commission came the first native labour ordinance. The state took on itself the task of moral regulation, the right to define what constituted "idleness." The legal rationale for forced labour was encoded in article one of the 1899 labour code. "All native inhabitants of the Portuguese overseas are subject to the moral and legal obligations to seek to acquire through work those things which they lack to subsist and to improve their own social conditions. They have full liberty to choose the means through which to comply with this obligation, but if they do not comply in some way, the public authorities may force them to comply." (Quoted in Isaacman & Isaacman 1983:34)

The Portuguese undoubtedly shared the fundamental attitude towards African society depicted in the Transvaal Labour Commission report in neighbouring South Africa a few years later in 1903.

> . . . the scarcity of labour is due first and foremost to the fact that the African native tribes are, for the most part, primitive, pastoral or agricultural communities who possess exceptional facilities for the regular and full supply of their animal wants, and whose standard of economic needs is extremely low.
>
> (Ashforth 1987:75)

Forms of Rule: Inventing the "Traditional"

Commissions of inquiry have historically been important tools for social regulation and legitimation. Commissions are part of an ongoing process of state formation, the state legitimizing itself through a "display" of the work of governing for all. Through a commission of inquiry, a particular problem can be worked up, a territory of social relations constituted with boundaries of authority set up and relations of communication, coordination and accountability established.[3]

Through the Government Commission in 1899 in Mozambique, a new dispensation of labour and land came to be legitimized. Within the framework of its inquiry, the commission constructed a particular kind of knowledge with a particular claim to truth. It solicited information from certain voices and excluded others, including those of African producers themselves.

Part of what the commission accomplished was to construct the African population as "native," an administrative category situated not only as "other" but also as "deficient." Regulation of language was an important dimension of this new dispensation, with both formal and informal social controls established about language domains.

A popular song from Inhambane province, for example, mocks the settler insistence that Africans say "bom dia" (good morning) to them in Portuguese. It recounts how men from Chigombe village like Macarite and Babuane have been put in prison for failure to do so.

> Listen to the song of Chigombe village
> It's tedious saying "bom dia" all the time
> Macarite and Babuane are in prison
> Because they didn't say "bom dia"
> They had to go to Quissico to say "bom dia"
>
> Popular Chope song
> Quissico district, Inhambane province
> (Quoted in Mondlane 1983:103)

In the case of Mozambique, the concept of "native" was constituted, embedded in a reconstructed "traditional" setting. The colonial state took on a set of institutional and accountability procedures to regulate the Native's "problem" of idleness into productivity, i.e. permanent availability as cheap labour for the colonial state. In Mozambique, where there were few voices of liberal dissent from the metropole to restrain the heavy hand of state coercion, the work of the commission to legitimize forced labour was almost superfluous. In neighbouring South Africa, however, with vociferous claims about native rights from missionary societies and reform groups, the "display" of the state through royal commissions as a means of legitimizing labour practices took on vital importance.[4]

An important aspect of state formation, then, was the establishment of the administrative structures to open up "native" social life to governance. In the areas not administered by European concessionary companies, three levels of administrative power subordinated to the governor-general were established. Immediately below the governor general were the district governors, usually military officers appointed by Lisbon. The districts were divided into European and non-European areas, with the councils of the European areas enjoying limited self-government. Even by the 1920s, fewer than 15,000 Europeans resided in Mozambique, most of them concentrated in the then Lourenço Marques and the other important port and railway centre of Beira. The African population by and large lived in rural subdistricts which, for administrative purposes, were further subdivided into localities. Each of the subdistricts and localities was governed by a Portuguese official, a "chefe de posto." In terms of formal schooling these Portuguese officials were all minimally educated and poorly trained, establishing petty tyrannies in which they had unchallenged power to accuse, apprehend, try and sentence their subjects. (Isaacman & Isaacman 1983:29)

Below the "chefe de posto" was a network of African collaborators. The local chieftaincy structure was already by this time both in disarray and disrepute as we have seen above. It had worked out a variegated "modus vivendi" with European colonial presence in patterns of trade, including slave trade and compliance with labour demands. Nonetheless, the chieftaincy structure was incorporated into the local government apparatus, the local chiefs becoming, in essence, paid functionaries of the colonial state. The "régulos" or senior chiefs were exempt from taxation and forced labour, in return for which they were expected to collect taxes, "recruit" labour, maintain order and settle minor disputes. Their perks of office included the right to use forced peasant labour on their own lands, higher prices for cash crops, recruitment bonuses and prizes such as cloth and bicycles for "stimulating" African production.

José Capela in his studies of labour in the colonial era described the layers of local government in this way:

> Local government extended down to Portuguese administrators in sparse "posts" who had virtually powers of life and death over their area of jurisdiction, whereafter the remnants of "traditional" authority were harnessed into the system. "Régulos," once chiefs . . . were confirmed or appointed to control local communities, scrutinize documentation, recruit labour, and collect taxes. They were assisted by "cipaios," black colonial police. They received a small allowance, perks, and exemptions from labour and tax, and privileged access to schooling for their sons. Many exercised a reign of terror among the populace; one practice was to take women into possession to compel tax payments.
>
> (Quoted in Johnston 1989:44)

As in other parts of southern Africa at the time, a reconstitution of "traditional" structures was a key element in modes of governance for the "native" community. Even peoples such as the Makonde in northern Mozambique who had lived historically without chiefs had a "tradition" of chieftaincy created for them by the colonial officials, who handpicked collaborators to fill the positions.[5]

An African police force of a particularly brutalized genre added to the arbitrary and repressive texture of the state at the local level. Hand in hand with the "chefe de posto" and the "régulo" were the "sipaios," made up of former colonial soldiers, sons of loyalist chiefs and ex-warriors, slavers and mercenaries who unhesitatingly carried out what the only slightly milder coercion of the "régulo" left incomplete. Arangatoni Mikiras, an agricultural worker who had lived and worked in the province of Tete during the colonial regime had this to say:

> People were put in chains and obliged to work -- it was forced labour. It started when boys were fourteen or fifteen years old. They had to go every year. Some were sent to one place and others to another. The administrator sent *cipaios* (local police) to get the people and bind them, and after they would be brought to the administration. Then the *recrutador* would ask them if they wanted to go with him -- and they were standing in front of him in chains! People were paid 100 escudos per month.
> (Quoted in Munslow 1983:35)

This construction of "native" and the "traditional" takes on particular importance around the question of land. Colonial sovereignty was being exercised not over a community of property-owning individuals with inalienable land rights as in "civilized" society, but over a collective group whose property rights were vested in the "tribe." The tribes, in turn, were ruled by their reconstituted "chiefs," now conveniently representing the colonial regime at local level. This construction of the "traditional" worked to make it difficult for Africans to act freely as property-owning individuals, employing labour and entering the market at will. It provided the mechanism for the colonial state to make African producers invisible as legitimate aspirants to the same rights as settler producers, situating them instead in a particular set of rights and obligations inhering in the community as a whole. This construction of the "native" allowed a characterization of the African population as "idle children" needing moral regulation and served to legitimize the growing labour demands by the state. A particular working up of "native" and "traditional" served to reorganize a whole dispensation of land and labour.

African producers were prevented from developing agriculture and were forced onto the labour market, then, by a variety of legislative mechanisms. In addition to land tenure restrictions, the colonial state did not allow African producers to employ labour. They received lower prices for their cash crops, and in regions such as Zambezia, they had labour obligations in lieu of taxes.

International pressure against forced labour in the Portuguese colonies began early and the labour code adopted in 1928, just after Salazar came to power, ostensibly put an end to forced labour except for penal correction and necessary public works. The new legislation spoke of giving Africans "full liberty of choosing the work which best suits them" and of "working to secure their livelihood and of thereby contributing to the welfare of humanity." (Isaacman & Isaacman 1983:41) Yet in 1930, another piece of taxation legislation was passed which created a situation that obliged most men to work at least a six month contract per year. In 1942, the governor-general issued a decree to close existing loopholes in the legislation and lock the forced labour system yet more firmly into place. The definition of "idle" was made to include all men between the ages of 18-25 who had not done a contract in South Africa or Rhodesia for the previous six months, were not at the time employed by a foreign firm or the state, and were not cultivating cotton or rice.

Cheap Labour for the South African Mines

Complementary to the "chibalo" system in regulating labour was the system of migrant labour. The final decades of the nineteenth century brought discoveries of gold in the Rand and marked the beginning of Mozambique's domination by South Africa. With a fixed price for gold and high capital investment costs for imported equipment, the guarantee of profitability lay in abundant sources of cheap labour. The South African Chamber of Mines wanted to control and regulate labour migration as a means of preventing free competition for labour that could draw wages upward. A labour force freely selling its labour to the expanding labour market developing in South African agriculture, industry, commerce and mining could well force mine wages upwards. A mechanism to force mine labour to live and work in two different socio-economic environments was the answer. The regulation of both time (through contracts) and space (through limitations to mining compounds) for mine labourers precluded the kind of contact with the expanding South African economy that would have allowed free entry into the labour market. The construction of "native homelands" inside South Africa and the agreements worked out with South Africa's poorer neighbours to guarantee conditions for recruitment of short-term migrant labour suited admirably the purposes of the South African Chamber of Mines. (van Onselen 1980; Katzenellenbogen 1982; Marks and Rathbone (ed.) 1982; First 1983; Ashforth 1987)

The origins of migrant labour in South Africa date to well before the Portuguese consolidated their control over Mozambique in the colonial wars of 1885-87. By 1879, there were some 12,000 Mozambicans working in various parts of South Africa; by 1897, more than 60,000 were employed in the Rand alone. This practice of migrant labour was encouraged by a complex interplay between local chiefs and "numzane" or homestead owners, turning on control over land, cattle and brideprice. Labour extraction from young men not able to pay cattle bridewealth was controlled through this system.[6]

The supplies of labour through local chieftaincy structures were not sufficient to keep up with the development of reef mining and the enormous flows of cheap labour called for when deep-level mines opened up in 1895.

> These the Mocambican chiefs and "numzane" were unable to supply because their political position was dependent on the kinship system, with all its rights and obligations, and on the existing relations of production. They were thus constrained to protect the worker's wage and his domestic means of production. Colonialism was fettered by no such encumbrances, and it was only the colonial state, established after the defeat of the Gaza king Gungunyana in 1895, that was progressively able to free labour from its material possessions -- and from the rights and obligations embodied in the social relations of the old order. . . . only the colonial state was able to use organised violence to propel workers onto the market for, unlike the chiefs and "numzane," its only responsibility towards the workforce was to ensure the conditions of its physical reproduction. The colonial state was able to use the apparatus of government, army, police, prisons and chiefs working as government agents, together with the threat of forced labour and porterage, military conscription, compulsory cultivation, corporal punishment and imprisonment to coerce the workers onto the market, while at the same time restricting Africans to reserves where their access to a means of production outside of wage labour was strictly limited.
>
> (Harries 1982:158,159)

The entire southern third of Mozambique was drawn into the orbit of the South African economy, servicing its continuing need for cheap labour and for transport and shipping facilities. By the turn of the century, mining capital was employing 54,000 labourers, two thirds of whom came from Mozambique. The colonial government had steady sources of revenue from recruitment license fees, passport fees, and customs duties on goods imported by the returning miners. As a result of mining income, higher taxes were levied on southern Mozambique. In addition, major agreements were worked out concerning trans-shipping through Mozambican ports, with the result that by 1917, the single largest source of colonial income, amounting to one third of the state's revenue, came from customs duties and related trans-shipping charges linked to mining. (Isaacman & Isaacman 1983:36)

The colonial state's role in setting up institutions to rent out Mozambican labour to neighbouring countries through the contract labour system was clearly the most dramatic instance of state intervention in the labour process. For the African peasant producer in southern Mozambique, locked into a new system of bondage by the reconstructed chieftaincy cum local level colonial administrator, contract labour was experienced as a more attractive option than what the local economy had on offer. The "chibalo" system created a generalized climate of terror, since at any moment a peasant could be pulled from whatever activity he was carrying out and be forced to work on a state-imposed tasks, public or private. State legislation restricted the African population with regard to land, labour (both control of their own labour and employment of that of others), prices for their produce, and licenses and access to credit to trade. This effectively ruled out the option to survive as private producers. A 16-18 month contract in the mines with some cash income at the end of it looked attractive in comparison. Increased interest in imported commodities such as cloth and hand tools and bicycles also necessitated cash, something hard to come by with the artificially low prices offered to African producers for their cash crops.

There were severe restrictions of time and space for the migrant labourers. A contract lasted for a determinate number of months, with movement restricted to the space between the mine shafts and the hostels within the mining compound. This gave little opportunity for exploring job options on the larger South African labour market, although loopholes were clearly found and significant numbers of Mozambicans remained in South Africa. Restriction on movement also gave limited opportunity to compare mine wages for migrant workers with the wage levels of others working in the burgeoning South African economy. Whatever the judgment on South African mining wages compared with those in other sectors of the South African economy, mine wages in South Africa compared favourably to any kind of opportunity in Mozambique. With agricultural production for African producers systematically suppressed and wage labour controlled through the forced labour system, the option to take on a contract to the mines looked attractive indeed.

"Idle" Men and "Invisible" Women

If peasant men were declared "idle" unless engaged in contract labour or employed by a foreign firm, plantation owner or the colonial state to produce rice or cotton, the labour of peasant women remained below the horizon of visibility. The systems of forced labour and migrant labour were experienced differently by men and women. These systems had an enormous impact on family structures. Both were based on exploitation of labour power without taking any responsibility for its reproduction. "Chibalo" did not supply anything beyond the means for physical survival of the worker himself, and even that was at times precarious. As we have seen above, men of all ages were rounded up by the "régulos" and brought to the local administrator. The administrator either put them to work on state projects or handed them over to owners of tea and sisal plantations. No provision was made for their families. The money earned at best covered the taxes imposed by the regime. The entire burden for family subsistence fell on the women, placing them in key positions as food producers.

Migrant labour patterns had a similar effect, but took men away for even longer periods of time. Migrant labour came to signify a normal part of attaining manhood, referred to by labour recruiters in the 1890s as a "form of initiation" and by a missionary in 1891 as a "tour of duty." (Harries 1982:157)

> After a period of service in the mines, young men were treated with new respect as "gayisa," those who have returned from the mines and are a source of wealth. Red-coats, smoking-jackets, hats and trousers bought on the mines were the symbols of their new status. Men who remained at home and refused to work on the mines were denigrated as "mumparras," narrow-minded and ignorant provincials.
>
> (Harries 1982:158)

The traditional bride price payable in cattle came to be payable in goods brought back from trips to the mines. As the consumer goods demanded by prospective in-laws increased, more trips to the mines became necessary to pay off the inflated bride price. Goods unavailable in Mozambique became part of the package.

Mozambican writer and journalist Lina Magaia's short story "Mother," captures the role of mining contracts for women throughout southern Mozambique.

> He had left for Joni. It was his first journey to the Rand, where he worked for two years, returning home with enough money for the lobolo [bride price] and with a blouse, a skirt and other pretty things her friends envied. Nor did he forget to bring her a pair of shoes and a black beret which she adored.
>
> (Magaia 1990:M8)

The inflation of the bride price meant brides being abandoned with even greater frequency to labour alone on their farms. In the traditional division of labour in rural areas, men had played an important role in clearing fields and harvesting the crops. The physical absence of all able-bodied men over long periods of time resulted in a general decline in agricultural production. Women were left with the entire work load of both production and reproduction. There is no doubt that the amalgam of old and new forms of oppression resulted in consolidating women's subordinate position even more.

> Men's dependence on women to supply the subsistence needs of the family increased proportionately with their involvement in migrant labour, and, in this way, much of the exploitation involved in homestead production was passed on to women. By increasing the burden placed on women in the production process, the "numzane" increased the cadets' [young men] dependence on women to supplement their wage labour with the agricultural production needed to reproduce the family. This increased exploitation of women was an important reason conditioning the cadet's decision to return home with the brideprice necessary to complete his debt to the elders. For with migrant labour, the establishment and maintenance of the homestead came to rest almost entirely on its female members, and it was the product of their labour and fertility that gave to the cadets the possibility of entry into the dominant "numzane" grouping.
>
> (Harries 1982:158)

The export of labour power to South Africa clearly had an enormous impact on Mozambique's internal development. It was not only African peasant producers who were thwarted in their desire to cultivate the land and develop agriculture. Settlers and officials of the colonial government also felt the negative impact of migrant labour. In 1909, there were some expressions of a more generalized resistance to mine labour and South African domination. There was a move to establish Portuguese as the language of the Lourenço Marques port rather than English. Governor Cabral of Inhambane province complained about the lack of labour available for developing agriculture in that province. He cited Governor Cardoso's alarm at statistics indicating that between 1903 and 1906, some 75,370 men left Inhambane of whom only 43,885 returned. (Katzenellenbogen 1982:102) Cabral felt that the problems went beyond loss of labour power, however, and threatened the core of the civilizing mission itself.

> To the problems of depopulation was added that of "denationalization," of which "flagrant proof" could be found in that it was rare to find an African speaking Portuguese, whereas many adopted English names such as Jones or Siquespence. This was part of the loss of Portuguese prestige as the dominant race.
>
> (Katzenellenbogen 1982:103)

Cash Crops in the Colonial Economy

The regulatory and controlling practices of the state through "chibalo" and migrant labour took on yet another dimension after the Salazar regime had had time to further consolidate its power. There was a desire to establish the more classic colonial relationship with Mozambique. This meant introduction of forced cultivation of particular crops, thereby supplying raw materials for the metropole. Forced cotton production was introduced in 1938 to supply the raw materials for the newly established textile industry and compulsory rice cultivation for the towns four years later. Twelve Portuguese companies received monopoly rights over huge areas of Mozambique in which they forced peasants to grow cotton, whether propitious conditions for cotton production existed or not. In other areas such as Inhambane, a 50 metre plot for cotton production was established in each administrative unit. Shortly thereafter, every married couple was forced to cultivate a cotton field of eight metres. Beatings were handed out as punishment for failed crops. Only the wives of the cotton overseers and those in the military were exempt. Wives of "chibalo" workers and migrant workers were forced to leave food production on which family subsistence depended to grow cotton.

Cotton production grew steadily, reaching almost 46,000 tons near the end of the Salazar regime. The number of African peasants drawn into cotton production peaked at 791,000 in 1944 and later stabilized at about 500,000. Forced crop cultivation basically meant hunger for the African population. The Bishop of Beira commented as follows:

> Since the beginning of the cotton production, stretches of fertile land had stopped producing food for the population and there had been acute hunger in the region. In one of the dioceses the spectre of death had fallen over the population, because of lack of food. I know some districts where the Africans got for their harvest fifty to ninety escudos. In the same regions and localities, if the Africans had cultivated crops other than cotton, the same plots of land would have yielded a harvest of which they would have got two to four thousand escudos.
>
> (Quoted in Munslow 1983:36-7)

Women were ostensibly exempt from "chibalo," although this policy was frequently disregarded. They were very much involved, however, in forced production of cotton and rice. The forced cotton production necessitated dramatic changes in the peasant family division of labour. As a labour-intensive crop, cotton pulled labour away from subsistence production, accounting in large measure for the backwardness of this sector in producing both the food and other commodities needed by peasant families. In some cases, it led to a switch in peasant diet, with women forced to adopt hardy, drought-resistant cassava over the more labour demanding (and more nutritious) crops of sorghum or maize. Women and children were forced to guarantee family production of cotton and there were many instances of men running away from "chibalo" labour to assist their wives with the cotton harvest. The Archives of the Cotton Institute include a survey of Gaza Province done in 1941 which concludes that "50 percent of the women could not produce the forced cultures without seriously reducing food production." (Quoted in Isaacman & Isaacman 1983:54)

The colonial state, as late as 1959, noted in a confidential document that "the majority of the population is underfed" and went on to warn that "it is absolutely necessary that cotton producers have sufficient food to enable them to work." (Quoted in Isaacman & Isaacman 1983:55) The brutal super-exploitation of the labour force was such, then, that its very reproduction was in jeopardy.

"The Man the Whites Appointed Is the Son of a Nobody"

The Portuguese colonial regime was intent on refashioning Mozambique in its own image. In a manner characteristic of the colonial encounter, be it through representatives of church or state, there was an assumption of Africa as featureless, a "tabula rasa" without the social organization or artifacts of a civilization, a blank page on which to begin writing history. A sustained exercise was carried out to construct Africans as child-like, little distinct from the savage natural order that the African continent itself presented to European eyes.

Integral to the colonial project was a moral discourse working to create an almost unbridgeable chasm between savagery and civilization. This sustained exercise was a necessary fiction for the systematic assault on African resources that was about to take place, and particularly the massive shifts of human labour power that were to dislocate millions of lives throughout the region over the next century.[7]

In Mozambique, each district capital was replete with the architecture of empire. The district administrator's office and home, the church and parish offices, and later the doctor's home, were constructed in Portuguese style. They stood out in splendour, adjacent to the formal park areas that made up the town square. A "national" history was created over the years, with celebrations of Portugal's national days, the introduction of Portuguese culture, from regional folk dances and the epic poems of Camões, to city clubs offering the soulful music of the "fado" and sidewalk cafes with "vinho verde". There were innumerable large and small signallings of what "citizenship" in the Lusitanian empire signified. Clearly the school system which we shall look at in detail in the next chapter was a key factor in this process.

A series of institutions, forms and agencies were established, then, to superimpose a "national history" on the diverse social groupings throughout Mozambique, to project the idea of nation and regulate a social identity with all the pomp and circumstance, national monuments and heroes, imposition of a language and day to day administrative ordering to go with it. It was a project carried out, however, with such a crude hand that it was even less effective than in many other parts of Africa.

Yet to be written are the social histories from the African perspective, reconstructing what kind of purchase this civilizing project of the colonial state really had on individual and collective subjectivities. There is much to be learned about what sense of self was preserved and how feelings of inferiority and subordination were internalized or rejected.

Sérgio Vieira, a senior Frelimo leader and writer, opened up this question in an address to the Ministry of Education and Culture shortly after independence. He spelled out the colonial project in terms of its intention to create a colonial subject without capacity to locate itself historically, geographically and culturally. For Vieira, the colonized (not those subjected to colonization but those who assimilate it) are people without a temporal dimension. They are unable to locate themselves historically within their own society and unable to locate their own societies historically. The central historical reference point is the history of colonial conquest.

> This lack of historical dimension in a people is the result of a deliberate and planned action by colonialism. I can remember . . . a whole generation, mine included, who delighted in reading Frobenius because Frobenius, at a point in the introduction to *The History of African Civilization* had the following expression: "When the Portuguese arrived" -- it was to the coast of our country he was referring -- "they found a people civilized *to the marrow of their bones.*"
>
> For us, this was a phrase that became a watchword. And why did it become a watchword? . . . We were locating ourselves in time and space. . . . To locate ourselves time-wise was to seek to know where we came from historically, to know whether we brought a culture . . . a civilization within us, if we were bearers of history . . . or if we had been an abandoned branch of humanity . . . waiting for the magic wand of colonialism to arouse us into motion, into History, into the World.
>
> (Address by Sérgio Vieira to the Second Conference of the Ministry of Education and Culture, 1977)

Vieira goes on to argue that the colonized are also spatially dislocated, finding themselves "overseas" from a European "Metropole." In Mozambique, as throughout Africa, the mountains and rivers of the European colonial power were named as geographic wonders and not Africa's own majestic ranges and mighty rivers. Finally the colonized lack a cultural dimension, bringing an ignorance of the roots of their own personalities, having been taught to despise their Africanness.

While Vieira's reflections are some of the few to theorize about the deep feelings and meanings attached to colonial practices, there are many forms of protest against the colonial state's incursions into the fabric of day to day life. The tyrannies of the "régulo" were all-pervasive, with physical escape from the locality at times presenting itself as the only recourse. Contract labour, escape to urban employment or flight to neighbouring countries were three of the responses. Leduangane Maxafage, a worker in the Maputo City Council, described his flight from his village to what was then Lourenço Marques in this way:

> I came to work in Lourenço Marques because of "chibalo." I couldn't sleep in my own home. I lived like a dog going into the bush at night because there were so many police seizing people.
>
> (Quoted in Penvenne 1979b:5)

For those who didn't flee permanently, there were many other forms of resistance to tax collectors and labour recruiters such as falsification of age and marital status or temporary absences across neighbouring borders or into remote areas. The extensive history of protest is only now being reconstructed, and includes everything from actions of outright sabotage to daily ingenuity in outwitting the overseers' demands.

There were instances of widespread local rebellions such as the Barue rebellion of 1917-1921 in which seven ethnic groups united, with a force of 15,000 armed men. They were angered by their conditions of forced labour, increased taxation and mandatory cotton production. As if these conditions were not enough, they were also being conscripted into the army and policemen were sent to their villages raping the women at will. Two months after the insurrection had begun, spurred on by leadership from the Barue royal family and a network of spirit mediums claiming sacred medicines creating immunity from European bullets, the entire colonial administrative network throughout the southern zones of the Zambezi valley had been dismantled. (Isaacman & Isaacman 1983:67)

There were even instances of social banditry such as that of the legendary Mapondera. Mapondera was a local chief who fled arrest and operated a band of 100 on the border of Mozambique with southern

Rhodesia. He protected the local peasantry from both Rhodesian and Portuguese tax collectors and labour recruiters.

One of the most dramatic expressions of active resistance found in confidential memos in the archives of the Cotton Institute was a strike action carried out by women against forced cultivation. Seven thousand women organized a strike at Buzi in Sofala province in 1947 and refused to accept the cotton seeds the administrator had ordered to be distributed. They protested that with their men working on nearby sugar plantations, they had neither the time nor the labour to produce both cotton and food. According to the archives of the Beira delegation of the Cotton Institute, the local administrator offered in response an exemption from cotton production to pregnant women and women with more than four children! (Isaacman & Isaacman 1983:67)

Cultural forms of resistance were common in the rural areas, including both sculpture, music and dance. In the northern areas, the strong presence of the Catholic church made its impact at an early stage on local carving traditions. The striking ebony characterizations of the spirit world of Makonde mythology and religion gave way to lifeless and stereotyped carvings of religious themes. At times, however, elements of doubt or defiance were introduced. The madonna was given a demon to hold instead of the Christ child. A priest was carved with the feet of a wild animal. (Mondlane 1983:104)

The Chope, located in Inhambane province, developed songs of protest like this one.

> We are still angry; it's always the same story
> The oldest daughters must pay the tax
> Natanele tells the white man to leave him alone
> Natanele tells the white man to leave me be
> You, the elders must discuss our affairs
> For the man the whites appointed is the son of a nobody
> The Chope have lost the right to their own land
> Let me tell you about it.
>
> (Quoted in Mondlane 1983:183)

Workers in the Sena Sugar Estates in Zambezia composed work songs to voice their protests against brutal overseers. The embodiment of their rage in sexual terms is a striking characteristic of many of their songs.

> You are making us suffer
> Beating me up
> You, beating me up
> You, Mr. balls owner
> Your penis

You are making us suffer for nothing
Me, working for nothing
We've seen hardship with the sugar
Look we're getting just two hundred only

Getting three small cruzados only, your penis.
(Quoted in Isaacman & Isaacman 1983:69)

Rural women left behind by the migrant labourers also used cultural forms to voice their protest. Their work songs capture the experience of abandonment, vulnerability to the vagaries of in-laws, and the re-organization of production necessitated by absent male labour. One work song, recorded by Alpheus Manghezi of the Centre of African Studies at Eduardo Mondlane University as part of a larger project on migrant labour, spoke to the suffering of a newly married women left behind when her husband went off to the mines in "Joni." She had to endure a small hut with a leaky roof in a treeless open space and the daily beatings and insults from her in-laws.

Leader: Oh! oh on the flat bare place
Chorus: Stay there/remain there
Leader: Even if they leave me there
Chorus: Stay there/remain there
Leader: With the rains falling on me
Chorus: Remain there!
Leader: Even when they insult me/swear at me
Chorus: Remain there!
Leader: Even if they hit me/beat me up
Chorus: Remain there!
Leader: Even if they kick me
Chorus: Remain there!
Leader: Even if they bewitch me
Chorus: Remain there!
Leader: Even if they throw me out
Chorus: Remain there!
Leader: Oh! oh that flat bare place!
Chorus: Remain there!
"A Voz do Mineiro" in Estudos Africanos (1)1980

Not all the women left behind were so longsuffering. Another work song with the repeated chorus "Heyoo! Maghalangu" is a dialogue between the departing men and the women. Maghalangu is the local representative of the labour recruitment organization, WENELA (Witwatersrand Native Labour Association). The dialogue consists of banter back and forth. There are cautions to drive carefully to Joni so that the food for the trip won't spill, reminders by a wife to her departing husband not to forget to bring back pants for his son, and admonitions by a miner to his wife to take good care of his fields and crops. Fears are raised -- of Maghalangu taking away the village's sons to get killed in Joni, and of miners returning from Joni to find that their wives have run off with other men.

Clearly African languages themselves preserved an important space for preservation of a sense of safety, dignity and coherence. Despite their systematic denigration by the colonizers, African languages became the vehicles to sing and dance angers, fears and resentments engendered by the invasive repressive apparatus and the omnipresent moral tutelage of the colonial state.

The protest in the urban areas took different forms and was carried forward by different social groups. Two of its most visible forms were labour protests and writings by urban intellectuals, both as journalists and poets. These actions increased significantly in the period from 1910 to 1928, when the monarchy in Portugal gave way to a Republican regime.[8]

Various newspapers were published during this period, the most influential and long standing being "O Africano" (The African), published from 1908-1918 and its successor "O Brado Africano" (The African Cry), which began in 1918 and continued until its suspension in 1932. These papers were published in Portuguese and Ronga, a reflection of urban migration patterns to the national capital and the predominance of Ronga speaking southerners. These newspapers gave voice to the leading families of African and mulatto society. The most well known journalists writing in them were the Albasini brothers. Their father was a Portuguese ivory trader, whose African wife was the daughter of the Maxaquene "régulo." The father's brother became the Portuguese Vice-Consul in the Transvaal Republic. The relatively privileged position of the Albasini brothers did not prevent them from speaking for all African people, and they regularly used their journalistic voice to denounce the abuses of colonialism. Their news stories and commentaries highlighted four abuses -- "chibalo," working conditions for "free" labour, preferential treatment for white immigrants and the discrimination in educational opportunities for Africans.

The Albasinis had a sharp eye for the contradictions of colonial life. Their urban location following the flow of goods and people in and out of the colony brought a stinging critique of the distance between the high flown rhetoric of civilizing missions and the miserable life of the poverty-stricken Portuguese settlers who came to the colonies. Not for Mozambique the traditions of impeccable colonial administrators groomed in "Oxbridge" traditions. Portugal's own backwardness made it a problematic representative of the European "civilizing mission" -- and the sharp eyes of the black press were not slow in pointing this out.

> The common Portuguese, who is known as *mumadji* among the African population, always leaves Portugal with the fixed intention of a short stay in the land of the blacks to gather enough savings, and then to escape it all to return to Portugal, settle in and enjoy the wealth which he managed to accumulate, with God knows what sacrifices over two, three or four years.
>
> Are they aware there [in Portugal], of the deprivations that these men suffer in order to save that 300 or 400$000 reis? It is a poem of pain and misery. A veritable madness that some of them live through in an effort to fill their suitcases -- with those paltry pieces of metal. Gold Fever!
>
> They live in pigsties, without light, without air, some four or five together in order to cut costs. They customarily eat three persons from the same meal, because it costs less. In a squalid diner, soups or stews, which are more accurately puddles of warm water in which some five beans swim hopelessly in search of company. . . . These beans, whose horny consistency breaks the teeth of unsuspecting countrymen, force the stomach which ingests them to turn somersaults and to cry without hope.
>
> There they know nothing of what a driven spirit is capable of doing in the mania to make some money!
>
> (Quoted in Penvenne 1979a:7)

Such voices were silenced effectively after 1926, however, with the coming to power of Antonio Salazar.

Urban labour protest was also a regular form of resistance to the efforts to impose a new economic order and ethos in the colony. It manifested itself both through action and cultural expression. Its forms were embedded in a complex organization of production through relations of class, race/ethnicity and gender. As Jeanne Penvenne's studies on urban workers in Lourenço Marques from the beginning of the century until independence so richly document, there is no such thing as the Portuguese over against the African. In urban settings, the colonial relation was super-imposed on a fluidity and diversity of social relations where dimensions of class and gender and race were also operative. (Penvenne 1979 a,b)

Penvenne depicts a complex and shifting labour hierarchy with moments of competition during economic crises between various groupings. These included tensions between the Portuguese and Indian artisans, merchants and skilled and semi-skilled labourers, vying against each other for economic opportunities. Penvenne documents much negative propaganda against the Asians by the Portuguese, labelling them as conniving and intent on tricking the Africans.

There were also tensions between the Asians and the Africans over jobs and entrepreneurial opportunities. There were campaigns against Goans in the civil service, since they tended to fill the junior level bureaucratic positions the African population had to contend with first. There was resentment that the Goans received settler privileges like getting part of their payment in gold. There were also moments when "assimilados" campaigned to get European women out of the civil service and retail sales positions that they wanted for themselves. At a certain moment, the male settler community also joined in this move to relegate women to the home. (Penvenne 1979a:11)

The first efforts of black workers to organize can be dated to 1911, a year after the Republican government had come into power in the metropole. A General Union began to form in Lourenço Marques, meant to encompass all black workers from the lowliest porter through to the black workers in the civil service. It was short-lived, defeated by a combination of factors. Strong resistance from the colonial state and the white labour movement were two of them. Inexperience was a third. Many carried out their protest action against the pittance wages offered in urban employment by opting for migrant labour contracts in South Africa or Rhodesia.

Although the General Union did not succeed, there were regular albeit sporadic attempts to organize over the years, with strikes and work stoppages in different sectors as a regular occurrence. Employees of the Merchants' Association staged a work stoppage in 1913, followed by tram workers in 1917, railroad technicians in 1918 and employees at an engineering firm in 1919. From 1916-1918, several thousand domestic workers refused to comply with registration laws. (Isaacman & Isaacman 1983; Penvenne 1979a)

The burgeoning port of Lourenço Marques, the gateway linking South Africa's expanding mining, industry and agriculture to the larger world economy, was the scene of much labour militancy by both black and white workers. Felizberto Zavala's reconstruction of the work songs to accompany coal loading in the Lourenço Marques port captures the arduousness and humiliation of work conditions.

> Loku vaku lanja, lanja ka wena -- lanja . . .
> Maputukezi i male mi baku leyi -- lanja . . .
> [When they say heave that shovel, shovel -- heave . . .
> The Portuguese live by stealing our wages -- heave. . . .]
>
> (Quoted in Penvenne 1979a:cover)

Black workers were involved in seven major strikes from 1918-1921. The wave of strikes focused on wage demands and the refusal of the shipping and forwarding company to increase African wages to keep up with the post-war inflation in the colony.

> All strikes at the port followed the same broad pattern. Disgruntled workers, organized through informal grassroots networks, refused to work unless their wages were adjusted. As soon as they gathered in front of the main entrance to the port demanding better salaries and working conditions, the colonial governor sent in troops to smash the demonstration and arrest the leaders and used "chibalo" workers as strikebreakers to keep the port going. The strikes were always quickly broken, and even when the employers agreed to pay increases, they often reneged, as they did in the 1919 strike. Nevertheless, there were several port strikes in the 1920s and a number of less publicized work stoppages.
> (Isaacman & Isaacman 1983:71)

White workers in the port were also militant. In 1917, a general strike of all European personnel in the ports and railways of Lourenço Marques was called and a state of siege declared on the city. Again in 1925/26, strike actions were carried out by the European workers including sabotage of the railway track, resulting later in a derailment. Brutal repression followed, including placing bound strike leaders on a "phantom" train as a warning to others. Wives of the striking workers held a hunger march, carrying black flags throughout the streets of the city. They were violently dispersed by mounted troops and police.

With the overthrow of the Republican regime in 1926 and the establishment of the Salazar regime, which lasted until 1960, the rights to organize and strike were severely curtailed even for white workers. State-run "syndicates" replaced the trade unions. For the African workers, the increased restriction of space for labour protest had less effect, since the right to organize had not been theirs to begin with.

In 1933, African workers staged a bitter strike in protest against a 10-30 percent wage decrease. The mass walk-out resulted in an agreement to rescind the cuts. Once the returned workers returned to their jobs, however, they were locked inside the port, surrounded by police, forced to unload the ships and informed that the cuts would be maintained. There were strike actions periodically during the 1940s, 1950s and 1960s but the openly fascist nature of colonial rule, responding readily with brutal repression and coercion, made it difficult to sustain labour militancy. Many sought to avoid the poor working conditions for the urban work force by legally seeking contracts in neighbouring countries. Others fled the colony illegally. In the early years they sought employment and in the later years, they left to link up with the nationalist movements forming in neighbouring countries.

Under colonialism, then, a multiplicity of institutions, forms, agencies and discourses were established that turned on a moral vision of a world divided between the "civilized" and the "savage." The colonial regime made mastery of the Portuguese language one of the primary qualifications for the "native" to pass from the status of "indigenous" to that of "assimilated."[9] The status of "assimilado" was defined by law in Article 2 of Edict 317 in 1917:

> Article 2. Through distinguishing himself from the norm of the black race, an individual of that race or descended from it is considered assimilated to the Europeans on showing the following characteristics;
> a) Has entirely abandoned the habits and customs of the black race;
> b) Speaks, reads and writes the Portuguese language;
> c) Adopts monogamy;
> d) Exercises a profession, art or craft
>
> (Quoted in Johnston 1989:46)

The coming to power of Salazar in Portugal in 1926 and the establishment of a fascist regime in the metropole brought changes in the colonial policies. Under Salazar, "assimilation" was to be a very slow and highly selective process. In Mozambique and Angola, a more formalized "Regime do Indigenato" or "native" status was established. As we have seen above, this classification set out a series of state-regulated racial and ethnic distinctions that bound Africans into subordinate positions as "indigenous." Those classified as "indigenous" had to carry an identity card at all times, and were subject to a series of regulations that formed part of the new regime. These included forced labour obligations, subjection to customary law, residential restrictions to non-European areas, restrictions on movement to cinemas, bars and shops, and exclusion from certain areas after dark. (Mondlane 1983:41)

The legislation on language was made more rigorous in 1954 by introducing the need to speak "proper" Portuguese. This law remained on the books until 1961. (Johnston 1989:46) Language was indeed one of the most important instruments of colonial domination, no less so under Portuguese colonialism than in the French and British colonies. The language of the colonizer abounded in discursive practices, expressions and images, all of which served to establish the "civilizing mission" and moral project of the colonizer while at the same time inculcating complexes of racial inferiority and dependency in the colonized. Chris Searle, in his extremely rich exploration of the role of language in the process of revolution in Grenada, points to the centrality of linguistic imperialism.

FIGURE 3.1 Contemporary Woodcut of Colonial Exploitation
Jose Tangawizi, Mueda (Source: Egero 1987:51)

> Class is as much a part of the English language as its grammar and syntax. When the language exists and is used in the context of colonialism or neocolonialism it has the added dimensions of violent racism and imperialist hatred, from the coloniser to the colonised, and successively from the colonised to his own people and himself. Over the past three decades, as a result of the struggle for and process of decolonisation, the truth of cultural and specifically linguistic imperialism has been put many times in Africa, America and Asia. . . .
>
> (Searle 1984:xx)

As we have seen, then, the colonial authorities put in place a set of discursive practices to distance the "savage" from the "civilized." They constructed a "native" with a need to be guided to productive pursuits as a way to legitimize practices of forced and migrant labour. The consolidation of colonial rule resulted in profound erosion and/or destruction of the existing social organization of African producers. One target was language practices, the social communication emerging from the seasonal rhythms of planting and harvesting "machambas" (farms), the daily routines and rigours of fetching water and pounding corn, the rituals and celebrations of birth, marriage and death. These were language practices through which social communication flowed richly, through which experiences and feelings could be readily conveyed. The assimilated African was forced to put them aside for "proper" Portuguese.

"Proper" Portuguese meant the culture and language practices of the colonial governor, the district administrator and the plantation manager whose increasingly strong presence began to intrude directly on day to day life and speech. This intrusion included a systematic effort to denigrate and destroy African culture and languages. Economic survival in the social organization of production shaped by colonialism included buying into this new construction of self as "native," reproduced in important ways through language.

The regulation of labour was done mainly through the Portuguese variant of a pass-book. The "caderneta," to be presented on demand to officials by all "natives," contained the tax record and labour record of the African male, along with the names of his wives and children. In the event of the bearer's disappearance, wives and children were liable for payment of the annual taxes. Photographs and fingerprint identification were also included. The "caderneta" also included the bearer's legal place of residence. Appropriate authorization and stamps from the local administrator were required for moving from one part of the country to another. All aspects of the "caderneta" were subject to the arbitrary exercise of power of local level authorities. If papers were lost or found not to be in order, beating, jail or correctional labour were commonplace. Through this mechanism alone, all African males were forced to keep in close contact with the colonial administration.

The strength and arbitrariness of this control of African labour necessitated an equally strong ideological project to try to hold it in place. The principles running through the various pieces of legislation introduced over the years were clear. The goal of Portuguese colonial policy was to integrate native peoples into the Portuguese nation. This had to be done prudently and selectively, bearing in mind that the natives had a culture, social organization and law of their own, albeit primitive in relation to the glories of Portuguese civilization. Part of the obligation of the state was a paternal role, to protect the Africans in their primitive state against abuses and control of the settlers, to protect their property and supervise their labour contracts.[10]

For blacks, access to "Civilization" was restricted. Eligibility was limited to the tiny handful of Africans and mulattos able to read and write Portuguese, prepared to give up the rights and customs of the "black race," including polygamy, and were employed within the capitalist economy. A school certificate became a fundamental criteria for entry.

According to Silva Cunha, colonial theorist and scholar, two dominant ideas prevailed in colonial legislation.

> One of these is to guarantee the natural and unconditional rights of the native whose tutelage is confided to us . . . and to assure the gradual fulfilment of his moral and legal obligations to work, to be educated, and to improve himself . . . The other is to lead the natives, by the means appropriate to their rudimentary civilization -- so that the transformation from their own customs and their own habits may be gentle and gradual -- to the profitable development of their own activities and to their integration into the life of the colony, which is an extension of the mother country. The natives are not granted, because of the lack of practical application, the rights associated with our own constitutional life, if it may be called that, our political laws, our administrative, civil, commercial, and penal codes, our judicial system. We maintain for them a juridical system consistent with the state of their faculties, their primitive mentality, their feelings, their way of life, but at the same time we continue to encourage them constantly, by all appropriate means, to raise their level of existence.
> (Quoted in Duffy 1959:293)

Under the "Regime do Indigenato," citizenship for whites was automatic, although many of them would have been disqualified if the same criteria applied to the African population had been applied to the Portuguese settlers. Colonial literacy figures for Angola as late as 1966 indicate 90 percent illiteracy for Africans and 40 percent illiteracy for the settlers from Portugal! (Ferreira 1974:43) Mozambicans recount wryly how colonial settlers in Gaza province in the 1950s arrived with their shoes on the wrong feet. (Vieira 1977:11) Clearly the transformation of illiterate barefoot peasant immigrants from rural Portugal into models of "civilization" was not always easy to accomplish.

In addition to the many other arbitrary categorizations and indignities which locked Africans into place as uncivilized, deficiency in mastery of the language imposed by the colonizer was, by law, a reason to be denied the status of citizen. "Illiteracy" had became a fundamental element in classifying Africans as "indigenous." The system of state provided schooling, to which we shall now turn, was a powerful institution in holding this ideological construct in place.

Notes

1. Sérgio Vieira, a senior Frelimo Party leader who is currently Director of the Centre of African Studies at Eduardo Mondlane University gave an extraordinarily thought-provoking address entitled "The New Man is a Process" to the second conference of the Ministry of Education and Culture in 1977. In it, he reflected on the colonized consciousness as one in which the colonized are left without capacity to locate themselves in their own history, geography and culture. Unfortunately, the depth and sensitivity with which he analyzed the colonized sense of self was not in any way extended to gendered senses of self. The oblivion to questions of gender in the use of language about "the New Man" and descriptions that assume women's experiences to be identical with men's in the new society-in-the-making is to be found not only in Vieira's address but throughout Frelimo Party documents more generally. Yet another level of struggle will have to be waged in Mozambique to establish the gendered reality of social relations and the need for a language to describe them that does not render women invisible.

2. For excellent discussions of this period, see Isaacman & Isaacman:1983; Munslow 1983; Serra & Medeiros (eds.) 1983.

3. For an excellent discussion of commissions of inquiry over the years in South Africa, and the ways in which the state constructs frameworks of knowledge and objects of knowledge in specific institutional forms which enable state regulation, see Adam Ashforth. On the "Native Question:" A Reading of the Grand Tradition of Commissions of Inquiry. D. Phil dissertation. Oxford University, 1987. Other interesting studies on commissions of inquiry as state formation include Beng-Huat Chua's "Democracy as a Textual Accomplishment." *The Sociological Quarterly* 20 (August):541-549.

4. This whole question of the social construction of the "native" and the multiplicity of measures to regulate African participation in the cash economy in ways complementary to and not competitive with colonial interests is a fascinating one. Mechanisms are to be found through British and French colonial history, ranging from the imposition of "hut" taxes and state marketing boards to the inducements of foreign trading companies offering credit and consumer goods. In Ghana, for example, an export economy was introduced at the beginning of this century. which included a profound reorganization of the labour process into intense exploitation of land and labour within a cocoa monoculture. Trading companies such as the United Africa Company (Unilever) fanned out throughout the rural areas offering combinations of seeds, credit and consumer goods. Cocoa production rose from zero in 1882 to 50,000 tons in 1914 and upwards of 200,000 tons annually from 1925 onwards. A cocoa marketing board holding a monopoly over sales on world markets further served to channel profits away from African producers and traders. For a detailed study of how Ghana's economy was shaped to serve the needs of the British empire, see Judith Marshall. Ghana 1945-1966: The Political Economy of Dependency. Masters Thesis. Institute of Social Studies, The Hague. 1972 and Marshall 1976. For

studies in other parts of Africa, see Sumner 1981; Leys 1975; Brett 1973; Arrighi and Saul 1973 etc.

5. Isaacman & Isaacman 1983:29. For an exceedingly rich analysis of this same phenomenon in neighbouring South Africa, in which a "traditional" Africa is reconstructed in order to legitimize the construction of the administrative category of "native," see Ashforth 1987.

6. A detailed examination of the origins of the migrant labour system from Mozambique to South Africa goes much beyond the scope of this study. For an excellent analysis, see Patrick Harries. *Kinship, ideology and the nature of pre-colonial labour migration. Labour migration from the Delagoa Bay hinterland to South Africa up to 1895*. Marks and Rathbone (eds.) 1982.

7. I am drawing heavily on the excellent discussion of the moment of first encounter between European and African cultures in southern Africa by Jean and John Comaroff in their article, "Through the looking glass: colonial encounters of the first kind" (Comaroff & Comaroff 1988). The Comaroffs capture with rich detail the peculiar zeal of the early missionary expeditions by the London Missionary Society. They pose with clarity the important and often not entirely conscious role the missionaries played in mapping out the terrain and the new ethos of industrial capitalism, with its notions of time, work and the individual. They also show how the missionaries were often caught in scripts cast by the very African actors they thought themselves to be writing into history.

8. For a fuller discussion of the forms of urban protest, see Isaacman & Isaacman 1983:61-78 and the Mozambican history series written in the Department of History, Eduardo Mondlane University (Serra, Carlos & Eduardo Medeiros (eds.) *História de Moçambique. Volume 2 Agressão Imperialista* (1886/1930). Maputo: Cadernos Tempo, 1983:279-299.)

9. The tendency for slippage between "literacy" understood as the ability to read and write and "literacy" as the ability to speak, read and write Portuguese is evident from the outset, both in policy documents and official references to education in Mozambique. I will endeavour throughout this study to make more visible which language is being referred to and to distinguish between competencies in speaking, reading and writing these different languages, *and* the social settings for their use. A fuller socio-linguistic history remains to be reconstructed. It is urgently needed since questions of language, in Mozambique as elsewhere, are integrally linked to fundamental questions of knowledge and power.

10. The construction of "civilized" and "indigenous" under Salazar can be likened to the period in western Europe in which those in power signalled a division of social space between two distinct groups. There was, "Society," a small social world of shared kinship, service and values, self-defined with a shared moral code of etiquette, dress, address and manners. Outside of "Society," there were "les autres," "the black people." (Elias 1978)

4

"Schooling": Path from Indigenous to Assimilated?

> Rudimentary primary schooling is designed to civilize and nationalize the indigenous people of the colony, spreading the Portuguese language and Portuguese customs among them.
>
> Legislative Diploma 238, Article 7, 1930
> (Quoted in Hedges 1982:6; my translation)

> The aim of these plans and programmes shall be to make the native population national and moral, and to inculcate such work habits and skills for each sex as suit the conditions and requirements of the regional economies; moral education shall aim at curing laziness and preparing future rural workers and craftsmen to produce what they need to satisfy their own requirements and their social obligations.
>
> Missionary Status, Article 6, 1941
> (Quoted in Ferreira 1974:67)

> The girls who were sent to school were made to collect firewood and cultivate the fields. Only the boys were allowed to study. This was in the Santa Maria Mission.
>
> (Interview with Alicinda Macuacua, July 1985)

Under the colonial regime, passage from the status of "uncivilized native" to that of "citizen" rested on level of education and job status. At the same time, the totally inadequate provision of public schooling and limited job market made it obvious that there was no real commitment to creating conditions for large numbers to attain assimilation certificates. What was signalled as the path towards certified knowledge and citizenship effectively served over the years as an institution to certify ignorance and native status. As late as 1961, less than one percent of the African population had been legally assimilated.

The colonial school was a powerful ideological symbol, compelling in its promise of a path out of misery and backwardness yet at the same time, provoking revulsion and alienation by its denial of Mozambican culture and history. Its language policies were among its harshest, and even included employing monitors to catch and punish children who spoke their own languages rather than Portuguese within school boundaries!

Adults coming to literacy after independence brought strong and complex histories and feelings about language. They brought scars from the colonialist practices of denigration of African languages and ritual humiliation around efforts to master Portuguese. They also carried memories of popular practices of using their mother tongues as a way of preserving a space of respite from and resistance to colonial domination.

While a few adults had developed critical perspectives on schooling through experiences of education in the post-independence era, the great majority held the colonial ideas intact. This meant they brought to literacy deeply felt, albeit not often articulated, ideas about their own legitimacy in particular language domains. They also brought colonial attitudes about what was a "language" and what merely a "dialect" and which was appropriate for use in the classroom. The learners had definite ideas of how to do "schooling," of what were the appropriate classroom roles for both "teachers" and "students." These were all part of a social learning over the years about the role of schooling in society. A reconstruction of schooling under colonialism, then, becomes important as a reference point for contemporary experiences.

Changing Education Policies in the Colonies

Differing views emanated from Lisbon in the early years about the form of schooling that should be put into place in the colonies. There were also moments of marked disagreement between the views in Lisbon and those in Lourenço Marques. For a brief period in the second half of the nineteenth century, the Liberal regime in power in Lisbon made efforts to establish a single system of public schooling accessible to European and African alike. Elaborate plans were made for colonial education with the idea of scattering elementary schools throughout the provinces offering reading, writing, mathematics and Christian morality. Teachers were to be recruited locally. The provincial capitals were to have secondary schools with faculty to be sent from Portugal. A liberal vision of large-scale assimilation of the African population prevailed, in which Africans would be subject to the same laws and institutions operative in Portugal.

These policies, however, were typical of Portugal's mode of governance over the years, with pretensions far in excess of what it could, in fact, produce. These schools existed only on paper, not remotely connected with what was really happening in Mozambique. In 1865, the Minister of Marine and Overseas stated with some regret that although the legislation "fulfilled an important service . . . local difficulties, negligence, and imperfect organization annulled or paralysed its good effects." (Quoted in Duffy 1959:257)

Schooling as an important site of ideological contestation was evident from early times. Mouzinho de Albuquerque, a colonial official writing at the turn of the century, took a view markedly at odds with the liberal current emanating from Lisbon.

> . . . the education system was nonsense and folly. Eternally preoccupied about assimilation with the metropolis, schools were scattered along the coast; even in the interior, there were schools where improvised teachers claimed to offer primary instruction to native children. Attendance at these schools was minimal, even when they were turned over to secular priests; the profit derived, none. But, since the arrangement resembled what Portugal had, the Liberal spirit of symmetry was satisfied. The schools were a fiction. . . . As far as I am concerned, what we have to do to educate and civilize the 'indigena' is to develop his aptitude for manual labour in a practical way and take advantage of him for the exploitation of the province.
>
> (Quoted in Ferreira 1974:58)

By 1900, 1195 African and mulatto children attended schools, 607 of whom were in missionary schools, 146 in government schools, 412 in municipal schools and 30 in private institutions. By 1909, there were 48 primary schools for boys and 18 for girls, the great majority run by missionaries, along with some trade and agricultural schools. (Duffy 1959: 258)

With regard to mission schools, the late nineteenth century saw a predominance of "foreign" (non-Portuguese) Protestant missions carrying out activities of education and evangelization. The main missions involved were the Swiss, the American Methodists and the Anglicans. Many of them had links to counterparts in the neighbouring British colonies. The Protestant missions were viewed with a good deal of suspicion by the strongly Catholic colonial administration. They were suspect not just for being Protestant but also for their encouragement of literacy in Mozambican languages, and their bent towards anthropology. Both of these were seen to undermine the broader "nationalizing" project of the Portuguese in which language and assimilation were key features.

The growing presence of "foreign" Protestant missionaries in the early decades of the century reflected, in part, the general lack of money and personnel available through the Portuguese Catholic church. It was also related, however, to a particular moment of strong separation of church and state under the Republican regime which came into power in 1911 and ruled until 1926. During the fifteen years of the Portuguese Republic support for Catholic expansion was ruled out. Lisbon banned Catholic missions in the colonies from 1911 to 1919. Their promised replacement with lay mission schools did not materialize and so in 1919, the Catholic missions were allowed to resume their work.

The Portuguese Catholic church expanded its missions considerably in the 1920s, although they were still subject to administrative harassments from Republican minded officials. Brito Camacho, High Commissioner in Mozambique in the 1920s, made public accusations against the Catholic priests, accusing them of selling themselves and making ridiculous teachers, vowing that he would never give the assistance of his government to a mission programme which did no more than catechize the Africans. Camacho found that no one in Mozambique took education of the African with any seriousness. The municipal schools, back country schools and trade schools in the colony were empty and the teachers totally incompetent. (Duffy 1959:114, 259)

Writing later on the period, Brito Camacho in his book *Blacks and Whites* included this anecdote of a visit to a mission school outside of Lourenço Marques.

> The priest who says Mass is the same one who teaches school, and it seems to me that God fated him for neither of these jobs. I attended a class to see how it was taught. The first thing the teacher asked one of the little black students was "What are 'palavras esdruxulas' [words accented on the antepenultimate syllable]?" When the little boy did not answer, he asked him another question, "What are polysyllabic words?"
> I told the teacher that if this was the way he taught the black boys, they would easily come to know as much as the professor, but they would never know enough to start down the road of life.
>
> (Quoted in Duffy 1959:368)

The report made by the African Education Commission set up under the auspices of the Phelps-Stokes Fund and the foreign mission societies of North American and Europe also had little positive to say about Portuguese educational policy. Commission members visited Angola in 1921 and Mozambique in 1924. The Commission noted the hostility to

Protestant missions, the practice of excluding African languages from the schools, the levels of apathy and misunderstanding in provincial government circles, the lack of funds, and the absence of plans to encourage training for African teachers. It concluded that not only was the present state of education in Angola and Mozambique very backward in comparison with that of its neighbours, but also that there was "practically no basis for hope of any essential improvement of colonial policy." (Quoted in Duffy 1959:259)

Colonial Schools Under Salazar

By the time the Salazar regime established a state-sponsored schooling system in the colony, debate on education had increased. As with most social policies, the schooling policy did not appear in a void but in response to a specific situation of contestation that needed containment. In the period at the beginning of the century, schooling's power for liberation was recognized, both by colonizer and colonized. Portugal's claims to a civilizing mission were not unchallenged, and those with access to education were amongst the most vociferous in questioning their legitimacy.

By 1928, concern about the expectations created by education had been raised in a study on the labour force in Homoine district of Inhambane province in southern Mozambique. Too much access to schooling was seen as dangerous, creating expectations that could not be met.

> In the province of Mozambique. . . . we continue to make the usual mistake, the old system of assimilation. Because of this, there is already a super abundance of schooled natives in all the districts -- the assimilated -- who, since they are not all able to get a response to their demand for the right to be considered educated and nomination for a public position, are already trying to organize into class groupings and found newspapers to attack the duly constituted powers. Not far off is the demand for the right to carry out nationalist political propaganda, attacking and injuring the European race, similar to what has happened and is growing in our neighbouring English colonies.
>
> (Quoted in Hedges 1982:5; my translation)

The climate of contestation around education was even more pronounced in the urban areas. The work of Jeanne Penvenne (Penvenne 1979a) exploring African attitudes towards race and work in Lourenço Marques throughout this century indicates lively debate in the first quarter of the century among urban, educated Africans about Portugal's claims to a civilizing and colonizing missions, and indeed about Portugal's education policies. According to her informants and her study of the African press during this period, educated African and mulatto families in the urban areas at the turn of the century had great disdain for the Portuguese settlers, whom they referred to as "mumadji," perhaps most aptly translated as "poor white trash." Penvenne concludes that the African population saw the Portuguese institutions and forms for carrying out its "civilizing" mission as crude and ineffective compared to those carried out through the British/South Africa connection.

Penvenne quotes from the most articulate African voices, those of the newspapers "The African" and later its successor, "The African Cry," both of which were published in both Portuguese *and Ronga* (the predominant language of the three southern provinces). These papers compared British and Portuguese activities in the colonies. They favoured the British/South African policies over those of the Portuguese, who were seen to live off the backs of the black population. The British hired labour; the Portuguese conscripted theirs. The British provided direct benefits to the population through veterinarians organizing cattle dips or British migrant labour recruiters organizing jobs in the mines. The Portuguese merely collected taxes. Any material benefits they organized accrued only to the settlers.

One of the points of difference that triggered much critical comment was the unwillingness of the Portuguese to speak Mozambican languages. While Portuguese missionaries and health personnel ignored African languages, personnel of the two most prominent foreign missions and the already well-established labour recruitment organization, WENELA (Witwatersrand Native Labour Association) were fluent in local languages. In Maputo, the African population sought out mission hospitals over state hospitals, since in the mission hospitals, everyone from the receptionist to the surgeon spoke Ronga. (Penvenne 1979a:16)

Penvenne's interviews with older workers reflecting back on colonial times include references to the pain and shame of reprimands in schools and workplaces for speaking what the Portuguese referred to as the "language of the dogs." Some even went so far as to speak positively of the South African use of "fanakalo" or "lolo," the Lourenço Marques names for the conglomerate "lingua franca" of the mining industry.

The question of what it meant for South African or Rhodesian mine managers to converse in fanakalo and what the establishment of fanakalo as a "lingua franca" really accomplished bears much scrutiny. Few saw it in the positive light conveyed to Penvenne. Charles van Onselen in his study of mine labour in Rhodesia quotes the opinion of one early observer on the virtues of fanakalo.

> The jargon – it cannot be dignified with the name of language -- in general used in the mines is "Kitchen Kaffir," a villainous mixture of bad Dutch and worse Zulu interspersed with English oaths; the unfortunate native is supposed to understand this and he is frequently abused for "not knowing his own language!"
>
> (Quoted in van Onselen 1980:152)

Van Onselen goes on to make his own trenchant criticism, much at odds with the feelings expressed to Penvenne by older workers in Mozambique who saw adoptiong of fanakalo as a farsighted policy on the part of the British and South Africans compared to Portugal's rigid insistence on Portuguese.

> The colonised status of compound inhabitants was continuously reinforced in a thousand insidious ways. Daily life was even regulated by a system of communication which denied the workers any independence, coherence, maturity or comprehension: . . . the language used was the industrial "lingua franca, fanakalo" which dominated the mining industries in southern Africa and this bastard tongue lay at the base of much of the friction and violence in the compounds. . . .
>
> The effects on blacks of the disorientation induced by the use of this strange and inadequate "language," and the combination of demoralisation and resentment aroused by on-going colonisation in the compounds and the regime of violence there, were to do much to mould the nature of African response within the whole industrial setting of central Africa.
>
> (van Onselen 1980:152)

Certainly amongst the tiny urban population of educated black and mulatto families, the British and South African presence in Lourenço Marques served to highlight the backwardness of the Portuguese and the crudeness of their forms of governance.[1] Assimilation was a status severely discredited, since it so evidently meant, at best, only second-class citizenship. There were regular newspaper articles denouncing "assimilated" status as demeaning to the African and fraudulent, since the rights and privileges it was meant to guarantee were still subject to the colonial authorities' whim. (Penvenne 1979a)

The work of the Salazar regime to reorganize time and space in a way that legitimized a world of the "civilized", separate in every respect from the world of the "savage," became the more imperative as voices contesting the colonial regime and its claim to rule emerged more strongly. One of the last public voices querying Portugal's colonizing mission was that of the African press, before it was censored out of existence. "O Brado Africano" published a ringing editorial in 1932 entitled "Enough" which shows clearly how urban, educated

Mozambicans perceived their situation vis-a-vis colonial claims of civilizing missions.

> We are fed up to the teeth.
> Fed up with supporting you, with suffering the terrible
> consequences of your follies, your demands with the
> squandering misuse of your authority.
> We can no longer stand the pernicious effects of your
> political and administrative decisions.
> We are no longer willing to make greater and greater useless sacrifices . . .
> Enough . . .
> We want you to manifest, not by laws and decrees, but by deeds, your
> elementary obligations.
> We want to be treated as you treat yourself.
> We do not want the comforts with which you have surrounded
> yourselves at the cost of our sweat.
> We do not want your refined education . . . since we do not
> want a life dominated by the idea of robbing our fellow men . . .
> We prefer our savage state, which fills your mouths and your pockets.
> But we do want something . . .
> We want bread, we want light. . . .
> We don't want to pay for services which are of no use
> to us . . . for institutions whose benefits we never feel . . .
> We no longer want to suffer the bottomless pit of your
> excellent colonial administration!
> We want of you a more humane policy . . .
> We repeat that we don't want hunger, nor thirst, nor disease,
> nor discriminatory laws founded on the difference of colour.
> We have the scalpel ready.
> We shall dissect your work . . .
> We are daring, the result of ignorance.
> We shall learn how to use the scalpel . . .
> The gangrene you spread will infect us and later we will
> not have the strength to act. Now we do . . . It is the
> instinct for self-preservation. We are beasts of burden
> and like them we possess it . . .
> Enough, gentlemen. Change your ways. There still is time.
> (Quoted in Duffy 1959:306)

Amidst the climate of social unrest underlying these sentiments, clearly an institution of containment was necessary, one that could regulate social identity in a way that located Africans firmly within the orbit of Portuguese time, space and culture. State provided schooling was seen as the answer.[2]

A School System for the "Indigenous"

After 1930, then, a much more rigorous policy of education and assimilation was established by the Salazar regime, including state-sponsored schooling. The colonial regime's project of establishing "assimilado" status as something to be coveted, African incapacity to attain it as the problem and schooling as the solution is perhaps best understood as a project of social control. It was an ideological project, aimed at the reproduction of social classes of ruler and subordinated and at the same time a containment of the climate of contestation and unrest that the pre-Salazar period had unleashed.

A more classic colonial relationship with the Portuguese metropole and the, by then, consolidated Portuguese bourgeoisie was part of Salazar's project. This necessitated an education policy not only to control the African labour force but to groom the colonizers. There was a necessity to reproduce through education a settler class with the necessary skills and attitudes to govern and exploit the colony effectively, and a "people" ready to accept these claims to governance. Thus one strand of the education policy was that of a formal separation between schools for the settler's children and schools for the "indigenous," to establish more clearly distinctions between rulers and ruled.

The recommendations of education officials concerning public schooling were published in Lourenço Marques in *Schooling Annual*, 1930. These recommendations tackled both the question of separate systems for black and white and the keenly felt issue of control over the mission schools, still at this time predominantly in Protestant hands and deemed to be offering education of the wrong type and in the wrong languages.

> The increase in the civilized population of the Colony, particularly in Lourenço Marques, demanding an increasingly marked separation between the teaching for indigenous and civilized children, for the benefit of both, and the need to regulate the teaching carried out by the religious missions, gave birth . . . to all of the indigenous schooling in the Colony.
>
> (Quoted in Hedges 1982:5,6; my translation)

The public schooling system operated by the state for the children of the "civilized" was patterned after the primary and secondary schooling systems operating in Portugal itself. The schools were directed by the Ministry of National Education in Lisbon, which included within it a Department of Overseas Education.

> The official system essentially provided the colonists with government schooling up to the level and in the areas needed by the economy. The colonist was a low government functionary, a small farmer or trader, an

TABLE 4.1 Primary School Enrolment 1934-1974

	Public	Private (Protestant)	Mission (Roman Catholic)	Mission	Total
1934	3,505	372	493	49,263	53,633
1944	4,019	862	4,149	102,953	111,983
1945	8,683	1,130	6,797	220,799	237,389
1964	27,904	2,451	14,370	373,587	418,312
1974	623,771	13,053	-	-	636,824

Source: Adapted from Ministry of Education and Culture (INDE). 1980. Education Systems in Mozambique. (Quoted in Marshall 1985:162)

> artisan or skilled worker, often from an illiterate peasant background in Portugal, though usually destined to occupy a position above that he could expect in the metropole. Thus the schooling available even for the colonist was of low quality. Until the 1950s there was only one official general secondary school; and the secondary road for most was into commercial or industrial schooling.
>
> (Johnston 1989:47)

Enrolment was extremely small until the 1950s, when a massive influx of settlers from Portugal arrived. These was a 30 percent enrolment increase between 1954 and 1956 alone (Duffy 1959:314), with enrolment more than tripling over the ten year period between 1954 and 1964. These government elementary schools were open only to assimilated Africans. Even as late as 1954, there were only 322 Africans enroled in the government primary schools. (Duffy 1959:314)

By 1954, the public schooling system provided by the state included 71 primary schools, 12 elementary professional schools (a craft school offered as a perk to the sons of the "régulos"), two government technical schools and one government high school. There were no government teacher training institutions. (Duffy 1959:314)

The system of schooling that emerged under the Salazar regime was organized in such a way as to deny more access than it created and to fail more students than it passed, while at the same time blaming the victim. Each of the three levels eliminated almost the entire group of students who entered, sending them back to the families and communities that had placed them in school as certified failures.

The first level was a three year system of rudimentary education for Africans. According to the first article of Legislative Diploma 238 of 1930, the rudimentary stage had as its objective "gradually to lead the 'indigenous' from savage life to civilization . . . making him conscious of himself as Portuguese citizen and preparing him for life's battles, making him more useful to society and to himself." (Quoted in Hedges 1982:6) The 1930 legislation also laid down the precise curriculum for African education. Article 8 outlines its contents. They were to include:

a. Portuguese language
b. arithmetic and the metric system
c. history and geography of Portugal
d. design and manual work
e. physical education and hygiene
f. moral education and choral music

Specific instruction for geography and history teachers about how to teach were contained in the syllabus laid out in the *Schooling Annual* of the same year.

> Both the choice of history themes and the explanations given by the teacher must bear in mind the creation in the pupils of love for Portugal and legitimate pride in having been born in Portuguese territory.
>
> (Quoted in Hedges 1982:6; my translation)

The new system of rudimentary schooling was compulsory for all African children between the ages of seven and ten living within a three kilometre radius of a school. The number of schools expanded fairly rapidly, according to official statistics, with 154 primary schools in place in 1940, each with one partially trained teacher. (Hedges 1982:7)

Rudimentary schooling was comprised of "initiation," first class and second class. For those who successfully completed second class, it was possible to enter the primary schooling system comprised of third class, fourth class and "admission." The "admission" programme was geared to secondary school entrance requirements. Successful completion of this six year programme allowed entry into the "liceu" or secondary school. Maximum age for entry into the "liceu" was 13.

For Europeans and "assimilated," there was a four year programme (as of 1962, five) for entry into secondary school. The secondary school programme consisted of three cycles for a total of seven years, in preparation for university entrance.

For African students, the administrative hurdles to attain these educational levels were enormous. In addition to being forced to learn a foreign language, they had to meet age restrictions for entry into each level. Many African children began to study when they were already eight or nine. Schools were few, and at times too distant for younger children to reach on foot. Financial resources were scarce to buy the clothing necessary to send children to school. Few children successfully completed the primary school programme; of those who did, many were ruled ineligible for secondary schooling because of age restrictions.

If the barriers because of age restriction were not enough, there were, in fact, many others. For a peasant family immersed in the village level social relations so thoroughly regulated by the colonial regime, it was not just a question of having the financial means. Preferential treatment was given to the children of the "régulo" and other "traditional" leaders now functioning as local level functionaries of the colonial state. Talking with workers 35 years later about their experiences of primary schooling in rural districts in the fifties inevitably included a fresh flare of resentment about this injustice. Cristina Mavale, a 42 year old unskilled worker at CIM, had this to say:

> My father died when I was a child. After, I stayed with my grandparents. Senhora Judith knows how it was, eh? In those days, when it came time to study, it was the son of the "régulo" who went. . . .
>
> (Interview with Cristina Mavale, March 1986)

For many parents schooling posed an insuperable financial burden. A child in school meant a loss in family labour power, since children played important roles in tending cattle, fetching water and minding smaller children, all crucial tasks in family economies where the male was absent more often than not, doing either forced or contract labour. It also meant expenses for clothing and footwear.

> It wasn't a question of not wanting to study in colonial times. It was a question of power -- parents who were able to put their children in school. Everybody wanted schooling but not everybody had the means.
>
> (Interview with Leonor Benjamim, February 1986)

The policy decision on language of instruction created another huge administrative barrier. No account was taken of the need to learn a second language as a prerequisite for learning other subject matter. The total arbitrariness of this policy was evident. Ostensibly the rudimentary schooling programme was designed to introduce children to Portuguese. Nonetheless, in rural areas, mulatto and Asian children brought up speaking Portuguese as a first language were also placed in the rudimentary schools. In other areas, children of Asian or non-Portuguese European parents for whom Portuguese was a second language were allowed to start in the state primary schools. (Mondlane 1983:63)

Teaching in the schools for the "indigenous" was carried out entirely in Portuguese with the exception of the catechism which could be taught in the children's mother tongue. The inadequately trained teachers suffered great difficulties trying to teach the various disciplines in a language not spoken by the children. Many neglected the syllabus and contented themselves with filling classroom time with rote learning of the catechism in local languages. As one woman reflecting back on it put it:

> I went to school up to second class. There was a lot of doctrine and not much mathematics and Portuguese at the Cambine Mission. There was also a lot of work growing maize, peanuts and cassava to buy school materials.
>
> (Interview with Clementina Ofício, February 1986)

For those few "indigenous" students who did manage to complete their primary schooling, the administrative barriers for going on to secondary schooling were, if anything, even more formidable. Few were the missions schools that even offered the fifth year programme in preparation for secondary school. Fewer still were the parents who could send their children to the city and pay for them to attend a private school in preparation for secondary schooling.

The lower secondary schools were all in towns, necessitating that parents in rural areas arrange transport and boarding facilities. There were only three upper secondary schools, one in Beira and two in Lourenço Marques. In some cases, Protestant missions arranged for student hostels in these cities in which pupils from the rural areas could board.

If "indigenous" children in general were subjected to these multiple hurdles militating against educational success, the girls had yet more hurdles placed in front of them. On the one hand, the social construction of appropriate roles for women established by traditional African society -- and in no way challenged by Portuguese settler society -- meant that families ruled out schooling for their daughters. Few girls even got as far as the classroom door. Striking in the interviews with women doing adult basic education after independence was the pattern in the 1950s of the boys in the family having completed three or four years of primary schooling while the girls remained illiterate.

For those girls who did make it to the classroom, the opportunity to learn was still often out of reach because of gender. Women recalling their schooling experiences in the 1950s spoke of inordinate amounts of time spent doing tasks for the teachers such as cooking and cleaning in the teacher's house. Alicinda Macuacua, an unskilled worker who packages pasta in a Maputo factory, remained illiterate as a child, along with her three sisters, while her brother completed lower primary schooling. She can still recall vividly her experiences in the Santa Maria

Mission School where sexual discrimination meant that the girls who were sent there spent much of their time collecting firewood and farming. Only the boys really got a chance to study. (Interview with Alicinda Macuacua, July 1985)

Schooling and the Roman Catholic Church

A key aspect of the education policy under Salazar was the central role played by the Roman Catholic church. Basically, education for the African population came to be provided by the Catholic missions. The churches were seen as key in the civilizing mission with increasingly close collaboration between church and state established by legislation. Already in the Constitution of 1933, overseas Catholic missions and their training institutions were guaranteed protection and assistance from the state. They were recognized as "institutions of education, of assistance, and instruments of civilization." (Hedges 1982:7; my translation)

The privileged status already enjoyed by the Catholic missions after the accession to power of Salazar was formalized and institutionalized in the concordat signed with the Vatican in 1940. An annexed missionary accord was incorporated in the 1941 Missionary Statute, article 66, which entrusted all education intended for natives to missionary personnel and their auxiliaries. The two-fold objectives of education were clear:

> The aim of these plans and programmes shall be to make the native population national and moral, and to inculcate such work habits and skills for each sex as suit the conditions and requirements of the regional economies; moral education shall aim at curing laziness and preparing future rural workers and craftsmen to produce what they need to satisfy their own requirements and their social obligations. The education of the indigenous population shall thus be essentially nationalist and practical, the native then being able to gain a living for himself and his family; and it shall take due account of the social conditions and psychology of the populations for whom it is intended.
>
> (Quoted in Ferreira 1974:67)

The schools were the vehicle par excellence to inculcate this sense of identity with the glory of the Portuguese empire. They worked to create a social identity, a locating of the African within time and space measured against the hallowed rights of being a "citizen," within the larger "nation." Thus education was to turn the African into a "true Portuguese," ready to accept Portuguese rule. It was to train good agricultural workers and craftsmen useful to the colonial economy. There was much stress on the pomp and circumstance of nationhood and an almost mystical reiteration of Portugal's vocation as civilizer with a special mission to the land of the "discoveries."

The educational policies and practices established in the colonies are not to be wondered at when one considers what was happening within metropolitan Portugal itself.[3] The "estado Novo" (New State) established by the 1933 Constitution, shortly after Salazar's accession to power, set out guidelines for education in which there should be:

> . . . a reduction of programmes to allow for concentration on "fundamentals," an emphasis on "applied knowledge" [this meant on design and manual work for boys and domestic activities for girls] and "all principles are to indicate ideas of country, family and the love of birthplace."
>
> (Quoted in Stoer 1981:336)

The missions were authorized to offer schooling in the colonies but the actual funds for physical expansion of the missions -- for staff housing, school classrooms, workshops and transport -- were not provided by the state. Instead the colonial state sanctioned close collaboration between the missions and local state officials who made land and labour available in abundance. A variation of the system of forced labour, "chibalo" was established in the mission schools.

> Pupils came to be used as a free source of labour for agricultural production, especially rice and cotton, subsequently sold to improve mission finances. This form of exploitation, a kind of forced labour extracted by the missions in the guise of payment for education -- which many rural parents wanted for their children despite the difficulties and costs -- came to be known as "Xipadre." (Xibalo in the mission fields.) Often parents had to supply the hoes of their children so exploited, and in addition contribute sacks of maize and beans -- also supposedly in payment for the education received, but in reality a tithe of agricultural production which the mission could dispose of for profit as it saw fit. The close collaboration of church and local administration was shown in the disposal of "Xibalo" and prison labour; the Catholic missions received Xibalo for their farms, and on the other hand, allowed "recruitment" of older pupils by the administration before their dispersal home.
>
> (Hedges 1982:9,10)

During the two decades after 1940, the Roman Catholic missions expanded dramatically. Senior figures in the church hierarchy were paid the salaries and allowances of colonial officials. Schools and missions came to receive some financial support. Control of teacher training for the "indigenous" was entrusted to the Roman Catholic missions as well, with all preparation of teaching staff at all levels to be carried out in colleges and schools established by the Prelates in accordance with the Governor of the colony. All personnel of these training institutions were to be Portuguese.

This close collaboration between the state and the Roman Catholic church was tantamount to a frontal attack on the "foreign" missions, much suspect for the ideological content of their education over the years. The Protestant missions were seen to be too liberal, with a propensity to validate African languages and culture and generally encourage education for Africans in a way that gave them a tendency to be "uppity." These attitudes continued unabated, up to the end of colonial rule in Mozambique, according to Eduardo Mondlane, first president of the Mozambique Liberation Front, FRELIMO.

> Since the seventeenth century, foreign missionaries have been suspected of "denationalizing the natives," and of acting as advance agents for foreign governments. When these missionaries are Protestant, fears and resentments are multiplied. Consequently, for many years the Protestant missions in Mozambique have been hampered and quite often thwarted by a powerful combination of the Portuguese Catholic clergy and officials of the colonial government. From time to time, public statements are made by high officials of the colonial government attacking Protestant missions, accusing them of fomenting anti-Portuguese sentiments amongst the African population.
>
> (Mondlane 1983:71)

TABLE 4.2 Mission Expansion 1940 to 1960

	1940	*1950*	*1960*
Catholic missions	296	851	2000
"Foreign" missions	41	39	27

Source: Hedges 1982:10

TABLE 4.3 Primary School Enrolments and Pass Rates 1940 to 1960

	1940	*1950*	*1960*
Total enrolment	50,000	232,923	379,068
Passes	1,844	2,985	10,448
Percent	3.6%	1.2%	2.7%

Source: Adapted from Hedges 1982:10

In the period from 1940 to 1960, the Catholic missions expanded dramatically while the "foreign" missions were reduced. The numbers of schools in the Catholic mission system by 1954 included 1,356 rudimentary schools, 55 primary schools, 51 elementary professional schools and four teacher training institutions. (Duffy 1959:314)

Schooling for Subordination

Whether measured by the intake of "indigenous" students to the system, pass rates, or entry to the next level, the results show a system little guaranteed to make education accessible or relevant to Africans. Even by 1959, there were only 392,796 children in the schooling programme for African children, now called "Adaptation Schooling." Of these, only 6,928 managed to move on to primary school. (Mondlane 1983:65) In 1960, there were only 30 African students in a student body of more than 1000 at the main secondary school in Lourenço Marques, Liceu Salazar. On the eve of independence in 1975, primary school enrolment was still only slightly over 600,000 in a population of 10.5 million.

The failure rates were staggeringly high. It would seem, then, that less than 3.5 percent of those entering rudimentary schooling actually completed it successfully. Striking is the fact that the pass rate for comparable levels in the surviving Protestant schools was 25-28 percent. (Hedges 1982:10)

What is perhaps astonishing is how oblivious the Portuguese leaders, both in church and state, were to the signs of the times. In 1960, at the same time that other African countries were gaining their independence and nationalist leaders from Mozambique had begun to group to form the Mozambique Liberation Front, the Portuguese prelate, Gouveia, was still writing pastoral letters in the tones of the 1920s.

> . . . we intend to reach the native population extensively and in depth to teach people to read, write and count, not to make doctors of them. . . . The schools are necessary, yes, but schools where the native is taught the path of human dignity and the greatness of the nation that protects him.
> (Quoted in Hedges 1982:14)

Dramatic changes were in the offing. The nationalist protest had strengthened, dramatized by the armed revolt in Angola in 1961. By 1964, the three movements of Mozambican nationalists that had formed in newly independent neighbouring countries joined together to form the Mozambique Liberation Front. FRELIMO launched an armed struggle for national independence in 1964.

The Portuguese economy was also changing greatly, opening up to foreign investment as a way to fortify against the nationalist assault, and in so doing, creating the need for a work force with new kinds of skills. Colonial policies were also subject to review. The "Estatuto Indigena" was abolished, and with it, compliance with the Missionary Statute and the practice of educational institutions only for Africans. Primary school was made compulsory for all children between six and twelve.

Secondary schools were expanded. From 1918 to 1958 there had been only one secondary school. By 1962 there were six official secondary schools and another 26 private secondary schools. This growth was still mainly in response to settler needs with the settler population growing from 54,000 in 1950 to 97,000 in 1960 to 163,000 in 1970. (Egero 1987:49) By 1973, on the eve of independence, only 27 percent of the general secondary school enrolment was African. (Azevedo 1977:199)

New technical schools were also created. Here African enrolment was slightly higher. In 1964/5, the school-age population of 11-19 was 97 percent African. The general secondary enrolment, however, was only 8 percent African while enrolment in the various technical schools was 20 percent African. The crafts and trades schools catered almost entirely to Africans, with 92 percent of their students being of African origin. In addition to the trade schools run by the state, the missions set up a lot of post-primary trade schools for Africans in the rural districts offering training in welding, carpentry, auto repairs and agriculture.

A university was established in 1963 offering general studies with a stress on natural science. A faculty of economics was added in 1970. Even by 1972, 83 percent of the students were in science or commerce. (Johnston 1989:61)

A small but significant group of Mozambican students was able to exercise the right of all citizens to sit for exams that allowed access to educational institutions anywhere in the Portuguese "Nation." Those who went to Portugal to do social science met others from the Portuguese colonies in Angola and Guinea-Bissau and encountered an intellectual

TABLE 4.4 Educational Qualifications 1970 (in percentages)

	Total	*Male*	*Female*
University	0.1	0.1	0.1
Secondary school	0.9	1.2	0.7
Primary school	9.0	13.0	6.0
Illiterate	90.0	86.0	93.0

Source: Adapted from Johnston 1989:63

and political milieu in which radical ideas flourished. This group, although small, made an important impact in shaping the direction of the emerging liberation movements and linking them together. The Portuguese were not slow to see this danger. The colonial government "barred all education abroad to Mozambican young men for fear they might acquire ideas of freedom and independence. Hence, more than 90 percent of Mozambican students abroad had no Portuguese passports and left the county in an aura of absolute secrecy." (Azevedo 1977:198)

For well-to-do settlers, Johannesburg vied with Portugal as the metropole. For many, the economic links that bound Mozambique to South Africa were reinforced with cultural and social links.

> Aside from the obvious economic ties, South Africa was to Mozambique's rich an oasis of modern cities and shops, gleaming hospitals and well-appointed schools. Many sent their children to study in South Africa. Some did so because it was closer and cheaper than sending them to Portugal. But others chose South Africa because they considered it a model society.
>
> While youngsters who studied in Portugal often returned with non-racialist, anti-colonial ideas nurtured on European campuses, those back from South Africa were typically imbued with admiration for the "big neighbour" and its hardnosed apartheid policies.
>
> (Machado da Graça and Massingue 1990:M6)

Educational provision for adults also expanded during the 1960s and 1970s, particularly through the missions. Night school enrolment expanded, many of the students being young people too old to do their basic primary education in the day schools. Enrolment fluctuated widely from year to year. The pass rate was abysmally low for the effort, averaging only 24 percent over the years.

In the mid-1960s, the colonial government came forward with a new initiative, SEE, an external education service for adults. SEE worked in two broad fields, one for the promotion of women and the other for the diffusion of the Portuguese language. It developed teaching materials in areas like nutrition, hygiene and civics as well as course for "detribalized

TABLE 4.5 Adult Primary Schooling 1963-1973

Year	*1963/4*	*1964/5*	*1965/6*	*1966/7*	*1968/9*	*1972/3*
Enrolment	16,055	9,751	10,818	12,623	20,222	10,288
Completion	2,588	1,931	4,026	3,493	2,622	3,784

Source: DPSEM, 1964-1973. Quoted in Johnston 1989:207

women." The SEE document, "The Situation of Detribalized Women," provides notes for a teachers' manual for a women's course being organized in Beira in 1964 and makes very clear SEE's objectives.

> It is useful to arrange attractive material to maintain and intensify the conversation with the [women] pupils and, above all, it is not permitted that, once they are able to speak our tongue, they speak the native language in front of us. They should be made to see the advantages of speaking Portuguese with each other -- the language which can upraise them, and indeed, the only one which socially has value amongst us, the Portuguese [people] that we all are: black, white, yellow, or of any other race.
>
> (Quoted in Johnston 1989:62)

Language once again emerges as a key issue of social control. SEE with its programme of education for adults is clearly, like the school system for children and youth, an important institution for state regulation of racial and ethnic relations.

The new education policy altered its discourse marginally to make the shift from church to state sponsorship, playing down the Christianizing mission and substituting a somewhat mystified vision of Lusitanian nationhood and a multi-continental Portugal. The contents of the texts were to a degree Africanized, including images of African life in rural areas and towns. There was a stress on visual images showing harmonious relations of Africans and whites, especially in the primary grades. The glorification of Portuguese "discoveries" was already a strong theme by third and fourth grade history, however, with Portuguese ships on the textbook covers. One textbook had the title "Sails for Christ." The other quoted the Portuguese epic poet Camões, " . . . and if there were more worlds they would reach them." (Quoted in Ferreira 1974:86)

The social construction of "schooling" is extremely interesting to analyze. Schooling was posed as the path out of the misery of the "indigenous status." The lived experience of daily brutality and crude exploitation at the hands of the colonial state was worked up ideologically as the "problem" of being "indigenous," of being, by nature, of an inferior race, brutish, totally lacking in culture. The "problem" of being "indigenous" could be resolved by something called "schooling." "Schooling," however, meant a special system for Africans, replete with bureaucratic and administrative categories that made it extremely difficult to succeed.

Certainly reflecting back on education under colonialism, Mozambicans were very clear about its shortcomings. Gabriel Maurício Nantimbo, a former pupil at Inbuho mission school had this to say:

> I studied at the missions, but we weren't well taught. In the first place, they taught us only what they wanted us to learn – the catechism; they didn't want us to learn other things. Then every morning we had to work on the mission land. They said our fathers didn't pay for our food or our school things. The missions also received money from the government, and our families paid them fees. After 1958 our parents even had to buy the hoes with which we cultivated the mission land.
>
> (Quoted in Mondlane 1983:72)

The diplomas for successful completion of schooling within this system communicate its aims very clearly. Designed in 1937, the diplomas were still in use in 1966. The ideological project is not hard to decipher. Schooling is for male, white children, resolutely holding up the flag of the Portuguese fatherland. The Bible and the faith provide a solid foundation, the soil from which an abundance of produce, more typical of Portugal than Mozambique, can flourish. The schools, replete with the pomp and circumstance of flag-raising, the national anthem, drilling for national holidays and songs for visiting dignitaries, played a key role in shaping social identity. Schools served as an important institution in the creation of political subjects, within the larger project of state formation.

A document presented to UNESCO shortly after independence by the Mozambique Liberation Front put it succinctly:

> In sum, beyond the boundaries of the areas liberated by FRELIMO, all schools were based on racism, divisionism, elitism, individualism, obscurantism and contempt for all things African. Many a Mozambican who managed to surmount the many obstacles to secondary or higher education did so at the cost of turning himself into a little black Portuguese, the docile instrument of colonialism, whose ambition was to live like a settler, in whose image he was created.

The Colonial Education System: Success or Failure?

How are we to evaluate the colonial school system? Evidently it was not successful if we assume it to have been established to give mass access to knowledge and skills. Few were the African children who had access to it. The illiteracy rate at independence in 1975 was estimated at 90 percent.

The adults who lived through this period have now passed through a process of social revolution. It is not easy to reconstruct the powerful hold the colonial school had on the local population. People look back on colonial institutions with a critical appreciation more related to contemporary events than to a genuine reconstruction of how such institutions

Diploma

DE HABILITAÇÃO NO ENSINO PRIMÁRIO (4ª CLASSE)

Certifico que

Jorge Matitimelane Novunga

FILHO DE Cufesse

E DE Uazumene Saile

NASCIDO EM ... DE ... DE 1935 NA FREGUESIA DE Vamuza, CONCELHO OU CIRCUNSCRIÇÃO DE Chibuto - Gaza

PRESTOU AS PROVAS

DE EXAME DA 4ª CLASSE DO ENSINO PRIMÁRIO EM 4 DE Julho DE 1966 E

Foi aprovado

COM ...

Lourenço Marques, 8 DE Agosto DE 1966

O Director Escolar Adjunto

REPUBLICA PORTUGUESA

MARTINS BARATA 1937

FIGURE 4.1 Primary School Diploma Lourenço Marques, 1966

worked on their lives forty or fifty years ago.

Illiterate parents struggling to send their children to school in the 1940s and 1950s did not record in documentary forms their reactions to the role of the school in their community. There are no "home and school" archives to aid us in reconstructing. The African press which had been so vociferous in its criticisms of earlier forms of schooling was effectively silenced under the Salazar regime. Indeed we have suggested above that the advent of a public schooling system was, at least in part, meant to contain the kinds of questioning and social unrest of the first decades of the century. The accounts from missionaries are from people involved themselves as dispensers of education. It is not simple, then, to give an account of the successes or failures of the colonial school system, much less of how Mozambicans at the time experienced the massive lack of access to it or the massive number of failures within it.

Perhaps a closer look at the colonial schools in terms of regulating the labour force and providing skills training gives a slightly different picture. The missions tended to have very substantial agricultural holdings and also large workshops ranging from car repairs to carpentry and metal work. This meant that the many students who left as certified failures in terms of the literary skills evaluated in school exams and needed as a prerequisite for "assimilated" status, were, in fact, fed back into their communities with new practical skills. They could be drawn through "chibalo" to apply their skills on the plantations or on state building projects or road construction. Indeed older pupils were recruited directly from the schools to forced labour contracts. Any positive features of this are measured only from the colonial side; for the African pupil, the skill acquisition gained through "xipadre" was not recognized as a qualification for permanent work. This skilling component of schooling simply made the labour force to be drawn into forced labour a more competent one.

Perhaps the more interesting assessment of the colonial education system, however, is one that does not look for schooling to be a mechanism for individual advancement, particularly for the popular classes. It looks neither for academic qualifications or skills training from schooling but sees schooling primarily as an ideological project.

In many societies public schooling systems have been introduced as instruments of social control. They have been key instruments in creating a social identity as "citizen" within a particular organization of time and space defined as "nation." (Corrigan, Curtis, Lanning 1987) Schooling has proved itself an effective mechanism for both rulers and subordinated to become convinced of the appropriateness of their "station." The assessment of individual worth certified by the school comes to be accepted. The school's day to day regulation of parameters, of the possible ways of speaking, thinking, doing, comes to be internalized.

There are real doubts as to whether the Portuguese colonial regime was sufficiently skilled at governing to be able to establish a school system that enjoyed this kind of legitimacy from the governed. Many would question whether schooling contributed positively to the ideological "glue" bonding rulers and ruled into a nation.

It is clear that at least for some of the urban dwellers, the project of establishing "assimilation" as desirable and schooling as the path to it never gained widespread legitimacy. The contradictions were too evident. Assimilated Africans in the urban areas were known as "pocket whites" or "paper whites" since their status depended on the paper which they had to keep on their person at all time, to be produced on demand. There were practical reasons for choosing to become assimilated, however, that had little to do with belief in Portugal's exaggerated claim to be guardian of "civilization."

> From the writings of the first African to receive the so-called *alvara de assimilação*, assimilation certificate, in 1917 to interviews with contemporary Mozambicans who filed for assimilation certificates in the years immediately preceding their abolition as part of the paper reforms of 1961-1962, it is clear that the assimilation certification was sought, often grudgingly, in order to facilitate upward mobility, minimize harassment and hopefully open opportunities for one's children. The obvious inequality of having to verify one's equality with a document to be carried on one's person and presented upon demand to white authorities at all times was a sore point from the start, but the legal and economic privileges carried by the status were sufficient to convince some 700 Mozambicans in the years up to 1954 to take out assimilation papers in the Lourenço Marques courts.
>
> (Penvenne 1979a:12)

Many rejected out of hand Portugal's claim as gate-keeper to civilization. At the same time they saw the assimilation certificate as a practical necessity.[4]

> I always carried the documents of a native, because I am a native. I am a Negro after all, aren't I. But after a long time I also became an *assimilado*, and like the majority of natives here what convinced me was the possibility of earning a bit more money – it was for this reason alone. . . . Those who were not *assimilados* were Negros after all, and as such they always earned a pittance.
>
> (Quoted in Penvenne 1979a:14)

The decision whether to opt for the assimilation certificate or not was open to a tiny handful of urban wage workers at best. As indicated earlier, even by the beginning of the 1960s, less than two percent of the population was assimilated.

For the vast majority of the African population in Mozambique, the option to become a "paper white" was well beyond their grasp. They were subjected to another textually-mediated form of rule. This was the hated "caderneta", or pass book, a document with enormous power over their lives. For Africans, it was obligatory to have the "caderneta" on your person at all times even in the most remote and dispersed rural communities. It was a text that bound African producers to the colonial state as if with an umbilical cord. Through it, words and texts and signatures took on a new power, with literacy linked to a world both desired and feared.

The "caderneta" created a documentary existence. It transformed rural producers, tied by complex links into their own nexus of social relationships in family and community, into administrative categories of taxpayers and labour units. The redefinition of spatial boundaries was accomplished through the "caderneta." Free movement from one area to another was restricted, except with express authorization of the local administrator written into the "caderneta."

The reordering of time for peasant producers was also accomplished through this textually mediated form of rule. The "caderneta" included a record of labour activity. Family production was made invisible as a legitimate use of time, falling under the category of "idle time." The local administrator was responsible for defining and controlling time spent in "idleness." The only legitimate uses of time were time spent in contract South Africa and Rhodesia, time spent in "chibalo", or forced labour, and time spent in wage employment. The rich and complex texture of rural production and society were totally transformed through the regulation of labour accomplished through the textually mediated discourse turning on "idleness."

Both oral and written forms of literacy, then, came to have an inordinate power over people's lives, one whose humiliating effects they could do little to control. The contract labourers in the mines were declared deficient and even punished for not knowing "their own language" -- fanakalo. Children arriving in schools were expected to learn in a language of instruction they had no way of knowing and which the school system did not propose to teach. Adults put thumb prints as substitutes for signatures on "cadernetas" that forced them to be fugitives in their own land, going underground or into exile to escape the labour obligations forced upon them. Through all of this, the power of literacy was consolidated.

Portugal's continued readiness for heavy-handed mechanisms to coerce the governed much surpassed any repertoire of forms for winning their consent. The transparency of the coercion meant that many Mozambicans simply calculated themselves how to play the system, developing well-honed survival skills over the years. Their murmurings and resentments were channelled to forms of cultural resistance, songs and dances in popular forms, often camouflaged in languages inaccessible to the colonizer. Others denied the legitimacy of Portugal's claims by opting out of colonial society altogether. Increasing numbers in the late sixties and early seventies escaped to neighbouring countries and joined up with FRELIMO to fight for independence. The liberated zones created in northern Mozambique became the crucible to begin to reconstruct the definitions of time and space and culture that Portuguese colonialism had tried so systematically to rob and destroy.

Notes

1. The popular ranking of who was the best colonizer persisted over the years. During the era of collaboration among the armies from the illegal Smith regime, fascist Portugal and apartheid South Africa, there were many references to a pecking order. Popular ranking within the region at popularlevel gave the British highest marks, followed by the South Africans, then the Rhodesians, and only at the bottom, the Portuguese. An expression in Portuguese used in Mozambique to this day about doing things up for show is "Para o ingles ver," literally, "For the English to see."

2. State provision of mass education at a moment of social change characterized by currents of contestation and unrest is certainly not unique to Mozambique. In many countries in Europe and North America, the first part of the nineteenth century saw a fear of mass education and its power to make the masses uppity and undisciplined, challenging the traditional deference to the elite. By mid-nineteenth century, literacy and education on both sides of the Atlantic had become a key feature in establishing control in society. The new ethos of capitalism with its ideas of property and production was woven into a moral project, making the school a key institution in shaping social identity and regulating class, race/ethnicity and gender. Schooling served to create political subjects, to transform the lives of the students to the point of accepting the existing political organization of society as "natural." (Graff 1979; Corrigan, Curtis, Lanning 1987)

3. For an interesting analysis of education in Portugal itself, see Stoer 1981.

4. Interviews with contemporary urban workers on their educational histories during my field work in 1985/86 included a number of people who spoke of

having stopped at third class because to do fourth class was to take on assimilated status. Further work is needed to reconstruct in more detail how this classification worked, both in urban and rural settings and during different periods of colonial history.

5

Literacy, Popular State and People's Power

> The People's Schools emerged at the moment when the population discovered, after participating in the literacy classes, that the methods used in the centres were different from the methods used in the formal school system. . . . At the time they identified the education system in place as being colonial. The population saw that, compared with the teaching in the colonial schools, the teaching in the literacy centres was more adapted to reality, to the socio-cultural context and political moment they were living.
>
> (Interview with Henrique N'Guiraze,
> Literacy organizer, Zambézia, 1975-77)

> The literacy centre became the nucleus for really important social interaction, and cultural activity that, in effect, marked a profound break with traditional society. It had many new aspects which were cause for both marvel and confusion. It was a moment of real ideological agitation at the base, which contributed massively to the great popularity and wide dissemination of FRELIMO's ideas. Even today this is reflected in people's language.
>
> (Interview with José Cardoso,
> Literacy organizer, Gaza, 1975-77)

The coup of April 1974 brought Portuguese colonialism to a dramatic end. The effectiveness of the liberation wars in Mozambique, Guinea-Bissau and Angola was a central factor in the minds of the middle-rank military officers who staged it. In early September, less than five months later, the Lusaka Accords were signed in Zambia establishing September 25 as the date for a transitional government composed of both FRELIMO and Portuguese representatives. This marked a radical break in the forms, both of governing and being governed.

The period in preparation for national independence on June 25, 1975, was one characterized by an explosion of popular energy. The murmurings and resentments that had formerly found expression largely through cultural forms now became part of an extended public conversation throughout the country, much of it taking place in the literacy centres and "People's Schools." With the broad literacy movement that emerged throughout Mozambique in the period immediately before and after independence came a dramatic recasting of what it meant to be illiterate.

The public discourse on literacy shifted dramatically. The backwardness of Portuguese colonialism was a major focus. It had failed to carry out any kind of socio-economic development of the colony, fostering ignorance and backwardness over the 500 years of presence in Mozambique.[1] The colonial state had signalled literacy as a category of deficiency, related to the natural state of the African as brutish and uncivilized. Now illiteracy took on a new meaning as a socially created state of deprivation, the result of a historic denial of access to education that had intentionally created ignorance in an entire people.

The watchwords of Samora Machel, president of FRELIMO, to the Mozambican people immediately after the signing of the Lusaka Accords were "Study, produce and fight." These were taken as serious marching orders in preparation for independence and a broad, popular literacy movement emerged throughout the country. It caught up in its wake many who, until that time, had had no channel to signal their support for an independent Mozambique.

José Cardoso, at the time a settler's son studying in a Portuguese university, was one of those who returned home to become part of the process. He became a literacy organizer in Gaza and later became head of the national literacy services in the Ministry of Education. His reflections almost fifteen years later on that moment in which he, and many other young, educated, urban Mozambicans, were drawn into the political process reconstruct something of the times.

> Samora's speech after Lusaka was very important in galvanizing the groups of sympathizers who had emerged in various places which led, later, to the Dynamizing Groups. Above all it meant they had a contact with the political line of FRELIMO. . . . As a result of an intense phase of spreading anti-colonial ideas, there was a process of massive expansion of schooling which was, in a way, spontaneous. . . . There was an interesting problem of distrust in the official school system, seen as colonial. Linked to this was the introduction of a tendency to speak local languages in the "People's Schools."
>
> (Interview with José Cardoso, February 1986)

The choice by FRELIMO to launch literacy activities was entirely consistent with the experiences of FRELIMO in the liberated territories. There, mass access to education was one of the tangible forms of the new society being built, one that touched deeply a people who, through the long decades of colonial rule, had been derided for their ignorance yet systematically prevented from access to schooling. Education in the liberated zones included literacy for both children and adults. It also included rich experiences of popular education at community level. These served as important reference points for action during the tumultuous days leading up to and following national independence on June 25, 1975.

Education During the Armed Struggle

The liberation struggle itself had brought forward different needs and expectations for literacy and popular education. The various strands of Mozambican nationalism that merged to form FRELIMO in 1964 under the leadership of Eduardo Mondlane, placed a great value on education. As their plans to mount an armed struggle from neighbouring Tanzania and Zambia into the northern provinces took shape, the need for a training programme for the liberation army loomed large. This involved not only the technical aspects of waging the war, demanding as these were, especially, as the war progressed to more sophisticated weapons and logistics. More fundamental, however, was the political aspect. If the soldiers coming from different regions throughout the country were to act as a cohesive force, if they were to gain the confidence of northern villagers terrorized by colonial repression, they needed a clear understanding of what they were fighting for, who they were fighting and why. This raised basic questions about tribe, race, gender, class, ideology and nation.

Language had emerged as a central question. Mozambicans from different regions and language groups throughout the country had fled the daily oppression and humiliation of forced labour and the "caderneta" to fight against Portuguese colonialism. The armed struggle brought them together with a new sense of national unity born of a common enemy, but they had no means of social communication. The demands of the armed struggle, from the language of instruction in training to the language of FRELIMO Congress documents to mold three nationalist movements into one all necessitated decisions about language. Choice of any one Mozambican language immediately privileged a particular ethnic group, marginalizing all the Mozambicans outside the language group chosen, and thus working against the very national unity so earnestly desired. After lengthy deliberation, Portuguese, the language of the colonial oppressor, was chosen as the official language.

Reflecting back on it four years after independence in 1979, during the "First National Seminar on the Teaching of the Portuguese Language," a senior FRELIMO leader recalled it as a decision thought through with care, which was taken as a "unanimous and tactical" decision. As he saw it, the armed struggle "putting side by side Mozambicans of different regions, with different cultures and languages of their own, was the first great factor in creating national unity." The need for a common means of social communication was paramount. The decision to opt for Portuguese was not determined by cultural traditions. "It was a tactical decision, with a perspective that the future fully confirmed as being the only correct one. . . a political decision, the result of deep thought and consideration." (Quoted in Searle 1984:4)

The option to take over the colonizer's language was a painful one, but one that did bring a number of immediate advantages.

> As the operational language of the liberation war, Portuguese, gave the basis of a common military language of command and co-ordination. It allowed the liberation forces to 'know the enemy better,' as well as giving greater capacity to understand and apply military strategy and the technology of war. It gave FRELIMO a language to deal with certain concepts that were untranslatable in the African languages. Portuguese colonialism had not allowed the Mozambican people any real penetration into the world of science and technology. The liberation forces needed not only soldiers who were also technicians, engineers and strategists, but thinkers with the necessary skills to analyze FRELIMO's ideological foundation of Marxism-Leninism.
>
> (Searle 1984:4)

Over the decade of armed struggle, Portuguese ceased to be just the language of the oppressor. The women and men in FRELIMO transformed the Portuguese language, making it their own. A new political culture emerged with songs, with poetry, with rituals and celebrations, with slogans like "A luta continua." Portuguese words took on new resonances unknown in metropolitan Portugal or beyond the liberated zones. One was "responsavel," literally the one charged with responsibility for a given task, with connotations of lateral and participatory decision-making rather than hierarchical chains of command. Another word that gained currency during the armed struggle was the adjective "engajado," referring to people engaged in, caught up in, committed to the revolutionary process. Songs were written celebrating the power of the "bazooka." Poems like "When bullets begin to flower" (Dickinson [ed.] 1972) captured the reality of a people's war leading to "people's power."

Words and knowledge came together in a new way. Sérgio Vieira in his poem, "Four Parts of a Poem of Education Left Incomplete" puts it this way:

> at night in the bases
> deciphering letters
> in the shadow of mango trees,
> spelling out words
> under the cry of bombs
> scribbling sentences. . .
>
> word was made bullet
> and the bullet was guided by the word. . .
>
> from words
> hurricanes were born
> which annihilated the companies.
>
> With the sentences they wanted to hide from us
> we lit the great fire
> of the People's war.
>
> (Quoted in Searle 1984:4,5)

The armed struggle rapidly created liberated areas where there was an enormous thirst for education. Just two years after the beginning of the armed struggle in Cabo Delgado province in 1964, a network of bush schools was already established. More than 10,000 children were enroled in FRELIMO primary schools by 1967. At the end of that year, ten teachers started to work setting up schools in Niassa and soon another 2000 students were enroled. Refugee children brought from Niassa to the Tunduru camp in Tanzania made it necessary to establish primary schooling there, and many children were later brought from the liberated zones to Tunduru to do their upper primary schooling. (Munslow 1983:99) By 1972, there were about 190 primary schools operating in the liberated territories with 250 teachers and an enrolment of about 20,000 pupils, most of them in 1st or 2nd grade. (Johnston 1989:78) Secondary schooling was set up in the Mozambique Institute in Dar es Salaam. Education in fact, became a central terrain of contestation during the intense internal struggles within FRELIMO during the late 1960s.[2]

The conflict erupted dramatically at the Mozambique Institute in Dar es Salaam where secondary schooling had been organized in the mid-1960s as an alternative to the schooling offered at the Kurasini

International Education Centre (KIEC). KIEC catered to refugee students in Tanzania and offered an education totally unlinked to Mozambican realities, one with possibilities of scholarships abroad. The elitist notions and individual ambitions fostered by KIEC put it at odds with FRELIMO's need for future cadres to carry on a national liberation struggle.

FRELIMO looked to its new secondary school as an alternative way to train cadres. The reality of the situation, however, was that most of the students had never been to the liberated areas and distanced themselves from the armed struggle. Many did see scholarships abroad as the logical continuation of their training. The argument for not "wasting" the students in the bush life of the liberated areas but instead preparing them for post-independence high level posts centred around Mateus Gwenjere. Gwenjere was a Roman Catholic priest who had joined FRELIMO at the end of 1967, bringing with him a group of his seminary students from Beira. Gwenjere had mobilized the students to come with the promise of scholarships. He encouraged them to defy the 1966 Central Committee decision whereby secondary school graduates spent at least a year inside Mozambique actively participating in the struggle. He also argued that those in power were afraid of creating more trained Mozambicans because it would put their own positions of leadership in jeopardy. He also fomented racism, demanding the removal of four of the Mozambique Institute's teachers and its director simply because they were white, and therefore "not Mozambican."

The ultimately victorious group within FRELIMO had a very different vision. Its definition of "Mozambican" encompassed all Mozambicans fighting to end colonialism, including white Mozambicans. It saw the fundamental goal of education as serving the people. In line with this vision was the necessity for students to return to the liberated areas before advancing for further study.

The conflicts in education were linked inextricably with the deep internal struggles in the movement at this time. Would the liberation movement simply create a nationalist party that would replace a white elite with a black elite or would it set in motion a more far-reaching social transformation to create structures with real popular control. As a result of these conflicts came a decision to close the school for two years. The fact that the nationalist movement itself radicalized and that education issues were a key focus of these internal struggles sharpened the perception of the role of education in establishing people's power. It forced a recognition that knowledge and skill are classed, raced and gendered acquisitions.[3]

New Forms of Popular Education

Discussions about education in the liberated areas have tended to reduce education to these embryonic forms of state-sponsored schooling. There were also, however, vital and dynamic educational forms that began to emerge in the communities linked to FRELIMO that are very much within the tradition of popular education as it has emerged in other parts of the world, particularly in Latin America.[4] One of the most important new form of education established in the liberated areas was the weekly village "meeting." This drew together all villagers with FRELIMO leaders in a kind of community forum that was both an educational process and an experience of direct, face-to-face democracy, all in the context of dramatically changing conditions for production and defence. The village meeting provided a new form for adults to be together and to think collectively about the transforming of their circumstances and themselves.

The pedagogy of leadership of FRELIMO at the time was one that was "good at learning," and that meant being good at listening and validating peasant experiences.[5] It was more a pedagogy of questions than of answers. The weekly meeting in the villages of the liberated zones were often prolonged affairs, some lasting eight and ten hours. Everybody spoke on a subject before any action could be taken. For villagers used to the arbitrary power of the Portuguese administrative apparatus, an open invitation to voice their ideas and concerns marked a radical shift. For women and young people, the shift was doubly dramatic. Traditional forms of subordination had ruled out speaking in public for women and created very restricted roles for youth. Elders held the privileged position.

In these meetings, the ravages of colonialism in shaping people to view themselves and their worlds in distorted ways could be addressed. The weekly meeting provided the occasion for peasant women and men to begin to take apart the constructs of colonialism, the way peasant workers had been despised, blackness repudiated, tribal differences manipulated and women silenced. Eliza Sumahili, a woman drawn into FRELIMO as a militant, described the changes for her personally in this way:

> I gained a wide experience of speaking to men and the public in general, of communicating, and I stopped feeling afraid, which is what I felt whilst living at home. Traditionally in my village, a girl could never speak with either a man or a boy. . . . Now we discuss on equal footing.
>
> (Quoted in Munslow 1983:145)

A process was set in motion whereby the social construction of a new reality could take place, engendering new ways of seeing, of saying, of being.

The war itself created the form. Peasant women and men and children in the underdeveloped hinterlands of Cabo Delgado, Niassa and, later, Tete were the human resources available, and their willingness to support FRELIMO and endure the reprisals of the colonial state was a necessary component for the advance of the struggle. Peasant energies and initiatives and creativity were the only resources available and the question of how to release these energies was paramount. There was no use thinking about machines, money, trained cadres, technology or infrastructure. Mobilizing the human resources for creating the new Mozambique was the only thing worth discussing. FRELIMO's first president, Eduardo Mondlane, pointed to these peasant energies as key.

> The people are constantly encouraged to clear more land for cultivation and to grow more food, and this campaign has been so successful that, despite the hazards and upheavals of the war, more land is actually under cultivation today than there was during the colonial administration. Even after the first year of war, more food was being produced than before. Now in some areas, as at Ngazela, 80 percent of the land cultivated had not previously been productive.
>
> The greatest impetus to production has clearly come from the abolition of the companies, and from the fact that the people now themselves profit from their work. Two other factors are also important. One is the work of the party in advising, encouraging and explaining the needs of the struggle, and in providing essential pieces of equipment like hoes and pangas. The other, linked with this, is the development of new methods of organization, principally the cooperative.
>
> (Mondlane 1983:172)

The village meeting as educational forum set in motion a critical discourse that relocated the peasants' position of subordination. Both external domination and internal power struggles were subjected to scrutiny. The collaboration of the local chief with the colonial regime came into question, for example. In some cases, these local chiefs, freed from the direct link with the colonial administration, proved ready to institute equally repressive and exploitative relations themselves. In Cabo Delgado this reached the extent of employing peasant labour on lands reclaimed from the Portuguese and treating the peasants to another version of forced labour.

Patriarchal forms, along with forms venerating age, were very much intact in the first forms of local government to appear in the liberated areas. The "chairmen" of the villages, the name having been adopted from neighbouring Tanzania, propounded a local authority based in part on traditional authority and in part on the maintenance of colonial structures but with black Mozambicans now as administrators. A Council of Elders was formed at an early stage which pitted itself against the Central Committee. Later, in the four year period from 1966 to 1969 when the internal struggle within FRELIMO gained momentum, there were tensions between those wielding power in the Department of the Interior which had responsibility for administration in the liberated zones and those in the Department of Defence.

These power struggles were played out through the village meetings. The chiefs whose support had been so critical at an earlier stage began to block the development of genuine social transformation.

> Chiefs and elders, who in traditional society exercised absolute authority over women and youths, impeded the full participation of these social groups in the revolution. They rejected women's right to participate in the armed struggle and defended the brideprice system, child marriage and polygamy. Emancipation of women would affect the power of the elders to control, buy and sell women who were both producers and reproducers in traditional society. . . . The revolutionaries within the movement argued that all should participate in the liberation struggle and share more equally in decision making be they women, youths or elders. Young men in the FPLM and young girls in the Women's Detachment and militia had *won* the right to have their voices heard, and were no longer prepared to accept the traditional system of blind obedience to the elders. By the end of 1967 the movement's publication was able to report: "Now an awareness had developed for the establishment of new institutions which put more stress on political devotion than on traditional legitimacy of power."
>
> (Munslow 1983:106)

In many areas, then, the village meeting created a new sense of power and a new basis for legitimacy. The traditional chiefs were replaced as chairpersons of the villages. Elections were held for committees of women and men and youth. It was these elected representatives who organized collective production, presided over public meetings, set up local courts that began to establish new notions of justice, participated in district and provincial assemblies and helped to organize people's militia units. (Isaacman & Isaacman 1983:93)

The village meeting, then, was a social form that was profoundly educational, a way for peasants who had endured the indignities of a ubiquitous colonial state structured down to sub-sub-chiefs in the tiniest settlements, to construct a new sense of the possible. The colonial state had shaped a sense of self as inferior and without civilization, naming peasant producers as "idle," subjecting them to forced labour and forced cultivation. The village meeting created space for a collective re-naming of self and society, a resumption by peasant women and men of their own social life. It engendered a "social literacy," empowering women and men to see themselves and their experiences as useful and interesting, the real resources for building a new Mozambican society *and* advancing the war. New cultural forms, forms of language, and forms of symbolic representation emerged, all of which were rooted in the collective experiences of women and men and children, fighting and producing and studying. A new "civil society" based on "people's power" began to emerge.

The war was the crucible. The complete resistance of Portuguese colonialism to all nationalist aspirations, despite the advanced state of decolonization throughout the rest of the African continent, left Mozambicans with no choice but to fight with arms for national independence. In areas freed from Portuguese control, there was a lacuna of power created. The old systems of administration and control had ended. The attempts to put in their place new exploitative systems had been exposed. It was in the context of this radical rupture with the old, this social space created by the war, that new forms emerged.

The material conditions in the liberated areas continued to be very difficult but people "had more" by "being more." And people's "being more," being free from the daily pain and humiliation of colonial servitude was a big factor. As Joaquim Maquival, a young FRELIMO militant who had been fighting over wide areas of the country, put it:

> The war has changed the people's situation. Where the war has already broken out, the people are no longer beaten, there are no longer taxes which exploit the people, the people are not humiliated. There are hardships but this is the price of victory.
>
> (Quoted in Mondlane 1983:187)

With the triumph in the Second Congress of 1968 of those advocating the more deeply rooted social transformation of a prolonged people's war, an even greater stress was placed on mobilization and popular participation. The pedagogy of leadership envisioned was not one of hierarchical structures and one way communication. There was a conception of "revolution from below," alluded to in Central Committee discussions as early as 1966 in the wake of the coup in Ghana that ousted Kwame Nkrumah. An article in the FRELIMO publication "Mozambique Revolution" put it this way:

> . . . fundamentally it is necessary to encourage the people to partake in the political life of the country. Further it is necessary to reject a concept in which the revolution (socialism) is built by an active nucleus of leaders who think, create and give everything and are followed by a passive mass who limit themselves to receiving and executing. This concept is the result of a weak political conscience and expresses a lack of confidence in the fighting and revolutionary capacity of the people. This is the lesson that recent events in Africa teaches.
>
> (Quoted in Munslow 1983:102,103)

Much greater stress was put on the liberated zones as the embryo of new forms of production, health, education and popular participation which would later be transplanted back to an independent Mozambique. The concept of "people's power" gained currency. The new forms of popular social organization in the liberated areas became known, then, as institutions of "people's power." Noted Africanist Basil Davidson visited the liberated zones and attended the Second Congress as one of FRELIMO's guests. His sense of what FRELIMO meant by "people's power" at that time was conveyed in his subsequent article, "The Revolution of People's Power: Notes on Mozambique 1969." "The basic principle is that every community should organise itself to analyze its own problems and possibilities, find appropriate solutions and policies and act to bring these solutions and policies into force." (Davidson 1979:127)

The victory of those advocating, "people's power" had a number of consequences for education. The text of the Second Congress resolution on education set out clearly the new emphases.

> On education
> (1) Development of primary schools shall be accelerated.
> (2) Teacher training programme for primary school shall be developed in order to raise rapidly its numbers and its technical level.
> (3) Intensive literacy campaigns among the masses of the people, men, women, old and young people shall be promoted.
> (4) Special courses for raising rapidly the level of knowledge of the militants shall be organized.
> (5) Young Mozambican women shall be encouraged to complete at least primary school education.
> (6) Production centres shall be created at every school place for self-maintenance.
> (7) A system shall be established which shall make it possible for the students to interrupt temporarily their studies in order to participate in teaching and literacy campaigns.

(8) It shall be the duty of all Mozambican students to take part, whenever it may be deemed necessary, in the various tasks of the struggle for national liberation.
(9) Development of schools of political training shall be promoted.

(Mondlane 1983 193,194)

New ideas emerged about the link between study and production and between school and community. The schools in the liberated areas were to include the establishment of production centres, with much more stress on self-reliance. In addition, the schools were to engage even more vigorously in production tasks in the community at large, with active programmes to combat the notion of a division between hand and brain. Elitist notions of schooling as a channel out of productive activities into a management or administrative strata were discouraged.

Schooling as a process to groom an elite was challenged by new and active roles of the students in teaching others. It became common throughout the liberated areas for those who could read and write, however minimally, to teach those who could not. Students with only the equivalent of third or fourth grade education themselves often delayed a further year of study for themselves, devoting a year to bringing along another wave of children by day and a group of adults by night.

At the second national conference of the Department of Education and Culture in 1970, President Samora Machel explained FRELIMO's position:

> . . . to us education does not mean teaching how to read and write, creating an elite group of graduates, with no direct relationship to our objectives. . . . Just as one can wage an armed struggle without carrying out a revolution, one can also learn without educating oneself in a revolutionary way.
>
> (Machel 1974:39)

By 1974, the number of children in the four year primary school programme in the various provinces was well over 20,000. More than 300 students were enroled in the 5th-8th year classes at Bagamoyo. Training courses for primary teachers had been running since 1972. More than 100 students were doing post-secondary level courses abroad on FRELIMO scholarships.

The FRELIMO Secondary School, now reopened and based in Bagamoyo, up the coast from Dar es Salaam, also played an important role in these educational activities. It was common for students to return from Bagamoyo to the liberated zones. The Bagamoyo school was instructed in 1972 to prepare literacy materials both for students and teachers. Entire classes from the secondary school were put through a week-long training course and then spent their long vacation in the liberated areas doing literacy between 1972 and 1974.

The embryo of a new education system was well in place, then, by the time of the coup in Portugal. A Department of Education and Culture had been established in FRELIMO and national conferences had taken place in 1968 and again towards the end of 1970, drawing together educators from throughout the liberated areas. In February 1973, a first national pedagogic seminar had been held, analyzing programmes and teaching methods. At the time of the coup in April 1974, educators from throughout the liberated areas were gathered together in the first literacy seminar. (FRELIMO 1976:16)

Post-Coup Mozambique: "Study, Produce and Fight"

These traditions from the liberated areas which freed people's energies to find solutions to their own problems were all drawn on in the immediate post-coup and post-independence era. Literacy seems to have been the central activity into which those identifying with FRELIMO placed their hopes and energies. It was an unusual moment, characterized by massive changes and confusing currents as old systems broke down, and new symbols and forms and languages gained hold. A language of hope emerged, espousing justice over privilege, solidarity over individualism and the collective over the private. Radical egalitarianism was the order of the day. The same people whose lives and communities had been subjected to a multiplicity of forms and institutions and discourses by state and church labelling them as "ignorant" and "idle" were suddenly caught up in a totally new disposition of power and knowledge. From one day to the next, they became the builders of "people's power," the resources for socialist construction. They were not "stupid" but "made ignorant," not "idle" but "denied opportunity."

> The Mozambican people were the victims of ignorance and obscurantism, originating from the Portuguese colonial system in power in our country. . . . to better exploit us it was necessary to keep the people in ignorance, unable to perceive their miserable condition. As a consequence of this we have the fabulous percentage of illiteracy which exists in our country.
>
> (Report on Literacy from Tete province 1976:1; my translation[6])

Ordinary people suddenly saw themselves as legitimate actors in public social spaces hitherto out of bounds. The desire for education was intense, both for those long denied it and for those who had had access to it and now were caught up in a process of making it available to others. In any case, the official schools were in disarray, with the mass exodus of Portuguese settlers already gaining momentum.

The new sense of mastery over social space meant that people felt free to organize their own education. Those needing schooling in a given community took the initiative to organize it, finding their own way to finance books, locate teachers and arrange for classrooms. There were no experts. Those with a little education felt free to offer what they had to others, and indeed especially in rural communities where educated people were scarce, real pressures were put on people to do so. The report from Tete province captures the tone of this period, and the central role that literacy played in the period leading up to independence.

> Our combat in this area [literacy] should not countenance retreats nor puff itself up with victories which are registered in tiny concentrations of population. We must count on the efforts of all those who have had the opportunity to study; they "must be the match that lights the flame that is the people" and their vision must be broad enough to encompass Mozambique from the Rovuma to the Maputo.
>
> (Report on literacy from Tete province 1975:1)

All kinds of individuals and organizations rose to the challenge, particularly in the larger centres. Provincial reports prepared for a National Seminar on Literacy held in Ribáuè in April 1975, two months before independence, document the beginnings of literacy in each province. This seminar was one of several aimed at organizing a national education system. It brought together for the first time FRELIMO cadres from the liberated areas and frontline state and those working inside the country. The literacy seminar was held in Ribáuè, where the students and staff from the old Bagamoyo Secondary School in Tanzania had relocated. Delegations from all ten provinces were present.

In Lourenço Marques, the capital, activities began in August 1974, four months after the coup and a month before the Lusaka Accords recognizing FRELIMO as the effective power to govern Mozambique. In addition to FRELIMO militants, other organizations, both old and new, were involved in literacy. These included the Associação Africana de Moçambique (African Association of Mozambique), the Associação Académica de Moçambique (Academic Association of Mozambique) and the Centro Popular de Alfabetização (Popular Literacy Centre), all of which organized classes. In addition, the Centro Associativo dos Negros (Black Contact Centre) organized a training course for monitors and a group of young people volunteered to teach literacy to soldiers stationed in Lourenço Marques.

With the establishment of the transitional government on September 25, 1974, came the formation of Dynamizing Groups. As we have seen, the GDs were formed throughout the country, in workplaces, communities, schools and other social sectors. These activists were in part self-selected and in part appointed by FRELIMO, serving as a vital point of contact between FRELIMO and local level organizational structures, facilitating communication both from the top down and from the bottom up. The GDs were organized with a secretary and assistant secretary and "responsibles" for various sectors including mobilization and organization, information and propaganda, education and culture, women, social affairs, production, commerce and finance. They were charged with the task of mobilizing fellow workers and neighbours in collective social, economic and cultural activities.

Literacy became one of the central activities of the GDs. The literacy sub-commissions of the GDs were organized from the base up, through locality and district structures and on to provincial level. This provided a lot of new impetus for literacy activities throughout each province.

At least one member of the GD had to be a woman. In many cases the women were turned to only on questions directly related to women and family affairs -- or worse still, automatically assumed to be the provider of food for all GD functions! Still there is no doubt that the GDs were the vehicle that gave many women outside the liberated territories their first experience of meetings, group decision-making and speaking in public. For the first time, women saw themselves as subjects shaping a social reality themselves rather than simply as objects being shaped by it.[7]

> Above all else, the Dynamizing Groups served as schools in which to learn democratic skills and class unity. Community meetings, organized by Dynamizing Groups on a regular basis, provided a forum for involving citizens in the study and debate of the critical issues facing Mozambique. Throughout the country, participants examined such diverse topics as the divisive effects of tribalism, the need for an alliance between workers and peasants, the problems of national reconstruction, the reasons for combatting the oppression of women, the necessity for vigilance against agents of the Rhodesian government, and the value of collective action. In addition, Dynamizing Group members explained to the populace important government directives and newly initiated national programmes and discussed ways to mobilize them more effectively for collective activities.
>
> (Isaacman & Isaacman 1983:117)

In Sofala, literacy was launched in the district of Beira in June 1974 and spread rapidly to other districts in the province. The report to the Ribáuè meetings refers to mobilization for literacy through the use of posters, wall newspapers, radio programmes and mass meetings, first organized by FRELIMO and later by the Dynamizing Groups. The report also refers to mobilization through individual contacts in the community by the literacy monitors themselves, by those in charge of Education and Culture *and* by the actual literacy students. The Sofala report also mentions training two separate groups of monitors, one group for mobilization and organizational work and another to do the actual teaching.

In Sofala, as elsewhere, the methodology for literacy was locally determined. The range of options throughout the country included adaptation of the materials already prepared in the Bagamoyo Secondary School for the student literacy campaigns in the liberated zones, use of existing primary school texts, and development of materials with variants on a Paulo Freire methodology based on a code of "generative" words derived from the social milieu of the students. There were also reports of centres that began by rote teaching vowels, and then moved on to consonants, words and phrases.

In Sofala, materials were based on a local inventory of generative words. It is interesting to note those that were chosen, an index of the themes deemed most resonant in the midst of the radical disruption brought about by the coup. They included "FRELIMO, people, food, capulana (African cloth), factory, maize, comrade, building block, cane, work, health and beer."

The Sofala document also makes reference to adaptations of materials published by FRELIMO's Department of Education and Culture, citing problems in their use because they had already been outpaced by events and did not refer to the important themes of the moment, namely, "people's power, FRELIMO structures and national reconstruction." (Report on literacy from Manica and Sofala 1975:4) The report concludes that in Sofala and Manica, the adjoining province, some 20,000 became literate through the classes organized by FRELIMO in this period.

The report from Tete province indicates that literacy activities as such were carried out only in the provincial capital. In the districts, schooling was available to adults through night schools taught by teachers who worked with children during the day. Again the decentralized character of the campaigns and the space for local initiatives is striking in the report. In Tete, the first training course for literacy teachers was led by a group set up two months earlier to study the best way to launch literacy in Tete city. The groups studied various texts and had the opportunity to meet with people doing literacy in Lourenço Marques and Beira as well as with people linked to the Department of Education and Culture of FRELIMO who recounted their experiences with literacy in the liberated areas. The report indicates that the method used was an adaption of the Paulo Freire method. (Report on literacy from Tete province 1975:3) Generative words were chosen. A dialogue was then initiated around these words. Next the words were written on the blackboard, divided into syllables and the syllabic families arranged into a discoveries chart in which the students could seek out new words.

The learners themselves were active as problem solvers for the literacy centres. The shortages of funds in the district to buy supplies were resolved by the learners. In Angónia, they decided to contribute the equivalent of one day's pay to literacy. The report indicates that the literacy students themselves administered the fund, and no distinctions were made between those paying a little, those paying a lot, and the unemployed who put in nothing. In a rural district, the students organized themselves to bring maize to sell at harvest time in order to buy supplies for the literacy classes.

In a profound sense the broader political process itself was the teacher, with all those involved, the learners, monitors and organizers, caught up in it. Their interaction took forms very different from typical classroom activities and teacher-student power roles.

> In many units, above all in the provincial capital, cultural gatherings were held to bring teachers and students together, both participating actively. Political themes are also discussed in these gatherings. They make an immense contribution towards breaking down the differences, that can exist between monitors and students, and as well are a big help in awakening each person's creative initiatives.
>
> (Report on literacy in Tete province 1975:5)

In many cases it was hard to distinguish between adult literacy and expanded primary schooling for children. In Sofala, early literacy activities were carried out by a group of students, teachers and workers who formed the "Comissão Contra a Discriminação da Criança e Para a Alfabetização." (Commission Against Anti-child Discrimination and for Literacy). The report from densely-populated Nampula province, bastion of the Portuguese military up to the end of the war, refers to phenomenal numbers of new schools throughout the districts for both children and adults. In Mecuburi district alone, 290 new schools were functioning with 16,000 pupils. In another district, Erati, there were 300 monitors at work with 14,400 students. The report indicates that the Dynamizing Groups were completely unable to keep up with the demand for schools, teachers and teaching materials. Local populations were undeterred when their requests were not met. They proceeded to build schools themselves and choose teachers locally with at least second or third class. The report goes on to detail the kinds of problems such a spontaneous mass movement posed for inexperienced activists with few means at their disposal.

The reports generally depict an ambience with high energy levels and dedication abounding. On balance, it seems to have been a rich experience. In Nampula, as in Tete, new forms developed beyond the literacy classroom in which the monitors were students and the broader political process the teacher. Also striking is the degree of autonomy in each province, with those immediately involved tackling the fundamental questions from content and methodology to organization and finance, rather than simply executing programmes defined centrally.

In Nampula, the monitors continued their training after the short initial courses, holding meetings on Sunday afternoons to trade experiences. The report speaks of these meetings as useful in capturing the monitor's own interest in the teaching themes. In the Nampula report, as at other points in the documentation prepared for the Ribáuè Seminar, the question of language comes up. In Nampula, it was tackled by using Macua, the local language, in the theme discussions and gradually introducing Portuguese. Another rich aspect of these Sunday sessions was the validation of local culture, with the literacy teachers participating in identifying stories, riddles and proverbs from the area to weave into the political discussions of the daily themes.

> During the courses, efforts were made to have the monitors develop a critical consciousness about the concrete situations and problems of the people. To this end, the future teacher presented reports during the sessions about contacts and conversations had with people in the various communities, including future literacy students. This work permitted the monitors to do a survey of the vocabulary in popular use and the generative codes in preparation for the collective discussions. At the same time it allowed the monitors to appreciate the real problems of the people seen from the side of the most exploited.
>
> (Report from Nampula province 1975:5)

Inhambane province in southern Mozambique also presents interesting questions in its report. In response to the call to do literacy throughout the districts, work began based on the FRELIMO manual. The Inhambane activists discovered that without monitors well prepared, this method gave few results. The group based in the provincial capital set itself the task of reorganizing the teaching methodology and divided into two groups, one charged with the task of studying how to teach spoken Portuguese and the other, with the task of restructuring the method for teaching to read and write. Group one came forward with a plan to introduce carefully chosen words drawn from the daily life of the people, work on their pronunciation and begin to build small phrases and sentences with them as an approach to learning to speak Portuguese. Group two proposed an adaptation of the method in the FRELIMO manual, using generative words out of which would come a theme discussion and creation of new words. A selection of generative words was made for Inhambane district. The report indicates that 48,289 people were involved in literacy activities in the province.

A Bottom-up Literacy Movement

Henrique N'Guiraze was a secondary school teacher in Morrumbala district of Zambézia when he got caught up in mobilizing the population for literacy. Looking back ten years later on the events of 1975, N'Guiraze singles out the directive from President Samora Machel to the waiting population in Mozambique after the Lusaka Accords as key.

> As a secondary school teacher, I think the movement must have begun with the speech of President Samora and certain documents from FRELIMO in circulation which included the directive to "Study, produce and fight." I think that directive was really valued at that moment. After that speech what we saw was, don't ask me how, but the truth was that from one day to the next, and through the initiative of individuals, schools for adults began to appear on all sides. There was willingness by anybody with any learning to offer freely to teach literacy.
>
> Although there was no uniform methodology, books or programme, everybody invented words with a certain socio-political content based on the local situation. It could be ten words, for example, of this type. Based on these, they tried to motivate people to try to learn. There were brief meetings and courses about literacy at times organized by missionaries. As for the character of these courses, they were very influenced by Paulo Freire. In fact there was much talk about the concept of conscientization.
>
> (Interview with Henrique N'Guiraze, 1985)

It was a period in which the social space for participation was wide open to all those identifying with the FRELIMO project for construction of an independent Mozambique. In several provinces, progressive forces within the Roman Catholic church made their presence felt. Zambézia, along with Manica, Tete and Nampula, were the provinces where literacy action was generated as well from the churches; in other provinces such as Maputo and Gaza, the churches were little evident as a force in literacy.

> Literacy began as a generalized movement immediately after the coup. But I have actually had contact with cases where groups were able to work in semi-clandestine conditions even during the colonial period. I know, for

> example, of the movement that existed in Manica through the Burgos Fathers, one of whom today occupies a position of responsibility in the field of literacy. . . . He and others of the same group had representatives in Sofala and in Tete. We can say that there were small nuclei where this group was active.
>
> (Interview with Henrique N'Guiraze, 1985)

In Zambézia, in the final years of colonialism, the Roman Catholic church had established various education centres that offered both post-primary schooling for young people and vocational training programmes for workers in general. These centres seem to have enjoyed a certain amount of trust from the local community, and in the period leading up to independence, became important centres for promoting literacy.

In N'Guiraze's area, he, as a secondary school teacher trained in a mission school, went to a literacy course organized by missionaries and returned to mobilize his students to teach. Their school was responsible for 27 centres and mounted a literacy coordination centre in the school. In the afternoons, groups of students went twice weekly to each centre to give classes. They had no books but based their teaching and studying on the local situation.

In the adjoining district of Gilé, literacy activities were also begun at an early stage. Here a particularly dynamic Italian priest, Doménico Liuzzi, organized a network of literacy centres and had the ambitious plan of eradicating illiteracy completely in the district of Gilé within five years.

The Dynamizing Groups were an important feature in the organization of literacy in Zambézia.

> Because of the way the Dynamizing Groups emerged, their members had a lot of influence in the local situation. They were chosen by the people themselves, and because of this had a certain political authority. Really, when they called for participation in literacy, there was general acceptance by the people. But, at the same time, maybe because there had been no opportunity to study during the colonial period, the population had a certain fear of the desire to study. They put pressure on those in the GD to find ways for people to study, such as supplying paper and teachers, who at that time we called monitors. These monitors at one point had to be chosen by the students themselves. On this question, the students were very demanding. They chose people they knew and generally did not accept individuals of the same age. They chose people from whom they hoped to learn a lot.
>
> (Interview with Henrique N'Guiraze, 1985)

In Zambézia, as elsewhere, the distinction between literacy for adults and for children was somewhat blurred. The population saw no sense in studying as adults if schooling for their children was not guaranteed. At a certain point the literacy schools became "People's Schools." Adult students began pulling their children out of the still existent official schools, which were seen as symbols of colonialism. While the official schools had 80,000 registered in primary schools, the People's Schools had 200,000. This number more than doubled during the latter part of 1975. (Interview with Henrique N'Guiraze, 1985)

In the "People's Schools" the population had a degree of control over the selection of the teacher and over the content to be taught. Some of them taught in local languages. In general, they were seen to be closely linked to the local reality, the socio-cultural ambience and the moment politically that people were living.

Literacy seems to have been the key activity for those with some degree of education who had not been linked to FRELIMO previously to make contact. Clearly students at the time saw it as highly relevant, perhaps more so than their studies. In Zambézia, senior secondary students were an important part of the labour force for teaching literacy. The fact that the academic year was switched in such a way as to leave six months without classes in 1975 prompted even more students to devote themselves to literacy.

Without doubt, then, anyone with education was drawn towards literacy. Some offered themselves for opportunist reasons, recognizing FRELIMO as the new force in power and hoping to ingratiate themselves. Others offered themselves as literacy teachers out of a genuine commitment to the broader process, but in so doing also made themselves visible as activists of political confidence. There is no doubt that the literacy movement operated as a kind of filter, many going from it to other activities. As José Cardoso suggested, literacy served as a kind of trampoline, and also as a process for the "remission of sins!"

Be that as it may, there is no doubt that a very vibrant mass movement for literacy emerged from 1974-1976. Official estimates suggest that as many as 500,000 may have become literate during this period. (Fonseca 1983:2) The degree of community participation and control, the active role of the learners in organizing their own education activities, the diversity of teaching methodologies and materials in use, the emphasis on basing content on local realities, the experimentation with local languages in teaching and the forms for creating a dynamic monitor/student relationship all mark it as an extremely interesting moment in the history of literacy in Mozambique.[8]

State Provision of Education and People's Power

During the eight months of the Transitional government, the mass literacy movement was by no means the only activity of vital interest. There were feverish initiatives at multiple levels as FRELIMO prepared to take over the governing of the country. Creation of the state education service was but one of the many tasks. The Ministry of Education of the Transitional Government was headed by the secretary of FRELIMO's own Department of Education and Culture, Gideon Ndobe. The seminar on literacy two months before formal independence was one of several such seminars in preparation for the new post-independence education policies and programmes. Each seminar called together FRELIMO education cadres and educators who had been working in the colonial institutions and selected representatives from related sectors to map out guidelines for future work. Those attending the national seminars then returned to their respective provinces to organize similar discussions at provincial level.

The literacy seminar had been preceded by a National Seminar on Education held in Beira in January 1975. This event brought together, for the first time, primary and secondary school teachers from the official schools of the colonial era and FRELIMO cadres working in education. An intense ten days of study and discussion ensued. People I spoke to a year later, during my first visit after independence, still spoke of the meeting with emotion, recalling the shock created by FRELIMO's work methods of active participation and discussion. For teachers coming out of the almost entirely closed colonial system, this was indeed a radical departure.

Out of this seminar came the decision to discard the entire colonial syllabus and throw out all of the textbooks. New programmes for first to eleventh class were to be drawn up and put into practice immediately. Religious studies were removed from the curriculum and political education and manual work introduced. New political/administrative structures were established in the school. The huge challenge to the teachers from the colonial schools was obvious.

> . . . accustomed to simply giving lessons in the classroom, they now have not only to build new kinds of relations with their pupils but also to incorporate their teaching and their education within the community as a whole. The school must be the dynamic factor in the community and its pupils and teachers must be in permanent contact with the local population, learning from them, working with them, and in this way never forgetting why it is they are studying and teaching.
>
> (FRELIMO 1976:8)

Perhaps less evident at the time was the challenge the new moment presented to the FRELIMO cadres themselves. They were faced with organizational problems on a scale and complexity much beyond what the liberated areas had presented. They were also dealing with a very different context. There was open contestation between old and new values, forms and languages. The culture of colonialism/capitalism held daily skirmishes for ascendancy with the new culture of liberation. Not all FRELIMO cadres kept to the moral high ground when suddenly confronted with peace time options and urban life. The confrontation were both subtle and blunt.[9]

Yet another seminar during the transitional government tackled the question of technical education, bringing together teachers and senior representatives from the Ministry to discuss how to bring technical training in line with national priorities. In this, as in other seminars, the work method was that of starting from experience. There was an analysis of technical education in the past and the development of education by FRELIMO, as a solid starting point for understanding present difficulties and finding solutions. (FRELIMO 1976:20) Recommendations were made to build up a network of agricultural, commercial and industrial schools that were less theoretical and more practical, organized in modules allowing easy entry and exit to and from the workplace, less discriminatory against women and more oriented to rural development. (FRELIMO 1976:9)

National independence was celebrated on June 25, 1975. One month afterwards came the nationalizations, of land, health services, funeral and legal services, rentable property, and also education. A national Ministry of Education and Culture was created, ending the practice of multiple school systems, state, private and church. The organizational chart shows clearly the intentions of the new ministry, and the formidable weight of its task.

The heaviness of the task increased even more to the degree that placement of FRELIMO cadres experienced in education diminished sharply just as the new national education services were established. This was not from lack of appreciation of education's vital importance but stemmed from the crisis caused by the massive outflow of settlers and the desperate shortage of human resources to manage the complexity and scale of the inherited socio-economic infrastructure. Added to the mix was a peculiar pressure to maintain all of this infrastructure intact, seen both internally and externally as a necessary proof of capacity to govern by these "bush rebels" now in power. Key education cadres suddenly found themselves running banks and ports.

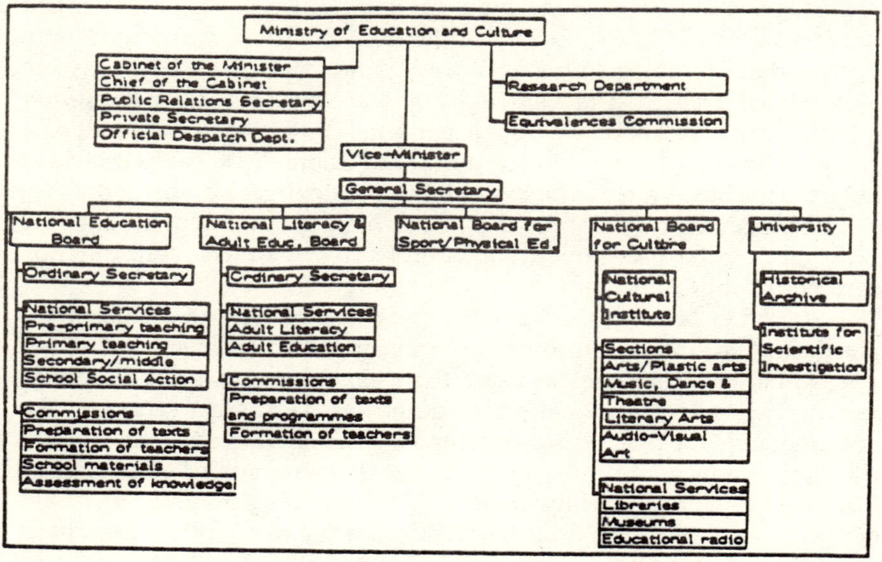

FIGURE 5.1 Organizational Chart, Ministry of Education and Culture, 1976

State-sponsored Literacy

The Ministry of Education set up a National Directorate of Literacy and Adult Education in 1976 which later became simply the National Directorate of Adult Education (DNEA). It began with only three staff members, but these numbers gradually expanded, including the addition of a team from Tanzania and a handful of internationalists. The result of the Ribáuè Seminar almost a year earlier provided guidelines for the fledgling directorate. By 1976, literacy activities in many provinces were basically on hold, waiting for directives and inputs from the newly created state literacy services. The support services anticipated included funding, teaching materials and training programmes.

The main conclusions from the Ribáuè Seminar concerning methodology included:

- methods based on an analysis of Mozambican realities, dominant economic and cultural activities, and choice of vocabulary accordingly;
- flexibility, in line with changing realities and critical inputs of both monitors and students;
- no single rigid method should be adopted. Instead a political discussion turning on a motivating word or phrase, if possible

reinforced with a picture, should lead to the presentation of a key word and its syllabic families, concluding with the discovery of new words from these syllables;

- Portuguese should be used. Where local languages are in use, they should become languages of support, gradually leading to Portuguese.

(INDE 1983:7)

The first year of activities of the newly created Directorate included a national survey to determine the scale of illiteracy. Interestingly neither capacity to speak Portuguese nor numbers literate in other languages seems to have been included in the data collected. Writing a literacy primer was tackled by a team made up of people from different sectors including teachers, students and some who had done literacy through the Academic Association. They came up with a programme based on ten themes related to the revolutionary process and its socio-economic conquests, from which phrases and key words were derived. An analysis of the material early in 1977 identified significant organizational and technical weaknesses. A Commission for Programmes and Texts was established which worked from May 1977 to January 1978 on modifying the material and organizing a manual.

The finalized version of the national primer consisted of ten lessons, each with a theme summed up in a key phrase and a key word. Some of the specific lesson themes included "The people's war is just." "The School belongs to the people." "Defending health is the duty of the people." The themes were designed to promote active discussion on vital issues in workplace and community and contribute to the larger political process.

TABLE 5.1 Selected Comparative Literacy Statistics

Country Number illiterate	*Population at independence/ liberation*	*Percent illiterate*
Cuba 1,652,000	7.0 million	23.6%
Nicaragua 722,716	2.0 million	50.35 %
Tanzania 6,750,000	9.0 million	75 %
Angola 6,800,000	8.0 million	85 %
Mozambique 9,540,000	10.6 million	90 %

Sources: Bhola 1984; Fordham (ed) 1983; Arnove 1986.

Far from being narrowly functional or purely work-oriented, they ranged from concrete aspects of the armed struggle to broader themes of cultural affirmation.

The manual for literacy teachers gave general suggestions on how to develop the lessons. It was a formidably large volume that also included extensive background information on broader themes related to health, agriculture, housing and appropriate technology. It also contained the outline for the mathematics programme.

Given the fact of 90 percent illiteracy in a scattered, predominantly rural population of 10.6 million, there was no way that a national literacy programme could do anything other than envisage a series of campaigns. The option of eradicating illiteracy in a single mass-based campaign as in Cuba, and later in Nicaragua, was simply not there.

The First National Literacy Campaign was launched in July 1978 and took as its target group 100,000 workers in key sectors of organized production, including industrial and rural workers in factories, businesses, state farms and cooperatives. In addition deputies to the People's Assemblies and members of the defence and security forces were included. Women were also prominent in this phase of literacy activities, with the Organization of Mozambican Women (OMM) playing a very dynamic role in organizing literacy activities, particularly those included as part of the training programmes for OMM activists throughout the country.

The campaign was launched with ceremonies throughout the country. District and provincial officials made speeches to open it, with speech guidelines supplied from the national office, including a definition of the purpose of literacy:

> The central purpose of literacy for adults is to liberate the creative initiatives of the working classes, by equipping them with basic scientific knowledge and instruments of analysis, which permit their best and full participation in the construction of a socialist society in our country.
>
> (Basic orientations for speeches to open the
> 1st National Literacy Campaign DNEA, 1978)

In Maputo itself, the campaign was opened by President Samora Machel in a massive gathering of workers in the national railway complex, CFM. The campaign had an enrolment of 130,000 from the priority sectors and an equally large number from non-priority sectors, mainly at community level. A first national evaluation was carried out in November 1978, just four months after the campaign began. Since many people were already involved in programmes of literacy throughout the country when the campaign was officially launched, it was assumed that many would pass. In fact, the results were very low. This related in part to the complexity of the test itself and in part to the unfamiliarity with administering and writing tests. The period of the campaign was extended to 18 months and a second improved test was given in which 140,000 of the 260,000 registered in the campaign passed.

The Second National Literacy Campaign was launched on February 16, 1980. The opening was timed to coincide with the opening of the academic year of the formal school system. This campaign targeted 200,000 men and women, with the objective of eradicating illiteracy in the following sectors:

- permanent workers in units of industrial and agricultural production
- Frelimo Party members
- deputies to the People's Assemblies at all levels
- leaders in the mass organizations, particularly the Organization of Mozambican Women, OMM

In the Second National Literacy Campaign 120,000 of the 290,000 initially enrolled succeeded in passing.

As for post-literacy, two approaches were taken. Mass campaigns for post-literacy began in 1980. Of the 140,000 who passed literacy in 1979, 87,000 were enroled in post-literacy, a programme of adult basic education. Completion of post-literacy was designed to give the equivalent of lower primary schooling. The other approach was the, establishment of residential courses for workers where post-literacy courses giving the equivalent of the third and fourth year of primary schooling were offered. Later some centres offered accelerated courses for the fifth and sixth years of general schooling. In addition to the centres

TABLE 5.2 Literacy Campaign Results 1979-1982

	1st Campaign 1978/1979	*2nd Campaign 1980*	*3rd Campaign 1981*	*4th Campaign 1982*
Initial Enrolment	300,000	290,000[a]	246,500	200,364
Final Enrolment	264,067	253,188	161,193	82,675
Examined	315,478	198,579	117,277	54,984
Pass target	100,000	200,000	200,000	200,000
Passed	139,369	119,394	61,095	37,430

[a] Estimate

Source: Adapted from Lind 1985:2

run by the Ministry of Education, some workplaces offered these accelerated programmes of general schooling. The Ministry of Public Works and Housing, for example, had a training programme in which unskilled workers with fourth class could spend a year in the training centre and come out with both sixth class standing in general education and a first qualification as a skilled worker.

Within these results, it is very difficult to differentiate distinct groups. The statistics published by the DNEA itself did not distinguish literacy results for women from those for men, or those of urban dwellers from those in the rural areas. The 1980 Census makes some contribution towards discrimination. Within the 72.2 percent of the total population that was illiterate in 1980, 59 percent of the illiterates were male and 84.6 percent were female. The illiteracy rate for women from 15-19 was 66.7 percent, moving up to 83.2 percent for the women from 20-24, 91 percent of the women from 25-39 and 95.9 percent of the women from 40-59.

While 72.2 percent of the population in general was illiterate, there were important differences between urban and rural areas. In the urban areas, only 40.3 percent of the population was illiterate while in the rural areas, the illiterate population was 77.1 percent. By far the highest rates of illiteracy were to be found among rural woman, with 94.6 percent of those in the 25-39 year age range illiterate and 97.7 percent of those in the 40-59 year range. Even among 10-14 year old girls in the rural areas, the illiteracy rate was 70.5 percent whereas urban girls from 10-14 had only a 31.9 percent illiteracy rate. (Conselho Coordenador de Recenseamento 1983)

In the period in 1976 and 1977, the Mozambican Women's Organization had put particular stress on literacy for women, and had organized special residential courses for their own provincial and district level OMM activists. These early OMM courses, which drew women away from their normal responsibilities to concentrate only on literacy had had phenomenally high results. For the women who came, the course marked a dramatic expansion of their worlds, starting from

TABLE 5.3 Post-literacy Campaign Results 1980-82

	1st Campaign 1980	*2nd Campaign 1981*	*3rd Campaign 1982*	*4th Campaign 1983*
Enroled	87,000	144,000	87,000	40,000
Passed	26,000	28,000	25,000	15,000

Source: National Directorate of Adult Education, Ministry of Education, Maputo, 1984.

airplane travel to reach the national capital to a three month period of new experiences. The women doing the courses progressed remarkably. They were freed to concentrate only on studying, recognizing how their newly acquired speaking, reading and writing work could feed into their regional organizing of other women. They got enormous support from the national OMM staff during the course including regular Friday night newspaper reading sessions and exposure to new places and ideas through films and study trips to local factories, museums, and child care centres.

None of these conditions could be duplicated easily at provincial and district level and OMM participation in the national campaigns dwindled over the years. The decision to concentrate literacy in organized work places rather than the community by definition cut down dramatically on the number of women involved in literacy. Of the 5.6 million economically active at the time the second campaign was launched, 2.9 million were women. More than 2.8 million of them were agricultural workers, however, almost all of whom were in the family sector and therefore outside the target area of the literacy campaigns. Women accounted for only 23,064 of the 346,794 industrial workers, 510 of the 42,121 construction workers, 2,206 of the workers in the transport and communications sector and 21,590 of the 112,244 workers in commerce. Even in the social sectors like health and education where women tended to be concentrated, only 6,736 of the 32,207 workers registered in education were women and 4,932 of the 15,186 workers registered in health. (Conselho Coordenador do Recenseamento 1983:33)

The official literacy campaigns, then, shifted the locus of literacy from community to workplace. They also shifted the teachers from community volunteers, including many secondary school students and literate adults, to workplace appointees, whose voluntariness came increasingly into question over the years. The DNEA guidelines were that people with a minimum of four years of schooling should teach literacy while post-literacy should be taught by those with a minimum of six years of schooling. By and large, the teachers were fellow-workers although some large enterprises with many illiterates and difficulties in finding minimally qualified teachers began to admit new workers just to teach literacy. The teachers were given a 21 day pre-service training course organized by literacy instructors at provincial and district levels. These were meant to be followed up by in-service training consisting of working visits to literacy centres by the pedagogical support staff and occasional seminars and refresher courses. Additional pedagogical support was given through an audio-visual department which provided weekly radio programmes aimed at both mobilization and technical support for teachers. There was also a broadsheet for the newly literate entitled "Keep Studying."

Literacy services were gradually set up in each of the ten provinces and later Maputo city. They included a head, a staff person each for literacy and adult education services, a staff person in charge of audio-visual services and teams of instructors, one for pre-service training and the other for in-service training and pedagogical support. At district level there was also a literacy team consisting of three or four people to carry out all of the necessary tasks, both educational and pedagogical.

A National Commission for Literacy and Adult Education was set up as the supreme coordinating body for the campaigns, composed of representatives of party, workplace, mass organizations, key ministries and the Ministry of Education and Culture itself. The Commission was presided over by the Minister of Education and was scheduled to meet three times a year to deliberate over the operation of the campaigns and to determine policy guidelines. This Commission and its provincial and district counterparts never functioned effectively, however, either not meeting at all or meeting with different representatives each time, or meeting only for ritual occasions of launching campaigns or awarding certificates. The Commissions did not grapple with the very real day to day problems of the campaigns.[10]

With flagging results, measures were taken to underscore the responsibility of the economic sectors in guaranteeing basic education for their workers. The Council of Ministers passed Law 1/81 at the beginning of 1981, making it obligatory for workplaces to provide opportunities for education for their work forces. The law created a clear tri-partite division of responsibility for literacy among workplace administration, education officials and Frelimo Party/mass organizations. Human resource departments were to be created in the economic sectors that would assume responsibility for planning and organizing literacy and post-literacy for their workers. The role of education staff was that of setting norms and methodologies and evaluating. The party and mass organizations had the major role of mobilizing. The actual coordination, organization, execution and control rested with the workplace administration.

The numbers successfully completing the literacy programme and passing the exam declined dramatically after 1980. The official explanation of why the campaigns were in such difficulties touches on a number of very complex factors. The reasons cited included inflated numbers in 1979/80, reflecting already literate adults needing certification, campaigns moving successively to rural areas and hence incorporating people with less ability to speak Portuguese, major intensification of the war mounted by South African-backed insurgents, catastrophic droughts and floods, and limitations of the teachers. Other reasons cited included lack of a "literate environment" and reading matter for post-literacy as well as abandonment by literacy teachers seeking paid employment.

An evaluation undertaken by Agneta Lind, a Swedish literacy specialist working with the DNEA, also included hierarchical structures in the DNEA and the tendency to centralization and one-way, top-down communication as important factors.

> The DNEA never had enough contact with the situation at grassroots level, in order to be able to act adequately and efficiently. . . . Linked to this problem is the fact that the campaigns were too rigidly and centrally programmed. It was, however, judged difficult to rely on more flexibility at lower levels, due to the lack of personnel with enough education and training for more decentralized comprehensive solutions.
>
> (Lind 1985:6)

Another fundamental problem she signals is the profound ambivalence between viewing literacy as a mass campaign with political objectives for increased participatory democracy and viewing literacy as the beginning of formal schooling for adults with technical-professional objectives. The decision to target centres of organized production rather than the community shifted literacy very much to a discourse around skills, training and higher productivity. The aim was to attain certification of basic primary schooling and thereby have access to the general system of education and technical training courses. This, of course, had an enormous impact on the teachers, the students and all those involved in literacy. (Lind 1985:10)

A New National Education System (NES)

Despite the signs that the mass campaigns were in serious difficulties, the DNEA was, by 1982, drawn fully into a global educational reform programme. "The National Education System is an essential element of the long-term battle to win economic independence," said Minister of Education Graca Machel, in presenting the proposal for the NES to the National People's Assembly in October 1981. She went on to say that what had functioned up until then was a series of education and training activities inherited at independence in which only the contents and programmes had been altered, leaving intact the broader structures. This had allowed each to develop at its own pace with its own mechanisms of organization, methodology, inspection and evaluation. What was desired was a coherent national system with interacting and compatible components and an integral link to the socio-economic development of the country.

The NES proposal consisted of five inter-locking sub-systems, namely, general education, adult education, technical/vocational education, teacher training and higher education. There was a four-tier structure of primary, secondary, post-secondary and higher education, with a plan to introduce the NES in phases starting with the introduction in 1983 of the first grade of general education and the first two years of adult education.

The adult education sub-system was targeted for those 15 years and over. It consisted of a first phase, basic adult literacy, followed by a graded programme of primary education. The literacy component was of two years duration, taking into account the special teaching and learning problems of literacy in a second language. The first, second and third year were all mass based, to be offered in workplace and community literacy centres. They were designed to take the learner to the stage where a reversion back to illiteracy was impossible. From fourth year on, the adult education programme was to shift to night school or to workplace-based schools offering secondary level studies. Adults were meant to be able to move freely into technical schools, teacher training and finally university programmes. The option for a graded sub-system of adult education, closely articulated with the sub-systems of general and technical education, pushed literacy and post-literacy even more firmly away from popular education and in the direction of formal schooling.

The literacy curriculum of the NES included both language skills and mathematics. The content of the new language programme reflected a shift from the themes of the national liberation struggle to the themes of national reconstruction. The units of the first year programme touched on such themes as organizing cooperatives, women's participation in development, care of machines, basic notions of post-natal care and solidarity in the anti-apartheid struggle. Methodologically the fact of literacy in a second language was taken with utmost seriousness. Basic literacy was stretched out over a two year programme with six two hour class sessions to consolidate each new family of sounds. For example, the key word "sabao" (soap) and the phrase "Soap is good for washing the baby" are used to introduce sa se si so su and ba be bi bo bu. Short sentences speak of washing the baby daily, taking the baby to the well-baby clinic regularly, feeding the baby breast milk, introducing the baby to soup, banana and papaya and washing the baby's clothes

TABLE 5.4 National Education System *

	Primary	*Secondary*	*Pre-University*	*University*
General Education	7 years	3 years	2 years	4-6 years
General Adult Teacher Training	-	-	3 years	4 years
Technical Education (youth)	-	3 years	3 years	4-6 years
Technical Education (adults)	-	4 years	4 years	4-6 years
Technical teacher training	-	-	4 years	5 years
Adult Education	5 years	2 years	2 years	4-6 years
Adult Pre-University (Accelerated)		3 years for both Sec. & Pre-univ.		4-6 years

* National Education System to be introduced in phases between 1983 and 1994

Source: Adapted from Ministry of Education/INDE 1982:24

carefully. Thus thematic content was introduced while working on words formed with the new syllabic families. In this particular unit, the words included "sopa" (soup), "banana" (banana), "saudé" (health) and "bébé" (baby).

The two hour teaching session included a substantial portion of time each day for oral skills, including dialogues, role plays, socio-dramas and structural exercises. The decision to introduce this component resulted from the testing of the materials during 1982 and the recognition that doing literacy in a second language necessitated real attention to learning to *speak* Portuguese. Classroom observation during 1983, when the new materials were introduced, seemed to indicate that these methods, while they may have been appropriate for the learners' needs, were well beyond the teachers' skills. Real limitations on the part of the volunteer teachers were evident, whether in facilitating discussions aimed at building critical consciousness or in using language teaching methods that allowed students to master spoken Portuguese.[11]

The teachers' manuals were simplified. They were set up so that each double page opened with the material from the learner's book on one page and the step by step suggestions of how to teach the lesson opposite to it. The lessons included activities working on speaking skills, reading skills and writing skills. There were tests built into the materials to try to measure progress on the one hand and familiarize learners with doing simple tests on the other.

All efforts were focused on writing the new curriculum materials and on training programmes to introduce them to the teachers. No attention was paid to organization of the literacy centres and learners. Meanwhile, the numbers involved in the literacy programmes continued to decline. In the first two national campaigns, 140,000 and 120,000 had passed the literacy exam. Only 60,000 had passed the exam in 1981 and by 1982, the number was down to 40,000. By then, a substantial infrastructure had been built. The adult education personnel at national and provincial level and throughout the 115 districts of the country were servicing what was, in fact, a very small number of people.

In 1983, those just beginning literacy followed the new first year programme. Those who had passed literacy in 1982 entered the new second year programme. About 31,000 passed the first year exam and 15,000 passed the second year. (DNEA 1984) This was just slightly over the 40,000 who had passed first year alone in 1982. The last campaign using the old adult education materials was held for repeaters and those accessing the system from the general primary school system. Slightly over 15,000 passed.

As indicated above, all attention in planning the new Adult Education Sub-system had been concentrated on pedagogical questions with little or no attention paid to organizational aspects. Meanwhile, in many workplace adult education centres, the planning and organization problems had become insurmountable. The close monitoring of progress with the new materials made it clear that the results registered from past campaigns often did not indicate pedagogical failure as such. In other words, the high failure rates from earlier campaigns were not to be interpreted as failure by individual workers who had duly completed the programmes of studies, done the final test and not been able to pass it. More common were the organizational failures. There were many literacy centres functioning only minimally, with irregular class sessions covering only a tiny portion of the programme of studies. Inadequately prepared teachers tended to get little support for their efforts, abandoned save for the occasional inspection visit. These inspections often included rants about absenteeism for the few who were actually present. Education staff was also prone to make very critical comments about the inadequacy of the volunteer teachers and the inability of the learners, leaving behind very demoralized teachers and learners.

Perhaps even more fundamental in its consequences for literacy, however, was the seriousness of the war and economic crisis. There were profound disruptions in every province by RENAMO terrorist actions. The economic destabilization tactics being carried out by South Africa were creating havoc with foreign exchange. The disinformation campaigns were creating a climate of rumour and intrigue, making people anxious about the future of the country and the ability of the FRELIMO government to survive. With the impact of the international economic crisis and severe drought conditions added to the mix, survival was very much on the agenda. It was not a climate that was propitious for literacy.

The Literacy Teacher: Educating the Educators

> The task of teachers and cadres in education is an extraordinarily delicate one because like us, they grew up and were formed in the old world, and carry within them many bad habits and defects, a lot of individualism and ambition, many corrupt and superstitious attitudes. . . . Teachers and cadres must behave like the doctor who, before approaching the patient in the operating theatre, disinfects and sterilises himself so as not to infect the patient.
>
> (Machel 1974:22)

> The materialist doctrine that men are products of circumstances and upbringing, and that, therefore, changed men are products of other circumstances and changed upbringing, forgets that it is men that change circumstances, and that the educator himself needs educating.
>
> (Marx III Thesis on Feuerbach 1845)

The teachers in the mass literacy campaigns launched after 1978 were regularly cited as one of the fundamental weaknesses of the campaigns. The evaluation of the first campaign pointed to the difficulties encountered by the teachers in employing the methods proposed, methods based on actual dialogue with the students.

> In general, the method proposed was not applied. In practice, the teaching was most close to traditional-colonial methods, based on the schooling experiences of the literacy teachers, with characteristics of repetition and memorization. This leads to a mechanical learning, instead of establishing comprehension, reflection and creative application of the materials.
>
> (INDE 1983:14)

Such difficulties, of course, are not unique to Mozambique, and can be found in many other experiences of literacy. Linda Harasim had this comment to make concerning Guinea Bissau:

> The Freire method is centred on a literacy animator who coordinates the cultural circle. The animator is to be a polyvalent agent, integrating political mobilization, health and preventive medicine, agriculture and community development with literacy work, and should be a highly conscious person who can talk with the people and return to them in an organized form what they themselves have offered in a disorganized form. . . . The volunteers for the literacy work came from the primary and secondary schools. They had neither the training nor the expertise to be political agitators, literacy teachers and community developers at the same time.
>
> (Harasim 1983:369/370)

Sheryl Hirshon's moving and humorous account of her experiences as a literacy coordinator in Nicaragua point to the same thing.

> "The Dialogue."
> It was Step 1 in every lesson, and by far the most difficult to conduct. The brigadistas found it a frustrating and confusing assignment. What was it for? Certainly *they'd* never been taught that way. In all too many of the classes it was done badly, or ignored altogether. Saturday after Saturday we spent trying to make them see its importance and master the subtleties of conducting it. "It has to be a conversation, not a lecture. And it has to come from the campesinos themselves, from their experiences. It has to be their thoughts. Look, everyone likes to talk about their experiences if they think the other person is interested. With the photo and your encouragement, they will get over their feelings of intimidation. But you have to think of questions which will unlock their experiences, then get them thinking about them."
>
> (Hirshon 1983:104)

Teachers and their tendency to reproduce the manner in which they themselves were taught is a common problem in educational activities anywhere. These tendencies became more acute in Mozambique, however, with the national campaigns. In the spontaneous literacy movement at independence, both monitors and literacy students were caught up in new configurations of power and knowledge embedded in "people's power." The community control of these schools and the role of the literacy learners in organizing their own schooling and vetting their own teachers were key aspects. So was the sentiment of anger at the creation of ignorance by colonialism, a healthy corrective to the notion of the illiterate as deficient. The broader political process was the real teacher. The dynamic of the teaching-learning situation was far from that of formal school classrooms behind which lies all the authority of the state.

By the time of the national campaigns, however, there were strong tendencies towards formalizing literacy and establishing once again classroom practices based on the imposition of a language, a way of speaking it, and a definition of knowledge bounded by prescribed texts. The teachers were key factors in establishing these forms of schooling, a tendency which only increased over the years.

At CIM, for example, these tendencies were strongly in evidence. The choice to make the literacy programme part of the "school," seeing it as just the first step in the educational pyramid, was one sign of this formalizing tendency. While it valorized literacy at one level, it also located it within a framework of "schooling" that brought with it many expectations from teachers, students and factory administrators. The classroom process was one in which the teachers often reproduced the worst of their own experiences of authoritarian schooling, effectively robbing the students of any possibility of finding in the literacy classroom a space for voices and a rediscovery of words.

With the state-sponsored literacy campaigns, the "illiterate" became, again, an administrative category, albeit to be resolved by a paternalistic socialist state rather than a fascist colonial one. Workers drawn into literacy, whether as students or as teachers, found themselves within an institution that validated neither of them as real resources for socialist construction.

The recruitment and training of the teachers for the campaigns was, in fact, fraught with difficulties. First, few workers were genuinely recruited to teach through anything approaching persuasion. Once it became obligatory by law to provide adult basic education in the workplace, management in most cases simply allocated workers to teach literacy just as they would to any other area of factory or farm activity. Workers who were to teach attended three to six week courses held in the months before the campaign at provincial training centres or in the workplace itself. Some workers actually arrived at the courses offered by the DNEA thinking they were going to a professional up-grading course. Only on arrival did they find that they were being trained to teach literacy!

If teachers teach as they have been taught, they also teach as they have been trained. The training courses did little to provide an alternative experience of pedagogy. There was nothing in the training programme to counter the vertical structuring, rote learning and all-powerful role of the teacher with a learner-centred pedagogy concerned about empowerment.

The courses for those being trained to teach literacy systematically stripped them of their own experiences as workers and as adults, along with any curiosity, ideas or motivation they might possibly have had about literacy. The training courses themselves made the trainees into "pupils" interacting with "teachers" in classic molds. The worker/trainees had their own experiences of subordination as pupils reproduced for them. Diagnostic tests were given on arrival in both Portuguese and mathematics. Most workers used few language or mathematics skills on the job and got very poor results on the test. Much was made of the low quality of these results, certifying the inadequacy of the trainee as the first step in the training process.

The poor results were real enough. The workers, whether products of colonial schools or the overcrowded schools with undertrained teachers during the explosion of education in the early years of independence, had very little command of either language or mathematics skills. Many of them had had no need to read, write or count in their jobs and, at best, read the newspaper. Many of them spoke little Portuguese on the job as well, since informal contact with fellow workers was usually in the local language of the region.

While the lack of language and mathematics skills was real enough, the question was whether tests were the appropriate way to start dealing with these weaknesses. As the first activity in the training course, the tests served to confirm the workers' sense of their own inadequacy, especially in this new (and usually unasked for) task as teachers. It also established the power of the trainer, not as colleague and friend to be counted on for support in the new task of literacy but as the authority figure, the inspector. Rather than being encouraged to share what they did know with fellow workers and learn more in the process, as had been the case in the earlier mass campaigns, the trainees first experience in the training course was to have their own lack of knowledge confirmed. Whatever resources they brought as adult workers, their life experiences, their work skills, their political consciousness were of no interest. Their poor language and math skills defined them as deficient.

The training courses, far from establishing a flexible workshop format and an active link between classroom talk and life experiences, established a rigid time-table of disciplines to be given in 55 minute periods, usually six per day. The disciplines included general teaching methods, teaching methods for language and mathematics, organization and psycho-pedagogy. They also included programmes to up-grade the teachers themselves in basic language and mathematics skills. Support texts were often handed out and the evaluation tended to be one that encouraged memorization of these texts. Each discipline was evaluated with an exam.

The courses operated in provincial centres for literacy staff training. Strict boarding school routines were replicated in these centres with housing in dormitories, complete with inspection for tidiness. There were marks for attendance and punctuality at classes. Formal requests had to be made for week-end leave even when there were no classes during the week-ends and the trainees lived in the town where the courses were being held. Adults workers, used to controlling their own lives and time (at least when off the shop floor), were placed in a boarding school regime with a time-table for waking up, washing, flag-raising, meals, classes, cultural activities and recreation. The set of internal rules and regulations of the centre reinforced the trainees' sense of powerlessness, stripping them of their normal capacities as adults in organizing their lives.

The trainers established extremely formal classroom procedures with students rising when the trainer entered and departed, and in many cases, also standing up to answer questions. The formalization of the authority and power of the trainer was very strong in establishing relations of hierarchy and subordination.

There was no contact with real classes and real illiterate students during the training. The practice teaching sessions with fellow-workers were far from the actual conditions of a literacy classroom. It was virtually impossible to simulate the formidable challenge in engaging illiterate workers. The barrier posed by language was one, given that many spoke only minimal Portuguese. The social learning of how to "do class," making the workers into passive recipients for what the teachers "gave" was another.

The training courses included no experience of another way of "doing class," despite much discussion in general methodology about the deficiencies of colonial pedagogy and the need for active, participatory methods rather than lectures and rote learning. This contradiction was so evident at one of the national level courses for provincial trainers that the trainees made criticisms of it in their evaluation of the course. They then returned to their own provinces, however, and imposed the same orthodoxy of lectures and dictations in the provincial centres. All was in its place when the teacher was positioned at the front of the room, and the students were in rows, ready to receive.

Mozambique's difficulties with teacher training should not be seen as surprising. The approaches to teaching taken by teachers throughout the world are determined through some combination of their own experiences as pupils, their professional education and their actual experiences of teaching. (Dale 1977:50) The teachers' own experiences as pupils are potent forces. Imitative practices from their own experiences in a very powerful institution are fundamental. A kind of social knowledge, almost an oral tradition, of how to do "schooling" prevails. The established means for doing the job of teaching are taken as common sense knowledge and applied. For Mozambican teachers, this meant drawing on experiences either in colonial classrooms or in overcrowded primary schools with untrained teachers immediately after independence. Both were far from the dynamic vision of classroom interaction and community engagement envisioned by the Ministry of Education and Culture.

As for professional training, the courses in the literacy training centres or in improvised conditions in the districts, just reproduced more of the same. There was nothing in the training experience that actually gave the trainees a concrete experience of active participation, horizontal rather than vertical communication, a pedagogy of questions rather than of answers.

The classroom realities faced by the literacy teachers also shaped their teaching. If in "western" classrooms, ideas of participatory methods often flounder when faced with class size or student attitudes that put basic control on the agenda, the literacy classrooms in Mozambique shaped the teachers' way of teaching in another manner. The passivity and silence of the learners was a powerful force. Many workers were there by decision of their section head rather than by persuasion. Often they were hungry and tired. All were locked into silence by an idea of classroom decorum socially learned. Many were very inhibited by their lack of command of the Portuguese language. Women were doubly oppressed, fearing also to speak out in front of men, and at the request of a male teacher. The inexperienced teacher tended to fill the silence with his or her own voice -- mini-lectures on hygiene, cooperatives, endless repetitions of closed questions demanding only a chorus of "yes" or "no" from the students. Rarely was anything approaching the rich naming of experiences, the deconstruction of one way of seeing and the construction of another, to be observed.

Clearly being posed in this situation were fundamental pedagogical questions turning on theories of knowledge and popular power.

> . . . "pedagogy" is a more complex and extensive term than "teaching," referring to the integration in practice of particular curriculum content and design, classroom strategies and techniques, a time and space for the practice of these new strategies and techniques, and evaluation purposes and methods. All of these aspects of educational practice come together in the realities of what happens in classrooms. Together they organize a view of how a teacher's work within an institutional context specifies a particular version of what knowledge is of most worth, what it means to know something, and how we might construct representations of

> ourselves, others, and our physical and social environment. In other words, talk about pedagogy is simultaneously talk about the details of what students and others might do together *and* the cultural politics such practices support. To propose a pedagogy is to propose a political vision.
> (Simon 1987:371)

The pedagogy of the earlier literacy movement had proposed a political vision, one that had begun to validate the lives and experiences of those who had been subordinated by colonialism. Collective renamings of situations and selves constructed under colonialism had been integral to it, in the heady moments of independence, with its new disposition of power and knowledge. The seeds of a new pedagogy were to be found in this movement, a "pedagogy of empowerment" that challenged old discourses that subordinated and marginalized people for being peasants or workers, for being black, for being female.

A "pedagogy of empowerment" had emerged strongly at independence -- and then receded again. The content of the educational programme established after independence continued to reflect ideas about building "people's power," replete with new values of participation, collectivity and internationalism. At the same time, old forms, antithetical to local control and spaces for self-education, reasserted themselves. The changes in content, then, were not matched by changes in forms. Styles of schooling prevailed in the literacy classroom in which old categorizations, old power/subordination roles were played out. Students were once again silenced. There were strong tendencies for literacy to become formalized and bureaucratized, with the new moral order of dedicated and disciplined Mozambican workers and peasants constructing socialism defined centrally. Pronouncements from the political leadership substituted a vital process of empowerment at the grassroots.

The teachers were key in establishing this, a situation not unique to Mozambique by any means. Henry Giroux in his analysis of North American teacher training, points to the same phenomenon.

> In many respects teacher-education programs have simply not given teachers the conceptual tools they need in order to view knowledge as problematic, as a historically conditioned, socially constructed phenomenon. Similarly, the objectification of knowledge is usually accompanied by the objectification of the classroom social encounter. Knowledge is not just content; its use also suggests specific kinds of classroom social relationships. When knowledge is seen as objective and "out there," it is usually accompanied by top-to-bottom forms of pedagogy in which there is little dialogue or interaction. . . . But the way pupils construct meaning, the importance of subjectivity, and the value of

> knowledge outside of the 'rationality' of strict science are important dimensions of the process of curriculum and instruction. These modes of knowing represent important pedagogical principles that future educators need to understand in order to be able to shape their *own* lives in a self-determining manner. . . . Knowledge in the technocratic rationality view is defined and used so as to be separated from the lived histories and biographies not only of teachers but of students. . . . Thus knowledge is used not only to mask the role that it plays in shaping how people view themselves and others, it also serves to ignore how important the relationship is among knowledge, context and learning.
>
> (Giroux 1980:19)

The real irony is that the teachers themselves were also silenced. Their own positions of subordination within workplace hierarchies as junior staff allocated to literacy often ran counter to their own job expectations. Many of them compared their own "dead end" as literacy teachers over against other colleagues with the same educational level who had entered with them and were now in professional training courses which were perceived as having a future. Ministry of Education officials saw them only as part of the problem, their low academic and professional levels contributing to the students' learning problems. No discussion of the poor results in literacy was complete without public laments about the inadequacies and limited competence of the voluntary/conscripted literacy teachers!

Clearly, then, the process of literacy in post-independence Mozambique passed through various phases, echoing the larger political process. Forms of genuine people's power, paternalistic forms of revolution from above, and cruder forms of silencing and subordination in the name of the larger socialist project vied with each other. These struggles played themselves out in multiple settings, with a diversity of results. These struggles can perhaps best be understood by looking in detail at the actual practices of literacy in one workplace. It is to a detailed study of an urban factory literacy centre and the meanings of literacy for the women and men in that setting that we will now turn.

Notes

1. The complexity of this historical moment should not be understated. The fomenting of anti-colonial sentiment was part of a larger FRELIMO project linked to questions of race and class. FRELIMO took pains to establish the enemy as the colonial regime and not the Portuguese people as such. This was, at least in part, linked to a concern to legitimize the presence of those settlers who opted to stay to build an independent Mozambique. Given the nature of the coup, the progressive cast of the officers who made it, it was not so difficult to give substance to a Portuguese "people" equally liberated from a fascist regime.

FRELIMO signalled clearly and worked hard at the base to establish that the question was not one of black against white. It was equally clear that its project did pit the popular classes against the privileged. The question was one of class, not race. The clear signalling of this aspect resulted in a massive flight of the settlers, with 90 percent of them departing within a few years of independence. What is interesting is the comparisons between Mozambique's policies at independence and those of Zimbabwe a few years later. Popular lore in the region suggests that Samora Machel was one of those who counselled Robert Mugabe to find ways to make the settlers stay on. Whatever may have been said, Mugabe's first years in office seemed to include acute awareness of the need for the Zimbabwean state to face two ways, walking the tightrope between faithfulness to a popular project within while at the same time having to avoid signals to alarm its powerful apartheid neighbour. There is no doubt that, for South Africa, the fate of a handful of Portuguese settlers was of far less consequence than the fate of the British settlers in Rhodesia. And indeed given the profoundly racist biases of the northern hemisphere, the fate of "kith and kin" takes on a symbolic importance well beyond the region.

2. The expectations actually raised by schooling deserve close scrutiny in Mozambique as elsewhere. Clearly the concept of schooling and what it brings is a social construction. Under colonialism, it had been the path to assimilated status. At the Mozambique Institute, this rapidly got translated into schooling for scholarships abroad and grooming for government positions after independence. What would be of interest is an exploration of peasant conceptions of schooling as a good for their children and how much this is always linked with departure from the rural areas, preparation for the city. Certainly in other countries in Africa, the social construction of "schooling" sees it not as a way to transform rural or urban production processes but as a way out of the field and the factory, from work clothes and shop floor drudgery to the office with suit and pen.

3. For a fuller discussion of these struggles, see Marshall, Judith. "Making Education Revolutionary" in John Saul (ed.). *A Difficult Road: The Transition to Socialism in Mozambique*. New York; Monthly Review Press, 1985 as well as Munslow 1983; Isaacman & Isaacman 1983; Egero 1986; Egero 1987.

4. Currently there are initiatives to give the concept of popular education a more precise meaning after more than a decade of rather loose usage. (Jara 1981; Arruda 1982; Torres 1983; Castillo and Latapi 1983) A common reference point for those claiming to do popular education has been the writings of Paulo Freire, based on experiences in Brazil and Chile in the 1960s and 1970s and in Sao Tome, Tanzania and Guinea Bissau in the 1980s. (Freire 1970, 1973, 1975,1987a, 1987b) Freire's notions of education for critical consciousness, a pedagogy of the oppressed, cultural action, the psycho-social method, the contrast between banking education and problem-solving education have all become widely known. Many and diverse practices would claim to be within the Freirian method. Recent work has tended to sharpen the definition of popular education to include a more explicit commitment to subordinated sectors, a process of "creating" knowledge rather than "transmitting" knowledge, and the construction

of new forms of people's power in a revitalized "civil society." (Brandão 1987; Torres 1986)

5. For the notion of a "pedagogy of leadership" I am indebted to Jose Luis Coraggio in his insightful discussion of the educational role of the political leadership in the process of transition in Nicaragua. (Fagen, Deere & Coraggio 1986) Sayer and Corrigan make the point strongly about "being good at learning" as a paramount necessity for political leadership within a process of social transformation, drawing particularly on the Chinese experience and conceptualization of this process. (Corrigan and Sayer 1984:140)

6. All subsequent translations from the documents submitted to the National Seminar on Literacy in Ribáuè in April 1975 are mine.

7. Gordon West's studies on education in Nicaragua show striking similarities. The state schools of the old regime were characterized by little access and high failure rates along with programmes integrating poor youth into the repressive apparatus of the old Somoza regime. In dramatic contrast was the widespread popular education movement linked to Christian base communities, neighbourhood improvement associations, union efforts and networks of FSLN supports establishing "safe" houses for guerrillas and information. West makes the point that the neighbourhood organizations established by these educational efforts were often the only "government" operating, as services were cut, factories shut, etc. "In this situation, popular education in the committees not only made the revolution possible, they suggested a possible new politics, a reformulation of education, and exemplified an alternative strategy of social development: a social structure where citizens taught each other, and provided the needed resources to develop their immediate social environment." (West 1987)

8. The vibrant mass movement in Mozambique at independence seems to have slipped below the horizon of visibility in official documents. Ministry of Education accounts about the experience of literacy in Mozambique devote at best a paragraph to this period, although the accounts include estimates that more people became literate at this time than in all the subsequent national campaigns. The paper presented by a Ministry of Education official to a recent conference in Germany on literacy described the early literacy activities in this way. "As a result of FRELIMO's drive, thousands of Mozambicans threw themselves enthusiastically into literacy and schooling. Despite the lack of adequate textbooks and without any central guidance or planning, popular initiatives encouraged the campaign and a wide section of the population participated - statistics gathered later indicate that more than 500,000 people learned to read and write at this time. The majority of these people were in urban and semi-urban areas where the lack of human and material resources was not as great." (Fonseca 1983:2) The invisibility of this earlier moment is lamentable in that it could and should be an important reference point for contemporary movements of renewal within literacy such as that emanating from the training programmes in Manga (see Chapter 9).

9. For a fascinating study of this process of change in the secondary schools in the immediate post-independence period, see Chris Searle. *We're Building the New School! Diary of a Teacher in Mozambique*. 1981. London: Zed Press. Here the

texture of the struggle between old and new is documented with humour and wisdom in the classrooms and surrounding community of Nampula.

10. For a detailed analysis of the functioning of the literacy campaigns, see Agneta Lind's *O Desafio da Alfabetização*. Stockholm: SIDA Education division documents No. 27, December 1985 and her recent doctoral dissertation, *Adult Literacy. Lessons and Promises Mozambican Literacy Campaigns 1978-1982* (1988). Lind worked with the DNEA from 1979-1983, during the last seven months of which she worked with Mozambican colleagues on a general evaluation of the first four literacy campaigns. The SIDA document gives a comprehensive evaluation of the 2nd, 3rd and 4th literacy campaigns run from 1980 to 1982 and the dissertation analyzes the campaigns in greater depth.

11. My own involvement in the National Directorate of Adult Education began at this time, as part of the team involved in testing the new materials in Michafutene, with particular responsibility for the training programmes. The articulation between the team working on the new curriculum materials and other structures, both those in the training and organization departments of the DNEA and those working in the literacy sector in INDE, was fraught with difficulties. The decision to include a strong component of Portuguese as a second language methodology was hotly debated, done at the last moment without opportunity for testing, and very inadequately presented in the training programmes. The courses organized by the training department functioned in a very formal context with "banking methods" prevailing and thus gave little space for the trainees to really grapple adequately with the new methods.

6

Time for "Schooling" at CIM

I'd like to do fifth class. My problem is the time. I get home too late to do the cleaning and feed the children. A woman is always being squeezed. She's always in the middle, always given orders

(Amélia Cossa, Warehouse 6, 43 years)
Passed fourth class in 1984
Never enrolled in fifth class

The problem is -- it's not worth it to go to classes because there comes a time when the job puts the squeeze on you.

(Bernardo Taimo, Workshops, 44 years)
Passed first year with 100% in 1982
Passed second year with 93% in 1983
Did not attend in 1984/5

The institutional arrangement of time and space for a "school" within a factory setting is a curious one. The institutional forms of the school are superimposed on the already established factory discipline.[1] In CIM, as in other work-place settings, the literacy programme sponsored by the state took uneasy account of prior arrangements of time in terms of either production rhythms per se or the daily routines of factory life including meals, rest, transport and social interaction.

The CIM "school," like all schools in all societies, had a set of organizational forms, practices, agents and documents, an institutional arrangement of time and space. As Michel Foucault makes clear in his studies of power, an institution like the CIM "school" can be seen as a kind of "block" of regulated and concerted systems. The internal life of the school is minutely regulated. Foucault points to the relations of schooling and power, to how an educational institution functions as a particular kind of space, organizing people into particular social relations as teachers and learners, each with their own function and clearly defined character. From this emerges a set of power relations and kinds of communication.

The types of behaviour generated by the school are created through a whole ensemble of regulated communications. The kinds of communications linked to doing school include "lessons, questions and answers, orders, exhortations, coded signs of obedience, differentiation marks of the "value" of each person and of the level of knowledge." (Foucault 1982:787) The political space of schooling also includes a whole series of power processes operative in an education institution. These include "enclosure, surveillance, reward and punishment, the pyramidal hierarchy." (Foucault 1982:787)

School Time at CIM

A study of "schooling" at CIM, then, means looking at the institutional organization of time and space.[2] By 1985/86, the organization of time at the CIM "school," as in other workplace literacy settings, was determined by a school year controlled nationally and run concurrently with the state school system. Although both dwindling participation in literacy and regular reports from field visits pointed to the fact that a set calendar of this sort in no way responded to the realities of organizing literacy in the workplace, the fiction persisted that it was possible to run national literacy programmes with a set calendar as you did the general school system.

School time at CIM was also organized around daily lessons in a standardized curriculum for adults. This programme of studies was introduced in 1983, as we have seen above, and was part of the Adult Education Sub-system of the National Education System. The first stage of the graded programme for adults consisted of three years of literacy and post/literacy which were meant to be the "equivalent" of basic primary education. This block of basic primary education curriculum for children extended from Class 1 to Class 5.

The CIM, "school" offered literacy and post-literacy programmes during the day and upper primary and secondary programmes at night. It was linked formally to the Matola Secondary School, one of a number of workplace satellite schools. The programmes available at CIM were identical to those offered in other city night schools. These programmes differed only marginally from the day school programme for young people in the General Education Sub-system.

The second and third year programmes of the Adult Education Sub-system were taken as the beginners level on the educational ladder within this multi-stream system. They shared the same formalities and the same organizational forms of graded contents, timetables, knowledge divided into subject areas, set text books, daily lessons, attendance requirements and exams.

The organizational forms of secondary schooling spilled over into literacy. The literacy teachers adopted the white smocks favoured by teachers in the secondary schools. Whatever practical value they had for protection from chalk dust were far superseded by their symbolic value. For both students and teachers, they signalled formal classrooms with authoritative teachers' voices lecturing, filling empty heads with wisdom, all of which would be returned verbatim for the exam.

The school year began on February 16 and continued until mid-November, when a nationally organized evaluation process was held with standardized exams. For the workplace-based literacy centres, the first date tended to be only minimally operative. Few were the centres, even the well-organized ones like CIM, that really could begin classes effectively in mid-February. Aside from the organizational problems of having books and teachers in place, many work-places found that a mid-February starting date conflicted with collective vacations or harvest time or a peak production period. These factors were totally outside the control of the Ministry of Education in a country with widely different climatic conditions from north to south, and widely diverse industries. Still, the notion that the adult education programmes could operate just as any other sub-system within the National Education System persisted.[3]

My Time and Role(s) as Participant Observer

Organization of my own time at CIM became more problematic once I arrived back as a full-time researcher. On arrival it was automatically assumed that I would be part of the staff of the training section which had responsibility for the school. Once I started to spend each day at CIM, I was given a desk in the Social Services Department, where the training section was located. My immediate colleagues were Samuel Zita, who headed the training section, and two other staff members, Aurélio Tembe and Lopes Chigoiane. I had met Aurélio Tembe when I first visited CIM while on national staff. He was still director of the school which was now offering Class 6 for the first time and had dropped first year of adult education. Those workers still at first year level were either working in shifts, multiple repeaters or deemed too old. The plan was to add Class 7, the first year of secondary schooling, in 1986, and drop second year of the Adult Education Sub-system.

The other immediate colleague was my old friend, Lopes Chigoiane, with whom I'd done the photo story. He was now teaching second year literacy and, at night, was a student in sixth class. The training section shared its space with two clerks from the Social Services Department in an inner office that linked the three other offices of that Department. It was therefore an excellent vantage point for observing the inner workings of one department.

My CIM day began at 7:10 a.m. as I waited outside my apartment in central Maputo. My request to CIM for transport had resulted in a daily ride to work in the senior staff car pool. Other CIM managers and workers were transported in a fleet of buses and trucks that regularly circled the far-flung residential areas of the city, picking up and depositing workers from multiple shifts.

Our car pool included Abdul Carimo, Director of Economy and Human Resources, Angélica Aguilera, a Chilean cooperant heading the Social Services Department, and when she left, José Manjate, the new head, and Albino Massingarela, a recent graduate of a technical institute. Massingarela was second in command at the mill, headed by Domingos Chinguvo, a veteran worker with fourth class.

The morning conversations covered every conceivable subject from bandit attacks to whether capitalist countries had queues, from recipes for banana cakes when CIM warehouses were full of over-ripe bananas to Mozambique's long-term potential for growing wheat. Out of these conversations came a strong rapport, particularly with Carimo, and a tremendous amount of general knowledge about the day to day preoccupations of the CIM staff.

I normally spent the first part of the morning at my desk in the training section or in one of the many sections of the factory interviewing and/or observing students. The work at my desk in the training section included gathering data on enrollment and attendance and exam results, analyzing reports on literacy activities and writing up observations. It also included many conversations with Zita and Aurélio and Lopes, since they automatically included me in discussions and decision-making about literacy during the time I was there. In turn, I shared highlights from the interviews with them regularly.

My role had many complicated aspects. The ease with which I was accepted and cast as part of the training department team made it easy to integrate into factory life. On the other hand, it placed me squarely within management structures. It also assumed that I represented and defended the ministry programme of adult education just when I wanted to generate conversations in which informants would begin to indicate their own ways of making sense of literacy. I did not want people to tell me what they thought I would want to hear, assuming me to be a representative of the DNEA. It was the more tricky because there was no active district education office presence at CIM. In the whole time I was there, there was only one brief visit by an official from the city staff. Assumptions certainly existed, however, about what the DNEA intended adult education to be, and I was seen as a representative of it.

In addition to sharing observations and data, I also continued to take an active role in resolving day to day problems, all of which built up trust and rapport. Going to battle with CIM against the city education officials to get school supplies from the provincial office undoubtedly helped to build up trust. The trust was presumably further developed by the fact that I constantly promoted critical discussions and cast myself in a training and support role rather than one of inspection and control.

My own location in the power relations organized through class, race/ethnicity, gender and age all played important roles in shaping my interactions with people at CIM. The "reality" of the CIM community that opened up to me in these extended conversations and interactions with its members is best understood not as *the* truth about CIM. It is *a* truth, a reading of the meanings attached to literacy and factory life derived from the explanations offered to me, all within the context of my own specificity as participant-observer. If I had been a male researcher, a black researcher, a researcher without any gray hair, presumably these factors would have triggered a different extended conversation, and hence a different reading of the CIM reality.

I spent about 15 hours every week in carrying out extended interviews. They were done first with all of the students who had been enrolled in 1985, including drop-outs. I then extended the interviews to students who had already completed fourth class, both those who had continued studying and those who had not. I tried to do the interviews in the sections at a slow enough pace that I would have the better part of a week in a given section and thus an opportunity for observation of the work of the section as I carried out the interviews. Normally the department head would set up a table and chair or a desk somewhere in the section. At times, we simply took chairs outside under a tree. In the pasta factory, the interviews worked out well because the table and chair provided were in the midst of the packaging operations and gave me a good opportunity to observe the assembly line bagging macaroni and spaghetti. In other cases such as the Mill, however, the desk and chairs provided were in the offices of the Mill management and the workers seemed to feel quite inhibited. With "bosses" within hearing distance a power dynamic seemed to be in place that had a strong impact on the flow of the interview. There were few interviews done with workers in the Mill, since shift work made it the remaining bastion of illiteracy with few participants in the classes. Those workers with whom I did speak seemed far less relaxed in the interviews, some of which may have indicated distance from any idea of what literacy was all about. At least part of it, however, seemed to come from a setting of having the Mill management team in close proximity.

The first interviews were done with informants I had already come to know through classroom observation as "talkative." They were entirely open-ended. From them, I began to see some recurring patterns and devised an interview form that served as a kind of discussion guide. The interviews normally took about two hours. A handful with particularly reticent informants or in circumstances not conducive to relaxed conversations took only about an hour. At the other end, however, there were several with particularly insightful informants that resulted in 3-4 hours of rich conversation.

The interview began with a set of factual questions about name, date of birth, etc. I could have taken information from the files, but these simple questions seemed to set people at ease. The interview then clustered around work experience at CIM (since when, in what part of the factory, doing what, for what pay), around family education (of parents, siblings, children, including present occupations, value and expectations of education), around languages spoken, read or written, around reasons for wanting to do literacy and feelings about progress in literacy, around participation in other organizations in the factory, and any other areas that emerged, including an opportunity to put questions to me.

One aspect later included had to do with a discussion around the uses of literacy. I discovered in chatting with people about languages spoken and read and written that the post-literacy students were not aware that, having learned to read and write in Portuguese, they could now begin to tackle reading in Changana, their mother tongue. I began to include a simple phrase in Changana as a way of enabling them to discover that their newly acquired reading skills could be applied to reading their own first language!

From ll:00 until 4:00, I spent most of the time in classroom. observation. The second year classes were held from ll:00 to 1:00 while the two sections of third year met from 11:00 to 1:00 and 1:00 to 4:00. I tried to arrive as the students did, in order to have an opportunity to chat with them informally before the classes began. When the classes started, I sat in one of the desks at the back of the classroom, taking notes about particular aspects of the class.

It was difficult to separate my various observer roles. On the one hand, I was noting down problems and weaknesses in the curriculum materials themselves out of an old role as part of the curriculum team. Secondly I was noting down strengths and weaknesses of the teachers in their handling of the materials, relating this not so much to individual assessments of the teachers from an "inspector" role but more to implications for training and ways to improve the pre-service training courses. Thirdly, I was observing carefully the behaviour of the students themselves. Given the tendency on the part of the teachers to dominate completely each lesson, asking at best closed questions that demanded yes and no answers in chorus, there was little to note down in terms of individual contributions from the students.

The classes included a period of time for written work in each lesson. The manual gave instructions for the teacher to circulate at this time and give individual help to the students. During our visits in 1983/84 as national and provincial staff members, we had opted to join the teachers in making the rounds desk by desk. This was done in part to be able to monitor the kinds of difficulties the students were encountering. It was also part of the in-service training for the teachers, demonstrating a style of interaction based on support, discovery and encouragement rather than corrections or supplying the "right" answer. I chose to follow that same style, using this opportunity for individual contact and encouragement. It was also a survival mechanism for me -- since, otherwise, I would have had a period of two and three hours of sitting and observing a process that was never very dynamic and often painful and infuriating because it was so antithetical to what we had envisioned when we wrote the materials.

I tried to use each walk from one section of the factory to another, and the daily stroll from the school at one end of the extensive factory complex to the dining room at the other as an opportunity to talk informally to as many people as possible. The lunch break was the only time that was generally recognized as "free time," when it was legitimate to stop and talk to people. Conversations struck up with workers at other times, apart from those in the context of the interviews, were always carried out with a note of tension. With middle and upper management, there was no problem, but with workers themselves, stopping work to talk to the researcher necessitated "permission." In order not to get the workers in trouble, or my colleagues in the Social Services Department who were not supposed to let a "stranger" roam the premises at will, I tried to maintain the ground rules of seeking formal permission before entering a section and limiting informal chats with workers to break times. This is not to suggest that the workers did not arrange plenty of moments to talk among themselves. The highly visible conversations with the foreign researcher, however, were mutually recognized as likely to cause problems.

The final hour each day at CIM found me back at my desk. This was usually spent in beginning to write up observations about the day's events and interacting with the level of excitement of the Social Affairs Department in late afternoon as bread was delivered for the workers to take home. This supply of bread to workers was a new feature of factory life after the opening of CIM's commercial bakery. Given the acute shortages of food, bread distribution became the high point of each afternoon's activities, with a flurry of arrival, distribution, payment for fluctuating numbers of loaves and wrapping to take home.

Sorting out my role as participant observer, then, was not always easy, nor always of my own choosing. During the first weeks of the research, I happened to sit down in the staff dining room beside Mário Morais, a senior Ministry of Labour staff person doing a study at CIM. Morais was also a senior official in the OTM, the Mozambican Workers Organization. He was immediately very enthused about my study of literacy, seeing it as a way for the OTM to learn, through the presence of an "expert" in its midst, how to give effective support to literacy. His first question to me was "What are the appropriate indicators to know how things are going in literacy?"

He was very aware that when the OTM was asked what it was doing about literacy in a given workplace, the OTM representative simply went to management. Management indicated how many classes there were, how many registered, how many passing and failing, and the OTM proceeded to report this as what OTM was doing in literacy. Morais was sure there were other indicators -- and I fed in immediately some of my initial observations, and what I thought it might begin to look like if OTM seriously defended the right of the worker to study. I alerted him to the real organizational problems and the number of workers who could not attend classes regularly because of work demands. I also alerted him to serious organizational problems in the ministry, such that students at times faced exams for which they hadn't had the books. I also mentioned the perception by workers of literacy as a dead end and the need for the OTM to promote training packages in which literacy would give entry to vocational training leading to increased skills, higher wages and better jobs.

> Today Mário Morais caught up with me as I went off to an interview and introduced me to Comrade Tembe who is responsible for organization in the OTM, and Comrade Inácio who is a party assistant. He proposed to them that they make use of my presence at CIM to organize a series of work sessions on literacy. These would look at what literacy is, reasons for absences and failures etc. The response of Tembe from OTM was very bureaucratic. He said he would inform the OTM Secretary and have him indicate someone to accompany what I was doing.

> Mário disagreed -- and explained that he was hoping for a more informal process. He also wanted to be present himself and proposed work sessions in which, without undue concern for hierarchies, everybody would participate actively. He then made some interesting observations about Mozambique, speaking of errors made since 1975 in formalizing things, establishing hierarchies. He recounted a conversation with Macamo, the Secretary General of the OTM, about all of this. Macamo, according to Morais, offered two reasons for the excessive formalities. The first was that OTM officials insisted on formalities as a tactic to maintain inaccessibility and thus hide their own incompetence. The second had to do with Mozambican culture. "Nobody speaks directly with the 'régulo' [local chief]. You always go through intermediaries before you finally get to him."
>
> (Field Notes, January 7, 1986)

Three work sessions were proposed, and the first one took place on January 17. Morais could not be there but a group of fourteen people including management, party, and representatives of the organizations of workers, women and youth attended. I had planned it in my best "popular educator" style with plenty of participation, with fond memories of sessions in Nicaragua using these methods. I envisaged a quick introduction of myself and how the idea of the sessions had emerged. Then I planned to ask those who had come to work in smaller groups, looking at the experience of literacy at CIM over the past decade and analyzing the successes and difficulties with respect to participation, teaching materials, incentives, the role of women in literacy, and the role of the Party and the mass organizations in literacy. The results of the small group sessions were then to be discussed collectively, followed by a slide tape presentation on the experience of literacy in other parts of Mozambique. The slide tape show was one I had developed for use in Canada, but had shown to colleagues in the DNEA where it had prompted much discussion.

Delays in arrival got us off to a late start. The work in the small groups was done, although not in a particularly dynamic fashion. In truth, few of them had anything to say about literacy because they were really distant from it. In addition, I had forgotten that what Nicaraguans do at the drop of a hat, organizing themselves into small buzz group, is rare in Mozambique these days. In the immediate post-independence era of the GDs, many such discussions took place. Now the very idea of an unstructured discussion, without guidelines set and the "correct answer" signalled was already highly novel. We had started so late that I decided to do the collective discussion of the results of the small group discussions during the next session.

The slide tape show did capture people's interest, but I was struck by the fact that, for many, it was the first time they had ever seen slides used in this way. They were really bowled over by visual presentations of their reality in and of itself, leave aside content, never mind critical analysis.

> Today was the day for the second work session with the OTM. I had prepared for it, already feeling that the thing was not going to go. I got there and nobody had come. . . . Second thoughts allowed that it might not have been all my fault! Underlying it all is a lot of uncertainty from the OTM as to what this is all about. They have a lot to do -- and this thing of literacy is not seen as a top priority. It was definitely Mário Morais' enthusiasm that got it established at all, and when neither he nor the secretary of OTM came to the first session, the thing weakened.
>
> It's interesting. Everything that you do to establish a process less authoritarian, less directive, appears as a signal of uncertainty as to how to proceed, almost as weakness. The expectation is for something already defined, with a leader providing all the answers. When the one doing the session signals another way of working, it becomes difficult. My refusal to play the role of expert was hard for them to understand.
>
> OJM, the youth organization, has no idea about literacy. The two OJM women who came . . . were totally at a loss. . . . Seemingly it had never entered their heads that literacy was something OJM could/should play a role in. The OMM sent Amélia Cossa from the sacks warehouse. She is an OMM activist and someone who completed fourth class in the CIM literacy programme a few years back. She was very timid when faced with the group who came to the work session. There in the warehouse, Amélia is a dynamic, even aggressive lady. When I went there with beer cans which the warehouse head makes into cups last week, she was in a teasing mood, and wanted to know why I hadn't brought full cans. She demanded to know when I was coming to interview her. There in the warehouse, she obviously feels in control. As the only woman who has managed to do fourth grade, she feels stronger than the women still doing literacy. Put the same woman in a meeting with the senior managers and she signals "stress" dramatically. I was struck by the body language, a timidness, a silencing -- a tremendous contrast to her aggressive presence last week as "queen" of the sacks warehouse.
>
> (Field Notes, January 23, 1986)

There were a couple of abortive attempts to re-schedule the session with the OTM people, and then I decided to leave it. The Secretary was absent almost constantly, working to organize a big food workers meeting. I decided that if it was a high enough priority for them, they would get back to me. They didn't!

The "School Year"

February 16 was designated nationally as starting date for the school year. When I arrived to begin work at CIM in May, 1985, I was informed that the starting date for classes that year had been much delayed. The new books for the third year programme had arrived only at the end of March; the programme began only in early April, a full six weeks late. The second volumes of the language and mathematics books did not arrive at all.

In 1986, CIM was able to begin classes only one week after the prescribed starting date, with books and basic supplies more or less in hand. This was unusual, and in part the result of my inputs. The CIM school director had put in the requisition for books and teaching materials well before the opening of the school year. Nonetheless, a saga of futile trips and much frustration was endured before the material actually arrived.

Creating "time" to do literacy within the framework of the formal education system was an enormous struggle. It had relatively modest dimensions in CIM with its high level of organization, availability of transport and presence of an "agitator." In many literacy centres, this same sequence of events would have delayed the books and supplies for several months rather than several weeks.

> Yet another trip out to the factory -- everybody a bit bad-tempered because the car arrived late. Talking with Aurélio, [the director of the school], this morning made me even more irritable. . . . How can he only now come to the conclusion that we are going to need a new teacher, after three straight weeks of talking about 3 classes? Still worse is the question of school supplies. The person at the school supply depot of the City Directorate of Education and Culture said yesterday, "They'll be available only from February 17th on. We're still receiving the materials. They'll be distributed first to the primary schools." How long will this go on in Mozambique -- Frelimo Party and Ministry talking of education for workers as top priority and then, in practice, giving all priority to the general system.
>
> (Field Notes, February 2, 1986)

> First Day of Classes
> Aurélio went to the opening of a professional training course. Zita [head of the training department] forgot to pass by the "school." Carlos, the teacher from last year who is off to work in the Mahotas, came. The new teacher did not appear. About 15 workers turned up at 11 o'clock. They were left waiting outside. Finally they came into the classroom at 11.25 just to have their classes indicated to them. They were informed that the timetable was identical with that of 1985 -- despite hot debate all week

within the Social Services Department about how to timetable the third year programme, which is based on 12 rather than 10 hours per week. The books still aren't here. Zita requisitioned a cheque today so that they can be picked up tomorrow. He has not been informed about the problems with the third year timetable.

(Field Notes, February 17, 1986)

Second Day of Classes
A message from the National Directorate of Education in response to my memo to the Director alerting her to what was happening in the city office as literacy centres tried to get their supplies. The memo says that the way to get school materials is to make a requisition and join to it a credential from the city education officer in charge of the zone. I passed it on to Aurélio and Zita. They were surprised. "We've never done it like that before. We always made a requisition, along with a list of the workers who are registered in the classes." Has my intervention created a situation in which a response has become necessary? Is the city office is inventing new steps? I am full of curiosity -- whether it will really be necessary to present a credential from Mr. Mondlane, the person in charge of the zone. Aurélio's comment sums it up. "Do we really have to go looking for this man who is never in his office and never comes here to visit, just for him to write us a credential? After all, what does he know about CIM? If he wants to know how many workers CIM has ready to study, who does he ask? Us."

(Field Notes, February 18, 1986)

People went to the city office. They did get some sort of credential and proceeded to the stores office. There they were told that the stores office is open in the morning only to receive goods, and that they had to come back in the afternoon for distribution.

(Field Notes, February 20, 1986)

They got transport arranged again and went to the stores office with the credential, only to find themselves in the midst of a line-up - including people from the primary schools, still hoping to get their materials. The CIM people managed to get textbooks, pencils and erasers. Exercise books and pens are still missing.

(Field Notes, February 21, 1986)

Today the CIM car-pool failed -- so I got a ride out to Matola with my neighbour, Balate. He insisted on taking me for a quick tour of the BIC pen factory he manages. It is classic import substitution. Everything comes from abroad, -- the pellets of plastic, all the components and a series of machines which ingeniously assemble BIC pens. How much does Mozambique have to pay for the name? Balate insisted I take samples with me and sent me off with two big boxes of pens, one blue and one red, a

> treasure in a city of a million where the only place to buy a pen is on the black market.
>
> (Field Notes, February 25, 1986)

> The gift from Balate has come in handy. I gave it to the school, since the city education office has still not come through with pens, and the secondary school students really need them. Ironically, the red pens created most excitement -- apparently they make it possible for the teachers to mark the students' work in the "correct" way!
>
> (Field Notes, February 26, 1986)

The opening of the school year, then, approximates February 16, but often between the formal opening on that date and effective commencement of classes with books, pencils, pens and teachers in place, there is a time lag. No such flexibility characterizes the end of the school year. With or without books, with or without sufficient time to complete the programme of studies, the final exam is administered nationally on a fixed date in the middle of November.

Clearly these delays in starting the school year have major ramifications for what proportion of the programme of studies is actually covered prior to the final exam. In 1984, the CIM school did not complete the programme of studies. The teachers could not remember what point they had reached but recalled that they had not covered everything before the final exams.

In 1985, most of the second year programme was covered but only a very small portion of the third year programme because of problems in textbook distribution. The lesson material covered was as follows:

Second Year	Portuguese:	86/90 lessons
	Mathematics:	44/51 lessons
Third Year	Portuguese:	Vol.1 - 60/60 lessons
		Vol.2 - 0/67 lessons
	Mathematics:	Vol.1 - 43/49 lessons
		Vol.2 - 0/35 lessons
	Natural Science:	24/36 lessons

The new language and mathematics programmes for third year included second volumes whose publication and distribution were seriously delayed. These second volumes did not arrive at all and at CIM, not even all of the first mathematics book was covered. The final exam prepared by the Ministry was meant to take account of the fact that many centres had not received all of the books, and that some had gone back to using the old curriculum materials. Nonetheless, the failure rate was extremely high and some students at CIM indicated that there had been questions on the mathematics exam that they had not covered in classes.

In general, the problem of organizing literacy programmes with sufficient time to complete the programme of studies was an enormous one, not just at CIM but in all the work place literacy centres. The factors working against completion of the curriculum included not only delays in the arrivals of materials but also classes interrupted regularly because of everything from pay day and queues to buy soap or oil to collective vacations, shift work or harvesting campaigns. There was no control mechanism for monitoring how much of the programme was covered, but even in a centre as well organized as CIM, there were huge difficulties.

Delays in arrival of the books and interruption in classes were not the only factors that sent the student to the exams ill-prepared. I discovered that during the first year of the new third year programme in 1985, there had been a complete failure to understand how to do the timetabling. For first and second year, each week includes five two-hour lessons, three of Portuguese and two of mathematics. The third year manual assumed twelve rather than ten hours per week, divided into eight lessons of ninety minutes, four of Portuguese, three of math and one of natural sciences. The manual suggested two 90 minute lessons a day for four days a week to make up the twelve hours.

The CIM "school," however, had kept to the same schedule as the second year programme, i.e. one two-hour lesson each day. This meant that each lesson was two hours rather than 90 minutes, and each week consisted of five lessons instead of the eight programmed in the manual. The results at the end of 1985 were, of course, disappointing. The students had covered very little of the programme by the time the final exams were given. Only seven of the twenty-seven who did the exam passed. The average grade was only 33 percent. For the workers, this meant an experience of failure they certainly did not need. Only one of the students I spoke to had any recognition of the organizational problems in covering the curriculum as a factor.

> This year there was a problem with the exam. We arrived at the exam and found things which we had never seen before. The Natural Science book was a problem. This problem could have been the teacher's fault or our fault. A lot of us got into the habit of skipping natural science classes because we didn't understand a thing.
>
> (Luis Guache, waiter, Mess,
> Frelimo Party candidate, 47 years)

Most, however, gave explanations of their failure turning on their own inadequacy rather than on the organizational problems of no books and an only partially completed programme of studies. The feelings of Bernardo Gimo, a particularly dedicated machine operator in the Pasta Factory, captured the experience for many. Gimo was 46 years old and had worked at the factory for 25 years. When I asked him what he did, he said, "I'm a driver -- of a machine!" He went on to say that he had "learned as an apprentice but begun work as the 'chauffeur' in 1976." For reasons most probably related to shift work, Gimo did not do literacy until 1982, when he successfully passed first year. He then did second year of the new programme, failed it first time round but succeeded in passing the exam in 1984 with 85 percent in mathematics and 60 percent in Portuguese. He failed third year with very low marks.

> I just go to school because I'm here in the factory. Next year, I'm not going. I can't continue any more. It's not that I don't want to. I do. But I don't have any aptitude for studying. I began to study in colonial times but it didn't go anywhere. I don't want to abandon my work mates to go to school when attending school gives no results.
>
> (Interview with Bernardo Gimo, January 7, 1986)

In Gimo's account, there is neither recognition of his accomplishment in passing the first two years nor acknowledgment that he did third year during a year when there were no textbooks and only a tiny proportion of the programme was covered. When we talked about his studying giving no results during the interview, I asked him if his boss in the Pasta Factory could demand that he fill production quotas during a period of no raw materials. I think he understood the parallel -- but there was no let up in his attitude about his own inadequacies as a student, an attitude established during colonialism and still strongly present. For workers, then, the experience of literacy was often yet another experience of failure.

Permission to Go to Class -- A Daily Negotiation

> There are organizational problems. During a whole year, I only managed to attend two months of classes. It's not because I don't have a good head. If I could stay there for just six months, I'd have something firmly in my head. It's because I never have time to study. Three months only -- that's nothing.
>
> (Mário Joaquim, handler, 36 years)
> Passed first year in 1984
> Registered for second year in 1985
> Didn't do exam

I expected to find organizational problems at CIM in establishing a viable time for literacy within the factory, having seen this problem emerge elsewhere throughout the country. At CIM, the collision course between shift work and literacy classes was a highly visible example of this problem. Indeed, I discovered that the only pocket of illiteracy still intact at CIM was the Mill where shift work prevailed.

What was surprising, however, was to discover the ongoing negotiation of time for schooling that each worker-student had to face daily. There was little visibility to this strong tension between workers and shop floor and school officials around regulation of time for literacy. It was a constant feature, however, of the experience of literacy for the worker. It involved the development of survival techniques for the worker-students, negotiating contradictory pressures to be present both in the classroom and on the shop floor. These demands came not only from shop floor bosses and teachers but also from factory administrators, education officials, representatives of the Party and mass organizations -- and even fellow-workers.

There was a need to seek permission daily to go to class as part of each day's labour process. Thus participation in literacy required a daily reproduction of the relations of power and subordination between the shop floor boss and the individual worker specifically over the question of time for literacy classes.

For each section of the factory, the organization of school time in relation to production time posed different problems. The Pasta Factory tended to organize production around a kind of piece work system, where each work team had a production target to complete before going home. In many cases, the team, made up mainly of women, could finish before eleven, when literacy began, or certainly before one, when it ended. The women preferred to go home early and try to resolve some of the problems of survival in their households, rather than stay around for literacy. It was the more complicated in that if the group doing literacy left for classes at eleven, the others were delayed even more in their efforts to finish early. This created a fair bit of group pressure not to leave.

The Finished Products Warehouse organized production around teams of six to eight men, loading 50 kilo sacks of flour and maize meal into clients' trucks. Each loading operation involved a different mixture of conveyer belt and individual handling by the team members, depending on the location of the produce in the warehouse and the size of the truck. Here, participation in literacy meant breaking up the teams of handlers, creating both more onerous and also more dangerous working conditions for those in the now depleted teams. There were substantial periods when workers from the warehouse missed classes, because of the volume of work in the section. Clients became irate when they had done the paper work and still had long delays in actually loading up the produce.

> It's difficult, for those who handle sacks of grain here and then go to classes. You're very tired by the end of the day, and want to go home and rest. It's a hard sector. When I started, there were 16 upstairs and 16 below. Now we're very few. It's too much. When someone is sick, it's worse. And when people go off to classes, those who stay behind suffer. We can't do it. For those who stay behind, it's punishment.
>
> (Afonso Chipente, handler, 25 years)
> Passed fourth class in 1984
> Dropped out of fifth year in 1985

Others in the Finished Products Warehouse gave the same account of how impossible it was to find time for literacy. "I want to go to classes but my work doesn't permit it," explained António Muiambo, a handler who was 49 years old. He had passed first year after three tries. When I met him in 1985, he was in second year.

Muiambo had not studied as a child in the rural district of Manjacaze where he was born, nor during his years of work in South Africa. When he first started at CIM in 1977, he had not attended the school. With the reorganization of the schooling programme in 1982, however, Muiambo also began to study. There are no records of how many days he lost during the three years before he passed the first year exam. In 1985, however, he had missed no less than 86 days, or roughly four out of the nine months of classes. (Interview with António Muiambo, January 14, 1986) For Muiambo, the experience of literacy was that, on the one hand, the CIM management put his name on the enrollment list, but on the other hand, they reorganized his work sector, paring down the number of workers in such a way that two hour absences each day for literacy created an impossible situation for those left behind. Muiambo therefore missed a great number of classes -- and failed year after year.

Many workers in this section pointed to the same problem. Francisco Xiconela passed first year and then dropped out of classes. He attributed this to his work situation. "Yes, I missed a lot of classes. Our section is very small and we have a lot to do; we're only six people now." (Interview, February 10, 1986) For Alfredo Joel, the problem was that his absence for classes left his specific task uncovered for two hours each day. "My job is to pick out the torn sacks and substitute them. It's hard for me to leave the team to go to classes." (Interview, January 20, 1986)

Work in the Silos, where grain was off-loaded from railway cars, was also characterized by a constantly varying rhythm of production. This created enormous hardships for those trying to study. All of the shipments of wheat and maize coming into the Milling complex came from food aid, with little control over arrival dates. When shipments came in box cars from the port, there was maximum pressure to off load it quickly, because each day that the boxcar stayed at CIM meant additional payment. Many times the rolling stock was South African, and this meant payment in foreign exchange. Thus the normal routine was to add on extra shifts when there were cars to be unloaded and cancel out literacy attendance during these periods.

> If I can manage to study here until the end, I can pass. This business of being absent for several days or weeks at a time is no good. When you return, you've forgotten what you learned before.
>
> (Major Franguana, Warehouse 2, 48 years)
> Passed first year in 1983
> Failed second year in 1985

The Sacks Warehouse was located in the farthest corner of the factory complex. The workers there, all women except for the heads, had responsibility for sorting, cleaning and repairing sacks. It seemed to have a very lazy rhythm without any of the pressures felt in the heat and noise of the pasta lines, or the fury of conveyer belts and sweating bodies handling heavy sacks in the Silos and Finished Products Warehouse. Even here, however, time demands for production and schooling were in tension.

> A person can't go to the field for a day and then stay home for three months. You have to go and weed every day. In that way the crops will grow. In our sector we have a lot of work. When the Mill and the Pasta Factory need sacks, we have to guarantee them. If not, the work can't go ahead. On those days the women in the Sacks Warehouse are left without classes. But those from the sectors that attend get something. What can we do when we return? We are left behind. It's not a question of our bosses refusing to let us go. We ourselves see what there is work to do in the sector and stay to do it with our fellow workers.
>
> (Mónica Gabriel, Warehouse 2, 48 years)
> Passed first year in 1982
> Passed second year in 1984

What became clear over time was that the permission to do literacy was negotiated daily between shop floor bosses and workers, and amongst the workers themselves. While the factory was obligated by law to make basic education available to its work force, and from 1981 onwards, had to include literacy targets in its annual planning figures, this did not mean that literacy was lived by workers as their right. When fellow workers were sick or on vacation, when production was lagging behind, when there were jobs to be done that took the workers away from the factory, when there was a need to off-load railway cars of grain, or even more routine procedures such as filling orders, supplying sacks or drums of oil from one section of the factory to another, the first thing to be dropped was literacy.

Tension around time for literacy affected groups of workers in different ways, then, according to the section of the factory in which they were located. This was not the only factor, however, that differentiated the experience. For the workers in third year, the additional hours of classes kept them from arriving at the cafeteria on time. It was only during a class assembly two months into the term that the workers put forward this problem, and the need to alert the mess to the fact that a group of workers would be arriving late each day and needed to have their food set aside for them.

> The workers in the assembly raised a problem about the Mess. When they arrive there after class, the food is finished. The Mess staff makes something for them to eat but they then arrive back at their sectors only at 14:20 or 14:45 and catch it from their section heads. It's only now at this meeting, two months into the school year, that we hear of these problems with the Mess.
>
> (Field Notes, April 10, 1986)

The time-tabling of classes for higher levels was equally fraught with difficulties, even though secondary schooling was outside of work hours. Fifth class had been introduced in 1984, with one more class added on each year so that by 1986, workers could do up to seventh class in the CIM school. Up until 1986, classes were held entirely outside of work hours, beginning at 5:30 and continuing until 9:30 at night, four nights a week. The CIM workers doing night school were given a bread and tea ration before entering classes and transport home after they had finished. This put them in a decidedly advantageous position compared to other adults doing night school throughout the city who had to fend for themselves in finding transport to their schools, finding a way to eat, and ultimately finding a way home late at night.

For women, time for literacy posed special problems. For women workers who were nursing, a not unimportant category since most of the women interviewed showed a pattern of giving birth every two years, the timing of the literacy class conflicted with the time prescribed to go to the day care centre to feed their children. This added yet one more complication since health problems during pregnancy and maternity leave had already created major interruptions for many women.

For the few women at CIM who had successfully completed primary school, the time-tabling for fifth to seventh class virtually ruled out participation. Almost all of them had responsibilities for child care, water carrying, and evening meal preparation which necessitated leaving the factory at five. It was not even discussable to think of signing up for classes, and arriving home each evening only at ten o'clock.

Leonor Benjamim had had the chance to study as a child but went back to school at CIM in 1983 to get her certificate. She felt she could need it at any moment, since a day could come when she would be looking for work. Her logic was derived from the new CIM admissions policy whereby a worker had to have at least a primary school certificate in order to apply.

Leonor had worked for 20 years at CIM, starting in the Biscuit Factory in 1965 at the age of 17. She was currently a clerical assistant in the Workshop, and a member of the Frelimo Party, the OMM (Organization of Mozambican Women) and the OTM (Mozambican Worker's Organization)

> I really want to study but social conditions don't make this possible. Senhora Judith knows how it is with men. I'm alone there at the house. I don't have any household help. If I study here, I'll get home only at 9 or 10 at night. My husband is without food or water. He could decide to get another woman, saying "This woman is prepared to cook for me. You don't want to." These are the social problems we face. I want to study a lot. I'd like to do up to at least sixth grade -- but I can't because of the social situation. Employing somebody costs a lot. They demand a lot of money -- more than our salaries. My husband lets me work. Many husbands wouldn't do this. He accepts that we don't have children. Because of this, I can't stop being a good woman for him.
>
> (Leonor Benjamim, 37 years,
> Workshops clerical staff)

Amélia Cossa had also worked at CIM for many years, starting off weighing and packaging in the Pasta Factory in 1958 as a fifteen year old straight from Class 3 in a Maputo primary school. She had had jobs in various parts of the factory over the years and was now in the Sacks Warehouse. She had also gone back to get her certificate, and passed on the second try.

Night school posed insurmountable timing problems for her. She described her day as beginning at four in the morning when she got up for two hours of work on her "machamba" or family plot, seven days a week. Between six and seven, she prepared for work. From seven when the bus came until five-thirty when it deposited her at home, she was at CIM.

> I'd like to do fifth class. My problem is the time. I get home too late to do the cleaning and feed the children. A woman is always being squeezed. She's always in the middle, always given orders. When she gets home, she has to do this but can't do that or the other. She's the one who always gets ordered about.
>
> (Amélia Cossa, Warehouse 6, 43 years)
> Passed fourth class in 1984
> Has never enrolled in fifth

There had been a moment at the time of independence when fighting to make time for schooling was worth it. A primary school certificate meant something then, and for many had led to promotions. In a survey done in 1981/82 as the new management team began to tackle literacy as part of its strategy to build up a qualified work force, a questionnaire was filled out by 48 CIM workers. One question read: "Is it worthwhile to know how to read, write and count? Why?" The responses to the question were as follows:

To have a better job	- 12
To be a section head	- 12
To make the work easier	- 2
To solve problems easily	- 2
To discover new things	- 9
To increase knowledge	- 7
To know where you're going	- 1
To have a better life	- 2
To not be left behind	- 1
To be worth more	- 2
To help your family	- 4

(Source: CIM Archives 1981/2)

By 1985, however, attainment of sixth or even ninth class began to have less meaning. A new calculation of whether it was worth it to invest time in literacy had begun to emerge. There were no promotions or pay increases for increased education done "on the job." It was a difficulty fully recognized by management.

> The problem is that we cannot recognize success in literacy with greater responsibility or higher salaries. In the period after independence, many workers were promoted -- they filled positions of management even as illiterates because they knew the work. Now young people enter. We cannot take out the old workers because the young ones still have a lot to learn. They can have sixth class -- or even seventh or eighth -- but they are still far from being able to control the situation. Meanwhile the old-timers have already proved their worth. Studying to guarantee or maintain your

> place makes sense -- but to be promoted, you would have to study a lot. Just fourth class would not be enough to guarantee anything -- not even fifth or sixth.
>
> (Conversation with Cardoso Muendane, Industrial Director, January 15, 1986)

Discussions with other management staff confirmed the efforts that had been put into developing a stable labour force with at least minimum qualifications. Both the administrative and political structures had encouraged literacy, according to Angélica Aguilera, the former Director of Social Services. She recounted how Industrial Director Cardoso Muendane himself, someone who had been at CIM for many years, had done a whole series of meetings and interviews with workers to try to determine why people were not attending classes. "Behind the first responses of how much people want to study came, slowly, a second set of responses that began to show literacy as just a waste of time because it brings no concrete results." (Conversation with Angélica Aguilera, June 6, 1985)

The head of the Maintenance Department, Frechaut, was another person who had been active in organizing literacy with the Dynamizing Group in the early days. For him, there was no mystery as to why workers choose not to make a big effort to do literacy.

> Today at lunch was the first time Frechaut and I talked about literacy. I had already heard that he was a dynamic figure in literacy activities done in the era of the Dynamizing Group. He certainly sees the motivation question as one of workers calculating how to improve their lives.
>
> "Take, for example, the illiterate in the loading section. It's heavy work. It takes some muscles. An illiterate worker looks around and sees fellow-workers with fourth class or sixth class. What's the incentive to study? After all the years to reach sixth class, you do the same hard work and get the same low pay. Look at the Secretary of the OTM (Organization of Mozambican Workers). He had fourth class. Then he got a driver's license. Then he did sixth class. Each step of the way brought different work but it also brought more pay. He was motivated to study."
>
> (Field Notes, June 20, 1985)

Literacy for Job Security

Although the expectation that schooling could result in upward mobility dwindled, there seemed to be a clear recognition that literacy was necessary for employment security. Even without this being stated, the workers took the policy of requiring a minimum of fourth class for all new employees as the shape of the future. Literacy was seen as a means of guaranteeing job security. And more than one person posed it point blank in the interviews. "Senhora Judith, do you think an illiterate person could be employed at CIM nowadays?"

Even with sixth class, then, the likelihood of someone with ninth class appearing and earning more, even without knowing a thing about the running of the factory, was high. The workers were clearly concerned about this reality. Even Laurinda Zibia, the cleaner in the school who had not managed to finish second year, understood the problem.

> A person who starts work at CIM today has to know how to read and write. Today, if you don't know how to read, you don't enter this place. Today it's a question of "Do you have ninth class?" If not, there's no work. Those of us already inside fight to learn to read here at CIM.
>
> (Laurinda Zibia, cleaner, 36 years)
> Passed first year in 1983
> Subsequent studies interrupted by
> pregnancy/maternity leave.

There was clearly a lot of ambivalence about whether to spend the time on studying or not. Atália Macamo's musings point to the power of literacy, even in the face of evidence of its impotence.

> You earn the same, illiterate or with fourth grade. Even when you have fifth or sixth grade, you earn the same. I have friends who got to fourth grade -- but it didn't change anything. Even so, it's worth it. Maybe in another firm you can earn more with fourth grade. When people are educated, they have to do well.
>
> (Interview with Atália Macamo, July 14, 1985)

It Takes Time to Survive

At the same time the workers were recalculating the value of a literacy certificate in relation to increased pay or better jobs, there were new calculations about the time needed for survival schemes. As the security situation deteriorated and the economic crisis became more acute, the investment of time in education began to enter in conflict with time needed for these survival schemes. Many workers depended as much on their second and third jobs as on their first.

The war and the economic situation were never far from people's minds. In many conversations, workers spoke movingly of how hard it was to study with the pressing problems at hand. Momade Iaca, an older worker put it this way.

> You go to literacy classes just to be marked present. Your wits aren't there. They're at home with the problems of living. Your wits and your heart aren't there. At the end of each month, when the rations have run out, it's worse. You go out the door with your wife saying to you, "There's nothing here in the house to eat."
>
> (Momade Iaca, Supplies Dept., 50 years)
> Passed first year 1982; Passed second year
> in 1983 and fourth class in 1984

Both women and men were constantly preoccupied with the situation in their homes and the lack of food and clothing for their children. Moving from the bustle and noise of the shop floor to the quiet of the classroom, many of them suddenly focussed on going home at the end of the day to face nothing with which to prepare an evening meal for their families.

> When you think a lot about your life, you can't bring yourself to study. What do we have to eat in the house when I get home from work? Here I can go to the Mess and eat well. There at home we have nothing. Here in the factory I have a uniform, I have something to put on, but there at home, there is no clothing for the children.
>
> (Cristina Mavale, Sacks Warehouse, 42 years)
> Passed first year 1983
> Failed second year 1984
> Passed second year 1985

The inability of urban wages to guarantee the reproduction of the work force, while exacerbated by the crisis caused by the war and economic destabilization tactics of the apartheid regime, was not in itself a new situation. Urban wages had always been extremely low, and even in colonial days, as we have seen above, many workers found contracts in the mines in South Africa a more viable option. The interviews with the CIM workers found virtually all of them still actively attached to the rural economy. Many referred to wives who "did nothing." When further pressed, they explained that their wives did nothing "except tend a machamba." This "machamba" or family plot historically had been absolutely fundamental for reproduction of the work force, with basic foods such as maize, beans, cassava and sweet potatoes supplied through household production. It was this invisible work of women that allowed the patterns of semi-proletarianization, keeping urban wages low, and urban workers with one foot firmly embedded still in the peasant economy. (Roesch 1987; First 1983)

Many CIM workers spoke of wives who were there, on the land, or who divided their time between Maputo and their farms according to the agricultural seasons. Part of the present crisis was precisely the choking off of the city from that pattern of production. Terrorist attacks by RENAMO throughout the districts of Maputo, Gaza and Inhambane provinces made it impossible for families to travel freely back and forth.

On the face of it, one could ask why more workers did not leave a job paying only 3,300 meticais a month for the informal sector. The activities of the workers outside their CIM jobs as mechanics, plumbers and painters, or working with other family members to trade, breed ducks, tailor or make home brew, all netted incomes much beyond the CIM monthly wage. It became clear, however, that maintaining a position on the payroll at CIM went far beyond what that monthly wage itself represented. Full-time wage employment legitimized the workers' status as city residents and gave them access to the urban rations programme. Working in the informal sector did not.

The calculations between continuing in wage employment at CIM at 3,300 meticais per month, about enough to buy the oil and soap regularly missing from the city's monthly rationing scheme, and striking off into self-employment in the informal sector, were presumably also influenced by memories of "Operation Production." In mid-1983, in the name of dealing with Maputo's overcrowded situation and tackling "unproductive" city dwellers, large numbers of people without work cards and residence cards in order were sent off to underpopulated Niassa province in northern Mozambique. Now officially recognized as an enormous mistake, its memory presumably persuaded many workers to hold on to their wage employment even when salaries bore no relation to the cost of living in urban areas.

On the positive side, CIM employment provided vitally needed inputs for survival schemes. For many who lived near the factory in Matola, keeping pigs or ducks was an important source of income. Being a CIM worker meant that you had the right to buy animal rations each month. Many workers who earned only the minimum wage used the CIM connection as a means of having feed for ducks which they could sell on the parallel market at 1500-2000 meticais each. Others used CIM rations as the basis for setting up their wives as traders, selling off the factory produce of pasta, sweets or chocolate that each worker could buy each month, or setting up a home brew operation from maize. These "schemes" earned a great deal more than a CIM monthly salary. There was often a need to tend to these survival schemes in daylight hours, the more so as the security situation in Matola deteriorated making it hazardous to be around after dark. Many workers opted to leave aside secondary school studies and concentrate on economic activities.

> Many people began to raise pigs when CIM closed its farm and sold off the animals at reasonable prices. These days I get up at four and do chores before catching the bus to work. I fetch water, straw and feed for the pigs. When five in the afternoon rolls around, I'm off to fetch water again for the animals. I can't manage to look after my children on the salary I get -- it's the pigs that save us. What's the use of staying on after five to study when it's raising pigs that guarantees the situation for my children.
>
> (Fernando Murrija, 49 years)
> Head of wheat handling section
> Finished Products Warehouse

Alfredo Joel, a 47 year old handler in the Finished Products Warehouse, captured the dilemma of the CIM workers. As a young boy, he had come to Maputo from Zavala district in Inhambane. He remembered that there, "only the children of the 'régulo' got to go to school." In Maputo, he spent five years as a domestic and learned Portuguese. From 1961-1964, he was in the Portuguese army. After that he got his first contract to work in South Africa. He went five times to work in South Africa. In 1982, he started to work at CIM. He was in the Finished Products Warehouse on the minimum wage. His work there consisted of selecting out the torn sacks and substituting them for good ones. While at CIM, he had been able to do literacy. He passed the literacy exam in 1982 and took two years to pass the second year exam, but did so with high marks in 1984. He did not continue at the school, explaining that his work on the team in the Finished Products Warehouse is such that "it's difficult to leave the team."

His wife had a machamba on the outskirts of the city where she produced maize, beans and cassava. He had five children, three of them of school age.

> When you're studying, your heart is not in it. It's with your children back home who have no food or clothing. The black market is full of "capulanas" (African cloth) -- but how am I going to manage 6,000 meticais to buy one? I want to return to South Africa. I need to go there. I need clothing and shoes for the children. The money I get here doesn't do for anything.
>
> (Alfredo Joel, handler, 47 years)

The war being waged by the South African-backed insurgents was a constant pressure as well, integrally related to the worsening economic situation. During much of the time I was there, the residential areas of large numbers of workers had "bandit" activity as almost a nightly occurrence. Even if their own area was safe, most workers had families in the rural districts of the southern provinces, where ambushes and massacres were regular events.

> What's the use of my studying when my son who is young is not in school? He was in third grade in Gaza province. We had to flee from the bandits. They closed the school. Now they're insisting on a certificate to prove that he was in third grade. Do they think that the teachers had time to issue certificates before fleeing the bandits? The schools here in Matola today are just like the black market. If it were possible for me to get 5,000 meticais, my son would be studying.
>
> (Interview with Celina João, February, 1986)

With the deteriorating security situation came the decision in March 1986 to change the time of night school. A decision was made to begin classes at 4:30 in the afternoon, allowing half an hour of classes still within work time, and end them at 7:00, five nights a week instead of four. This coincided with the new shift plan that moved from three shifts of eight hours to two shifts of 12 hours. This permitted shift changes at 7:00 a.m. and 7:00 p.m., avoiding the need to transport workers in and out of their communities at ll:00 p.m.

"Motivation" : Do Workers Want to Study?

This daily negotiation of time for literacy, juggling competing demands of the factory school, the shop floor and family survival schemes, was completely invisible. The assumption on the part of school and factory administration, and indeed the teachers, was that attendance and punctuality were entirely controlled by the workers themselves. Absenteeism and lateness were seen as questions of individual motivation. The opening of the school year, for example, included speeches from management and party representatives, all of which focussed on the need for workers to avail themselves of the opportunity to study created for them by the factory. There were strong pleas for attendance and punctuality, as if the even stronger pressures on management to guarantee production did not enter into conflict with attendance and punctuality at literacy classes.

> OPENING THE SCHOOL YEAR
> The speeches from management and party and worker organization officials touched mainly on questions of discipline and attendance. Nobody left more motivated to study because it was useful for their lives.

> The teachers themselves also saw absences and lateness by the workers as questions of motivation, interpreting them as signs of a fundamental disinterest in literacy.
>
> (Field Notes, February 16, 1986)

> Today I met with the teachers to hear their thoughts about the two discussion documents. One of the most fascinating parts was their response to my observation that workers lacked self-confidence. Eduardo thinks it isn't a question of lack of self-confidence at all. It is really lack of interest. If you insist on an answer, the person is able to give a reply -- which for Eduardo proves that it was really a lack of interest.
>
> Lopes also thinks that absenteeism is intentional. He went on further to say that he thinks that when it gets to be time for classes, the workers calculate where there will be fewest demands on them during the next two hours, and make their decisions about attendance accordingly.
>
> Aurélio asked if this logic wouldn't be one for full attendance, since surely the classroom is virtually always less demanding than the sectors.
>
> (Field Notes, March 14, 1986)

What is interesting is the distance between the workers own accounts and those of managements and the teachers. The teachers assume the workers to be resistant to literacy, calculating how to do least. The workers' own accounts of their lives speak only of work demands from the sector, and also a sense of solidarity with fellow workers. They refer to occasions when they opt to stay in the section and work, knowing that their absence will make it difficult for their colleagues.

All of the workers accepted without question the appropriateness of having their shop floor boss' make the decision on attendance at literacy. It was as if attendance at literacy classes was just one among the many work orders that might be given for any particular day. There was no sense of having a right to study, or any way to protect your time to study from other demands.

> "Today there's not much work to do. You can go to school." That's how it is in our section. The head tells us when we can go.
>
> (Major Franguane, Warehouse 2)

> There are a lot of problems related to production. For our company not to lose money, we have to stay in the Silos and work.
>
> (Augusto Bernardo, handler, 38 years)
> Passed first year in 1982
> Passed second year despite 77 days absent in 1984
> Did not do third year in 1985

Even workers at third year level, ready to do exams that gave them a primary school leaving certificate, did not think it appropriate or possible to negotiate a decision to send them to work at another site the month before the exam, hence missing the final review and the exam itself.

> I didn't do the exam because I was sent to do a job in the Candy Factory. I counted on being able to take the exam at the second sitting but there wasn't one.
>
> (Fabião Cossa, welder's assistant, 38 years)
> Passed first year in 1982
> Passed second year in 1984
> Did not take third year exam in 1985

Many workers referred matter-of-factly to regular work demands that, by definition, ruled out attendance at literacy classes. The reasons were infinitely variable on any given day, and could range from plumbing to pineapples. For Luis Uamba, a 47 year old plumber who had passed his second year exam in 1984, the difficulty was related to his work as a plumber.

> My problem is that I have jobs regularly that take me away from the main factory [where the school is located].
>
> (Interview with Luis Uamba, March 8, 1986)

For Albertina Carlos, a 43 year old assistant in the kitchen, pineapples were the difficulty. Albertina had passed first year in 1982. She missed the 1983 exam because of being pregnant but successfully passed second year in 1984. In 1985, she once again missed the exam because of pregnancy and was having difficulty finding time to attend the third year classes in 1986.

> I want to study but the time-table doesn't allow it. We're very few workers in the Mess. On the days we serve pineapples for dessert, we have to cut them up. There's no way we can get to classes.
>
> (Interview with Albertina Carlos, January 12, 1986)

The worker/students were, then, subjected constantly to conflicting demands on their time. The school and party officials and workers' organization put pressures on them to attend classes and assumed absences as of their own making. The shop floor boss' role in impeding attendance at literacy classes was never a subject of discussion and surfaced only rarely in interviews.

Francisco Muchanga, for example, was a 37 year old mechanic's assistant. He had passed the first year exam in 1983 with a perfect score and a year later, gotten a 90 percent average on the second year exams. He was not able to do the third year exam.

> I was alone in the section during the month of the exam. The head said I couldn't leave. I tried to get support from the school. I talked to Pedro. He was our teacher in third year. No results.
>
> (Interview with Francisco Muchanga, February 10, 1986)

The negotiation by worker-students of permission from their shop floor bosses to attend classes was delicate. Even more delicate, however, was the negotiation of written authorization not to attend. Such authorizations were a necessity for the worker. The only way to escape the pressures from the teacher and the school director about absences was to have a note from your section head justifying them. This put the section heads in an awkward position. To furnish written justifications in the name of production priorities was to run the risk that they themselves would come under pressure from the management for not allowing their workers to study. The management, in turn, was subject to pressures from higher level Ministry of Industry quotas for literacy and party pressure to eradicate it.

Few students referred to the hassles of getting their absences justified; one can imagine, however, that many preferred to be viewed as delinquent and unmotivated rather than negotiate with their heads for written justifications which could ultimately cause problems for the section heads which would be played out against the workers.

> Our section is very small and we have a lot of work to do. I asked my head for a paper to justify my absence, but it wasn't given to me.
>
> (Francisco Xiconela, handler, 47 years
> Finished Products Warehouse)

The observation of individual women and men and their own accounts of their lives made the texture and diversity of time constraints on the workers quite visible. Making time for literacy was not simple. For some, the rational choice given limited energies and enormous needs was to dispense with literacy as of little use for the crisis situation they were living. What was interesting was that the official discourse persisted in constructing worker motivation as the reason, and this as somehow mysterious. My first contact with the Director General after I started to work at CIM, was a chance meeting as he shepherded a delegation on a tour of the factory. The immediate thought that came to his head was for my research to explain why the workers didn't come to literacy!

"School" Time and "Work" Time for the Teachers

Time for schooling for the teachers posed itself in very different ways. The four literacy teachers at CIM during the period of my research had very different work situations. Lopes Chigoiane, whom I had first met and worked with in 1984 when we did the photo story with the first year students, was now teaching second year. He was also a full-time CIM employee based in the training department. After being away from the factory for several months during 1985, training for the militia, he was back full-time. He divided his days between lesson preparation, teaching and the administrative and clerical tasks related to the school in general. He was also studying in the CIM night school, enrolled in sixth class. He seemed to handle his multiple roles with equanimity. His training for teaching was limited to the DNEA courses but he had a calm presence in the classroom and an instinct for teaching and picking up learning difficulties that made him quite effective.

Pedro Chivute, the third year teacher, was also a full-time worker at CIM. He had started work at CIM in 1981, with seventh class. He had also completed his formal training as a primary school teacher and had several years of teaching experience in a rural district school. He came to CIM to escape the teaching profession, but was admitted as a literacy teacher, with the understanding that, in his spare time, he would work in some sector of the factory. When I met him, he was doing clerical tasks in the Finished Products Warehouse in his non-teaching hours. Vague mention seemed to have been made of possibilities that in future he would get training in some specific area, a dream strongly held onto, nonetheless, by Pedro.

Four years later, Pedro was determined to get out. His performance in the classroom was one of boredom and arrogance, putting down the students, especially the women, with what to me seemed incredible cheek. In retrospect, perhaps it was in the hopes that I would report him and cause him to be removed from the classroom, his deepest desire. Pedro saw teaching as a dead end.

> I want to be in a sector where I have a profession, a future. Everybody who entered when I did already has done training -- they're clerks or ??? I'm the only one who has nothing. I have the right to be trained in something. It's not that I don't want to work. I want to -- but I have the right to get training in something.
>
> (Interview with Pedro Chivute, January 1986)

For Pedro, the high failure rates of the students were seen as threatening. He felt they were a negative reflection on him, and that they resulted from a situation created by the factory. The workers had other priorities, but since the factory made it mandatory for all workers up to the age of 45 to do literacy, they were compelled to come.

> Pedro: If people were to pass by the school, they would come to the conclusion that I'm not doing anything. What I'm doing is not showing any results. There is little success. The adults who come here have other priorities. They come only because the factory makes it mandatory for them to come. Look how it was last year. Hardly anybody passed.
>
> Judith: What do you think were the main reasons that only 7 of the 27 passed?
>
> Pedro: These things I've just mentioned are important factors.
>
> (Field Notes, January 16, 1986)

For Pedro, the fact of no books and completion of only a tiny proportion of the programme were not the most important factors. Much less were there reflections on the broader socio-economic situation that put survival questions on the agenda and made school certificates worthless. "Lack of motivation" of the workers, the fact of literacy being obligatory for them and not a matter of free choice were, for him, the central questions.

There were two other teachers during the period of my research. Carlos Mutimkuio was a second year teacher during 1985 but in 1986, was transferred from CIM to another centre. Eduardo Zucula taught in the Candy Factory during 1985 and in 1986, moved to the main factory complex to teach third year. Carlos and Eduardo were not CIM employees. They were both "professional educators," full time employees of the Ministry of Education for adult education. The title "professional educator" was a much inflated language to designate sixth class graduates with a six month training course in adult education.

The assumption of the planners when the course for "professional educators" was designed was of an expanding Adult Education Subsystem in which adults doing third year would need trained teachers, particularly in the communal villages and indeed, throughout the rural areas. The "professional educators" were therefore to be trained specifically to work in rural villages, teaching third year, giving support to first and second year teachers, and in general creating a dynamic presence of adult education in the countryside.

The reality was far different. Recruitment and training in the six month course had all the weaknesses of the shorter courses. Conditions of lodging and food were not easy to organize in the rural areas once the

1. Nome: ______________________

2. 

a mota

3. 

o pilão

4. 

a maçaroca

está	estão	é

5. A Rita está no Posto de Saúde.

6. Ela é mãe do Bernardo.

Hoje temos vacinas no Posto de Saúde.
As vacinas são para os nossos bebés.
Todos devem estar no Posto às onze horas.

7. A que horas há vacinas?

Há vacinas às onze horas.

8. Para quem são as vacinas?

As vacinas são para os bebés.

FIGURE 6.1 First Year Literacy Exam -- Portuguese

adult educators arrived, particularly with terrorist actions already so drastically altering the texture of rural life. The sixth class graduates, even if originally from rural areas, had had a taste of city life. Neither they nor their families thought placement in a rural village an attractive option. Nor were students for their classes readily forthcoming, with peasants struggling to survive the crisis even less predisposed than urban workers to make time for literacy.

The upshot was that many of the "professional educators" like Carlos and Eduardo were placed in urban centres instead. There most of them were greatly underemployed, responsible only for one class session per day. At the same time, they enjoyed the salary that had been allocated to the professional educators after the six month course of 6,000 meticais per month. This was not only almost twice as much as most of the students. It was also more than most other education officials at district level made, a factor that made their integration into the district structure even more problematic.

Carlos was 20 when he started working at CIM and came directly to CIM after his six month course. He was from Chibuto, a thriving district capital in Maputo province prior to the era of MNR attacks, and came from an educated family. His father was a guard in Chibuto and had second class, as did his mother. His two older brothers had fifth and ninth class respectively. One of his older sisters had seventh class and taught primary school. The sister his own age had fifth class. Carlos himself had completed sixth class and the six month course. He had registered in seventh class, but the Maputo school in which he had done sixth class could not locate his records and so he was forced to drop out of seventh class for lack of a school certificate! He had two younger brothers, one in sixth class where Carlos' older brother worked for the Ministry of Defence, and one in fifth class in Maputo.

Eduardo had come to CIM when he was just 18 and spent the first year teaching in the Candy Factory. He was then transferred to the main factory where in 1986 he taught mathematics in the third year programme. This occupied only a small part of each day. This left many hours alone in the staff room with the newspaper and the radio, preparing his own lessons and also his homework for the city night school where he was doing seventh class. When asked about his main problems in teaching he said they were the poor results, the difficulty in finding patience to explain things again and again, and the organizational problems like not receiving the books until April the year before. Eduardo got little support or supervision. His only contact with the City Directorate of Education and Culture to whom he was responsible was in a Saturday meeting for all professional educators.

For the four teachers, then, schooling represented very different things. They were not, however, pulled away from the classroom by conflicting demands on their time as were the worker-students.

Upward Mobility at CIM

In some sections, the conflicting demands about time for schooling and production were experienced by the workers as power struggles between themselves and their immediate bosses. Many of the section heads had only primary school certificates. As we have seen above, there was a concerted effort in 1981 to do an intensive course for lower level management, some of whom had never had the chance to study, others of whom needed their prior studies "certified." A group of 15 men did the course of whom five enrolled in the first year of lower secondary, the next year. Not one of them completed it successfully. Some actually did the exams and failed. Other did not qualify to write the exams because they had been absent too often.

It would seem that veteran workers in lower level management positions were not seriously threatened by new employees coming in with sixth or ninth class, because these new employees had absolutely no work experience. Even those coming from technical schools had not really had enough exposure to factory situations to be very competent. The real threat was the possibility of other veteran workers gaining academic qualifications, thereby having equal seniority *and* superior academic qualification to the existing section heads. Several workers spoke strongly of being thwarted in their desire to study by these power struggles.

> I completed fourth class here at CIM. I requested permission to study in 1984 and passed fifth class. I was working shifts. At times,the section head forbid me to go. The people in charge were not studying and they didn't want to let their subordinates get ahead of them in what they knew. I know a lot of people who want to study and can't. Many of them figure it out like this. Since they won't give me permission to study, studying or not studying amounts to the same thing. Even if you study, you stay in the same place. It's really not worth it to study. You already know that you aren't going to get any benefit from it. I can tell you how it was with my shift. We were ten. Five went to school and five stayed. We made a plan. But the management reduced the numbers. There was no way. Even when somebody went to the toilet, it was difficult for the others.
>
> I can also tell you how I came to leave my old section. In December 1985, after the exams, I went to Inhambane for vacation and returned later than January 1, when I should have been back. There were big problems with transport because of the bandits in that area. Since I was late returning, I had to provide a justification. The justification needed the signature of the section head. He demanded that I indicate whether I'd

> returned to study or to work, and gave me to understand that if I replied, "to study" I would be in trouble. I replied that I had returned to work. Later in February when classes began, I went to request permission to attend. This triggered another crisis. I finally went to the head of the Social Services Department. She got one of the staff from that department to speak with my section head. The result was that I was offered the possibility of doing a course and a transfer to another section.
>
> (Mário Muhai, 28 years)

Muhai, by the time he was transferred in 1985, had worked for six years at CIM. He had begun work at CIM when he was 19 and was doing a semi-skilled job in his section that involved some handling of figures on control sheets. The section hierarchy was seemingly happier to lose a young, experienced worker to another sector than to have him begin to compete with veteran workers for promotions.

Roberto Tivane was another worker who felt he was being blocked by his colleagues. Tivane had begun work at CIM in 1961 when he was just 18 years old. He worked for a year, left to work at another factory for four years, and returned to CIM in 1966. He worked in the Biscuit Factory and earned 570 escudos at the time. Shortly after independence, he was made a section head. His salary increased to 4,500 escudos in 1976. It has remained virtually at that level over the years, increasing only to 5,000. When the Biscuit Factory was closed down in 1982, Tivane moved to another section. He was made a section head there. Later he was given a semi-skilled job, inspecting and maintaining equipment. He also took up schooling at this time. Tivane had had a chance to go as far as third class as a child. In 1982, he did the adult education programme and got his certificate of basic primary schooling with high marks. He then proceeded to fifth class which he completed in 1983. During 1984 and 1985, he tried to complete sixth class, but felt only antagonism from his colleagues in the section.

> I did fourth class in 1982 and fifth class the following year. I was in sixth class in 1984 and 1985. I was working in shifts during this whole period and it was a hard life. When I did the shift that entered at eleven at night, I caught the bus for the three o'clock shift in order to go to classes at half past five. When we got out of classes, I went to sleep for a bit before starting the shift at eleven. My section head didn't support me very much and I had a lot of absences. In 1984, I didn't even do the exam. In 1985, a colleague went on vacation in the last month of classes and I had to work more to cover everything during his absence. I did the exams but I had lost the geometry classes and I failed mathematics.
>
> In our section of the factory, the majority of the heads have only fourth class. They don't want to see a worker from the section get to do sixth

> class. They do everything to stop him. I am taking a rest this year. Next year, I'll start again. I want to get to at least ninth class. I already have a son doing eleventh class at Francisco Manyanga school and a daughter who is in ninth class at Josina Machel school. I am doing everything to guarantee that they continue in their studies. If I bring up a President, a minister, an ambassador, a doctor, an engineer -- it's a contribution. My work will not have been in vain.
>
> (Interview with Roberto Tivane, March 6, 1986)

Schooling Time Measured in "Lessons"

Education was measured by the time spent in the classroom. The dynamic links between literacy and life, classroom and community, that had been part of the spontaneous literacy movement at the time of independence were long in the past. There was neither encouragement nor acceptance of individual ways of learning -- through, for example, independent lessons with spouses, children, or work mates. Time lost from classes was truly lost. There was no suggestion that workers go ahead on their own, catching up on the math exercises and reading lessons on their own time. There was no recognition that many adults had already had some access to schooling outside the factory and that others through home, community and work activities actually used reading and writing skills on a daily basis and therefore had a possibility of advancing at a rhythm apart from the "daily dose" administered by the teacher. There was no encouragement to use literacy skills in "life," no push to read newspapers, write letters, fill in forms, debate ideas, work out family budgets. To the degree that the curriculum materials pointed in these directions, the teachers seemed to take pains to keep the lessons at an abstract level, simulating the activity rather than trying to link the literacy classroom with day to day situations.

> At the time of the fifth Anniversary of state intervention into CIM, I brought a whole page from the daily newspaper, "Noticias" into the classroom and, in the moments before the class was to begin, gave it to Santos Nakale to read. He read it without any problem and was enjoying it since it was all about his workplace. On that afternoon, only one other person appeared. Nonetheless, the teacher, Lopes, suddenly cut off the newspaper reading to start the 'class' with two people. The idea that adult education is for life skills and not to pass an exam just doesn't exist.
>
> (Problematic Areas in ABE at CIM
> First Discussion Document March 1986)

Reflecting on it further, I suppose there was nothing in the teachers' experience to make them think such initiatives would be applauded. It

FIGURE 6.2 Making a Photostory – Lopes' "Modern Lesson"

is possible that my presence might even have thwarted spontaneous building on the newspaper article. Lopes might have felt that with me present as an observer, he had to "give" a lesson at all costs. The more likely explanation, however, is that complete fixation on "giving the lesson." The imperative of *the lesson* was not easy to set aside for Lopes or indeed any other teacher. I remember looking at the photo story again long after we had done it and discovering something written on the blackboard I hadn't seen before. Lopes had still felt the need to put a lesson heading up on the board that day. He obviously had not known quite what to call it, so put up:

> Date: June 23, 1984
> Subject: Portuguese -- Modern Lesson

For Lopes, an activity that stepped out of "giving" the packaged "lesson" and engaged the workers in using language skills to talk about their actual lives was a "modern lesson."

The only thing that constituted literacy was what happened in the classroom. "Giving" classes was the normal way to refer to the educational process. What was "measurable" in evaluating literacy was time spent in classes.

The major preoccupation of the national, provincial and district education offices was to monitor literacy attendance at literacy classes. Workers could not sit for the exams unless they had attended a certain percentage of classes. Education officers visiting literacy centres assessed the classes in terms of "participation," by which was meant not active teaching-learning activities but physical presence in the classroom.

The second method of evaluating literacy was through national exams which were held only once a year and tested only reading and writing and math skills. The repertoire of literacy skills having to do with communicative competence and critical consciousness were completely lost to view.

The teachers themselves, in Mozambique, as elsewhere, taught to the exam. A conversation with Aurélio, the school director, about the difficulties the teachers were having with the oral work and their tendency to jump over it for the reading and writing exercises brought the observation that the oral part was not on the exam. For Aurélio too, this was a valid reason to leave it out.

After months of observing lessons at CIM, the vision of literacy that interacted with the actual lives of the learners began to seem illusory, a fantasy of mine not connected with the real world. An incident along the way, however, rekindled the hopes for a different approach. Pedro was ill one day when I had brought Henrique N'Guiraze from Cabo Delgado province along to observe classes. N'Guiraze was the head of adult education services in that province at the time and curious to observe lessons and interact with learners in a setting not specially prepared for him as a senior official. Instead of cancelling the afternoon class, we decided to take advantage of N'Guiraze's presence and have him substitute.

> I sat in on N'Guiraze's afternoon session. Absolutely fascinating. In the hands of a teacher who knows where (s)he want to go with a particular session, and has a genuine interest in the students' experiences, the classroom atmosphere is totally different, with genuine participation, interest, humour. The lesson was on science and its contributions to agriculture -- improved seeds, pesticides and insecticides, etc. I tried to take it down verbatim.

N'Guiraze:	So how many seeds do you usually plant in one hole?
Student:	Three or four seeds.
N'Guiraze:	Why?
Student:	Well, you can't be sure if they're good seeds. Bugs get in them. Some won't germinate.
N'Guiraze:	But that's with local seeds isn't it? With treated seeds, how many do you plant in one hole?

Student:	Oh, just one.
N'Guiraze:	Why?
Student:	Well you can be sure it will grow.
N'Guiraze:	But if you don't have seeds you can count on, you have to put in three of four. Is that it?
Student:	Yes, or maybe even five.
N'Guiraze:	But now what happens if you plant five and four germinate. You've got four stalks of maize coming from the same hole. What do you do?
Students:	You do nothing! You just wait for them to grow and give you plenty of maize.
N'Guiraze:	But doesn't the agricultural technician advise you to leave just one, so you can grow one strong, healthy plant?
Student 1.	You mean take shoots of new maize and pull them out?
Student 2.	But if four germinate, you'll have more maize.
N'Guiraze:	But won't they crowd each other out? Isn't it better to have one healthy stalk?
Student:	You mean throw out shoots of new maize? That's unthinkable.

Finally a real dialogue about something of importance in their lives. All discussing. All animated. The desire to get into the discussion outweighed the inhibitions about Portuguese. Conclusions. First, the teacher is a huge factor. Second, these workers are truly peasants. I'm almost certain no discussion about urban industrial matters could have generated such interest.

(Field Notes, June 26, 1985)

The moments of reaffirming a pedagogy of empowerment, however, were few. In general, the institutional organization of time in the CIM "school" tended to rule out biography and local experience in favour of a graded curriculum taught for the purposes of reproduction in an exam. It also placed workers in a situation of complex and competing demands for their time, forcing them to work out a daily modus vivendi between the pressures of school and shop floor superiors and their own and their family's survival strategies.

Notes

1. Although it is a curious one, it is by no means a new form. As late as 1918, 50,000 children in England were educated in the half-time system in factory schools. (Corrigan and Gillespie 1978)

2. The division between time and space is somewhat arbitrary when, in fact, the two are so integrally related. It seems useful for analytical purposes, however, to separate them. This overall schema time/space/textuality draws heavily on the recent work on the political space of schooling by Philip Corrigan, Bruce Curtis, Robert Lanning in Witherspoon 1987.

3. By the early 1980s, the need to rethink the organizational forms and encourage much more diversity had become commonplace in reports and debate at national level. It is only now, however, in the context of the appointment of a new director and a movement to revitalize literacy coming from the pilot project in staff training at Manga, that there seems to be some energy to tackle this problem. Having adopted a system of graded curriculum and national exams, there is strong built-in resistance to freeing literacy centres to begin and end at different times throughout the year and to advance through the programme at different rhythms determined by local conditions. (These local conditions could even include enriching the programme by adding materials based on local realities and experiences.) There is even more resistance to rethinking evaluation, encouraging local setting of exams, or indeed dispensing with exams for the first years altogether and having an exam for the primary school certificate only.

7

Classrooms: Spaces for Regulated Communication(s)

> Take for example, an educational institution: the disposal of its space, the meticulous regulations which govern its internal life, the different activities which are organized there, the diverse persons who live there or meet one another, each with his [sic] own functions, his well-defined character. . . . The activity which ensures apprenticeship and the acquisitions of aptitudes or types of behaviour is developed there by means of a whole ensemble of regulated communications (lessons, questions and answers, orders, exhortations, coded signs of obedience, differentiation marks of the "value" of each person and of the levels of knowledge) and by the means of a whole series of power processes (enclosure, surveillance, reward and punishment, the pyramidal hierarchy).
>
> (Foucault 1982:787)

When I returned in 1985, the CIM "school" had been moved from the old Biscuit Factory into a long one-storey block of small rooms, tucked away along the far wall of the factory complex. The first office served as a general meeting room, followed by the offices of the Frelimo Party, the workers' organization, (OTM), the militia, the women's organization, (OMM) and the youth organization, (OJM). At the other end were offices for the grounds division. The rooms in the middle were taken up by the school, with teachers' rooms for both secondary and primary levels and two classrooms. The modesty of this newer cement block construction with metal sheet roofs stood out against the impressive scale and aura of permanence in the other buildings within the factory complex -- presumably a post-independence effort to "make space" for workers and their organizations.

Far from linking schooling with daily realities of workplace, home and community, the CIM classrooms were spaces reserved for very particular kinds of communication(s). And of course these regulated communications and power processes of the micro world of the CIM school were shaped by the disposition of power and knowledge in the larger macro society of Mozambique and southern Africa in which they were embedded.

At CIM, as in other literacy centres throughout Mozambique, all efforts were made to create a centre which, as much as possible, duplicated the forms of the schools in the formal education system. CIM, however, had more means at its disposal than most factories. The classrooms were organized in a way that would have been the envy of many workplaces -- and indeed official schools! Each classroom included a more than adequate number of adult size desks, a teacher's desk and chair and a blackboard. The physical arrangement of the classrooms was uniform: the teacher's desk was at the front of the classroom alongside the blackboard and a pointer. The students' desks were in rows. The students chose their places at the beginning of the school year and after that, went back to the same desk each day.

The classrooms were used only for schooling, with literacy and post-literacy classes occupying the space for the two or three hour lesson periods during the day, and secondary school students occupying the space at night.[1] Apart from these hours, the rooms were vacant.

The walls of the classrooms were completely bare. No graphics, clippings, calendars or material of any kind were to be found. The only people entering the classrooms were the teachers, the students and representatives of the Social Services Department. In the early days of literacy, there had been many working visits. Now, people from the Party, the women's organization and the workers' organization came by only on formal occasions like school openings or when they had foreign visitors to the factory to show around. Even the visits of Ministry of Education officials had dwindled to almost nothing. The only people entering regularly were the students, the teachers and the school Director.

Routines and Rituals for Regulated Communication(s)

The classroom was a space for regulated communication(s). It was characterized by routines and rituals within which the workers were silenced or found voices, through which their sense of competence or failure was reproduced. The regulated communications of the classroom included the imposition of a particular language -- Portuguese -- and, moreover, a "correct" way of speaking it. They also included the establishment of particular texts, the packaging of knowledge and learning into "lessons," the establishment of particular kinds of question and answer rituals, encoded signs of authority and obedience, and ways of placing value on certain kinds of knowledge and experience and denigrating others. All of these in concert constituted a form of "doing class." They included a number of practices for establishing ways of speaking and for silencing, for promoting or denying people a sense of legitimacy as participants in particular kinds of discursive practices. (Corrigan, Curtis and Lanning 1987; Freire and Shor 1987b; Simon 1987; Rockhill 1987)

The regulation of communication first, then, was based on the imposition of a language. The language option for the national literacy programme was Portuguese. As we have seen above, the decision to mount the national literacy campaigns in Portuguese had been taken when the first national literacy campaigns were launched in 1978. The reports to the Ribáuè Seminar in 1975 about the experiences of the various provinces in literacy referred to literacy centres teaching in local languages in some provinces and special studies being done in others about how to consolidate a spoken second language, i.e. Portuguese, as a basis for literacy. Nonetheless, the general recommendations from the seminar had included a recommendation that Portuguese should be used for literacy. Where local languages were in use, they should serve to support a gradual transition to Portuguese.

Schooling in the literacy classroom thus took people from the varying mixtures of mother tongue use and Portuguese that constituted their normal language practices in their homes and communities, and indeed on the shop floor, into a world in which the language being promoted was Portuguese. The distance between the classroom and daily languages practices varied considerably throughout the country. For rural Mozambicans, the distance was vast. They were put in the contradictory position of having to learn something not in use in everyday life. They could not use Portuguese without learning it, but neither could they learn it without using it.

For the CIM workers, dwelling in an urban environment, with children in schools where Portuguese was the language of instruction and a broader social environment that brought them into contact with Portuguese on a daily basis, the distance was not nearly so great. Geographic location was not the only factor, however, for different levels of familiarity and comfort with Portuguese. The whole panoply of gender, race and class locations also entered in.

Rigid imposition of Portuguese in the literacy class was not in compliance with specific policy directives of the Ministry of Education. The teachers, in fact, got mixed signals about language from the new curriculum materials introduced in 1983 as part of the curriculum reform. The language programme in the new literacy curriculum was designed to build growing skills and confidence in communicative practices. There had been intense debate within the team that designed and tested the new curriculum materials in 1982 about how to do literacy in a second language. The manuals recommended the promotion of first languages, especially for content discussions. The idea was to work according to the language skills of the actual participants. This was particularly encouraged in the first year programme.

Both the literacy teachers and learners, however, brought strong assumptions about Portuguese as the only language appropriate for the classroom. This was so internalized by the CIM workers themselves that I actually heard one chiding another for speaking "dialect," before the class began. "This is a school. You can't speak "landene" [dialect] here."

Many of the learners had had direct experience of colonial classrooms with their special monitors just to detect and punish students who reverted to African languages in the classroom. Others had had a social learning of how schooling was done that established immediately the question of language as a key factor. And of course the broader social context had included a powerful colonial discourse around becoming "civilized" and a legitimate "citizen" which turned on proficiency in the Portuguese language. This discourse included systematic denigration of African languages as belonging to a milieu of savagery and backwardness.

> The social value given to the Portuguese language and the Mozambican languages exacerbates learning difficulties. There is an acceptance of the colonial attitude in which Portuguese is a "language" while Changana and Ndau are merely "dialects." Portuguese is valued as the language of "civilization," of "Europe". . . while Changana and Xitsua are disparaged as bush dialects. The over-valuing of Portuguese and the under-valuing of the African languages serves to mystify the question of speaking Portuguese. It is not treated as a means of social communication; implicitly there is an assumption being made of Portuguese as the language of a higher strata, almost inaccessible by definition. Thus the educatees enter without the slightest confidence of their capacity to . . . master the Portuguese language.
>
> (Problematic Areas in ABE at CIM
> First Discussion Document, February 1985)

Typical conversations in the interviews with literacy students ran as follows:

Q. "What language can you speak?"
A. "I just speak "landene" [Changana word for dialect]."
Q. "But what are the names of the languages that you speak?"

A. "I just speak Bitonga and Changana."
Q. "And what else? (Pause) Don't you also speak Portuguese -- because that's what you and I are speaking right now."
A. "Oh, but I just speak it a little. And I don't speak it correctly."

The assumption by literacy teachers and learners that the only language to be spoken in the classroom was Portuguese served to silence a number of students. Although the literacy manual attempted to tackle frontally the question of literacy in a second language, and, as indicated above, explicitly suggested in the first year programme that each classroom use the combination of first language and second language appropriate for the language capacities of the students, this was not "heard" by the literacy trainers and teachers. The training programmes for the new materials touched on this point in presenting the language methodology. There were training sessions to sensitize the teachers to what literacy in a second language implied. A lesson was conducted with the trainees in a language they did not know -- in Macua for Ronga speakers or in English. This was done in an effort to have the trainees feel how it was to have the literacy teacher conduct the class in a language which the learners did not know how to speak. But obviously the suggestion of a highly flexible approach to first and second language use was not posed with sufficient weight, given the sensitivity of the question. In retrospect, it was completely unrealistic to think that volunteer teachers, unsure of their own capacities in either language, would find ways to do this effectively.

There was absolutely no attempt to recognize proficiency in first language skills as valuable while second language skills were being attained. Nor was there any effort to promote the application of new second language skills, for example new reading skills, to first languages usages like reading the bible or writing letters.

What does it mean to read?
I discovered today that people don't know that now they can read Portuguese, they can also begin to read Changana. It's a big discovery for them to find that they can read not just words in Portuguese but words in other languages, *including* their own first language. They thought they could only read the words they had already "had" in the textbooks!

I asked Aurélio to translate two phrases into Changana in order to have something to show people how they could apply their new reading skills to Changana. "Nini machamba a Manjacaze. Ningadzala a mavele, midzombula ni tinhala." It means, "I have a farm in Manjacaze. I grow onions, tomatoes and cassava." Interesting that Aurélio was so full of hesitations about doing the translation -- and went into an explanation of

> the complications between the various written forms of Changana and Ronga.
>
> (Field Notes, January 7, 1986)

Once armed with my new phrase, I had many people sound it out with their new-found reading skills during the interviews as part of the discussion about uses of literacy. With smiles mixing sheepishness and pleasure and other emotions harder to interpret, they suddenly clicked to the fact that they were reading something in their own mother tongues. It felt like a very emotionally loaded moment. I felt very conscious of my foreignness -- and the unusualness of foreigners stepping into that language world. Since I was the one who had written out the sentence in Changana and helped them read it, they were immediately intrigued with whether I knew more. The foreignness I felt was not resentment that I had intruded into their world but more a sense of wonder, that somehow through these symbols on a page that could be "read," our separate worlds had some connection through language.

The Quest for "Correct" Portuguese

As if the imposition of Portuguese was not already fraught with complexities, the classroom also insisted on a way of speaking Portuguese. It had to be "correct Portuguese." There was never a moment of free expression of ideas that transcended the preoccupation with correct usage. This meant that any discussion around theme and content took on a totally artificial character. The main preoccupation of both teacher and student was speech as a test of oral correctness rather than speech as a means of social communication. The notion of growing communicative competence as a legitimate goal in and of itself did not exist.

> Massingarela, the technician in the Mill, was talking today about the low educational level of the workers and told me about a general assembly in which a worker spoke up. One of the white directors stopped the meeting to note the poor quality of Portuguese spoken by the worker, asking what grade he had and giving a negative commentary on his mastery of the Portuguese language. It seemed to me like an amazingly insensitive thing for a director to do, knowing all too well how limited the opportunities had been for black Mozambicans to learn Portuguese, never mind how hard it was for them . . . to speak out in a public meeting.
>
> What was also interesting was that Massingarela, himself a black Mozambican, certainly did not tell me the story as a comment on the

insensitivity of the director. It was told as illustrative of the incapacity of the workers!

(Field Notes, March 12, 1986)

The inhibiting dictums of both the imposition of a language, and a "correct" way of speaking that language were powerful tools for silencing. The regulated communications of the classroom were further tilted in the direction of silencing by the tendency of the teachers to cut off any space for unstructured conversation.

As curriculum designers we had carried out intensive debates during the elaboration of the materials about how best to develop the kind of classroom atmosphere that would foster growing confidence and competence in language skills. As indicated earlier, a complete revision was made after testing the materials. A major oral component was added to each lesson plan. This took the form of conversations around teaching pictures, dialogues, and structural exercises. Given that the themes were drawn from community and workplace experiences of ordinary people, there was an assumption of classroom space becoming a place of much unregulated conversation through which students would validate their own life experiences and develop self-confidence in oral expression.

This did not, in fact, prove to be the case. For example, the first unit of the first year book began with greetings in Portuguese. When we wrote the materials, we imagined this daily routine of greetings as a moment for individual conversation with the students, for tapping into their daily lives and feelings. Many of us came from experiences of second language teaching. We anticipated working easily from these dialogues into natural conversations.

Teacher: "How are you?"
Student: "I'm sick today"
Teacher: "Oh, I'm sorry to hear it. What do you have?"

Student 1: "How are you this afternoon?"
Student 2: "I'm tired."
Student 1: "Oh, Why is that? What have you been doing to make you so tired?"

These were the kinds of interchanges we imagined, where there was no "correct" answer -- but only an account of one's experiences and feelings, opening the door to individual lives, leaving space for fantasy and humour. We imagined all of this building up confidence in communicative competence and serving to affirm the importance of the students' own lives and experiences.

In the daily classroom ritual, however, this got reduced to the entry routine of the teacher, with "Bom dia" (Good morning), "Como estao?" (How are you?), "Estamos bem." (We are fine), all repeated in chorus as done in the primary schools. The greetings dialogue of the first lesson got caught up in the daily ritual to reproduce the power relations between students and teacher.

The clusters of workers arrived from their various workplaces, hot, sweaty, and hungry. They took their places, dirty with grain dust or whitened with flour. They assumed silence to be the appropriate stance on arrival at their respective desks. Some looked over the lesson. There were always late arrivals, with workers from some sections coming into the classroom five to fifteen minutes after the starting time.

The teachers, meanwhile, were in the teachers' room next door. When an appropriate time had gone by for all of the students to arrive, the teachers, all of whom were male and a good deal younger than the workers, made their entrances. They dressed in what looked like white lab coats, an adoption of the old Portuguese uniform for the teacher. They took their places at the front, deposited their books on the teacher's desk and formally greeted the students with "Good morning" or "Good afternoon." The students responded with equal formality, in chorus.

The stress on greetings, meant by the curriculum writers to establish an atmosphere of informality and trust and growing confidence in oral skills, instead got incorporated into a classroom ritual of reproducing power. The entry routine between the learners and the literacy teachers was probably best understood as one of the coded signs of obedience in the classroom. It regulated social communications in such a way as to establish the hierarchical social relations of teachers and students. The students waited for the arrival of the teacher. The importance of who was to do the waiting established the position in the hierarchy of power. The all-knowing teachers, wearing the garb of office, arrived last. They certainly did not divulge that the weighty pursuits left behind in the teachers' room had less to do with the pursuit of learning or lesson preparation than in hearing out the Madonna song on the radio provided for listening to the national literacy programme!

Textbooks as Arbiters of Knowledge

The ritual greetings were just one of many organizational forms that established the literacy classroom as totally removed from the ordinary world, a place for regulated communications. The regulation of communication in the classroom was further consolidated by the use of a set of official textbooks for literacy and post-literacy. The only reading materials in the classrooms were the prescribed texts from the Ministry of Education. Other texts were non-existent nor was there any encouragement to bring texts to class such as newspapers or magazines, or indeed written documents that people were having trouble dealing with -- letters from the village or the mines in South Africa, children's report cards or bureaucratic forms.

The only writing that was done was in the language textbooks, which served as both readers and work books, and in the exercise books. This had the effect of making all other written materials irrelevant. Far from using the text as the springboard for reading and writing skills that could open up the world of written communications to the workers, the literacy teachers confined their work in the classrooms only to the official texts. As indicated earlier, even photo stories done by the workers about their own factory or a newspaper article about CIM were not perceived by the teachers as suitable material for "the lesson." Only the textbooks counted.

The methodology in the language texts was to introduce systematically the syllabic families of the Portuguese language through a key or generic word that tapped into people's life situations. The thematic material was drawn from the broader social process current in the early 1980s. The central characters in the first year book were part of an extended family in Tete province, one part of it living in a communal village and the other in a key industrial centre. The rural side of the family included Paulo, a leader in a newly created communal village. He and his wife, Aida, and daughter, Mena, along with grandparents Daúde and Lila were involved in activities like forming cooperatives, participating in literacy, organizing small-scale animal production or mobilizing village clean-up campaigns. All of the lessons echoed the then current initiatives by the Ministries of Agriculture, Health, Education etc. Nuno, Paulo's brother, was a coal miner at Moatize, where he also taught literacy. His wife, Odete, was a health worker who had adventures travelling about the province with her colleagues. The discourse of socialist transition pointed to new and dynamic roles for the popular classes, with women, workers, students and peasants all playing activist roles. The contents of the texts themselves promoted new values such as collective rather than individual solutions, equality, popular participation and internationalism.

One of the debates as the textbooks were being written was the tone. Some of us argued for more problematic situations, more grey areas and a few failures rather than everybody on the high road to socialist construction in their cooperatives, communal villages and literacy classes. Once the books were in use, a number of people noted that the lesson that invariably triggered the most lively class participation in the first year book was the one dealing with a drunkard beating his wife and squandering his pay. With the daily realities of MNR brutalities, drought and hunger, the high moral tone of the books got more and more out of tune with people's lived experiences.[2]

The generic word or theme drawn out of each teaching unit was illustrated by a teaching picture, meant to spark lively dialogues and ready links with the workers' own lives and experiences. Not so, however, in practice. This too become almost a ritual. A typical interchange looked like this:

Teacher:	"What do you see in the picture?"
Students:	"We see people."
Teacher:	"How many people do you see?"
Student:	"I see two men and a woman."

With luck, the dialogue would at least continue to identify what the people were doing. And indeed, conversations identifying people, objects and actions were useful enough for consolidating vocabulary and developing confidence in speaking ability. The step that never got made, however, was that of moving from identifying people and objects and actions to identifying life situations and problems, and from there, links to the workers' own lives. The one or two questions in the manual meant to serve as examples of the types of questions that could draw out these realities were rarely expanded, turning the dialogue into meaningless questions and answers, of little interest to students or teacher.

> The way the teachers use the teaching pictures is enough to make me weep. When I think of our vision as we wrote the books, the care in selecting the unit themes, the notion of rich conversations, schooling really linked with the workers' actual life situations -- and then observe day after day a kind of theatre where one plays teacher and the others play students, and they exchange meaningless questions and answers in a classroom ritual, all knowing that none of it has anything to do with their real lives and concerns!
>
> Thinking more about it, what happened with the design for the first lesson says it all. The teaching picture for Lesson 1, which introduces greetings in Portuguese, was intended to establish the pattern of social communication in the literacy classroom. Our idea was that it should show a teacher and student warmly greeting each other at the door -- no formal routine of entry here! What came out, however, was something quite different. The image of the teacher at the door greeting the student was not front and centre as we had conceived it. It has been relegated to the background. In the foreground is the image of schooling built up over years of colonial practices -- the passive, receptive posture of the obedient

> student waiting for knowledge to be deposited. When I was in grade one in a small town in Manitoba, this was called "Position One!"
>
> Lesson 1 shows the concept of "schooling" shared both by the literacy teachers and students -- and captures perfectly the social construction of schooling. The design got past us as we wrote the books, probably because we were under such enormous pressure to finish the first year book and get on with the book for second year. As I recall, the designer herself was in the midst of a family crisis, desperately trying to get to Portugal, and we were intent on trying to get minimally acceptable designs for 104 lessons from her before she left!
>
> (Field Notes, March 14, 1986)

Realistically, though, how could we have imagined the teachers would know how to interact differently, to cease being authority figures, guarantors of "*the answer*" when their own experiences of schooling clearly had been ones of transmission of knowledge always in extremely formal, vertical settings. Moreover the brief training programme for literacy teachers operated in just the same way.

FIGURE 7.1 Teaching Picture Lesson One

The style of interaction between the literacy instructor and the trainee was one of giving and receiving, active and passive, authority and powerlessness, bearer of knowledge and empty vessel. The subject was teaching methods rather than some other subject like history or geography, but the form reinforced all of the old stances. Nowhere had the teachers encountered an educational setting where the learners' ideas and experiences and voices were taken as central.

As we have seen above, there was a step in each lesson in which the students were called on to "discover" the new words they could make from the syllabic families already introduced. The teachers seemed to bypass this step systematically or else supply all the words themselves. The students were left believing they could only read the words they had already "had." The irony, of course, was that the theme materials and suggested lesson plans begged for a different treatment, linking the classrooms to the community, school with work. The theme materials all focused on real life situations of ordinary working people, albeit far less besieged with war and hunger, far more gloriously on a path of socialist construction, than the CIM workers.

The suggested lesson plans included writing actual letters, filling in real bureaucratic forms, reading the wall newspapers common in workplaces and villages. Nonetheless, the teachers assiduously avoided taking up these suggestions. Particularly in the first two years of the language programme, the teachers had the students repeat the reading texts in chorus until they were memorized, and than had them copy them several times in their exercise books, just to be sure they had "got it."

There was virtually no encouragement of creative writing. When the manual suggested it specifically, as, for example, in the unit on how to write letters, the teacher had the students copying the sample letter in the text rather than actually using new writing skills to write their own letters. To the degree that the curriculum materials pointed in the direction of concrete, usable language skills, the teachers seemed to take pains to keep the lessons at an abstract level. They simulated the activity rather than actively trying to link the literacy classroom with day to day situations.

> Only two people came to class today, and the teacher was sick. They're doing the teaching unit on letter writing and I felt a sense of elation that I would actually have a chance to work with a couple of them on writing real letters! Then Mondlane had to leave early. Cristina Mausse stayed and probably assumed we wouldn't do anything. I went through the steps of the suggested lesson plan and arrived at the activity of writing a letter to a friend. It's actually there in the plan. Cristina forms letters easily now and more or less copes with sounding out words by syllables. She decided

to write to her son in Xai Xai -- and actually succeeded in writing a really good letter. Afterwards she was brimming with satisfaction.

These things have to influence your attitude to literacy. She was almost dancing with happiness -- ready to put it in an envelope and send it off to Xai Xai. I learned later from some of her friends that she had showed it around to everybody in the factory before she sent it.

(Field Notes, March 3, 1986)

When a class assembly was organized late in the year, the students seemed to be somewhat aware of these circumscribed uses of their new language skills.

Class Assemblies
After several false starts, there was actually a class assembly in which the workers themselves got a chance to put forward their ideas about what was going on in literacy. Amazing how literacy silences the illiterate. Everybody talks about how to do literacy and the problems of literacy except the most vitally interested, the illiterates themselves.

The party and mass organization representatives were once again absent. Senora Leonor, the head of the party literacy committee, did not attend. Sansão, the new teacher, took the initiative of having them work in four groups. The proposed agenda for the group discussion about literacy included:

1. participation
2. time-table
3. teaching methods
4. other items

With regard to participation, they identified the position of the section head as key. With encouragement from the section head, as was the case in the health post, it is easy for the worker to study. Once again there was a listing of problems related to work demands. When there are too many trucks to load, people from the Finished Products Warehouse don't come. When there are too many patients to attend, the person from the Health Post is absent. When a colleague has a day off or goes on vacation, it becomes impossible to go to class.

There weren't too many ideas about teaching methods. In an exchange about things to read, it came out that the various post-cards I had taken such pains to send to the two classes during the four months we were in Brazil and Nicaragua had never gotten into the hands of the students. I didn't have the heart to pursue it and find whether they had stopped at the Social Services Department or in the teachers' room. Wherever they had stopped, the workers to whom they had been written had never seen them. So much for my efforts to stimulate interest in letters, and my

> strategy to keep up contact during my long absence so as not to break the momentum of building up trust etc! The workers did say that they thought it useful to write things, both on the blackboard and in their exercise books, so that these things could later be corrected by the teacher. They thought that in this way they could learn something and that this method would give much greater results than simply copying phrases out of the literacy text.
>
> (Field Notes, April 10, 1986)

During the period of my research, I experimented with the use of other texts outside the classroom, introducing "O Campo," a monthly publication of the Social Communications Offices of the Ministry of Information. "O Campo," which means "the countryside," was written in simple Portuguese with a popular style including plenty of graphics. It included regular sections on health care, environment and appropriate technology, plus a comic books, games and quizzes. I arranged to have these posted on bulletin boards in various sections of the factory where I had developed a good working relationship with the section head.

> I went by the Finished Products Warehouse this morning to change the clippings display on the bulletin board at the entrance. Mr. Gouveia, the section head, really liked the idea of having something to read up on the board, and said that many people stopped to read them. I wonder if it's true -- or is it said because it will please me.
>
> (Field Notes, February 2, 1986)

I suggested that the literacy teachers might also like to put them up in the classrooms and arranged for a bulletin board to be mounted. What got posted on it, however, was the daily time-table of classes and not the newspaper. Later the Social Services Department decided to get a subscription of 50 copies for CIM. The hardest task was to guard them for the literacy students, since the general dearth of reading matter made them a hot commodity, much desired by already literate CIM workers.

Knowledge and Learning Packaged in "Lessons"

The regulated communications of the CIM school included not just a language and a way of speaking it. They also included a packaging of knowledge in the form of lessons. The new literacy materials had each day's work programmed for the teacher. There were teaching units on given themes broken down into lesson units with suggested plans for activities during the 90-120 minute classes. The first year language programme, for example, had 104 lessons, with teaching units made up of 4-6 lessons for each broad content theme.

These detailed lesson plans were included after much debate within the team of curriculum writers during 1982. The first literacy teachers' manual had included only general guidelines. Literacy monitors, usually with less than ten days of pre-service training, had shown little capacity to develop the theme materials into teaching activities. On the other hand, step by step lesson plans were seen as too rigid, lending themselves to a very mechanical approach which could rob the teachers of whatever creativity they might be developing.

The classes observed at CIM underscored this danger. The lesson plans were followed with a fairly rigid orthodoxy, a packaging of knowledge in daily doses that allowed no space for unregulated communication to enter. The "lesson" ritual began with the routine of putting up a "heading" every day on the blackboard for the students to copy into their exercise books. It was never clear where this ritual originated. It was certainly not suggested in the literacy manual but seems to have been accepted classroom procedure in the official schools and hence deemed appropriate for literacy. This meant copying from the blackboard into individual exercise books the date, the lesson number and whatever the literacy teacher could derive from the lesson as its title or content. Often in mathematics, the exercise book entry would be something like, "Maputo, March 12, 1986, Subtraction with borrowing." The mathematics exercises were actually done in the mathematics textbook, so often there was either nothing alongside the heading or only the rough figuring for the answers in the book, neither being very useful for future reference. Nonetheless, this routine of doing the heading was taken with utmost seriousness.

I found Eduardo giving directions at the beginning of the school year that only the heading, i.e. the date and topic, were to be done with a pen. Anything else was to be written with a pencil, so that it could be erased. At the beginning of the year when there was a shortage of exercise books, the major consternation was about how to resolve the problem of the headings.

> Eduardo came late for the mathematics class, even though his sole task in the factory is to teach two and a half hours per day. Despite his late arrival, he has gone through the ritual of putting up the heading. Today it said:
>
> Lesson Number 4
> Summary, March 3, 1986
> Subject: Mathematics
> Conclusion of lesson 4 on natural numbers up to 100.000.
>
> (Field Notes, March 11, 1986)

What was interesting was the systematic deletion of all steps in the suggested lesson plan that took teachers out of a lecturing, authority role and involved active teaching methods and group work. Rote learning with drills using the pointer was the norm. Even the date and heading got drilled by individual students who came to the blackboard and had other students repeat the word indicated.

Ritualized Questions and Answers

The regulation of communications in the classroom was also characterized by a ritualized form of questions and answers.[3] This ritual was part of a discursive practice that assumed the teacher as the authority who, in all situations, had the "right" answer. Knowledge was taken to be a given, something already possessed by the teacher and not by the students.

The questions and answers in the classroom were word games in which the student tried to guess the right answer. The teachers played the students as you might play a fish on a line, giving positive encouragement for where the teacher wanted to take the interchange and dropping what was not of interest in arriving at a particular pre-defined answer.

In the classroom, this use of questions with a code of teacher's signals that guided students towards "THE RIGHT ANSWER" was not very deftly done. This was evident in the approach of the literacy teachers to the teaching pictures. The themes of the lessons, as indicated above, were derived from the day to day life of ordinary factory workers and rural producers at home and at work. They had been established through a consultative process with officials from various sectors including agriculture, housing and health. They included such themes as post-natal care, agricultural cooperatives, handling machines, women's participation in society etc.

These "discussions" in the hands of the inexperienced literacy teachers tended to be a series of closed questions, in which choruses of "yes" or "no" were the only response from the students. Given that those who ventured into a longer answer tended immediately to have their grammar or accent corrected in the interests of "speaking properly," these "discussions" tended to be ones in which the only voice heard was that of the teacher. The students were effectively silenced.

> Today Eduardo did, or better said, "gave" lesson 3 of the third year programme. He put up the inevitable heading on the board for the students to copy. Today it was:

Subject: Portuguese Lesson 3
Summary: Reading and interpretation of text

He then gave instructions about when to use pen and when to use pencil. Only headings, copies of passages and dictations can be written in pen. In the books themselves, where students write answers, only pencil can be used.

Then he "gave" the lesson about housing and various types of housing. To my surprise and consternation, all of the question and answer part about round houses, square houses, houses of thatch and wattle and houses of cement blocks and metal sheet roofs was slanted towards one conclusion only. His conclusion could be summed up as follows. Houses from local materials are inferior, relevant for the era before the "discovery" of superior building materials; cement block houses with metal sheet roofs are the best.

I cringe. CIM sits right next to an idle cement factory. The bandits cut off the limestone quarries ages ago and there is no raw material for production so all construction depends on imported cement. Every worker in the classroom knows how impossible it is to get cement. What little is imported goes for high priority projects; individual housing is way down the list.

But even apart from the current cement crisis, the housing policy in Mozambique was never one of cement block construction for all. The National Housing Directorate has worked for ten years now to encourage improved construction methods with local materials, hiring cooperants to work in that area and winning fame at international gatherings for its enlightened and realistic approaches to improved rural and urban housing, developing local construction techniques and materials. Here in our very own literacy classroom is Eduardo as the authority on housing, telling the workers that cement and metal sheeting are really "it."

(Field Notes, February 25, 1986)

Another major inhibiting factor in the question and answer ritual was the excessive formality deemed to be appropriate by both teachers and students. All communication was through the teacher with no direct conversation from one student to another. Despite the small numbers in the classes, the learners normally stood up to address the teacher, or raised hands and were formally recognized by name before they spoke.

The formalities clashed head on with the teaching activities of the new curriculum, not only in the language programme but also in mathematics. The mathematics programme included oral drills at the beginning of each lesson to develop skills in mental arithmetic. These were meant to be rapid-fire drills with the element of surprise keeping students on their toes, ready to respond instantly. In practice, a formal "Mr. João. What's 5 x 7?" was asked, after which Mr. João figured out the response to his question, stood up and gave it and sat down again. The others, meanwhile, sat back and relaxed.

There were ritual laments from the teachers about wanting more class participation. Meanwhile they actively silenced the few who ventured forward with an input or observation outside the teacher's game plan. Moments that could have been key for validation and empowerment were lost or turned into rejection and silencing instead.

> The reading text for the lesson was short. The manual suggested asking each student to read alone. Eduardo read it first; any challenge of discovery automatically ruled out for the students. Some will now memorize it rather than read it. They have difficulties with three words, "utilizar," "resistente" and "tecnica."[4]
>
> Eduardo puts two of the difficult words/phrases on the board for the students to study -- "técnica de construção" and "resistente." In the discussion, Celeste, the cleaner from the Mill who is often outspoken, suggests that "técnica de construção," in addition to meaning construction technique, also means a female technician. Eduardo does not pick up on Celeste's observation at all. He simply repeats that the correct meaning is "construction technique."
>
> This may indeed be true in the context of the text under study, but as an opportunity to acknowledge new roles for women (CIM actually does have several women who are technicians and one of the four technical directors is a woman), to pick up on an unsolicited observation from a student, from a woman . . . the moments lost make me weep!!! If they were only opportunities lost, it would already be bad. But they are more than that. Celeste was actively silenced. Her observation was dropped, made invalid, denied the stamp of authority of *the teacher*. Will she be up for more observations in class in the future? Given her feisty personality, maybe she will be -- but lots of other women will know not to risk it.
>
> (Field Notes, February 25, 1986)

The manual for the language programme, particularly in the second year, included a great deal of work in small groups. The instruction in the teacher's manual was to divide the class into groups of four or five with a mix of stronger and weaker students in each. Many lessons included a period of time working in groups, discussing, preparing a reading passage or class presentation, solving problems. The teachers at CIM, and indeed elsewhere, seemed to systematically alter this instruction and carry out the activity with the entire class. They seemed determined to maintain control themselves.

During the monitoring visits the year the materials were introduced, I had often asked teachers why they didn't have the students work in groups as suggested. I got answers like, "It makes too much noise."

"They'll teach each other errors." "It's uncontrolled." "I won't be able to correct them."

> Lesson Observation
> Lesson 22: Second Year Portuguese
> - 19 present
> - many replies in chorus
> - reading done by rows, which are called groups
> - instead of dividing into real working groups, the teacher directs all the work
> - instead of each group's working out its own answer, the teacher keeps control and gives them to understand that there is only one correct answer
> - much confusion between rows and groups. Leads me to believe they have never really worked in groups in this class.
>
> (Field Notes, May 6, 1984)

On the few occasions when work was really done in groups, the entire dynamic of the class shifted. There was a totally different body language from the students, and a totally different quality of participation. This had already been very evident in work done with the first year students at CIM in 1984, when I was still working in the training department of the Adult Education Directorate and giving pedagogical support to various literacy centres. We had seen that once the authority figure at the front of the classroom was removed, the workers began to interact with each other and visibly both relaxed *and* became animated. What was nice was how the connection of language and the world was immediately established. The high moral tone of the literacy texts, where everybody tended to be a model worker or peasant building socialism with few problems and grey areas, was left behind.

In addition to work in groups, the manual also suggested a variety of teaching-learning activities that were more active, and took the teacher out of an authority role. These also seemed to be systematically left out.

> June 12, 1985: "teacher skipped over the game"
> June 17, 1985: "Carlos jumped over the step of putting them to work in small groups to prepare a description of different provinces to present to the class"
> June 19, 1985: "Carlos didn't bring the bottles to show how to divide a 10 litre bottle into 5 bottles of 2 litres"
> June 26, 1985: "Aurélio, N'Guiraze and I chatted today about methods of teaching. We were left with the questions of why the active teaching methods are more or less systematically left out. Is it for lack of time, or because they don't have any conception of how to do them, and for that matter, why?"
>
> (Field Notes, June 12, 17, 19, 26, 1985)

Having seen this pattern during the first year the new materials were in use in 1983, we had already begun to introduce activities into the training programmes to familiarize the teachers with more active methods. The geography unit, for example, included a quiz. The simple mechanism of writing out the questions and drawing them from a hat, with opposing teams having the chance to reply and gain points for their team, immediately transformed the classroom. The first time we did it the trainees themselves got super excited at doing the quiz. In subsequent training courses we added a few harder questions to make it more of a challenge for the trainees, and let it serve as both a tool for teaching methods and a tool for content.

I had actually introduced this game in a mini-training session with the CIM teachers. They had seemed receptive but presumably understood it as a challenge and diversion for them, and not a method to use with their own students. The transfer back into the classroom did not happen. Active methods did not come easily. There was always a powerful tendency to revert back to formal lectures, with all in its place when the teacher was "giving" the lesson and the students were on "receiver mode."

In large measure, the teachers probably did not know either how or why to use these more active methods, and feared the lack of control that such activities engendered. The social construction of colonial schooling that turned on rote learning of the catechism and rigid discipline was still intact enough to make teaching methods that included fun highly suspect. Lack of time was probably just the pretext to cloak their fear of the unknown.

Classroom Codes of Authority and Obedience

The classroom as a space for regulated communications included coded signs of authority and obedience. The routines of entry and the formalities of being recognized to speak were two of the most obvious codes in operation. But in fact, the authority of the teacher was all-pervasive, dictating which book to open and when, when you could write in pencil and when in ink, who could speak and when, whether you could leave the classroom. Far from seeing learning as individual or collective projects of the learners themselves, the teachers saw themselves as the ultimate authorities on all matters. Absolute obedience was expected.

The student-teacher interaction around the exercises in the textbooks was another point where this relation of authority and obedience operated. The language, mathematics and natural science programmes included daily exercises -- filling in blanks, matching words, copying, dictations, multiple choice questions and, in second and third year, short paragraphs. The mathematics programme included both set exercises and a section of supplementary exercises for independent work. The students did these exercises in class time, with explanations from the teacher. Often the exercise was first explained and done on the board. When the students missed a class, the page remained blank. There was no encouragement for the student to catch up. Nor was there encouragement for the more apt students to do more. Once the exercises were done, the quicker students waited passively for collective corrections. Any initiative of the students to work ahead or write something in their exercise books was constrained.

Many of the language exercises, particularly the comprehension questions in second and third year, had the potential for several answers. The teachers, however, discouraged a diversity of answers. Answers were given in the teacher's manual as an aid for inexperienced teachers, but these tended to reinforce the tendency to accept only one reply, and further reinforce the authority of the teacher as arbiter of "THE ANSWER."

The relations of authority and obedience were reinforced even more by the style of corrections. One of the clearest codes of authority intact from colonial days was the teacher, red pen in hand, judging the correctness of the students' work day by day. The literacy manual tried to suggest another approach for adults. It questioned whether a red slash or cross through errors and a correct sign for right answers was appropriate. This occasioned consternation from the volunteer teachers, for whom the role of arbiter of correctness was central to their definition of teacher.

It was suggested in the manual that the teacher give individual attention to the students as they did their exercises, walking from student to student as the exercises were being done. In these strolls around the classroom to observe the learners' work, the literacy teachers showed an alarming predilection for supplying the answers rather than probing where difficulties and errors were coming from. The teachers were also often extremely brusque in their manner, far more ready to pounce on errors than to commend correct work, thus reinforcing workers' views of themselves as incompetent and unable to learn. This often took the form of irony.

Confronted with a correct exercise, the standard comment was along the lines of "See how simple that was." Faced with errors, there was little attempt to seek out the few correct answers for praise, tempering corrections with encouragement. The judgmental stance of the teacher led frequently to reinforcement of the students' sense of themselves as failures but both students and teachers seemed to accept the, at times almost dictatorial stance of the teacher, as entirely normal.

The class sessions observed gave ample opportunity to watch teachers not validating students' efforts. The repertoire for creating distance, silencing and putting students down was intact from the authoritarian classrooms of colonialism, expected from both sides.

> Observation of Lesson 24, Third Year Portuguese
> - 15 present
> - dialogue theme about donating blood
> - Pedro [the teacher] suggests those who don't have to give blood are "lucky"
> - Pedro asks for volunteers to read and two are forthcoming
> - both able to get through the passage without too many difficulties
>
> When they finish, Pedro gives his judgment -- "*Not very good!*" Pedro then has the whole class read together. Later Senhor João tries to read alone and has difficulties. Pedro makes him stop. Senhor Banze reads "I was" [estive] instead of "he was" [esteve]. Pedro makes him stop. Senhora Ana reads "I had" [tiveste] instead of "I was" [estiveste]. Pedro makes her stop. None of them has any idea what (s)he has done wrong. Later people succeed in giving answers to several of the questions. The final comment from Pedro on the lesson is "All of you are doing badly. This is a crisis."
>
> (Field Notes, June 15, 1985)

> Observation of Lesson 50, Second Year Portuguese
> - 7 present
> - photostories done in 1984 distributed
> - lots of spontaneous enthusiasm to get them and read
> - Aurélio dampened this a little by suggesting they should read it for homework!
>
> The photostories were just given out like that -- at my insistence finally. To what end except individual pleasure, I'm not sure -- though goodness knows a book just for pleasure is no bad thing. Senhor Santos can read it right through with no problems.
>
> (Field Notes, July 7, 1985)

> Observation of Lesson 46, Second Year Portuguese
> - 8 present
> - Senhor Alexandre was concentrating so hard on the lesson, copying a text into his notebook, that he didn't even see Carlos, the teacher, approach him
> - Senhor Amilcar took ages to write his name, "AMILCAR"
> - Carlos' reaction when it was done was to say "Goodness -- such handwriting. I really don't know. . . "

- Senhor Amilcar now sits, all the tension gone out of his body, leaving only a deep weariness. The body language expresses frustration and defeat.

(Field Notes, August 7, 1985)

The teachers' repertoire for encouragement and support, to help students begin to construct a new sense of self as able, competent, articulate, with life experiences that were valuable and important, was just not there. But then how could it be? What experiences had Carlos or Pedro ever had of a pedagogy that wasn't rigid, top-down, based on the transmission of knowledge? And it was all reinforced for them daily in their own night school classrooms and work relations at CIM or the Provincial Directorate of Education.

I found myself torn constantly between the students and the teachers. My feelings of sympathy for the teachers, knowing what their own experiences in the classroom had been and how little the literacy teacher training programme had done to provide alternatives for these authoritarian styles, were real enough. They were usually far surpassed, however, by my outrage at what the teachers did to the adult learners.

Afternoon

Am I being bitchy or are they being impossible? After an excellent day yesterday, today is a misery. While at one level it was useful to sit observing this morning, at another level the whole thing was ridiculous. The rigidness is what really drives me bananas. Carlos this morning with incessant drilling on a word like "artesanato" [handicraft] -- hardly essential to the workers' day to day needs. He seems to have a special dislike for Senhor Alexandre so even what little Alexandre manages to do right is never praised.

This afternoon it's a session with just two students, Senhor Santos and Senhora Isabel. Santos romps through the text from the lesson, having been interrupted by Carlos from reading the photostory. She has difficulties reading the text, and gets harassed by both Santos and Carlos together.

Carlos is working with them on the difficult words. Senhora Isabel is not able to read them. Carlos chides her. "This is very bad. We can't have only Santos reading. Senhora Isabel is also here. She has to read too." Then Senhor Santos gets in on the action. He also harasses her. She just gets more quiet still, and almost seems to grow smaller in front of our eyes as she withdraws into herself. Self-fulfilling prophecies fulfilled once again!

(Field Notes, July 7, 1985)

The women students seemed to be particular targets of these put downs by the teachers. I observed an amazing scene in one of Pedro's third year Portuguese classes one day. He had given the students a test, meant to help them prepare for the real test at the end. The men all managed to do it fairly readily. Three of the women stayed on long after most had gone, trying to complete the answers. Pedro, who must be more than six feet tall, came in and hovered over their desks impatiently at the end, demanding to know if they were finished. The women, looking somewhat defeated, shyly said they were, and handed in the tests. Glancing over their papers, Pedro commented. "Well, you've made a real fruit salad of it, haven't you." I could hardly believe my ears. So the two women left, confirmed in what they already knew about themselves and literacy -- hopeless cases.

> I was furious with Pedro today and the way he treated the women in the class over the exam. I caught up with him outside and told him in my best national training staff authoritative manner that this was absolutely not the right way to work in literacy and to correct students. It's strange. Whenever women are put down, I find myself reacting very fiercely, with none of the qualms about whether I should intervene, and how. Anyway, intervention with Pedro to what avail? This one I just happened to overhear, but I imagine the use of authority to put people down in this way is common enough.
>
> The problem is, Pedro himself doesn't believe they can learn. The notion of support and encouragement to tackle their shame and inhibitions is not his fix on how to be a teacher at all. He's the teacher. He "gave" it. "They" didn't "get" it. Clearly "they" are the problem.
>
> (Field Notes, June 16, 1985)

In the end, we were all caught up in the hierarchical structures. In such a moment of fury with Pedro about how he was putting the two women down, the repertoire of behaviour I drew on was the repertoire in common usage. I did not actually yell at him or threaten punishment but I did assume a stern senior national staff pose and lectured him about inappropriate methods. I did pull rank on him and virtually prohibited him from repeating this kind of behaviour. There was nothing horizontal or two-way about the kind of exchange between us.

Throughout the period of my field work, there were regular discussions with the CIM staff about how to link the classes with real life experiences of the workers and move them from being mini-lectures by the teachers, or ritualized questions and answers. Aurélio, the school director, was part of many of these discussions, and finally came to me one day to work out how we could enrich the second year lessons. The decision seemed to stem from the response by Abdul Carimo, Aurélio's director, to the study document. Carimo had included a comment to the effect that the teachers should break out of monotonous lesson routines and introduce new teaching methods like slides. Aurélio presumably now felt "authorized" to be "creative."

We set up a time and then sat down and went through the units one by one, adding an additional activity to each unit. The unit on health care was to include a visit from health extension staff with their new video on diarrhoea. The unit on tea production was to include real photos of Gurue tea plantation. The unit on colonialism was to include the wonderful photos from the CIM archives showing overweight, cigar-smoking settlers with their families at lavish parties in the dining room for whites only, while the blacks who slaved with endless sacks of flour and maize meal ate from tin plates in a warehouse. The unit on people's power was to include a new video on people's tribunals in urban Maputo. The unit on textile production was to include a visit to the neighbouring Texlom factory.

Aurélio seemed doubtful about how it would all work. I tried to steer us towards manageable things. I also arranged to take him around to the Ministry of Health and the Social Communication Office from where we were to get the newspaper subs for the students. I calculated that by taking him on these rounds, he would be able to put faces to the people working in the various sectors. I hoped that once he had experienced their enthusiasm at the prospect of getting their resources out to places like CIM, he would be more determined to make it work. I also tried to alert DNEA colleagues so that he might get some additional back-up from them. Subsequent letters, however, showed how hard it had proved to be.

> We are in the implementation phase of those supplementary activities to enrich the teaching units. The visit to Texlom failed. The authorization from management was delayed in getting to me. I didn't receive it until after the date we should have gone.
>
> (Letter from Aurélio Tembe, June 18, 1986)

> The work with the Ministry of Health did not take place, although we made a lot of efforts for it to happen. On the day set for it, after having organized everything, we were gathered with the literacy students from Petromoc (neighbouring factory) in the meeting room waiting for the Ministry of Health team. At the last moment, we at CIM did not have transport to go and pick them up and therefore nothing took place. I am really worried now and afraid to return to the Ministry of Health to explain how the problem of transport came up.
>
> (Letter from Aurélio Tembe, October 13, 1986)

Breaking out of lecture routines was not easy, then. Nor was it always simple to interpret what happened when a different kind of activity was introduced into the classroom. Creating opportunities for the students to be something other than passive recipients turned some on but was highly threatening to others.

> Today we did the activity with photographs to beef up the unit on tea production. We got photographs from the newspaper archives of the plantation at Gurue and passed them around to the small group of five who were present for the class. A couple of the designs in the book are actually based on these pictures, but clearly the photographs established these tea pickers at Gurue as part of the real world in a way that the illustrations in the books hadn't done at all. Basically, the pictures triggered very different responses. Mondlane got super turned on. He started to speculate about how tea got introduced into Mozambique in the first place. He queried whether the tea worker really picked 45 kilos a day as the text said, and wondered how many baskets constituted 45 kilos. Mondlane himself spends his days handling 50 kilo sacks of flour.
>
> In stark contrast, the two women were singularly passive. Henriqueta from the day care literally slept -- and justified it in terms of working shifts until 7 o'clock. Celeste was in her usual stance of "I can't." "I'm not able to." This, I have come to see, is not a statement in relation to a particular question, but a general posture in relation to all classroom activities. A question on day care centres on the tea plantation got through Henriqueta's barriers -- and suddenly a complete sentence, forgetting to be inhibited. What to conclude from it all? Hard to say.
>
> (Field Notes, April 2, 1986)

> I am still pondering the reaction of the two women. By chance I re-read Malina de Montis' account of their participatory research project in Nicaragua last night. (de Montis 1985) Some of it jumped out at me as the logical interpretation of yesterday. At a village called Regadio, a participatory research team working with the adult education department had carried out a project to try to see how to make the teaching materials more relevant to village needs and priorities. The local people had worked out a questionnaire and then community meetings had been held where a kind of resource inventory was made with identification of problems and possible development projects. de Montis spoke of how the villagers at Regadio had a tendency to complain of incapacitating headaches and shoulder or neck pains exactly at the moments of greatest analytical or reflective need in doing the research. Maybe that explains Henriqueta's response yesterday. It was really too much of a coincidence -- the scene of intimacy with five people handling photographs and talking about them, and Henriqueta literally nodding out. Probably it did feel infinitely more threatening to her -- an expectation of participation that was almost impossible to deny, given the intimacy of the situation. It was an invitation to have a voice and a form that made it hard to be anonymous and silent.
>
> (Field Notes, April 3 1986)

Whose Knowledge and Experience Is Valued?

The regulated communications of the classroom also included practices that valued certain kinds of knowledge and experience and denigrated others. The most obvious form of this had to do with oral language skills. All of the workers brought to the classroom spoken competence in at least one, and in many cases several, Mozambican languages. Many could also read or write in their mother tongues. About a third of the students interviewed indicated an ability to read or write Changana or another Mozambican language. Many of them had learned to do so in mission schools or through the church. Others had learned while on contract in the mines in South Africa. This knowledge, however, was not seen as valuable. These were merely "dialects," of no interest in the world of schooling, in practice banished from classroom use.

I had observed during 1983 that on the few occasions the students were encouraged to form new words from syllabic families, they had often thrown in words that were not Portuguese. This usually occasioned nervous laughter. In situations in which I was part of the staff observing team, I tried to intervene and demonstrate ways to give positive feed-back, underscoring the validity of the word in another language, finding the Portuguese equivalent or showing how you could form the words in English too. I am fairly certain, however, that the teachers left to their own devices, did not feel secure enough to accept non-Portuguese words as legitimate.

The question of validating certain kinds of knowledge went well beyond questions of language, fundamental as these were. The basic life experiences and skills of the workers tended to be systematically denied as valuable by the classroom experience. This was at odds with the recent history of the factory itself. The abrupt pre-independence flight of Portuguese technicians from 1973-1976 had created a rupture in the hierarchies of power and knowledge, a sudden opening in which there emerged a radical discourse recognizing competence even when not accompanied by certified schooling. During the colonial era, there had been virtually no opportunities for black workers to become qualified. Many CIM employees were highly skilled workers who had learned on the job, but had next to no formal schooling or professional training. Such workers, during the transitional government and first years of independence, were promoted to positions of responsibility, in recognition of their competence. Many were promoted to fill positions of management even as illiterates because they knew the work.

The professional training programmes for workers at CIM also put experience ahead of paper qualifications. When CIM did not have enough workers in the shops with fourth grade certificates to put into the training courses offered by the Ministry of Labour for welders, mechanics, carpenters etc., it set up its own internal training programme based on skills, waiving the formal qualifications for entry.

This dramatic shift of circumstances at independence had altered the parameters of the possible. Ordinary workers who had imagined only continuity in dreary routines of hard labour suddenly saw the possibilities of change. The intervention of the state in 1980 consolidated yet further this recognition of competence and knowledge through experience. The more highly trained Mozambican technicians brought in did not replace the veteran workers who had been made heads of the various sections of the factory.

> Today I talked with the head of the Mill, Domingos Chinguvo, who did third grade in colonial times and then did the exam at CIM to get his fourth grade standing in an accelerated course for cadres in 1982. He recounted how, when the settlers began to flee in 1973, he was named by the Portuguese engineer who stayed on as director to be in charge of certain activities in the Mill. "Little by little, I mastered it -- until I took charge of the whole Mill. Today I have an engineer to give me support."
> (Field Notes, January 22, 1986)

As we saw earlier, an inquiry into literacy carried out by the Social Services Department in 1981/82 showed that CIM workers at this time had high expectations of mobility within the factory. At that time they saw literacy playing a role in making this possible.

No worker interviewed during my stay at CIM in 1985/86 even hinted at expectations of becoming a section head. The situation had altered dramatically with the earlier space for mobility totally closed. In fact, literacy had become necessary just to hang on to your job and even sixth class guaranteed little in terms of improved work or wages.

The practices at CIM and those of the Ministry of Education were quite different with respect to paper credentials over against experience. Even in the first years of independence with such dramatic lacks of trained cadres, there had never been a move institutionally by the Ministry of Education to recognize mature students, or mix professional experience with formal studies as a basis for establishing equivalencies. On the contrary, the Ministry of Education had been quite rigid from the highest to the lowest levels. Even with regard to literacy itself, there was no stance of flexibility. There was no recognition that people might have learned sufficient reading and writing to pass the literacy exams in other settings, at home or in the community over the years, and that such people could be encouraged to do the exam and get the credential. The stance was quite the opposite. You not only had to register, but you also had to attend the classes in order to try the exam.

Not surprisingly, the general knowledge adults brought to the school was given even less recognition. The pre-service training programmes for the literacy teachers included some work on characterizing adult learners, differentiating them from children precisely by their store of empirical knowledge based on life experiences. Once within the classroom setting, however, the teachers did nothing to signal either the existence of this knowledge or its value.

Carlos, the second year teacher, had spent all his life in the city. Assuming his authority role as teacher he gave mini-lectures on things far beyond his own experience. I found him one day giving a lecture on how to clear fields with the local slash and burn method. He was presenting this to men and women, almost all of whom had lived in the rural areas. The learners could have given real accounts of their experiences, of fires that got out of control, of feasts from animals caught because they were disturbed by the flames, of children burned. But only Carlos spoke.

In another lesson I observed on child care, there was a step in the lesson in which the teacher was supposed to initiate a group discussion on local methods for controlling diarrhoea. Carlos, who was only 22 and had no children, felt no qualms about acting as the authority on raising children to his students, most of whom were in their thirties and forties, many having raised six or eight children. On this occasion, one of the students intervened shyly and volunteered that in her district of Zavora, on the coast in Inhambane province, they used coconut milk to cure diarrhoea. Carlos gave her no response. The teachers had little appreciation of the popular wisdom held by the students, and regularly interacted with them in a way that made the learners appear stupid and incompetent. The learners themselves, on entering the classroom, left behind any sense of themselves as competent adults with responsibilities in workplace, home and community. They readily assumed a posture of ignorance and passivity and defeat.

The sessions in the training programme on the psychology of the adult learner theorized about the wealth of popular wisdom possessed by workers and peasants and the need to take account of it in the teaching-learning process. The texts themselves were designed to draw on the life experiences of the workers. Often the lesson guide suggested asking the students to recount their own experiences -- of everything from how the liberation war was fought to local dances, how to construct houses from local materials to popular medicines.

The teachers themselves, however, shared none of this vision of literacy, and the possibility of constructing rather than transmitting knowledge. When the lesson plan suggested a discussion or work in groups that would draw on the students own ideas and experiences, these were invariably jumped over completely, or developed only as far as the two or three sample questions of the manual. The responses from the teacher clearly signalled that this was a simulated discussion, and not one based on genuine interest in the students' experiences or genuine valuing of their ideas. Having picked up signals that it was a classroom ritual and not a genuine exchange of information and ideas and experiences, the students had little to contribute.

There was only one occasion when I saw another dynamic at work. This was the occasion when Henrique N'Guiraze had substituted for Pedro Chivute and had succeeded in getting the whole group to speak in a very animated way about their experiences with treated and untreated seeds. At times the discussion got so animated that the students threw in contributions in Changana, seemingly without even being aware which language was being spoken.

N'Guiraze managed to carry out in practice the process we had envisioned when we worked on the curriculum. It was a process of building on the life experiences of the students, choosing the moment to systematize, to introduce the "theory," only after the reality had been opened up by the students themselves. N'Guiraze found ways to pose problems rather than provide answers. There was a kind of joint creation of new knowledge rather than simple transmission of old.

The evaluation mechanism for literacy was a strong factor militating for transmission of knowledge as defined by the texts rather than creating knowledge based on the students experiences. Measurement of literacy success was purely quantitative -- attendance and marks on the final exam. A conversation with Carlos just after he had done the six months training course for professional adult education teachers was telling. "The oral part is a waste of time. What's on the exam is just reading and writing." For Carlos, the rote learning of the reading passages of the literacy textbooks was assumed to be the best preparation for the exams and so the classroom communications were rigidly limited to the prescribed texts. There was no understanding that growing oral skills in the language in which you were learning to read and write might affect your progress.

Attendance and test scores were the only things to evaluate. From the general director to visitors from the education ministry staff, the Frelimo Party to the shop floor boss, the only measurement of literacy success was bodies in the classroom and scores on the written exams. Since there was neither a language to identify nor forms to measure literacy's impact on job productivity, childcare, community participation, family communications, status of women etc., there was a strong tendency built into the programme to reduce it to what was going to be measured.

The exam, then was a powerful form in determining what knowledge and experience was valued and in shaping what went on in the literacy classrooms. Teaching to the exam was the norm. This became the more negative in that the exams themselves were so unpredictable. The inexperienced literacy staff encountered major problems in setting, distributing and marking the exams.

> Today the third year students finished the tests sent to them by the city education office, another set of "training tests." It was a total fiasco. Pedro invited me to have a look at the tests when they arrived, saying: "I'm afraid of these tests. I hope they won't be too difficult."
>
> Duplicators, paper and ink were all in short supply so the tests were to be done from the blackboard. The idea of the city staff was to have the text written on the board for students to read, followed by fill in the blank comprehension questions. First, there wasn't enough blackboard space even for the text itself, never mind the questions. Then the students were told to copy the questions and fill in the blanks -- which in effect was a huge additional copying exercise for new writers, using up all the time available. Instead of using one of the types of questions common throughout the written exercises in the third year programme, the test used a kind of matching question that threw the students completely.
>
> The Natural Science paper was even worse. It was hopelessly abstract. "What is nature?" "How would you define a substance?" So of course they all did very badly, all felt completely defeated, and all assumed that it was their fault.
>
> Pedro's fear of the tests was well founded. For once we were in complete agreement. Or almost complete -- because he also situates the problem as his students' limited ability whereas I see the main problem as one of badly set tests.
>
> (Field Notes, July 8, 1985)

The methods of evaluating literacy success, then, played a powerful role in consolidating the value placed on certain kinds of knowledge and expertise, and making other kinds of knowledge and expertise entirely invisible. In practice, what the classroom experience and exams did, was to erase whatever knowledge and self-confidence the students had, as competent practitioners in their multiple worlds of work, home and community. Within the classroom, those areas of competence were invisible. When tested against the competence that the literacy programme was prepared to measure, most of the students became failures.

Literacy: A Socio-Political or Administrative Space?

Behind the forms of the school classroom and its peculiar organization of time and space was the set of inter-locking organizational hierarchies that made up the factory. There seemed to be a fundamental ambivalence about where to situate the school in the midst of these hierarchies. The operation of the school was the responsibility of the Training Section, a section with a history of movement between the Human Resources Department and the Social Services Department. When I started the research in May 1985, the training section had been moved into the Human Resources Department. This department was concerned mainly with questions of work categories, control and discipline, combining questions of personnel policy, hiring, firing and transfers with those of absenteeism, punctuality, theft, damage, etc. It tended to deal in purely administrative methods. The Social Services Department, on the other hand, dealt with a number of social programmes that directly benefitted the workers and had historically had a dynamic staff, responsive to new needs and opting for persuasion and mobilization ahead of administrative fiat.

The jumps in interpretation of what was happening in literacy, between bureaucratic impulses and political impulses was a constant. In one conversation with Carimo, the Director of Economy and Human Resources, I was astonished at the rapidity of the switches.

> I had an interesting conversation with Carimo today. He started with a very strong critique of education, suggesting that it was not really geared towards the workers but towards elites, a problem he saw as common in third world countries. He noted that the attention paid by the factory to workers' education and training was concentrated only at the level of secondary and tertiary education. This missed the needs of the great majority of the workers for adult basic education.
>
> He was very critical of how workplaces organized education for workers, including CIM, and said at one point, "We're very ready to demand things from the workers. But in terms of support, we're not there."
>
> But then a sudden jump, and a lot of strong words about punishments and how to force workers to study. I am left baffled at the switch.
>
> (Field Notes, June 29, 1985)

The ambivalence about where to locate the school and training section in the CIM organizational chart seemed to indicate the tension between literacy as a socio-political space and literacy as an administrative space. It had already shifted back and forth several times. The debates about where to house the training section surfaced once again with the appointment of a new head of the Department of Social Services.

> Carimo says the training section has to go into the Social Services Department again. It seems to have been bouncing back and forth ever since I've been at CIM. Carimo says it needs to get out of the Human Resources Department because that department has control and discipline functions with entirely bureaucratic methods. The Social Services Department has a different stance, much closer to the pulse of the workers, much less bureaucratic.
>
> (Field Notes, February 22, 1986)

Nonetheless, it seemed very difficult for CIM to discover ways of doing literacy that were not bureaucratic. The immediate post-independence era of frequent meetings and high energies for voluntary activities had long since gone. The practice by 1985 was not one of persuading workers to volunteer for literacy, either as students or teachers. The training sections had a listing of educational levels of all workers as part of its records, and the school director simply pulled out the names of the students in each sector needing to complete adult basic education and posted them. Assignment to attend school was not unlike assignment to other duties in the factory.

> The question of who participates in literacy and how is a staggering one. Zita informed me today that the Finished Products Warehouse says it can't send so many to literacy. It has too many work pressures. Literacy has to be outside of work hours. I know the newspaper has been publishing some complaints from CIM clients about long waits to load up their trucks with produce after doing the bureaucracy of requisition forms etc. So management gets pressured, both to increase production and to make time for literacy.
>
> Aurélio tells me later that we're going to a meeting to talk to the workers in the Finished Products Warehouse. I'm full of curiosity as I've never been able to observe management in direct contact with workers about literacy – but I'm also wondering if I want to be identified with this scene. So we go to the Finished Products Warehouse office, and I meet a senior official I've never met before, plus the regular section head, Gouveia. Gouveia, once the more senior official appears, is marginal to the discussion.
>
> The workers are called in. The man from outside the section doesn't know the workers by name, though many have been there more than 15 years. Several aren't present. They are on vacation – great planning for people who are supposed to be enroled in the school.

> The senior official goes through the list. Old people, i.e. more than 40 (sic!) are ruled out by definition. There is a semblance of a discussion of each case, but nothing remotely close to real joint decision-making. It is more concurrence with the slant already given by the senior official.
>
> I keep pushing the discussion towards looking at each person in terms of what they've done -- and manage to keep on the books a 42 year old man who has passed each year he has taken. I hope he makes it. At the end, he's the only worker still left in the room, and the two heads leave him standing as they complain about workers slacking off, leaving at ten for classes at eleven. I don't know -- maybe they do. I guess I'd push it to the limit if I were there -- there surely doesn't seem to be any semblance of workers' control at more meaningful levels -- so why not push the system to the limit?
>
> (Field Notes, February 21, 1986)

The management discourse around participation focused purely on individual motivation. It was assumed that drop outs and failures were straightforward indicators of lack of will. Moral harangues about attendance were seen as the antidotes, with administrative measures to back them up when necessary. There were no rewards for attendance at school, except the odd prize for a tiny handful of students with top marks. The punishments, however, were very severe.

> Today Aurélio showed me the rough draft of a letter about administrative measures to be taken for unjustified absences. I guess the bureaucrat only has instruments for punishment and no instruments for mobilization. Now, according to this memo, people who have unjustified absences are going to lose their rights to buy maize meal and bread and animal rations from the factory!
>
> (Field Notes, March 6, 1986)

Many punishments took the form of threat and were never put into practice. Indeed it would have been quite impossible to implement them without occasioning a major revolt from the workers. What is interesting, though, is the way that literacy administrators saw them as appropriate to propose.[5]

The question of why CIM workers participated in literacy or dropped out was by no means a new one. A lunch conversation with Angelica Aguilera, Head of the Social Services Department, shortly after I had begun at CIM pointed all too clearly to the complexities.

> Literacy is a huge problem. We've got workers who started with the Dynamizing Group back at independence. Then they did literacy in the first campaign [1978/9] -- and the second and third. Some of them have been at it for ten years and still haven't succeeded. You can't force them

> to keep coming. Last year we had workers who left their sections to go to literacy classes and hid behind the buildings until the classes ended. Then they returned to their sections. It got to the point that you almost had to force people bodily. This year, we've just dropped first year. You can't bring people to literacy by force.
>
> (Field Notes, June 20, 1985)

Clearly the question went well beyond straightforward notions of individual "motivation." The complex mixture of motivation and constraint, desire and fear engendered by literacy for each worker was rarely visible. The shop floor work process itself held out literacy as a path to training courses, promotions, and transfers to less back-breaking work. But life on the shop floor also made it virtually impossible to attend classes regularly without jeopardizing fellow-workers and production goals, leading at times to conflicts with shop floor bosses and internal struggles for power. And in fact, those who did succeed at literacy did not get the training, new placements and salary levels held out as incentives.

The acute social problems caused by the war and continued economic crisis were ritually mentioned as affecting literacy. The descriptions by the men and women at CIM of how they experienced this were powerful. They felt acutely the disjuncture between the CIM workplace with its systems of food, uniforms, transport and social services, not unlike the vision of model factories and development in the literacy texts, and their own lives. At home and in the community, hunger and a rapacious black market were turning many Mozambicans into hustlers and thieves for a bar of soap or a pair of shoes.

The desirability of literacy for women was ritually affirmed. What was invisible was the cost and constraints -- from old and still operative social learning about the inappropriateness for women to participate in public discourses to the bi-annual interruptions for child-bearing and daily demands of child-rearing so common amongst the women workers at CIM.

A factor absolutely unnamed in all the discussions of the push/pull of literacy was the possibility of an option against literacy taken by women, as protection from the humiliation of the classroom. I happened on a few situations where women were put in very embarrassing situations in the classroom, although none of the women put this humiliation into words in the interviews. I wondered about this when women in the Pasta Factory sent a mysterious message directed to me saying they did not want to continue studying. It crossed my mind that, for some of the older women in particular, it might be based on the daily classroom experience of feeling threatened and then humiliated -- at times not only by the male teachers but also by the male students. It was a message passed through many hands, however, and the possibility to probe deeper was made complicated by the response it got from the CIM bureaucracy.

> Senhor Aurélio, Director of the School told me that Samu Gudo, Head of the Pasta Factory, had informed Senhor Manjate, Head of the Social Service Department, that the women of the Pasta Factory wanted to inform Senhora Judith that they didn't want to study anymore.
>
> Senhor Mandlate told Senhor Aurélio to reply immediately that they have to put it in writing. The impulse seems always to have a justification for those who aren't studying and always to go for administrative methods.
>
> (Field Notes, February 25, 1986)

The working assumption was always that literacy was something good – and the more of it the better. The notion that the illiterate might opt against studying as a rational choice was rarely entertained. The implicit notion of the illiterate as deficient, lacking not just reading and writing skills but also judgment, maturity and wisdom about their own lives, made it difficult to accept them as decision makers. The image of the illiterate was never one of canny, urban survivors, calculating possible benefits from education certificates and the value schooling had in resolving the problems of their lives. The notion of illiterate workers making a conscious and carefully thought out decision to drop out of literacy was not even entertained.

There was an ongoing tension, then, between literacy as a political process concerned with participation and empowerment, and literacy as a bureaucratic process concerned with formal qualifications and certificates. But how could it be otherwise, given that the power relations in the literacy classroom were so firmly embedded in processes of power relations and communications within the interlocking hierarchies of the factory? It is within these power relations organized through class, race and gender that illiterate men and women made their calculations about the benefits of literacy to their lives.

Notes

1. Although part of the space was officially designated as space for the OMM and OJM, the organizations for women and youth respectively, the two rooms for the OMM and OJM were virtually unused by these organizations. Neither of them was in a particularly dynamic phase. The few meetings or activities that took

place while I was there made use of the general meeting room which was also used for Frelimo Party meetings, training activities, etc.

2. The question was sharpened for me further on the trip to Latin America where we came across some amazing literacy material for women from the Dominican Republic. Tomasa came to the city as a domestic and her first crisis was finding herself on the street, fired by her madam because she was pregnant by madam's husband. Back to the countryside, another equally unjust firing and many other adventures later, Tomasa finally ends up as a union activist with a good "companheiro" at her side who not only accepts her children but also does the dishes! Apparently this "soap-opera" approach to literacy, with plenty of real life pathos and crises leading up to the happy ending, had the students begging to take the books home to read more.

3. There are increasing numbers of excellent studies on classroom talk that focus on the very unequal communicative rights between students and teachers. The seminal work of Basil Bernstein in *Class, Codes and Control* (Bernstein 1973, 1977) has been taken up by many others, with important empirical work in school settings making clearer the functions of language in the classroom, ways of displaying knowledge and the cultural resources required to answer teachers' questions. (Hammersley 1977; Cazden, John & Hymes 1972; Heath 1983; Edwards 1980)

4. In Portuguese, technique is "técnica." But "técnica" is also the word for a female technician, as compared to "técnico," a male technician.

5. At one of the sugar plantations which I visited regularly in 1983, the school director had proposed to management that those who were consistently absent from literacy be thrown out of company housing. The newly appointed General Director, himself an educator, found himself in a position where he had to explain to his education staff that since literacy was a profoundly political action, it would be more appropriate to deal with it using political methods. He suggested a study to determine the real causes of drop-outs and some mobilization and persuasion rather than punishment. The result was a plan for kerosene lamps for night classes in the community, recognizing that cane cutters moving from field to field, hot and hungry after a shift of cutting, could not realistically down their tools and settle under a tree for two hours of literacy.

8

Power Differentiation in the CIM "Village"

In this "village," your sector is almost your prison. You're not able to get out of it.

(Alberto Sousa Moamba, 40 years
Grounds Department)

When I speak Portuguese and make mistakes, those who hear are amused. It's because I'm not white. For blacks, it's different.

(Celeste Tembe, Cleaner, Mill)

Sometimes something happens in the section and I think of alerting the head to it. But I keep quiet. For me, it's a problem -- how to have the courage to speak up to the people in management. The head who blows up just makes me shut up. . . . It's very complicated. I know the directors here are interested in the workers, but it's really difficult to find the words in Portuguese.

(Alexandre Mondlane, handler, 27 years
Finished Products Warehouse)

There's a group in the management, and in the political structures of the Party, OTM and OMM -- that's already quite comfortable in its position. The people in it aren't very active these days. There is virtually no activity at the base.

(Mario Chissano, operator, 37 years
Pasta Factory)

The school classroom with its particular organization of time and space was firmly embedded in a set of inter-locking organizational hierarchies that constituted the social relations of the factory and, indeed, of the larger society beyond it. Knowing or not knowing how to speak, read, write and count structured the interactions, practices and choices of the worker-students on a day to day basis, not just in the workplace but in their communities and in their families. People brought to the literacy classroom the hopes, desires and fears of literacy, shaped by their particular location within the larger society, a location shaped by a complex interface of power relations. These relations were organized primarily, if not exclusively, through categories of class, race and gender.

Literacy was by no means reducible, then, to a set of language skills equally accessible to all. There was a need to take into account the social relations in which these skills were embedded and embodied as prevailing discursive practices. At CIM, as elsewhere, access to literacy was differentially experienced according to class, gender, race, ethnicity age and location. The social construction of subjectivities as female or male, black or white, Mozambican or Portuguese, worker or management, urban or rural included differentiated senses of self as bearer of knowledge. Each learner brought to literacy that socially constructed sense of self. This included a definition of self as legitimate participant in some public discursive practices and not others, even if this inclusion or exclusion was not always a conscious one.

The very language chosen/imposed for literacy and the illiterate person's perception of access to/marginalization from particular practices as desirable/threatening was experienced from a determinate position within a set of power relations. Moreover, these knowledge and power relations were not specific to "literacy" but involved broader social and sexual relations. The literacy classroom, in other words, was firmly embedded in a set of social and political relations, ideological practices and symbolic meaning structures. (Corrigan, Curtis and Lanning 1987; Simon 1987; Lewis and Simon 1987; Rockhill 1987; Walsh 1987)

As we saw above the prevailing public discourse on literacy by the 1980s had come to frame literacy as a commodity. Provision of literacy had become a kind of investment in human capital, part of a larger package of rationalizing the workforce for maximum productivity. Literacy was treated as a composite of quantifiable knowledge and skills, that could be measured accurately and meaningfully on an exam. Literacy statistics were located in a developmentalist framework that assumed a direct, causal link between increased literacy and increased economic development. Illiterate people were perceived as having a deficiency.

There was an implicit assumption that the barriers to literacy had been irrevocably broken down with independence. The colonial regime had denied access to schooling to Mozambicans, while at the same time making all kinds of discursive practices out of bounds to Africans without the certified knowledge provided by schooling. The very language imposed by colonialism, Portuguese, had a set of boundaries around it defining who could legitimately speak it, within a powerful discourse of cultural superiority. As we have seen, the colonial state maintained a set of institutions and discourses of moral and social regulation to lock these boundaries into place. Thus a whole range of discursive practices was seen as beyond the capabilities of black Mozambicans, with female black Mozambicans even more circumscribed.

The nationalist movement had brought radical shifts in the discourse around knowledge and power. The nationalist discourse of the liberation struggle had challenged the colonial regime's cultural superiority profoundly. Independence brought a dramatic change in the parameters of the possible for ordinary Mozambicans. The extraordinary energy of popular participation in the 1975-1977 period had been triggered by this dramatic shift and at the same time created it. Ordinary Mozambican women and men suddenly saw themselves as participants in formerly out of bounds discursive practices, linked to the management of society at all levels.

This marked a radical break with the disposition of power and knowledge under colonialism. Suddenly positions of decision-making, action and authority were in the hands of those who had, in the old dispensation, been relegated to the margins. The call for participation in Dynamizing Groups and the ability of these groups to set up local structures of face-to-face democracy were key in all of this. Building local institutions of "people's power" was the order of the day.

As we have seen above, this explosion of popular energies included an enormous desire for education. In many ways, it was the broader socio-political process in which both students and teachers were inserted that set the tone for the spontaneous literacy movement that emerged. New forms of education were set up as alternatives to the official schools, and these were closely linked with emerging forms of people's power.

Even by 1977, however, the radical egalitarianism of social and political relations that had characterized the immediate post-independence period had begun to shift. The Third Congress of FRELIMO transformed the liberation movement into the Frelimo Party, a Marxist Leninist party defined as the leading force in society. The Dynamizing Groups were put on hold or phased out, replaced with a movement to build up a formal party structure instead. The release of energies and creativity and "ownership" that had characterized the Dynamizing Groups at their best, making ordinary people begin to feel in control of their own communities and workplaces, able to take initiatives to shape the "new" Mozambique, came to a halt. Once again, ways of being and doing were being defined from the top, albeit a paternalistic one rather than a repressive one. The channels defined for popular energies were the mass organizations for workers, women and youth. In fact, however, these organizations had little effective autonomy. Both their leadership and programmes were defined for them by party and state structures.

A new "statist" discourse focusing on development emerged. The decade from 1980 to 1990 was designated as the decade to defeat underdevelopment. The new discourse on development seemed to signal a strong shift towards the state as the central agent of development rather than collectivities of people in their diverse forms of "people's power."

President Samora Machel ushered in 1980 with a New Year's message on a very buoyant note. Machel established a kind of "social contract" with the people for a decade in which victory over underdevelopment would be won. With the triumph of Robert Mugabe in the Zimbabwe elections and the prospect of peace for the first time since the beginning of the armed struggle in 1964, there was a vision of a decade of dramatic changes. It was a decade which was to result in establishing an abundant supply of good food, decent housing, clothing and footwear, the country developed agriculturally with heavy industry established, an end to illiteracy and unemployment, and everyone with access to health care and education.

Even by the end of 1980, the mood of buoyant optimism had been replaced by rather somber tones. There was a steadily worsening foreign exchange crisis. The major political organizational offensive launched to wage war against the internal enemy highlighted many sectors not functioning effectively.

The political and organizational offensive gave very mixed messages about centralism and democracy. It came down hard on abuses of power, on illegality and on incompetence. It insisted on people's rights and on ordinary people as the ones to expose abuses of power. But it also strongly buttressed the positions of directors and departments heads in commanding roles, without any simultaneous strengthening of structures at the base to provide the constant check on new abuses of power. The mood to centralism, to work methods less through persuasion than administrative fiat, was strongly present. And the worsening economy and sharply increased attacks from South African backed insurgents served only to exacerbate the tendency to centralize decision making.[1]

By the end of 1980, it was clear that the socio-economic process was limping badly. The 1980 Plan was filled in only two of its five major sectors and lengthy discussions were held in the People's Assembly about how to make it work more effectively.

> In many cases one problem or shortcoming reinforces others and helps to create a negative cycle that will need several years to be broken . . . peasants and the family farming sector responded to calls by the

> authorities by increasing their production. At harvest time, however, there was not sufficient transport to take the products to be sold, and so production fell again. Following the Plan for 1981 is compulsory for all state, cooperative and private bodies included in it and measures will be taken against those who are responsible for failures to meet schedules and carry out tasks.
>
> (Aim Bulletin No. 54, 1980:6,7)

In all of this, a language of "must" and "compulsory" compliance emerged strongly. The state appeared more and more as the main agent of development, with the role of the people more and more as passive executors of directives issued through a top-down chain of command. Mozambique took on the classic attributes of many other governments throughout the African continent, a mixture of paternalism and benevolence that assumed all responsibility for economic and social development to rest with the state alone.

> The legitimacy of the state in articulating the goals of national development leads to a view of the state as the central agency in the realization of these goals -- the capacity accorded the state as the central agency of development necessarily entails (and legitimates) its right to mobilize resources, to decide how they are allocated and used. A characteristic feature of statist discourses of development, in fact, is that these two aspects -- the state's right to articulate the goals of national development and its capacity to pursue them -- are inextricably linked. They become mutually confirming assumptions of a particular mode of defining development.
>
> (Bernstein and Corrigan 1984:58)

In Mozambique, the institutions of people's power soon became a distant memory. The all-pervasive state left little room for civil society. A full-blown statist discourse on development emerged, with the state as some sort of benevolent technocrat, employing certain kinds of expertise which it used on behalf of the nation. The state, through its repertoire of development planning and administrative institutions thus appeared as the executive agency of the development process -- with the legitimate tasks of defining, planning and executing development tasks, on behalf of the beneficiaries of its policies, the rural poor, the illiterate, the working masses or even the nation as a whole. In agriculture, for example, rather than establishing an enabling environment, with policies on prices and marketing, and an extension service that would allow family farms or cooperatives to get on with production, the state itself tackled agriculture through multiple large projects.

State became definer of the problems and strategies, regulator of social relations, all in the name of some sort of collective subject -- the "povo" or the "workers and peasants." Meanwhile people at the base were robbed of their roles as agents of development, as in any way responsible for their own social life. The channels for popular participation such as the mass organizations for women, workers and youth and the professional organizations for teachers and journalists were themselves creations of the party and state, with party appointment of those in senior leadership positions within them and little to encourage critical debate or democratic practice.

The lack of promotion of basic civil rights -- of speech, of association, of the press -- was blurred by the benevolent and paternalistic stance of governance. The state governed on behalf of a collective subject, the "people." Within that collective subject there was little space for ordinary citizens, individually or in groupings of their own choosing, to take initiatives. State policy discourse was loudly in support of the popular sectors and the state made broad claims to expertise in accomplishing development on their behalf. The loudness of state claims to work for the interests of the popular sectors made it more difficult to challenge the state's all-pervasive role, even in the absence of mechanisms for active participation of the popular sectors in shaping public policy or organizational space to voice their demands in their own voices and in terms of their own making.

The mass media played an important role in reinforcing this display of state as prime mover with daily banner headlines of cooperation agreements, projects, arrivals of delegations of planners, experts and technicians. "Development" was a textual accomplishment, tangible in project documents and newspaper accounts of "developers" at work, in UNICEF, the World Bank, SIDA and CUSO. The production goals and plan targets contrasted starkly with what people in their homes and communities confronted on a daily basis. Far from experiencing the "development" promised in the "accords" and "plans," and "projects," most people endured growing shortages and hardships, against which they were powerless. Their ideas for solutions were rhetorically solicited; in fact they had very little space for action.

After 1980, then, a whole new discourse of "ten year plans" and "planning targets" came into vogue, a full-blown statist discourse on development. The main energies in literacy came to be focused on planning targets. Numbers dominated. The "metas" for enrolment and passes were the measure of literacy and not its capacity for empowerment, for promoting greater participation in community and workplace democracy.

As we have seen above, the project of global educational reform adopted at the time fed into this same discourse, focusing on educated workers as the human capital necessary for higher productivity. From the radical egalitarianism of the first phase of independence came a new stress on hierarchies of power, and clear identification of seniority in decision-making processes throughout the society. This was ostensibly done to tackle abuses of power and establish leadership accountability. The extreme formality and bureaucratization with which the leadership hierarchies surrounded themselves, however, tended to have the effect of distancing people from the authorities, whether in party or state structures. New hierarchies of knowledge and power began to consolidate, with the great majority once again relegated to the margins.

CIM workers, then, brought to the classroom particular desires and fears, hopes and constraints regarding literacy that were shaped by their locations in the shifting configurations of power and knowledge both within CIM and more broadly. For each person, it was a complex interface of gendered, aged, raced and classed lives. Meanwhile the prevailing discourses made these differences difficult for CIM workers to name. The Frelimo Party was committed to building a "non-racial society" and promoting the "full participation of women." At times, however, the rhetorical commitment to equality blurred the recognition of difference. There was little vocabulary with which people could name their daily interactions, practices and choices as shaped by power relations of inequality or by difference. The continuing power relations of subordination -- of women by men, of black Mozambicans by white Mozambicans, of the old by the young (or vice versa), of workers by management, of northerners by southerners -- were a daily experience but unnameable.

With regard to race, for example, the old political work of the armed struggle days to discuss race, was long since gone. It had been characterized by open and frequent discussion about who the real enemy was, about the place of white Mozambican patriots who were genuinely anti-colonial, about the fact that black Mozambicans were not above complicity with the Portuguese, selling out their own people. In the "non-racial Mozambique" created after independence, however, race as an explanatory category disappeared.

Meanwhile, within the "developmentalist," "technicist," human capital discourses that had come to prevail, formal qualifications and expertise were valued more and more. The claims to expertise from experience in the liberation struggle had long since disappeared. Increased power came to be placed in the hands of "experts," whose expertise was measured on purely formal qualifications. All too often this meant precisely those who had had the opportunity to study in colonial times and were already relatively privileged.

There was no public recognition of the raced and gendered construction of expertise, no reminders of who, historically, had had opportunity to study, to travel, to build up experience. The commitment to a non-racial society seemed to rule out strategies of equity or "affirmative action" targetting designated groups. Such strategies could have valued the "expertise" as such while simultaneously asserting publicly that those who had not had the opportunity to gain it, because of their race, gender or class, must now be given the opportunities to do so. In the absence of such discussions, more spaces were opened for murmurings and feelings of domination, particularly turning on race.

It is to the interface of these power relations and their effects on the experience of literacy that we now turn. As we have seen, there were persistent tensions between literacy as a linear, measurable, bureaucratic process and literacy as contexted and informed by political relations. The power relations in the classroom were firmly embedded and reproduced in the interlocking hierarchies of the factory and its power processes.

The regulated communications within the classroom and the power process within which the school was embedded shaped the experience of literacy profoundly, then, albeit not always visibly. It is to this question of literacy as a process to consolidate or challenge the interlocking sets of power hierarchies in the factory that we must now turn, analyzing more systematically the gendered, raced, aged and classed experience of schooling.

Locating the Researcher

Clearly I, as researcher, also had a location within these social relations of class, race and gender, and lived the tensions between the location attributed to me within the prevailing dispensations of power and the location which I tried to carve out for myself, consistent with my own commitment to the least powerful. Once I started to do regular participant observation in the classes, I found myself in many dilemmas in terms of how to handle my own location within the hierarchies of power at CIM as a middle class, white, female foreigner. This was made the more acute by my former role on the national literacy staff and the perception that behind me was all the weight of the Ministry of Education and, in turn, the state.

The CIM directorate, on my arrival, had immediately given me a desk in the Social Services Department, along with others from the training staff. They also incorporated me into the staff car-pool for senior staff, and the staff dining room for senior and middle officers of management, party and mass organizations. I was somewhat uneasy about being put in this position and felt I needed to take actions that showed a different stance and a commitment to the lives and concerns of the workers.

One immediate question was what role to play during the daily classes which were my main opportunity for contact with the learners themselves. I felt instinctively that things like the entry ritual of the literacy teacher into the literacy classroom each day was important in reproducing the power of the teacher over the students, and that this ritual was firmly embedded in all the interlocking hierarchies of power within CIM. Acceptance on my part of this practice could only be interpreted as acceptance and further consolidation of these power relations. On the other hand, failure to comply could be seen as a way of undermining the teacher's authority.

> Is there a bit of a power struggle between Carlos and myself that I've been oblivious to? Maybe. If all year you have a sense of your own power by being THE TEACHER, then suddenly you are eclipsed by a visitor/foreigner/national staff person, it could be tricky. I like to come early to chat as a way of building up confidence, but I need to see that this totally sabotages routines already established of formality, entering, silence, writing down the day's lessons, etc.
>
> (Field Notes, July 7, 1985)

Professionally, I felt that the establishment of formalities and hierarchies in the literacy classroom, of which the entry ritual was a part, was the antithesis of what needed to be created. I had complied with the formalities in my early years in Mozambique out of respect as a foreigner for Mozambican practices but was relieved to find the formalities increasingly a topic of debate in the literacy directorate. My concerns had been further strengthened by the lengthy discussions about these questions during the trip to Nicaragua and Brazil with the four Mozambican literacy instructors at the end of 1985. In some of the literacy centres we visited in Brazil, popular educators talked about taking pains to ensure that nothing that happened in the literacy centre was in any way similar to school. The Mozambican trainers had developed a full-blown critique of vertical structures by the end of the trip, ranging from the power hierarchy of teacher over learner in the classroom, trainer over trainee in the training programmes and senior staff over subordinate within the Ministry of Education itself. The appropriateness of my disorganizing the entry ritual was in part determined by knowing that my four travel companions were tackling these same questions in their experimental training centre at Manga.

I therefore opted out of the ritual entry to the literacy classroom, trying to arrive before the first student, and using the time to chat informally with the learners about everything from what the "bandits" had done in their area the night before to how many beers each worker would get at the 5th Anniversary party. There were conversations about children and a recurrent joke with Mondlane from the Finished Products Warehouse about how much I wanted his red baseball hat, a cherished possession from his brother in South Africa. Once I began to do the longer interviews, there was much more substance to chat about with each one, and a recurrent commentary from different workers about Senora Judith as our "friend."

On the days I drove the van that CUSO had provided for the national literacy office, I made a point of giving rides to those associated with the literacy programme. I also made a point of giving priority to the women, calling it the "women's van" and joking with the women about how women needed more places in this world where they got priority. This kind of bond with the women, the fact that the foreign, white researcher who drove a car really "saw" them and their lives and sought them out seemed to be an important component in establishing rapport and trust.

"Mama Only Lets the Boys Study"

Not knowing how to speak, read, write and count was clearly a gendered experience. Women and men experienced illiteracy differently. For the women in the literacy classes at CIM, whose ages ranged from 25 to 45, access to schooling for women was a new experience. Many of them brought to the literacy classroom as adults a childhood experience in the colonial era either of the classroom as out of bounds to girls or as a space in which boys were allowed to study while girls were channelled to other tasks deemed more appropriate to their sex.

As we have seen above, the regulation of sex and gender through schooling was an explicit aim of the missionary personnel and their auxiliaries to whom education of the "indigenous" was entrusted. The aims of education referred explicitly to inculcating work habits and skills appropriate to each sex.

What was interesting in the discussions with the women who grew up in this era was their matter of fact accounts of what this meant for their lives. All of the interviews included questions about the family history of education. Exclusion from education based on gender was common. Colonial hardships notwithstanding, their brothers had managed to get at least some primary schooling while they and their sisters generally had not.

Matilde Maboie was typical. She was a young woman of 30 working in the Pasta Factory as an unskilled labourer. She had begun at CIM when she was just 22 years old. Matilde had managed to complete second year at CIM as an adult in 1983 but was having trouble passing third year. She had missed many classes, however, coping with a four year old and year old twins. She explained why she was having to go to primary school as an adult while her two brothers had managed to do fifth and seventh class respectively. "In the colonial days, mama only let the boys study. Now I've done second year. Reading is not a problem. The problem is natural science." (Interview with Matilde Maboie, February 3, 1986)

Albertina Carlos, a 42 year old who was part of the kitchen staff, also spoke of not having had the chance to study as a young girl. Her three brothers had reached third, fourth and sixth class, while she and her sister had to begin their education as adults. Albertina had passed the literacy test with almost perfect scores in 1982. She had passed second class on a second try in 1984. When I met her in 1985, she was coping with a five year old, a two year old and an infant of two months. She had not tried the third year exam because of her pregnancy.

> I didn't study as a child. My father wouldn't let me. I don't know why. . . . In the colonial days, schooling wasn't for women. "Go to school to do what?" That's how it was seen.
>
> (Interview with Albertina Carlos, March 4, 1986)

A common theme from those who got to school was the disproportionate amount of time spent on studies as compared to doctrine and practical activities. For the girls, tasks outside the classroom were even more common than for boys. This was certainly true for Alicinda Macuacua, a 38 year old unskilled worker in the Pasta Factory. Alicinda's brother had managed to get his primary school certificate while she and her two sisters remained illiterate.

> The girls who were sent to school were made to collect firewood and cultivate the fields. Only the boys were allowed to study. This was in the Santa Maria Mission.
>
> (Interview with Alicinda Macuacua, August 22, 1985)

Clementina Oficio, a 45 year old unskilled worker in the Silos had much the same thing to say. She was enroled in the third year of the adult education programme at CIM, making up for lack of opportunity years before in the mission school.

> I went to school up to second class. There was a lot of doctrine and not much math and Portuguese at the Cambine Mission. There was also a lot of work growing maize, peanuts and cassava to buy school materials.
> (Interview with Clementina Oficio, February 10, 1986)

Essinete Gabriel, a 34 year old cleaner working in the Production Council offices, had a similar tale. Essinete's two brothers had managed to study as far as fourth and sixth class but she was trying to get her education through the factory. She had failed third year the year before in the midst of a pregnancy.

> I studied, but going to school in those days meant working in the fields. Afterwards I stayed home. Then I went to work to help out with the family.
> (Interview with Essinete Gabriel, March 11, 1986)

The lack of access to the school classroom for girls in colonial times was embedded in more global structures for silencing women. The patriarchal structures of traditional society relegated women to a position of complete subjugation. Part of the social content of the national liberation process had been a profound questioning of these patriarchal structures, with the liberated areas as a testing ground for new forms of participation by women. These began with women's having voices in village level assemblies and resulted in significant presence of women in all structures. This included the military where women formed a Women's Detachment and proved effective mobilizers as new areas were entered. (Isaacman & Isaacman 1983; Urdang 1985)

In the first years of independence, women were included in the Dynamizing Group structures and the Mozambican Women's Organization, OMM, expanded dramatically. The fact of women finally having a public voice was a recurrent theme in OMM gatherings. The visit of writer, Stephanie Urdang, to talk with women in Gaza province in the late 1970s underscored this point.[2]

> We have talked a lot. We have related many stories. But I must talk about something we seem to have forgotten. We have forgotten to say that women had no voice. Where matters were being discussed, there were no women. Men said women could not think. But after we got our independence, this changed. FRELIMO says that all of us, women and men, can develop our minds, all of us can work. FRELIMO knows that women can think very well, that women are as capable of making decisions. A woman can be somebody. In the past days we never had a chance to have a hall full of women talking about our lives. But today we can be together from morning to night discussing our problems.
> (Urdang 1985:350)

The post-independence upsurge of people's power brought to many women a new sense of self, a broadening of the parameters of possible ways of being and doing. They came to see themselves as legitimate and competent participants in discursive practices formerly perceived as out of bounds to women by a complex interface of patriarchal and colonial social regulation.

Some of the CIM women seemed well and truly to have left the old inhibitions behind. Celeste Tembe, an energetic cleaner from the Mill with a particularly brash style, seemed to be typical of this new generation. When I asked her why other women found it difficult to speak, she replied, "Many other women don't talk because they're embarrassed to try. What's there to be embarrassed about?" (Interview July 14, 1985) In the classroom, Celeste was always ready with a commentary or reply, at times to the discomfiture of the young men who taught.

Celeste had started to work in the factory in 1958. She had worked first in the assembly line making biscuits and later moved on to the Mill as a cleaner. She seemed to take a real pride in her work, which included the seemingly endless task of sweeping up spilled maize meal. She explained that it was not thrown away but used as animal feed, and that workers at CIM could also buy it. Celeste had started late in literacy because of shift work. She began in 1982, passed a year, failed a year, took a year off with a new baby and then completed second year, passing with an 80 percent average. Of the five of her eight children already in school, one had already reached third class, three had reached fifth class and one had done seventh class. Her husband, who worked in the neighbouring Cement Factory, had fifth class.

She said she had learned Portuguese under the old colonial bosses who spoke no Changana. She obviously felt at home with it, even to the extent of casual banter. I greeted her one day in passing, calling out, "How's everything over at the Mill?" "Everything is normal," was her response. "What does 'everything normal' mean at the Mill?" I joked. She immediately shot back, "It means everything is *clean*!"

But for women in the CIM school who were having trouble learning, the old shame and inhibition about speaking was still strong. There were constant reiterations of, "I can't speak Portuguese." "My head is too hard. Nothing enters it." Adelaide Mulengo, a 34 year old women who worked in the factory kitchens, found words to describe her own situation and that of colleagues similarly traumatized by the classroom process.

> I like to study but nothing stays in my head. When I close the book, my head also closes. I don't think I'll go anymore. I'm just going to irritate the teacher. Not even a little bit stays with me – nothing enters.

> Going to the blackboard at the front, getting up to read -- it's painful. The material enters a tiny bit but really not very much.
>
> (Interview with Adelaide Mulengo, February 3, 1986)

Adelaide was repeating third year and eventually dropped out.

At times in the classroom, when a turn for a questions or going to the board logically fell to one of the women most afflicted with shame, things reached a painful impasse. Short of physical coercion, nothing would persuade these women to try to give the answer. At times, this was handled gently by the teacher. There were other occasions when the teacher simply harassed the reluctant speaker. As indicated above, there were even occasions when the men in the class joined the male teacher in harassing the women!

The OMM at CIM tackled these questions with women from time to time. I was told that there had been meetings to discuss these "complexes" and to encourage the women to speak up in Portuguese, but none took place during the time I did my research. Gilda was one of the few women in the Pasta Factory who had managed to do sixth class. She was now in charge of the stores office in the Pasta Factory, and had given some thought to ways to support women. It was Gilda who had helped out with the translation in the one interview where it was needed -- and had done so in a way that really supported the woman being interviewed. Gilda said she now spoke only Portuguese with her colleagues, as a way of encouraging them to use Portuguese in situations outside of the classroom. She thought it was mainly a question of age, with the older women most locked into the old boundaries of silence.

It seemed, however, that old attitudes about women not speaking Portuguese and not speaking out in public were still in the air despite remarkable progress in altering the roles of women in society. Even in the relative sophistication of Maputo, the national capital, for black women to speak Portuguese in public was seen as a novelty. Delfina Sitõe was a competent and self-possessed attendant in the CIM first aid post. She was 39 years old and was following in the path of her sister who also worked at CIM and had completed fourth class there. Delfina spoke of her own experiences of speaking Portuguese in public and being ridiculed.

> A woman who doesn't speak Portuguese well can make a mistake and everybody else starts laughing. For example, this can happen. Two women can be talking Portuguese together on a bus. They don't speak it perfectly. Other passengers who overhear them start to laugh. That's why we're ashamed to speak.
>
> (Interview with Delfina Sitõe, February 9, 1986)

It was very difficult to distinguish between silence resulting from fear and silence resulting from not knowing Portuguese. And of course such distinctions were not necessarily useful since both inability and fear created equally definitive silences. Clearly the context of power relations played a determining role in whether women were silenced or found voices. And clearly the added factor of finding a voice in Portuguese rather than one's mother tongue compounded the problem immensely.

I had anticipated needing interpretation in many of the interviews, but found that the same women who, in the power context of the classroom, could manage barely a word, had a good command of Portuguese for a one to one situation with another woman. I had sought out classroom activists for the first interviews, especially women, calculating that the first unstructured interviews from which I was planning to devise an interview guide, should be with more articulate workers. In retrospect, I imagine that the "bush telegraph" of the CIM "village" probably got the word out that the conversations were not to be feared.

One of the early interviews was with Atália, a friend from the first weeks when the training section was still in the Human Resources Department. She was attached to the Sales Department next door where she worked as a cleaner. She also did light clerical work and had learned how to operate the telephone system. Atália's energy and irreverence caught my interest immediately and there was a lot of mutual enjoyment of jokes in the department. She had started at CIM in 1973 and was a party member as well as being active in OMM. She had just passed third year but did not enrol in night school to do lower secondary. This was partly because she was taking care of her daughter's baby and had to take it home from day care each evening. It was also because she had done third year during a year with only some of the books and anticipated that she would fare badly in the next level. I partially agreed with her assessment and encouraged the teachers to think about a make-up programme for the handful of students in her position, but this never happened.

Atália had many ideas when I asked her why she wanted to study. She had already learned how to read and write in Changana years earlier from her brothers and sisters. "It's better to have your own secrets. By reading and writing in Changana, you can avoid having your letters read by others." As for learning to read and write Portuguese, she had several thoughts, in an interesting mix of fact and fantasy.

> I want to travel. Someday I want to make a trip. I could go to Tete. I have a brother-in-law there. But if I go there, and have to travel by plane, arrive and find a hotel, I'll need to be able to read and write.

> You earn the same at CIM with or without literacy. Even with fifth or sixth class, you make the same. I have a friend who passed fourth class and she gets the same. But still it's worth it. Maybe in another company I could earn more. When people have an education, they don't suffer.
>
> (Conversation with Atália Macamo, June 21, 1985)

I asked Atália for her ideas about why other women had such difficulties in learning and such shame about speaking Portuguese. She pointed to the distinction between public and private domains, and language use in each.

> Some women really don't know how to speak Portuguese. Others are just embarrassed. As to why they have such complexes, how should I know? In my experience, women who don't work are especially afraid.
>
> (Interview with Atália Macamo, July 17, 1985)

This interpretation was echoed by others, including some of the men. The distinction between not speaking and not speaking Portuguese was often blurred in these discussions. This was not surprising since none of the three relationships that accounted for the triple silencing of women -- being women, being black and being workers -- was clearly named and discussed.

> Women have difficulties. Men get about. They travel to other places. They need to speak Portuguese. Women just stay at home. They don't travel. So that's why they don't talk.
>
> (Interview with Isac Cebola, handler
> 28 years Finished Products Warehouse)

Illiteracy: A World of Fear

Many of the interviews with the women underscored the circumscribed worlds and daily choices dictated to them by illiteracy. It was a world characterized by fear, with the desire for literacy clearly in part shaped by a yearning for more control over their day to day experiences in the home and community, and a belief that literacy somehow guaranteed this.

Cristina Mavale was a tall, quiet, slow-moving worker in the Sacks Warehouse who, to everyone's surprise including her own, passed the second year exam second time round with 80 percent. Her daughter was so pleased, she gave her mother a party to celebrate. Cristina also got prizes when the school year opened, including two coveted items, a pair of shoes and a capulana. Nonetheless, she had lots of difficulties keeping up with the third year programme. She later confided to me that two people in her warehouse, one man and one woman, had shunned her completely after she got her prizes, claiming that they had passed with equally high marks in earlier years and got nothing!

Cristina alluded to a world circumscribed by inhibitions for those without schooling. Her sense was that people who could speak and read and write could manage their social worlds at will, going anywhere, doing anything. She, like many others, spoke of fear in the world of the illiterate. There was fear of finding yourself in a military area, or at the wrong end of the city bus system or attacked by a fierce dog, for lack of ability to read signs. Clearly for many women, part of the desire for literacy was to feel more competent in the discursive practices of the urban world they now inhabited, far from the security of oral communications in their villages.

> With literacy, people don't earn more but everything they know is in their heads. They can go anywhere, do anything, ask for things, enter in. When people don't know reading and writing, they are afraid. A person could arrive somewhere, read a sign saying "Entry prohibited" and know not to enter the area. An illiterate person could wander into a military camp by mistake.
>
> (Interview with Cristina Mavale, March 20, 1986)

Laura Samuel, another older worker in the Sacks Warehouse, also alluded to the multiple difficulties of day to day life, and the way choices got shaped by lack of reading and writing skills. She had very practical reasons for wanting to learn. At the core of her reasons, however, was a fundamental sense of powerlessness and dependency to control her life without literacy.

> I really want to read and write. It's really necessary for me. When I go somewhere, there could be a sign saying "Beware of the dog." If I couldn't read, I could continue on and get bitten. I need to be able to go to the registry office and register the baby. Sometimes a stranger appears who isn't from around here and doesn't speak Changana. Without Portuguese, it's difficult. Also I'd like to be able to do things without asking for anybody's help.
>
> (Interview with Laura Samuel, February 9, 1986)

Clearly there was a lot of power attached to literacy. At times the sense of powerlessness of the illiterate facing the perils of the larger world seemed only a thinly veiled paradigm for the perils felt concerning immediate job security. Laurinda Zibia was the cleaner for the school. No day passed without a detailed account of her illnesses, part of a complicated history of pregnancy and health problems for her and her children. Her efforts in literacy were constantly interrupted by these illnesses, and even when she was well, she showed little anxiety to get to the classes. For Laurinda, a sense of powerlessness in the face of the larger world and the immediate world of employment at CIM seemed inextricably bound together.

> If you're travelling on the road, you could die. Maybe a sign says, "Entry forbidden." You could enter and die. Enter where you can't go.
>
> A person who enters now must know how to read and write. Now, if you don't know how to read, you don't enter here. Nowadays the question asked is, "Do you have ninth class?" If you don't, there's no work for you here.
>
> People struggle to learn to read inside here [CIM].
>
> (Interview with Laurinda Zibia, February 8, 1986)

Clearly literacy held out the hope of more control, moving more freely with street signs, bus signs, birth registrations, hospital forms. Celeste, the feisty cleaner in the mill, seemingly so full of confidence and certainly full of ready humour, confided her view of literacy one day.

> When I know how to read and write well, I'm going to do a whole lot of things. I'm going to send letters to my children [one worked in Swaziland] telling them what mama needs. I'm going to write things for the office. I'm going to do a lot of things. Schooling is the way to become somebody!
>
> (Interview with Celeste Tembe, July 14, 1985)

For some of the younger women, the combination of employment and literacy had taken them out of the circumscribed world of fears and inhibitions to a much greater sense of control and power over their immediate family situations. Serafina Alexander, one of the day care workers, started at CIM when she was 19, after her husband, a CIM worker, died. She had not studied as a child but began literacy at CIM in 1982. Despite the three children under the age of five produced in her new marriage, she had managed to get as far as third year by 1985. She missed the exam because of the birth of her youngest child.

> Literacy makes a difference. Since I've come to Maputo, I've had to ask people for directions. Now, at work, my department head sends something for our signatures and I sign it. I can also sign receipts.
>
> Once my husband sent me a note saying, "Meet me at the corner of July 24th and Lenin Avenue at four o'clock." No sooner said than done, off I went there to meet him. Afterwards, I was really pleased. This studying has its uses!
>
> (Interview with Serafina Alexander, March 4, 1986)

Literacy and Mothering

For many women, one of the immediate constraints of illiteracy was a sense of inadequacy in mothering. Many stated very explicitly that the main reason for wanting to study was to be able to help their children. Marte Francisco was a 27 year old operator in the Pasta Factory who had started at CIM in 1979. She had gotten into literacy when the new management reorganized it in 1981/82. She passed third class in 1985. She said that in her work as such, there was little need for reading and writing. The work consisted of loading boxes of pasta and sewing up sacks. Instructions given in Portuguese were the only points she can remember when Portuguese was necessary.

> The factory makes literacy obligatory but I also want to study. I need to know how to speak, read and write. At the hospital, it has been hard to explain my children's illnesses. We have visitors in the factory. They ask how many packets the pasta machine bags per hour. I don't know how to reply. With the children, I only speak Changana. If the children don't get places in school, they'll have to stay with their mother. Their mother is as dumb as an ox. They'll also be as dumb as oxen.
>
> (Interview with Marte Francisco, February 10, 1986)

A number of women referred specifically to the importance of speaking Portuguese at home for their children's success in schooling. Luisa António, a day care worker, put it this way. "I want the children to speak Portuguese at home. This makes them enter school with their heads already in good shape." (Interview, March 14, 1986) Luisa herself had passed first year but did not complete second year because of a pregnancy.

Her colleague in the day care centre, Cristina Mausse had the same idea. Cristina was 35 years old and had failed the second year exam. She could already manage better, however, claiming to know how to read the bus signs now and wanting to learn more so she could read letters. She was quite concerned about her children's schooling. "I have to speak Portuguese with the children to get them used to it." (Interview, March 1, 1986)

Manuel Gouveia, the veteran worker who was section head in the Finished Products Warehouse, mused on the question of women speaking Portuguese.

> There are women here who say they don't know how to speak Portuguese. But at home, they insist that their children speak Portuguese. And who is doing the teaching? They are!
>
> (Field Notes, January 12, 1986)

If the practices and choices of the women were shaped by their global sense of a fearful world beyond the circumscribed space they could control, they were also shaped in very concrete ways by their reproductive functions. The fact of giving birth every two years made a claim on women's time and energy that left little for projects like literacy. In a group of 37 women interviewed, 22 had had at least one year of their studies interrupted because of pregnancy and/or maternity leave and/or illnesses of toddlers. Comments like these were commonplace. "I didn't get to do the exam. I lost a lot of classes. The baby was sick." "Last year I couldn't cope with literacy because of the baby." "I was pregnant last year -- but this year I'm going to study."

The "First Discussion Document" took up this theme, suggesting that if women were going to be encouraged to have children and at the same time study, then clearly literacy for women workers would take at least twice as long as men. This theme was not picked up in any of the discussions, except to suggest more information on birth control. Indeed many of the interviews included discussion on methods of contraception emerging out of women's descriptions of their own families or of years of study lost because of child-rearing.

The structural constraints related to reproduction did not have to do only with childbirth and child-rearing. Full responsibility for the domestic sphere rested with the women. A double shift was the daily lot for almost all of them, alleviated only partially by the extended family system and the CIM daycare centre. The great strides of the Frelimo Party and the OMM in encouraging women into the public sphere and into the work force had not been matched by any initiatives to examine the work processes in the reproductive sphere. Women continued with the full weight of responsibility for reproduction of the labour force, including both child-rearing and all household tasks.

Celeste Mujovo, a young woman of 29 who was a cleaner in the Accounting Department, spoke of her double shift beginning before sunrise. The CIM bus picked her up at six in the morning. Before that she was up cooking, fetching water and washing clothes for her five children aged eleven, six, five, three and two. She worked until five and then returned home for a round of evening duties. This was typical.

Many like Amélia Cossa, the OMM activist in the Sacks Warehouse who had recently completed fourth class, found themselves experiencing a strange mixture of liberation along with constraints and classic forms of subjugation.

> I'd like to enrol in fifth class. My problem is the time-table. I arrive back too late from classes to clean the house and feed the children.

> Women are always squeezed. They are always in the middle – always ordered about. When you get home, you have to do this and you can't do that. A woman is someone always ordered about. In colonial days, women did not have an active voice. They didn't have the right to speak in meetings, to discuss things at home. They were always waiting for someone to give them orders.
>
> At CIM women now have voices. Now there's a head for the women. Women can be found in the various offices. Senhora Elsa is one of the directors. Senhora Leonor is a clerk in the Shops offices. There's a woman technician in the Electricity Department.
>
> In 1981, there were two women who taught. One was very patient; the other wasn't. Men have more patience. When a sector is headed by a woman, it runs better.
>
> (Interview with Amélia Cossa, February 13, 1986)

Women, then, came to the process of literacy bringing with them an experience of daily interactions, practices and choices shaped by their ability to speak, read and write. Their experience was different from that of the men. Women brought a subjectivity shaped by a colonial and patriarchal legacy that circumscribed their sense of possible ways of being and doing. This had been challenged in important ways by new forms introduced with independence, but at other points it was firmly intact. For many women, silencing and the discovery of voices were experienced most sharply in terms of gender.

"For Blacks, It's Different"

Within the mosaic of power relations in which the literacy students were integrated, literacy was also differentially experienced according to race and class. The occasions when direct reference to race were made were few. The one very explicit occasion that came up was so stark and powerful, however, that it reinforced my sense that being black was an explanatory tool for many different levels of experience. The incident came up in the class assembly. In an effort to encourage people about speaking Portuguese, I mistakenly likened my experiences in learning Portuguese as a second language with theirs. This happened at the end of the research project, with a climate of trust already firmly established. It was the ever alert Celeste who named the major difference between our experiences.

> Senhora Cristina: Speaking Portuguese is a big problem for most of us.
>
> Senhora Judith: But the best way to learn is to speak. It's all practice. Portuguese is not my mother tongue either. When I speak, I make lots of

> mistakes. Even now after many years. But I speak -- and you understand me. We communicate -- and that's what a language is for.
>
> Senhora Celeste; But it's not the same thing for us. Senhora Judith can talk and make mistakes and nobody treats it as a joke. It's because you're white. When I speak and make mistakes, those who hear are amused. It's because I'm not white. For blacks, it's different.
>
> (Field Notes, April 10, 1986)

I was left pondering. How many occasions in the day to day lives of the black workers were interpreted with those words -- "For blacks, it's different"? How many events in my own day to day life were actually shaped for me because of the power I enjoyed being white, a power attributed to me and enjoyed by me, just because of the colour of my skin. How often did I assume that "that's how it is," "that's how it works" -- when actually it "is" and "worked" that way only for me as white and was totally different as an experience for blacks?

All of the black workers at CIM had grown up in the colonial era with its powerful regulation of race and ethnicity through the establishment of assimilated status and indigenous status, as we have seen above. They had been shaped as subjects to see and sense themselves in particular ways and not to see and sense themselves in other ways.

If the social and political content of the national liberation struggle had radically challenged the position of women, it had been even more thorough in its challenge to subordination by race. With the establishment of the FRELIMO government in power, black Mozambicans had assumed positions of power and begun to participate at all levels in the management of their economy and society. At the same time, Mozambicans of Portuguese origin and Asian origin were urged to stay. Some of the top FRELIMO leaders were white. From the Council of Ministers to the local football club or block committee, Mozambicans of all racial and ethnic origins were to be found together.

The work on racism had tended to stop after independence, with the significant achievements on racism leading up to independence being captured in the capsule formula of now being a "non-racial" society. The heightened public awareness at independence of education and skill as having to do less with natural capacity than with historical opportunity dwindled. The politics of a "non-racial" society seemingly precluded public naming of the historic advantages enjoyed by non-black Mozambicans which were such a significant factor in their present day roles. Nor did the commitment to constructing a "non-racial" society seem to allow any kind of affirmative action programme for black Mozambicans as new stresses on professional qualifications emerged.

Race as a public explanatory category and as an area needing constant political work receded, while at the same time many people confided privately the view that racism was growing.

At CIM, as we have seen, the colonial era was one of white managers in privileged positions, enjoying the perks of office, from command of all sections of the huge complex to their own bar and dining room. Black workers were given few opportunities to become skilled workers, no role in management and a warehouse with poor food for their meals. Even those who had learned on the job and had a thorough knowledge of the workings of their own sections were not recognized. In effect, these workers kept the factory running but without any formal acknowledgment of their roles. Officially they were invisible.

When the colonial glue came unstuck, all of this changed radically almost overnight. Black workers had long had the knowledge of how to run factories but no power. With the flight of the Portuguese, they suddenly found themselves in positions as department heads, or heads of entire production areas. A huge space opened and black Mozambicans were drawn into discursive practices, particularly around factory management, from which they had been totally excluded.

A decade later, the interface between class and race was more difficult to decipher. CIM, as all other Mozambican factories, reflected the racial composition of Mozambican society, with blacks, whites, Asians and Mozambicans of mixed origin. At one level, this was taken as just another example of how a non-racial society can work. But CIM also reflected the tendencies throughout Mozambique to move from the radical egalitarianism of the first years of independence to more formalized power structures. So along with the pyramidal structure of factory management, each of the multiple institutions in the factory had its hierarchy duly recognized. This included the Frelimo Party itself, and the mass organizations for workers, women and youth. Each of them had vertical structures firmly in place.

The general inexperience and habits of passivity coming out of centuries without any kind of democratic practice on the agenda made it hard for these structures to work. The Frelimo Party Secretary, Fenias Matsinhe, reported to the 5th Anniversary celebrations on the growth of the Party at CIM, not only in numerical terms but in capability to give leadership. He spoke of moving from a situation in 1980 where 75 percent of the party members were illiterate to a situation today where only 18 of the 104 members had less than fourth class. He also spoke with pride of the fact that each member of the Party had a specific task within the ten working groups of the Party Cell. These included working groups for the wall newspaper outside the dining hall, for political study, for production questions and for adult education, etc.

Certainly the working group for adult education was not working. The ever-irreverent Atália had already commented on my meetings with its head, Leonor, saying, "What would she know? She's never put her foot in the classroom!" Indeed, as we have seen above, when pressed to act as a Party cadre in giving the workers an opportunity to reflect on literacy in a class assembly, Leonor had deferred to the school director. One wondered how many other Party structures were just there on paper with no actual meetings, work programmes, capacity to solve problems. And indeed, being there "only on paper" was relevant to the workings of the power relations in the factory, since having the titles and perks of office meant a formalization of yet another structure of power that left the ordinary worker outside, without access and without a voice.

The hierarchies of power and the role of the party as an instrument to give voice to workers were seemingly entirely unproblematic for the Party head at CIM. Even his comments about recruitment to the Party were solidly entrenched in a vertical ordering of the factory.

> In the area of mobilization, hard work was done to select the best workers (most dedicated, disciplined and exemplary) to become candidates for Party membership. Since 1980, more than 40 comrades have come into the Party Cell, including: Directors, Engineers, Technicians, Skilled Workers and youth with high school certificates, guaranteeing a continuity of party work in the enterprise.
>
> (CIM 1985b:4)

Some workers voiced cynical comments about opportunism amongst those in middle and upper management who were prepared to admit privately they did not care about socialism or the Frelimo Party but were going to become members because that was the way to guarantee promotions.

Not surprisingly the hierarchies of power at CIM also reproduced in some important ways the racial hierarchies of the colonial era. Given that acquisitions of skill and expertise are intimately connected to the interface of race and class, one had at CIM a management structure filled with those who had had most access to schooling in the past. A disproportionate number of them were both male and white. The general director was a white Mozambican who had had opportunity to attend university abroad. The three directors immediately under him included a black male industrial director, a white female chemical director and a male director of economy and human resources of Indian origin. All three were recent graduates of technical institutes. At the next echelon of power, there were four Mozambicans who were white or of mixed racial origin in a group of about twelve.

The placement of three directors who had graduated recently from technical institutes, along with other technical graduates in key sectors like the Mill and the Pasta Factory, was part of the larger strategy of state intervention in CIM. Few were the industries with such a concentration of human resources. A strong management team had been created along with a set of working conditions and social benefits for the workers that had made CIM into a model of efficiency, productivity and sound management. The workers recognized this -- and there were many comments acknowledging that the CIM directors had the workers' interests at heart. Yet in many ways CIM workers seem to have been as much silenced by the paternalistic benevolence of the new order as they had been by the crude abuses of power of the old.

One of the most moving depictions of workers struggling with fear and silence in the face of hierarchies of benevolent management was given by Alexandre Mondlane, a worker in the Finished Products Warehouse. Mondlane had worked at CIM since independence, entering when he was only 17. He was from Manjacaze district and had come to Maputo as a youth, learning Portuguese by working as a domestic. He had worked in shifts for many years in the Mill, filling and sewing up sacks of flour. When he was transferred to the Finished Products Warehouse in 1984, he began to study. He passed first year in 1984, and after two tries, passed second year in 1986.

> Those of us who grew up under colonialism had a bad time. We lost our mothers and our fathers; we had to look after the cattle. We had no time to go to school.
>
> When you get into an enterprise with good conditions, you have to take advantage. We're here working at CIM but not all our section heads create conditions for us to study. Some say no. "When you go we're left short-handed. You can't go." There are others who force you to go -- and later you see that it was a good thing.
>
> When you begin to study, it's hard. You don't have any idea of the reason why. Later you begin to see and you're glad you were forced to go. It's good. If you go to another company, you can manage.
>
> Look at me. I know Manjacaze and Maputo only. I'd like to go to Boane and Namaacha. My heart wants to go there. I'd like to go to see how they live, what they plant. But I'm afraid to go. How can I ask for directions, get information? With Portuguese, I'll be able to ask, to read the signs. Many trips we'd like to make are difficult because we can't read and write. Even conversations are sometimes difficult. We don't pronounce things well.
>
> We may want to say what we think but since colonialism taught us not to speak up, that's it. We are afraid to speak out. We might say something

> wrong -- and then everything would collapse on our heads. It was better to stay silent. That was our experience.
>
> When I worked as a domestic, it was the same thing. The lady taught me to speak Portuguese. She explained all the tasks of the house in Portuguese. She showed me how to cook, how to iron, how to water the garden, all in Portuguese, and I learned. She used to return home and ask if everything was alright. I always said yes. Something could have happened that day. For example, I could have had the bad luck to break a cup. But I would never tell her -- because you never knew how she was going to react. Days later, she would discover it. Sometimes she reacted calmly, explaining that I needed to take more care, especially when the dishes were soapy. Other times she blew up. You never knew. That's why I kept silent.
>
> And it's the same thing here at CIM. You never know how the head is going to react. Sometimes there is something that happens in the sector and I think of alerting the head to it. But I keep quiet. For me, it's a problem. How to have the courage to speak up to the people in management. The head who blows up just makes me shut up. I'm just afraid. The fear remains.
>
> When we workers are together, we're fine. Nobody is going to correct my error, say that's not how to pronounce it. When it's Portuguese, it's different. If I am having difficulties at work, I have to figure out how to say it all in Portuguese. It's very complicated. I know the directors here are interested, but it's really difficult to find the words in Portuguese.
>
> (Interview with Alexandre Mondlane, June 12, 1985)

The workings of race within and between these hierarchies, was clearly important in shaping subjectivities, and hence practices and choices. The colonial experience of arbitrary power in the hands of white madams and bosses seemed to be an active reference point for Mondlane, even ten years after independence. It seems reasonable to expect that a good deal of the colonial experience of regulation of social identity on racial lines was still operative, albeit not a matter for public discussion in a "non-racial society." One was left with the question of how the disproportionate number of white Mozambicans in management structures acted on the situation.

I assumed that my own whiteness as a researcher limited the possibilities for black informants to speak readily about their feelings with regard to race. Clearly the fact of my being a woman had created immediate expectations of a commonality of experiences from the CIM women. There were frequent comments like "Senhora Judith knows how it is, eh?" to preface commentaries and observations. Implicit was the assumption that we were both situated in some common space and experienced the world in some common ways by virtue of being women. I assumed that the fact of my not being black closed down spaces for sharing of common experiences of how the world got put together for people who were black.

Closure of communication for being white was not experienced with anything like the intensity of spaces opening up because of being female. Small incidents, however, made me intensely aware that there was a constant process of locating oneself organized through race. One was the conversation with a young worker whom I happened to come across on the CIM grounds wearing an ear-ring I had lost earlier in the week. I started to comment on it but even before the words were fully out of my mouth, I suddenly picked up from his face and those of his mates that I had stumbled onto familiar -- and dangerous -- ground.

The "white madam" was accusing the "black worker" of theft. It was a known situation, one in which they assumed total powerlessness -- and totally arbitrary power in my hands because of my whiteness. From their faces I felt they had slotted me as the "white madam" against whose claims there was no defence. I thought I read a mixture of anger and resentment, but also a profound resignation. "That's how it is." "That's how it works." "For blacks, it's different."

I rapidly backtracked, explaining that I knew it had dropped off somewhere in the factory and that it had only sentimental value. I proposed giving him another one in exchange -- and felt as if I had gone a little way towards deconstructing the stereotypes we had so suddenly played out.

I happened to be giving a ride to a black engineer from the Mill when we next met, me with ear-ring tucked in my purse. I felt as if the engineer thought me completely crazy to be dealing with trivia like ear-rings with unskilled workers. I knew I could not reconstruct for him in words the intensity of the reactions I had felt and the intensity of the "white madam/black thief" scenario I had suddenly created. We drove in silence, I preferring at that moment to be seen as foreign and eccentric.

It was a small enough interaction in itself. It made me realize again, however, how much being black, and situating oneself in terms of blackness or whiteness, was central to the sense-making repertoire for all of those working at CIM.

"Studying Means Staying in the Same Place"

The hopes, fears and desires linked to literacy were not only shaped by gender and race. They were also shaped by class. CIM workers, along with all Mozambican workers, had experienced a radical opening of space a decade earlier. The convulsions of this immediate pre- and post-independence period brought about dramatic shifts in the power relations in each workplace. During these heady years, workers had been invited to participate actively in workers assemblies and forms of direct participation in decision-making. In some factories, the mass exodus of the settlers resulted in periods of direct worker control. In others, the management cooperated fully with the new Dynamizing Group structures. Workers were drawn into rounds of meetings, rallies and voluntary work days. They had input into decision-making on all manner of policy questions formerly the prerogative of management, from technical innovations to annual plans and methods of discipline. (Sketchley 1985)

At CIM the continued presence of the old management after independence meant that the space for worker involvement was a highly contested space. The colonial management style had been anything but participatory. Women workers interviewed in 1980 recalled with horror their former working conditions.

> The heads of the sections were Portuguese. We were not free to get on with our work, but were constantly overseen and criticized. The Portuguese woman who oversaw the Biscuit Factory would regularly beat the workers on any pretext. If a biscuit dropped onto the floor, she would beat the offender. If she called one of the workers and the worker didn't get to her quickly enough, she would hit her.
>
> After 1969 the situation relaxed a little, maybe because of the war, one of the workers hypothesized. They felt they couldn't antagonize the Mozambicans too much.
>
> (Urdang 1980:14)

After independence, as we have seen above, a few CIM workers made breathtaking leaps from the shop floor into positions of management. On the other hand, the administration cooperated very little with the Dynamizing Group structure. The period from 1975-1980 was one of intensive struggles for power between the Administration, the Production Council, the Dynamizing Group, and, after 1977, the newly created Frelimo Party Cell.

The report of the Party Secretary, Fenias Matsinhe, on the occasion of the 5th Anniversary of state intervention in 1985 hints at the complex struggles that went on.

> The former administration of CIM did not welcome the establishment of the Party Cell. It did everything to delimit its functions. Relations with the Party Cell and the Production Council at the time were very negative. Divisions and complexes of superiority and inferiority reigned freely. There was a spirit of lack of confidence and paternalism. The administration did not participate in the meetings with either the political

> or the organizational structures. This was a way of blocking the participation of these structures, and by extension, the workers, in the life of the factory.
>
> These administrators feared the strength and the mobilization of the workers as well as their organizational forms. They showed a complete lack of interest in resolving the problems of the great majority of workers, limiting themselves to false promises and demagoguery. They also made clandestine promotions of some Mozambican workers.
>
> These administrators, however, found themselves at times with no escape from the spirited demands of the workers. They abandoned the enterprise, only to be replaced by other administrators with new ideas.... At this time some workers, tendentiously, organized themselves into a group called the Elders Group (Grupo de Madodas). They alleged that the party cell was not able to resolve the workers' problems. This group had as its sole objective a confrontation with the administration of the enterprise, forcing it to resolve the workers' problems, particularly the question of salaries.
>
> (CIM 1985b:3)

Veronica Sumbane, a worker in the Social Services Department, had become a strong FRELIMO activist after 1975. She spoke with journalist Stephanie Urdang about her experiences in 1979, a year after being elected secretary of the newly created Frelimo Party Cell at CIM.

> When the party secretary, Veronica Sumbane, talked about the problems, she gave voice to a sense of malaise. She spoke of the special difficulties that had emerged during the past year. Before, they used to have political education meetings, they read revolutionary magazines, and there were regular party meetings. "When I try to call a meeting the first question the workers ask is: 'Are you going to discuss what to do about the low salaries?' When I say no, they don't want to come."
>
> The commitment to political education petered out, and brigades of the district's political structures seldom visited the factory any more. "They only come to know the problems," she said, "they don't come to solve them." They would listen, assure the workers they'd be back to iron them out and then not return. Even the acceptance of a woman's leadership of the party cell was not necessarily a sign of progress, she said. "The men had no reaction," she explained. "People are not deeply involved in party work just now. They are apathetic."
>
> And OMM? Isn't there support for OMM among the women: No, Sumbane regretted. There was a secretary of OMM at the beginning, but she was appointed the Provincial Secretary for Maputo. The biggest complaint of the women is around the wages. They don't like the fact that they earn such a low wage and that it is less than the men. It really distresses them. So they keep asking OMM to look into it. Promises have been made. But they remained promises. "We are still asking and they are

> still studying. This is why the women don't support the OMM." She has troubles herself with the workers. Because she is the party leader they think she must be earning more than they. Sometimes on pay day they ask to see her receipt. "I show them. They can see than I earn the same as they do but there is still tension. The secretary of the Production Council had the same problem before he left for a training course in Cuba. He earned a little more -- 3,500 meticais per month -- because he worked the machines. They were sure he was earning 8,000!"
>
> (Urdang 1980:15,16)

These open struggles at CIM were tackled finally with the intervention by the state in 1980 and the establishment of a team of some of the best managerial, administrative and technical resources that Mozambique had at its disposal. The salary question was not resolved except for the women, but a great deal of attention was paid to developing a much broadened benefits package. These were just a component of a much larger effort to take hold of the, by then, failing enterprise and get it back into good working order.

By 1985/86, this new order was well established, far removed from the dramatic shifts in power relations a decade earlier. In this new order, the sense of mobility within the factory, the space for workers as workers to move into management positions or upgrade themselves in the workforce from drudgery and back-breaking labour to jobs as skilled workers or clerical workers had long since disappeared.

The new team of management, administrative and technical cadres was firmly in place at top and middle levels, with key sectors like the Mill and the Pasta Factory and the Administration headed jointly by veteran workers promoted in the early days and newly trained graduates of the Industrial and Commercial Institutes. There was a great deal of fluidity in personnel at middle levels, with many workers abandoning CIM for more lucrative positions in the private sector. Others, including technicians and skilled workers migrated (often illegally) to neighbouring Swaziland and South Africa. They went in quest of jobs that were more viable for their own and their family's survival amidst the ongoing war and economic crisis. At lower levels, many workers felt trapped and there were some real struggles for power for the positions available.

Alberto Sousa Moamba, a 40 year old worker in the Grounds Department, put forcefully the feeling echoed in less eloquent ways by other workers.

> I didn't study as a child. I took care of the cattle. The factory undervalues me but when I leave here, I could have some knowledge to take with me. I started out here carrying sacks. Then I was a driver's assistant. Later I trained for three months to be a fire fighter.

> I requested work in another sector to learn a trade. In this "village," your sector is almost your prison. You're not able to get out of it. I want to transfer – but they won't let me, because there's no substitute for me. I work alone.
>
> (Interview with Alberto Sousa Moamba
> 40 years Grounds Department firefighter)

Moamba had started working in CIM in 1973. He had studied a bit during a contract in South Africa and did literacy in the early years. In 1985, he successfully passed from fifth to sixth class and was enroled in sixth class when I met him. He had earned the same salary throughout this entire period.

I had not met him before and he treated the interview with unusual formality. When I asked as I usually did if he had any questions to put to me, he asked me to convey two inter-connected concerns to those "at the top." "People who come from outside with sixth class do well here at CIM and get more salary just because they come from outside." The other concern was a complaint. "I don't like the way they jump over people who do fifth and sixth grade in CIM. For example, in the Finished Products Warehouse. . . . "

Even some of the very young workers were resigned to staying in the same place and hence saw little value in studying. A 25 year old handler in the Finished Products Warehouse saw it this way.

> Aurélio [school director] called me in the other day asking me why I hadn't registered. He instructed me to enrol. But many of us have our doubts. At our age, what's more studying going to bring. We can go and study. But at my age, I'm not going to be moved from here again.
>
> (Interview with Afonso Chipente, March 3, 1986)

All knew that literacy was not a straightforward path to promotions and salary increases. And indeed factory management itself complained about this. The CIM management staff operated within a set of government wage policies that included a strict wage freeze. The ability to promote, to change categories recognizing more education and training, was blocked for management too.

The larger context of constraints notwithstanding, workers' experiences within the hierarchies of power in different sections of the factory varied tremendously. Some workers encountered support and encouragement to study while others were blocked. This led to much variation in how workers put together the question of schooling and work. Muchuchuane António Sambo, a labourer in the Mill, simply said, "There's a conflict between work and school. You can't win them all. You lose schooling but you keep your job." (Interview March 19, 1986)

For a select few, schooling meshed with expanding parameters in their jobs; for most it was a dead end or even actively blocked. The success story of CIM in terms of young workers on the rise was Francisco Cossa, a 29 year old mechanical welder. Cossa had come to Maputo from Bilene district in 1968 at the age of twelve. He had become a car mechanic's apprentice and later worked for the city bus company for a time. He dreamed of working on machines so started at CIM in 1975 as a machine operator in the Candy Factory. He did fourth class at CIM and asked for a transfer to work in the Shops. In 1984, he successfully completed both fifth class and a professional course in mechanical welding. By 1986, he was doing seventh class at the CIM night school and working to sort out the bugs in the new equipment just installed in the industrial bakery. He had many insightful comments to make about schooling for workers at CIM.

> There was a time when factories began to organize schools. It was a victory for us workers. At CIM, they organized all of this for us -- good teachers and good conditions.
>
> As an adult it's not easy. An adult has a lot of problems. You have to plan your life, to organize time to study and time to deal with your personal problems.
>
> Lots of people drop out because of age. They also think they know all about their sector. 'I already know my job -- it's not worth it to study more.'
>
> In colonial days, going beyond third grade meant entering the road to assimilation. Many of us stopped.
>
> I saw that I needed more -- language, things in math like percentages. I saw that being a student was worth it. Fourth class brought a lot of new things into my life. But what most excited me was the course in mechanical welding. It was a really complicated course. I really needed sixth class to do it -- but I passed. When you study, a lot of things open up to you. You feel like a new person. You're really free.
>
> You have to make the future -- and not think only of the present. My ambition is to be a technical engineer.
>
> (Interview with Francisco Cossa, February 9, 1986)

Few workers had the mix of personal drive and sectoral support that Cossa did. As we have seen above, some workers trying to improve their positions through schooling found that the way was blocked by workers who had been drawn into lower management positions as section heads. These workers perceived the rising education levels of their subordinates as direct threats to their own positions of power.

For the section heads too, the situation was extremely difficult. The war had disrupted their lives and put economic survival on the agenda in dramatic ways. Studying to hold at bay veteran workers who were making their way up the education ladder did not always fit in. Fernando Murrija, the 49 year old head of the wheat products loading section in the Finished Products Warehouse, had held this position since 1974. He was from Manhiça, a rich farming district two hours north of Maputo, now full of "bandit" activity. The family plot in Manhiça had always been a major source of food inputs for their city household and also extra income.

Murrija had passed fourth class in 1983, having failed on his first try in 1982. He enroled in fifth class, but later dropped out, claiming a family death as reason to interrupt his studies. Later in the conversation, he warmed up to the subject and spoke of the real reasons he had rejected schooling.

> My children can't survive on the salary I get. It's only raising animals that saves us. What's the use of my staying after hours to study when it's the pigs that guarantee my family's survival. I expect one of my sons to marry soon and I'll have to contribute to the marriage. With my salary, there's nothing to give.
>
> My wife is in Manhiça. I'm here alone. There is a lot of clothing available in Manhiça in return for cashews. But there's nobody there to harvest the cashews. The district is almost empty. Everybody has fled to the city.
>
> A lot of us began to raise animals when CIM sold its pig farm and offered pigs for sale at accessible prices. I get up at four. I have to fetch water, hay and food. I return at five in the afternoon to fetch water again.
>
> (Interview with Fernando Murrija, March 10, 1986)

Clearly, then, for contemporary CIM workers, there was little perception of a space for improving one's situation through education. The old expectations of schooling as a mechanism of upward mobility, providing the credential to get up and out of a situation -- rural drudgery, urban sweat shops -- no longer held.

For the great majority of workers, there were no uses for speaking, reading and writing skills in the workplace itself. One handler from the Finished Products Warehouse, where workers spent their days heaving 50 kilo sacks, made this wry comment: "The study needed for that sector is just brute strength!"

The organizational structures for worker participation in the factory which might have drawn on new skills and knowledge were at a low ebb. In the early days of independence, with Dynamizing Group activities at their height in both workplace and community, there had been a need for women and men to know how to speak up in meetings, how to analyze and debate. There had been a vision of schooling linked to work place and community issues, a place to gain skills that could transform work places into places of innovation and participation and control by workers themselves.

In some factories, the first planning process involved the workers fully and necessitated not only a capacity to speak but also to read and to deal with figures. The participatory democracy in practice at the base created the occasions to put new literacy skills to immediate use. In the era of my research, however, there was very little life at the base in terms of workers' participation and control. The worker involvement in planning and production strategies that had characterized the post-independence period was gone, with decision-making about planning and production once more firmly the prerogative of management

The Director General spoke frankly about his strategy in taking over the management of CIM in his report during the 5th Anniversary celebrations. He also referred to the minimal functioning of structures at the base.

> The main task that we confronted was to establish correct working relations with the Party Cells that existed then and the Production Councils. We needed these to allow us to define jointly the priority actions to be undertaken and how to mobilize the workers for them. . . .
>
> To ensure the authority of the new management in all sectors of work, it was imperative that middle management at the various levels take up roles as heads and learn how to transmit the directives of management to their subordinates. The practice of Management Collectives was the instrument used in this case although up to today it has been difficult for the lowest levels of the hierarchy to meet with the frequency desired.
>
> (CIM 1985a:3)

In fact, the collectives at the lowest level did not meet at all. The workers had very little voice in the day to day running of the factory. As we have seen above, many reverted to silence rather than risk what was still experienced as the arbitrary power of a head. The fact that the collectives within each sector had ceased to meet, and that workers' input was never invited by their section heads about work problems and work methods left this arbitrary power of the head intact.

There were few meetings with the workers, then, and those that did take place had little active worker input. Some workers felt that they simply "rubber stamped" decisions already taken at "the top." One worker spoke somewhat cynically about the populist style of the directors, even suggesting that it wasn't by chance that when they wanted worker agreement on a tough decision, they called on the popular industrial director, who was black, and had him conduct the meeting in Changana. This was seen as a strategy saved for decisions about which management expected some worker resistance, like the one to change the shifts from eight to twelve hours.

All meetings or activities or allocations of benefits further consolidated the existing hierarchies of power. Rank in the hierarchies was reproduced daily in the factory routines around everything from modes of transport to get to work to the number of loaves of bread carried home. It was a system operated openly, and senior staff quite publicly carried home the additional perks that they were allowed such as gas for their stoves, and a monthly quota of beer, both in short supply throughout the city.

Everything allocated through the factory was duly noted as part of the complex power interplay. While I was at CIM, word came that there would be clothing available for purchase by workers in a number of key sectors. This type of distribution of scarce goods through workplace structures was one of the mechanisms for contending with the black market. The CIM workers were included in the distribution and were duly transported to the store where the clothing was on sale.

The workers were informed that they would be divided into three categories. The first category was comprised of directors and senior management, including senior official in the party and the workers', women's and youth organizations. The second category was that of full-time workers with no disciplinary actions against them. The third category was casual workers and full-time workers with some kind of disciplinary action on their record. Each category had the right to buy different items, the number and quality of items diminishing from category one to category three.

Once word got out, an angry rumour started around CIM that the CIM management itself had devised these categories and that the higher ups at CIM got extra pants rightfully belonging to the workers. In fact, the directive to divide into categories had not originated at CIM. These kinds of distribution in which the top of the hierarchy got the best and the most were quite widespread by this time. In part, they served as mechanisms to hold on to senior managers and technicians who were looking at other possibilities on the job market. Foreign companies and agencies paying in dollars were very attractive since the market for purchases in local currency was almost non-existent.

Whatever the reasons, distributions like this were a long way from the radical egalitarianism of the early days when such allocations were worked out on the basis of need. This obviously fed into a latent resentment amongst the workers. A few workers were openly critical.

> There is a practice of always privileging more those who are already privileged. Everything there is goes first to the senior echelons and then to the base. Notions of working towards equality or guaranteeing

> resources first for those who most need them doesn't enter the game. It's simply, first to the structures, from the directors to the heads -- and only at the last to the simple workers. There's a group -- in the management, and in the political structures of the Party, OTM and OMM -- that's already quite comfortable in its position. The people in it aren't very active these days. There is virtually no activity at the base.
>
> (Interview with Mário Chissano, January 16, 1986)

The structures organized specifically to give workers an effective political instrument did little to alleviate the problem. The newly created workers' organization, OTM, was meant to give the workers a means for voicing their concerns and demands, but rapidly established both work methods and an integration with management and party that simply added another structure to the already top heavy, top down power relations of the factory.

The replies of the workers in the interviews to questions about membership in the Party and mass organizations and what that entailed pointed clearly to the problems. The OTM was clearly not experienced as a voice for workers' concerns.

> Yes I'm a member but I still haven't caught on to what it means.
>
> (Interview with Augusto Maibasse, March 6, 1986)

> Yes, but I still haven't received the card.
>
> (Interview with Francisco Cuco, March 10, 1986)

> Yes, I handed in the money and photo.
>
> (Interview with Jaime Vilanculos, February 24, 1986)

A few workers had the idea that OTM existed to defend the workers but they were not very clear how.

> I don't know what it is. In fact I asked what the trade union was. They said they'd have to explain. For someone here, the OTM defends that person when something happens. For someone not in the trade union, it's straight to the street.
>
> (Interview with Alexandre Jossias, March 4, 1986)

> I don't really know how to respond. They said to us that we had to become members. Afterwards, we accepted. We are always paying dues month after month -- and we have cards. For those who aren't members, if they have problems, there is nothing to resolve their problems. If there is a shortage of work, the trade union has to fight to guarantee employ-

> ment. Even here, whoever is not a member of the trade union can only resolve problems directly with the management.
>
> (Interview with Aurélio Malhusse, March 2, 1986)

The introduction of the OTM, then, as the workers' organization, did nothing to alleviate the situation of workers' dwindling participation at the base. Its most tangible impact on workers' lives seemed to be its bureaucratic form -- photos, membership cards and dues. There was certainly little sense of a new space for workers to channel their problems and concerns about their work situation or social life. It had no autonomy as an organization to actually represent workers' demands and carry out collective bargaining.

Hopes, Fears and Hierarchies of Power

Ordinary workers at CIM, then, brought hopes and fears to literacy shaped by their daily experiences of subordination to multiple hierarchies within CIM. The expectations of what literacy could do for their lives were influenced by the spaces opened up by literacy. The experiences of work mates who increased their skills and got school certificates, and the degree to which this increased schooling altered their positions in the relations of power within CIM was an important basis for establishing expectations of literacy. The closing down again of the discursive practices around worker control of production and social conditions that had begun to open up after independence also narrowed the expectations of what literacy could bring.

As we have seen, then, the expectations brought to the literacy classroom were based on gendered, raced and classed experiences of the power of literacy, in the home, community and workplace. Not knowing how to speak, read, write and count shaped interactions, practices and choices as workers within the hierarchies of power both at work and in the community.

The experience of literacy at CIM thus takes on an importance beyond the confines of one factory. Just as the "school" was embedded in the interlocking hierarchies of power and knowledge of the larger CIM complex, so CIM itself was embedded in a broader political project of socialist construction in Mozambique. The lives of the CIM workers and their experiences of literacy cannot be understood without seeing how CIM was shaped by, and shaped, the rough and uneven process of socialist construction during this period.

Measured in terms of making education accessible to workers, CIM's activities in literacy over the years were an important accomplishment. Posed in the broader context of creating rather than transmitting knowledge, of encouraging working people to develop a capacity to locate themselves in their times and space/places and legitimate their activities and inter-relatedness, the experience is fraught with contradictions. It points us to some of the most vexing problems of socialist construction.

Notes

1. For interesting discussions of the tensions between democracy and centralism during this period, see Saul(ed.) 1985, Egero 1987, Johnston 1989, Marshall 1991.

2. Urdang is a journalist who has written extensively on the role of women in the liberation struggles and in post-independence societies in Africa. She is author of *Fighting Two Colonialisms: Women in Guinea-Bissau* (New York: Monthly Review Press, 1979), The Last Transition? Women and Development in John Saul (ed.). *A Difficult Road: The Transition to Socialism in Mozambique* (New York: Monthly Review Press, 1985), and *And Still They Dance* (New York: Monthly Review Press, 1988).

9

Literacy and the Practice of Democracy

Empowerment literally means to give ability to, to permit or enable. When we hear the word empowerment used in education, it is usually being employed in the spirit of critique. Its referent is the identification of oppressive and unjust relations within which there is an unwarranted limitation placed on human action, feeling, and thought. Such limitations are seen as constraining a person from the opportunity to participate on equal terms with other members of a group or community to whom have accrued the socially defined status of "the privileged"/"the competent." To empower in this perspective is to counter the power of some people or groups to make others "mute." To empower is to enable those who have been silenced to speak. It is to enable the self-affirming expression of experiences mediated by one's history, language, and traditions. It is to enable those who have been marginalized economically and culturally to claim in both respects a status as full participating members of a community.

(Simon 1987:374)

In the first phase, we received . . . directives vertically, how we had to do this or that. We were simply executors of programmes from the top. . . . In this second phase, we have improved a lot. . . . We are able to carry out a community study. Now we know how to do a training programme. . . Difficult as it may be, we're the ones who are doing it. Pedagogically, we are the ones responsible for it. We're autonomous. It's us -- both for the successes and the failures.

(Interview with Domingos Chigarire
Staff Trainer, Manga Pilot Project, August 1987)

> It is now a moment of transformation. We [the OTM] emerged as part of the party. Now we have to speak with our own voice.
> (Interview with Alberto Sebastiao, August 1990)

> Some people, arguing as ever that we are illiterate, incapable, ignorant and above all, almost all women, sum it up by saying that we don't know how to manage our property, our land. They say that with the PRE, [structural adjustment programme] what is important is private initiative.
> (Celina Cossa, Maputo Cooperative Leader, March 1990)

The experience of literacy in Mozambique over the years has been characterized by strikingly different moments. Within and between these moments, however, is a common thread. There has been a recurrent tension between moments of popular control in which ordinary people have played central roles in defining their own educational project over against moments when educators, administrators, planners and other "experts" have assumed as theirs the prerogative of definition and provision of education.

The struggles over literacy have been embedded in much broader struggles over competing visions of the social order. One is a vision of participatory democracy, a social order promoting local expressions of "people's power." Here ordinary citizens exercise their roles as stakeholders in shaping and controlling public policy through a vital "civil society." This civil society is made up of a multiplicity of local organizations representing sectoral and regional interests, interacting autonomously with both state and political parties.

Another is a vision of a society of "experts" and consenting masses. Here power and knowledge rest with a minority who claim their position in managing society and controlling information on behalf of others by their superior merit. In a participatory democracy, the objective of literacy is to learn to govern -- from below. In a society of experts, the objective of literacy is to learn to be governed -- from above.

Building Socialism Within a Capitalist Ethos

The tension between literacy for empowerment and literacy for social regulation are a reflection, then, of the broader tensions within FRELIMO's project of socialist transformation. In Mozambique, as in any other country embarking on a project of socialist reconstruction, the path proved to be both jagged and uneven, marked by advances and retreats and holds. This was so for many reasons. An important and not always recognized one was that Mozambique, like any other country setting out on a socialist path, did not start from some sort of "tabula rasa." It was located in the real historical world, in a real geo-political time and space which both created possibilities and dictated constraints.

Samora Machel, first president of Mozambique, acknowledged on various occasions that Portugal's intransigence in trying to maintain its colonies was an important factor in creating possibilities for the liberation movement to radicalize. Without the resistance to decolonization from Portugal, it would have been impossible to move beyond a simple national liberation struggle to a struggle for social transformation. The geo-political time and space also imposed serious constraints. One was the extreme state of underdevelopment inherited at independence. Another was Mozambique's firm and long-standing integration into the regional economy of southern Africa, with its social organization of racial capitalism and its domination by the powerful apartheid state of South Africa. Integration into such a regional economy clearly meant that Mozambique's efforts to redirect its resources for the benefit of its own people and to challenge the use of racial categories in the organization of production brought an immediate counter-attack.

For Mozambique, this meant a project of constructing socialism under siege. In retrospect, the concerted and expanding actions to prevent Mozambique from advancing on its socialist option seem abundantly clear. These were first organized from Rhodesia and took the form of sporadic terrorist attacks along the border starting in 1976. In 1980, with the creation of an independent Zimbabwe, action against Mozambique was organized from South Africa. The systematic campaign of low intensity warfare only faintly discernible in the first two years after independence was already obvious by mid-1977. Mozambique alerted international forums such as the United Nations and the Non-aligned Movement, to the heightening regional tensions. Internally, a booklet entitled *How the Enemy Acts. A Political Analysis of the Socio-economic Situation of the Country* was widely circulated.

> We are witnessing the operationalization of a vast plan which corresponds to the current tactics of imperialism against popular governments. . . It is a combination of aggression, subversion, economic sabotage and general destabilization. Its aim is to affect the living conditions of the masses, create shortages, and in general to build discontentment on a broad scale.
> (Frelimo Party 1977; my translation)

Over the next few years these pressures increased greatly, although their origins remained somewhat blurred. The slowness in establishing a clear definition and characterization of the source of the destabilization had several explanations. In part the explanation lay in Mozambique's complicated multiple dependencies, historically subordinated not only to

Portugal but also to Britain and the powerful white settler regimes in South Africa and Rhodesia. Another dimension was the desire of the still fledgling FRELIMO government not to provoke South Africa unnecessarily by signalling its role, particularly over against South Africa's strong denials of complicity. Not for Mozambique the clarity of U.S.-Nicaragua relations, with U.S. President Reagan as a self-avowed "contra." In fact, the systematic actions pitted against Mozambique under South Africa's "Total Strategy" adopted in 1980 closely resembled the low intensity warfare being carried out against Nicaragua.

> LIW [low intensity warfare] seeks first to crack the logic of the revolution, deciphering its internal cohesion and understanding the tactics it employs to advance its interests, and then to devise a strategy that will warp this logic, undoing its internal cohesion and rendering its tactics ineffective -- in short turning the revolution against itself. LIW is extremely flexible; its tactics are made to suit the conditions of each conflict. . . . The war against Nicaragua is thus aimed at delegitimizing, isolating, and suffocating the Revolution to the point where it is no longer considered a viable political alternative in the eyes of the population. At the same time, an attempt is made to legitimate and stabilize the counterrevolutionary alternative to revolution.
>
> (Robinson and Norsworthy 1985:15,16)

Mozambique was forced increasingly, then, onto the defensive. It had to contend on a daily basis with a combination of outright attacks from South African Defence Forces, widespread terrorist actions in every province from South Africa's surrogate force, RENAMO, economic sabotage and destabilization and a disinformation campaign designed to frame the issue both in the region and internationally as an east-west conflict, and to denigrate Mozambique's option for socialism.

The construction of socialism under siege, however, was not the only reason for a jagged and uneven path. A post-revolutionary social formation may be one where capitalist forces have been deprived of their monopoly over the means of production and labour power has ceased to be purely a commodity. In addition, however, to the significant sectors where production in capitalist forms remained intact, there is also a continuation of the capitalist ethos throughout the society. Capitalism, after all, is never just a mode of production. It is a mode of "life."

There were extensive productive, moral, cultural and habitual bases of power of the former ruling classes in Mozambique that remained to be transformed. Neither the forces of production (narrowly conceived) nor the purely legal forms of property control could be separated from the richly variegated texture of political, cultural and other social relations which made that capitalist production possible. And this texture was the more complex still to transform in a situation like that of Mozambique where the consolidation of capitalist forms had been only partial.

The struggle between capitalism and socialism was not assured by the simple fact of taking power, however much FRELIMO's victory after ten years of armed struggle against Portuguese colonialism seemed to indicate that it might be. Transition is always a two-way street and a regression to some variant of capitalist forms is always as real a possibility as consolidation along a socialist path.[1]

The pervasiveness of the capitalist/colonialist culture was a key impediment in Mozambique's efforts to consolidate its revolutionary process. This culture was diametrically opposed to "people's power" and worked to distance people from initiatives for popular control. The social relations of productive forces specific to capitalism permeated the categories of thought, sense of human capacity and repertoire of social forms in Mozambique. It was this ethos of capitalism that needed to be deconstructed by all, including the leaders!

When FRELIMO took power initially there was a strong sense of the distinctiveness of institutions of "people's power" over against those of capitalism. There was widespread recognition that intrinsic to capitalism was a deep distrust of popular initiatives and energies and hence a fetish about the need for "experts," for doctors, architects, lawyers -- and also teachers.

It was this reality that prompted Samora Machel to speak on independence day of inheriting a colonial state whose apparatus was "in its nature, composition and methods, a profoundly retrograde and reactionary structure which has to be completely revolutionized in order to be put at the service of the masses." (Machel 1975) An interview given a year later included reflections on this process of establishing "people's power." A central question was the difficulty of finding "expertise" and "technical competence" which was not coupled with the profound distrust of popular solutions so central to the capitalist ethos.

> There are manoeuvres of the local bourgeoisie which have already failed. Thus, some of that group had thought that after the takeover of power, and after a period of time had elapsed, FRELIMO would have a great need for qualified personnel and that it would be among the "evolues" [those that had "evolved"] that we would be obliged to look for such personnel. They thought in this way to lay hold of the state apparatus and to block or distort our projects.
>
> But we haven't such an overwhelming need for technicians and administrative personnel (of which the bourgeoisie has many more than FRELIMO). We aren't afraid, in the first phase, of making the state a little less efficient, in order that it can safeguard its popular inspiration and its popular character. This is always preferable to having a state which is

> efficient in theory but entirely in the hands of the petty bourgeoisie because in the latter case we would find ourselves completely dependent upon our class enemy. How many African countries have experienced this phenomenon and thus fallen into the hands of privileged classes!
>
> We will destroy all the structures and tendencies which are characteristic of the capitalist system. It's the people who must take over everything since the only ones "qualified" in our country are the people, the people who have struggled for liberation.
>
> (Machel 1976)

The new forms of people's power established in the liberated territories and the "qualified" personnel tempered in the armed struggle encountered a hostile climate, once they reached Maputo. After an initial euphoric phase characterized by endless meetings and critical debates about all inherited forms and discourses, the weight of old claims for ways of doing and being began to reappear. "Authoritative" voices with fixed notions of technical expertise, international "standards" and legal correctness began to reassert themselves. The problems in the day to day running of a country of more than ten million were on a scale and complexity very different from the problems of running a liberation war and building up rudimentary socio-economic structures within a war economy. Sceptics, both inside and outside, were judging the bush rebels' capacity to govern by their maintenance of the very institutions they were most keen to dismantle and replace.

Within a year of independence, senior FRELIMO leaders were giving more sober assessments of the weight of inherited structures. Oscar Monteiro's speech to open the First National Conference on the State Apparatus in 1976 attests to this.

> In his message to the nation at the swearing in of the Transitional Government, Comrade President Samora defined it as the first government which represented the mass of the people, and as the executive arm of FRELIMO, he attributed the following tasks to it: to decolonize structures and mentalities; to extend people's democratic power to the whole country; to function in close liaison with the workers. We can see now that instead of communicating our experience to the entire country, instead of impressing upon the state apparatus throughout Mozambique the popular and revolutionary character that it had assumed in the liberated areas, we were swamped by the administrative machinery left behind by colonialism. Instead of giving direction, we were controlled and directed.
>
> (Quoted in Saul (ed.) 1985:86)

"Victory" included dealing with a lot of inherited state forms -- agencies, institutions, practices and discourses -- that had regulated the day to day running of society under colonialism. Finding new forms and "qualified" personnel from the armed struggle to tackle them was not easy, particularly from a population that was 90 percent illiterate. People of confidence from the era of the armed struggle often proved very vulnerable. The political expertise they had gained from the liberated zones was often ineffective in countering claims of organizational and technical competence from those they were now called on to direct and supervise.

> Today . . . the necessity to fill posts and positions in the new state apparatus and in the firms make the urban middle class the principal source of capable personnel. Particularly in the city it functions as the link between the vanguard and the base. . . . Not only do large numbers of bureaucrats of the old regime remain in place, but also new officials have been admitted to fill space . . . not according to political-ideological training but principally because of their know-how, certainly learnt in colonial times.
>
> (Correia and Homem 1977:177,205)

Four years later, in 1980, President Samora Machel in an address to the Council of Ministers returned to reflect on these same problems.

> The state apparatus is the principal site of a bureaucratic petty-bourgeoisie created by colonial-capitalism during its last years of existence, which today is the principal depository of its values, conceptions, habits, methods of work, of its ideology and therefore its practice. This same state apparatus is the fundamental instrument for the application of the Party political line in all social domains; it is, thus, the central instrument for the construction of socialism in our country.
>
> (Council of Ministers 1980)

Party and state, then, had become inextricably intermingled, and those dominating the state apparatus had no trust in popular solutions.

The old ways of seeing the world, the cultural ethos of capitalism, did not, then, disappear overnight. In the years after independence, there was a persistent tendency in Mozambique for new groups of "civilizers" to emerge, based within the state apparatus, and claiming expertise for programmes of national development. Many proved as incapable as their colonial predecessors in tapping the real energies and resources of the popular sectors. Ultimately their paternalistic stance and propensity to "make the revolution" for others proved as deadening to popular energies and initiatives as the heavy hand of colonialism ever was.

This kind of tension between a society managed by top-down directives from "experts" and a society based on establishing institutions of "people's power" and popular democracy is fundamental to the question of socialist construction. It therefore becomes instructive to trace these tensions over the years in Mozambique between a political discourse on literacy with the illiterate viewed as important human resources (with work methods based on participation and empowerment) over against a bureaucratic discourse on literacy with illiterates viewed as administrative categories (with work methods based on top-down orders and administrative fiat).

Literacy -- Learning to Govern or Learning to Be Governed

Certainly in the period immediately before and after independence literacy was a profoundly political and cultural question. A dramatic new space was opened up by the coup in Portugal. Women and men throughout Mozambique suddenly assumed responsibility for their own lives, in their communities and in their workplaces. This extended from neighbourhood security and street-cleaning to projects of self-education. The broad literacy movement that emerged was a vital component of this process.

It was a moment of strong community control, within a process of empowerment, building on the post-coup release of energies of very ordinary people. Women and men throughout Mozambique were "given their heads" after centuries of colonial humiliation. A space opened in which people's collective skills and energies could be channelled into assuming responsibility for their own social life, taking initiatives to create their own day to day development. The richness, diversity and high energy of the broad, spontaneous, learner-centred literacy movement around 1975 contrasts sharply with later experiences of literacy.

The decision to mount mass, state-sponsored literacy campaigns was understood as a mechanism for giving more support to literacy initiatives. Many provincial delegations in their reports to the Ribáuè Seminar just prior to independence in 1975 put in strong pleas for support from the Ministry of Education and Culture soon to be established, particularly in terms of funding, training and teaching materials. What is not clear is whether there was debate about how the state should provide this support. Was there questioning about whether it was appropriate to house literacy within the Ministry of Education and Culture rather than in party structures or in an autonomous literacy commission? Were there any voices pushing for strengthening non-government initiatives as well?

In all probability the dangers of formalization and bureaucratization of literacy were not immediately evident. In 1976 and 1977, there was a vision of a transformed formal schooling system which would link school with community and study with production, making the school itself an active centre of face to face democracy and a dynamic force for development initiatives throughout rural districts and urban neighbourhoods. Thus the possibility of literacy's having a tendency to become bureaucratized by becoming part of state-sponsored educational services did not loom as a danger.

The new FRELIMO government accepted the challenge of literacy but did so in a way that funnelled the diversity of the community-controlled literacy movement into a single government-sponsored programme. There were institutions of an embryonic civil society which had strengthened their own organizational capacity and popular base through involvement in literacy in the immediate pre- and post-independence period. These included churches, student groups, nationalist associations, cultural groups, women's groups and community groups. By 1977, however, literacy action by these groups was essentially on hold, waiting for the new government literacy programmes to emerge.

There is little documentation to reconstruct the kinds of policy debates around the establishment of a national literacy service, either from FRELIMO or from other institutions participating in literacy at the time. Some clues about the thinking in FRELIMO circles may be gleaned from a document reflecting on the seminar on literacy which had taken place in April 1974 at the FRELIMO Secondary School in Bagamoyo, Tanzania, just as news of the coup emerged. Valentina Peixoto's report on this seminar (Peixoto n.d.) indicates far-ranging discussions about the problems being confronted in literacy teaching in the liberated areas. Difficulties in getting beyond rote drilling of ABCs and tensions between literacy methods and second language methods were central points of debate. Adaptation of the methodological approach of Paulo Freire was discussed as a possible solution. The reasons for its rejection are revealing. The first was the problem of second language teaching and how to conduct generative discussions in a second language. Secondly there was a perceived tension between the need for generative themes to serve the general purposes of the nation and the Freirean approach which derived generative themes from local issues of immediate relevance to particular groups of learners. The third reason to reject the Freirean approach was perhaps most telling of all and had to do with power. "Another fundamental problem for the organization of programmes of this type [Freirean] is the problem of the *control of power*, which, as it is so obvious, we will not discuss here." (Peixoto n.d.:19) Emphasis in the original). The assumptions being made about the vital role of language and literacy in state formation, governance and social control could hardly be more clearly stated.

The option of a single campaign to eradicate illiteracy was obviously not available in a country of more than ten million, nine million of whom were illiterate. There is nothing in the archives, however, that indicates policy debate around the decision to make workers in centres of organized production the primary target group for the national campaigns. In fact, it was an option that had profound implications. Situations of organized production were, in fact, not plentiful in Mozambique at this time. By far the main body of the labour force, and certainly most illiterate workers, were to be found in family sector agriculture or in the informal sector of the economy, accessible only through community programmes.

The policy decision to target organized sectors of production served to institutionalize a whole series of biases, privileging urban over rural, industrial workers over those in agriculture, wage labour over against the informal sector, men over women, and workplace over community. This series of biases is what Philip Corrigan, Harvie Ramsay and Derek Sayer refer to as the "Bolshevik paradigm" in their fascinating study of the processes of socialist construction in the Soviet Union and China. They suggest that this privileging of industry over agriculture, urban over rural etc. is fundamental to the cultural forms of capitalist society as it has developed historically. They argue that only in China, was there an attempt at certain moments to break radically with these forms and begin to construct new forms of social relations profoundly different than those that characterize capitalist culture. (Corrigan, Ramsay, Sayer 1978)

In Mozambique, local initiatives from the bottom up gave way to top-down directives. Implicitly if not explicitly, an argument turning on "human capital" and a linear connection between increased schooling and increased productivity was built into the state-sponsored programmes from the outset.

The detailed historical reconstruction of the transition from promotion of literacy by the Dynamizing Groups to campaigns organized by the Ministry of Education and Culture has not yet been carried out. It would seem that at least in some provinces, the impact of the state-sponsored programme on local initiatives of "people's power" was quite negative. In Zambezia, for example, where a broad movement of People's Schools had flourished in 1975 and early 1976, the establishment of Ministry of Education schools and adult literacy programmes seems to have been done with little consideration for community control over existing literacy activities.

> These "people's schools" later had to be recognized by the Ministry itself, sending those monitors who had shown some teaching ability to training courses. Some of these schools were later formalized and turned into

> primary schools. In this regard, a certain reaction from the population was evident. They saw the intervention of the Ministry of Education as a bureaucratization of teaching, as if it was a question of taking power from the population over the control of these schools.
>
> (Interview with Henrique N'Guiraze, 1985)

This is not to suggest that the spontaneous movement to create schooling had indefinite capacity to continue and consolidate, in Zambezia or elsewhere. In part, the initial euphoria could not be sustained. There was a real feeling in the air in those pre- and post-independence days that everything could be done -- and done immediately. This included the rapid eradication of illiteracy. Even by the time of the Ribáuè Seminar, some provincial representatives indicated a discovery that there was no "quick-fix" approach to illiteracy. Volunteers prepared to work for one or two years had become tired. The time span for learning reading and writing skills was clearly longer than expected either by the learners or the literacy teachers and organizers. More sober assessments of the deep-set problems surrounding literacy and "people's power" began to emerge.

The Dynamizing Groups which had been such an important force in promoting literacy began to wield less power. In part this was due to a natural attrition rate. The GDs had been sought out by secret sympathizers, unable to link up openly with FRELIMO until this time. Many of them had proved their political trustworthiness and gone on to other important tasks. The GDs had also been sought out by opportunists, some of whom were later expelled, others of whom continued in leadership positions, operating with as dictatorial and arbitrary a manner as anything the colonialists had dispensed.

Political decisions were taken about state and party in Mozambique that included a decision to phase out the Dynamizing Groups. The III Congress of FRELIMO in 1977 transformed the liberation movement into a Marxist-Leninist party, with a programme to establish party cells at the base. This fundamentally diluted the power of the GDs. Though they were still maintained, the legitimacy they had enjoyed as the right arm of FRELIMO was now seriously eroded and/or confused, both by the newly emerging Frelimo Party structures and the new state structures.

> The big difference that exists. . . is that the Party is present in terms of defining and giving political orientation that people study. But in terms of a physical presence at local level, it's not there. Maybe this is one of the big difficulties that we meet in terms of participation of the population. This factor was acute when literacy passed over to be controlled by the Ministry of Education. Here there was a conflict. Who is in command? The Ministry of Education said they were in command and the GD said it's us

> in charge because we know the problems. But since the state apparatus is privileged in terms of the means at its disposal, I think the idea (which I would even call an erroneous conception) that literacy is an administrative task of the state prevailed.
>
> (Interview with Henrique N'Guiraze, 1985)

The problems of definition of roles and lines of accountability between party, state, Dynamizing Groups and the mass organizations of women, workers and youth were complex. They were made the more difficult still by the inexperience of party members which translated itself into rigid stands and fear to adapt directives to local conditions. The Frelimo Party was by no means unaware of these problems and efforts were made in the party to counter the mechanical and inflexible way party representatives carried out their tasks.

FIGURE 9.1 "Mobilisation is done in a mechanical way, without attention to the concrete situation."

By 1981, the "Cell Bulletin" published for party members included campaigns to counter top-down methods. Cartoons showed the party member, with suit and car, haranguing peasant women with the words, "It's necessary to increase production. More cotton means more clothing for our people." The thoughts passing through the women's heads went unvoiced. "But last year's cotton hasn't even been collected yet." "I thought he came to say something about the truck we requested." (Quoted in Egero 1987:117)

In the field of education, there was an early shift away from the "people's schools" that had begun to emerge.[2] This shift meant that instead of people acting locally to define and organize their own forms of education, a paternalistic state began to act on their behalf.

> People offered voluntarily to give their contribution to the task of literacy. Because of the enthusiasm that characterized the movement, the notion existed at that time that literacy would not be an activity stretched out over a long period of time. Maybe because of the information they had about other campaigns, some thought that we could make the majority of the population literate in three to five years. That's why people appeared offering to teach during this period as a national task, without demanding payment.
>
> Clearly, in this situation, the real number of illiterates existing in the country was not taken into account. Maybe there was a bit of utopia in that period. But one way or another, I interpret it as a positive sentiment because, in fact, there was a strong consciousness and interest in education. . . . It was a question of facing the situation with courage and finding a way to advance. . . .
>
> When the monitors from the "people's schools" were integrated into the formal system of education, they also became bureaucratized and were drawn into the methods that predominated, which were from the colonial period. The population for its part began to see literacy as something, I wouldn't say imposed, but that came from the top down. It became a task of the state, carried out by functionaries. In this way, literacy ceased to be seen as an action emanating from the people, from their concrete reality.
>
> (Interview with Henrique N'Guiraze, 1985)

If the first national literacy campaign was still a little ambiguous in situating literacy between schooling and new forms of "people's power," the subsequent campaigns came down clearly on the side of schooling. As we have seen at CIM, the practice of centralized literacy with a standard programme, texts, exams and calendar grew more and more distant from community and workplace realities.

Organizing time for literacy within a workplace setting, even one operating as efficiently as CIM, was fraught with difficulties. In many other workplaces, even the pretence of a literacy programme was dropped by the mid-1980s, with classes organized only on the occasion of the infrequent visits by officials.

The very real difficulties in combining literacy with production were not tackled as organizational and political questions. They were reduced to administrative questions and tackled with administrative measures. The state intervened with a Council of Ministers' decree, Law 1/81, in January 1981 that made literacy mandatory in each workplace and gave directives for the establishment of human resource departments with special literacy sections.

The law defined the responsibilities of each of the three main bodies involved in literacy -- the education ministry, workplace management and party/mass organizations. The Ministry of Education's role was reduced to a normative and methodological one. The role of the Party was to work in close collaboration with the human resources department. Responsibility for coordinating, planning, implementing and controlling the activities of literacy and post-literacy fell to the human resources departments. There was no role envisaged for the community or the illiterate themselves!

Through Law 1/81, it became mandatory to include literacy targets as part of the state plan. Article 4 read as follows:

> The annual plan of each economic, social or service unit must include a register and target figures for literacy and adult education. In particular, the annual plan must include the total of workers to become literate and to be integrated into adult education activities and the human, material and financial resources to allocate to this end.
>
> (Law 1/81 Council of Ministers)

The establishment of a literacy law as a response to dwindling numbers in the literacy campaigns came during a period in which formal, hierarchical style took hold in a number of sectors. The National Planning Commission became extremely powerful. Centralized, top-down planning prevailed. Plan targets became a powerful accountability structure, reducing illiterates to administrative categories and literacy to a numbers game in many areas. The earlier language of persuasion and literacy for critical consciousness no longer existed. "Metas," the plan targets, dominated the discourse.

In subsequent self-criticisms such as those during the IV Congress in April 1983, the Frelimo Party offered a number of reasons for over-centralization and top-down methods. One was a desperate attempt to deal with the lack of trained cadres. Another was the crisis management mentality in the face of war, drought and destabilization. All of these pushed for more rather than less centralization.

The report to the IV Congress by the Central Committee also put forward another reason -- the prominence of a group of aspiring bourgeoisie in the state structures with a profound disbelief in the capacities of ordinary people.

> [T]hey try to distort the class character of our revolution by transforming it into a technocratic process through which they can control power. This social stratum actively opposes any measures that aim at simplifying organisation and methods, democratising leadership or increasing the workers' share in planning and controlling production. Because of their book-learning, aspirants to the bourgeoisie despise solutions from the people. They are unable to learn from the people. So they reject the experience of the liberated areas. They reject the small-scale projects that require the intelligence, sensitivity and understanding of the people and prefer the projects that come ready made from abroad.
>
> (Frelimo Party 1983:72)

Yet despite the clear identification of the class character of those employed by the state, the Frelimo Party persisted in viewing the state structures as the main vehicle for social change. The call to popular vigilance over the state structures by workers and peasants had little substance without, at the same time, creating a space for autonomous organizations at popular level through which that vigilance could be practised.

A Movement to Revitalize Literacy

The IV Congress, then, aired strong criticisms of top-down communications and work methods with no faith in the capacity of ordinary people to organize and take decisions at local level. In its wake came a somewhat tenuous movement toward a more popular project. There was a renewed policy commitment in agriculture towards the family and cooperative sectors rather than state farms. Amongst literacy staff there was a concern to create a more learner-centred approach rooted in contemporary realities of the community and workplace centres with a serious strategy for tackling literacy in the rural areas.

The directives from the IV Congress put decentralization on the agenda and the district as the base for planning. For literacy this was meant to mark the beginning of a planning process workplace by workplace, recognizing production rhythms as basic parameters and social conditions of the workers during difficult times as paramount.

Within these constraints, the idea was to build in a good deal more flexibility, and a process of involvement and ownership of literacy through the planning process. There was an attempt to move away from an administrative approach to literacy and see workers once again as vital resources for development.

A group of people within the DNEA began to work on plans for a pilot centre for staff training as the starting point for changes in literacy. The initial discussions centred on changes of content in the literacy training programmes and how to equip volunteer teachers to teach differently. A huge question rapidly emerged, however, once the discussions began to tackle how to change the methodology of the training courses. If literacy teachers needed an experience of a pedagogy of empowerment during their own training as an alternative to teaching models based on the authoritarian classrooms of their own education, where were the trainers to come from? There was a need for a training staff with a critical vision of education, skills in a pedagogy of empowerment and a commitment to revitalizing literacy. But who was to train the trainers?

Exposure to other ways of doing and thinking about literacy emerged as one possible strategy. Some of the provincial training instructors who had shown themselves most dynamic during the introduction of the new curriculum materials were to make up the staff team at the pilot centre. Two groups made up of a mixture of these provincial instructors and national training staff, were selected to make study visits. One group went to Nicaragua, Brazil and Argentina for four months. The other group spent two month in Guinea Bissau and Portugal.[3] A third group worked in the national office in Maputo, planning and strategizing and preparing resource materials.

The four months of group travel and exchanges of experiences with popular educators in Latin America in which I also participated were very intensive. All four Mozambicans were travelling outside Mozambique for the first time. This brought the fundamental questioning that occurs on anyone's first trip to another culture. With it comes the revelation that "how it's done," is historically and socially created rather than the natural order of things, be it dancing, eating, expressing emotions -- or organizing literacy!

In Nicaragua, there was the instant identification with another struggle for survival. As in Mozambique, the dream of creating a different kind of society and the first steps in establishing "people's power" were pitted against a combination of externally backed insurgents spreading terror throughout the countryside, massive economic destabilization, natural disasters and constant disinformation campaigns.

As in Mozambique, unarmed village literacy teachers and health workers were under regular attack by the insurgents.

There were moments of self-recognition. The Nicaraguans asked if Mozambicans had to work against "machismo," identifying this as a key struggle in Nicaragua and throughout Latin America. Once the term, "machismo," was explained, the Mozambicans readily admitted that this was a struggle in Mozambique too. And indeed an important part of the dynamic during the trip both within the group itself and in interactions with Nicaraguan and Brazilian counterparts had to do with gender -- and how questions of silencing and empowerment played themselves out in a different way for women than men.

There were the painful moments of finding racism in other parts of the world, through meeting with the black consciousness movement in Brazil and Nicaraguans from the Atlantic coast communities who were of African origin. "Why is it that black people are always at the bottom of the heap?" was the plaintive question one day.

The study visits created dramatic results. The Mozambican literacy instructors who did them brought back a new energy, vision and critical framework to apply to literacy. The travellers also developed a new sense of themselves as part of a larger movement of popular education. Domingos Chigarire, one of the four who went to Latin America, put it this way.

> Here [Latin America] I saw another style of relations between educator and educatee, between junior staff members and those at the top. I saw that these relations were key to determining a process. I have been in a vertical situation and didn't see any way out of it. I thought that's how it was and how it would always be. Now I've seen something different and I am returning, determined to fight for change.
>
> I think this kind of visit is very important. Many of our literacy teachers don't know that there are illiterate people in other countries. It really gives them encouragement. When I return, I'm going to put a lot of energy into my work because I know I'm not alone in this struggle.
>
> (Marshall 1990b)

The three groups, two of whom had travelled seeking other experiences of literacy while the third prepared materials in the national office in Maputo, proceeded to Manga, near Beira, at the beginning of 1986. They were filled with anxiety about whether it would actually be possible to put their new ideas into practice. At Manga a renovated training centre awaited them. With strong support from the newly appointed National Director of Adult Education, Teresa Veloso and excellent back-up from project coordinator, Aldovanda Martins, the staff team at Manga thought, debated, sang, acted, danced and dialogued their way to a new methodology for literacy and adult education during 1986. They prepared programme guidelines, and did an experimental run through and evaluation of three different types of courses. These included a dramatically revamped ten month course for "professional educators," a short term course for "voluntary" literacy teachers and a refresher course for provincial and district instructors.

Through it all, a pedagogy of empowerment began to emerge. Giving voice to the trainees was seen as central to the training programmes. The four who visited Latin America, on the eve of their return, were very concerned not to arrive back as "experts." Helena Francisco put it this way. "If we arrive as people from the outside and just inform, we're going to move ahead without hearing the ideas of people there. We can't arrive there as people who come with all the answers." To which fellow-traveller Chigarire replied: "We have to find a way to build on the knowledge there in Mozambique, to get our cadres, those who are there, to voice their experiences first."

Gradually the Manga classrooms came to be seen not as spaces to fill with the instructor's voice transmitting knowledge and directives but spaces for interaction with the trainees and problem-posing, out of which would come collective creation of knowledge. The trainers themselves were enthused with the process and in the first courses, worked from dawn till midnight, day after day. The high energy levels emerged at least in part from their own exhilaration at having the space to develop something that was really theirs. The testimony of their colleagues is significant.

> I've known them since 1982. When they got back from their trip to Nicaragua and Brazil, they weren't the same people. They'd seen a different life, another way to do adult education. They brought nice things back with them -- that's true. But best of all, they brought back a determination to pass on all their new ideas and insights to those of us who'd stayed behind.
>
> (Quoted in Marshall 1990b)

The centre brought about a dramatic reversal in its approach to staff training, then, starting with the experiences of the trainees as fundamental. In a complete switch from the old style of top-down directives, the starting point for the courses was the real situations faced by trainees in their day to day work in the districts -- pedagogical, organizational, political, social and professional. The critique of formal hierarchies and top-down methods extended into the classroom itself. New methodologies giving voice to the trainees/learners were on the agenda. It also extended into the collective life of the training centre, where the Manga staff trainers opted to share a common dining room with the trainees. This decision to end the hierarchy in the training centre itself, with no special food or china for the staff, was one of the most talked about innovations!

A growing capacity for pedagogical analysis began to emerge, with the real questions of knowledge and power understood as central. In a discussion about whether it was appropriate for a staff member from the district education office visiting a rural centre to do a model lesson, for example, António Gonçalves, the trainer responsible for pedagogy and one of those who had travelled to Nicaragua and Brazil, mused along these lines.

> For me, it's an interesting question. It poses the whole dilemma of the role of the instructor. The instructor tends to be seen as the authority, the one who knows how to do it, the one with the answers. We have to discover how the instructor can interact with the adult education teachers in a way that has the teachers themselves sharing in coming to the solution.
>
> (Marshall & McCord 1987)

It is obviously very difficult to measure the impact of this movement for revitalization. The training team itself recounted some resistance from those in positions of power in the hierarchies of education. Indeed some senior provincial staff visiting the centre questioned the common dining room and interpreted a Manga instructor's request for input from participants in the classroom as an indication that the instructor was weak and did not have the answers himself!

The energies and enthusiasms from those who had done courses at Manga seemed far stronger than any resistance encountered. Manga had provided a space to name experiences of silencing and subordination. It gave the course participants a critical framework into which they could situate their experiences in the districts and was very empowering. A strong mystique developed around "being at Manga" and the trainees began networking to give each other mutual support as they tried to introduce the new methodology into their provinces.

Some provincial literacy staff were highly enthusiastic about the impact of the Manga project on provincial work. Guilhermina Macabi, a Maputo city staff person, was one.

> There's a lot of movement going on in this project. Before, there was no respect for literacy, but this project has succeeded in creating interest. ... The big success was curriculum for the training programmes. The instructors themselves were able to plan these programmes. The methods are flexible. Things are always changing. People are stimulated to improve their own work plans. These gymnastics of developing the training

> curriculum allow people to develop. People have become dynamic through this project.
>
> The project makes a person work. It makes demands on your head, your initiatives, in an on-going process of planning, implementation and evaluation. The value of the knowledge people bring is recognized. Nobody is stupid.
>
> The way we used to work was monotonous and boring. People were flabby, with no creativity. When the people returned from the Manga course to Llanguene centre here in Maputo, things changed. Maria Bona, the woman who had attended, came back transformed. She worked tirelessly, she agitated, she brought us together.
>
> (Marshall 1990a:107)

The larger context of continued war and deepening economic crisis made it extremely difficult, however, for the Manga network to keep up the momentum. Efforts to promote community education programmes with an alternative pedagogy had to contend with low levels of interest in literacy. Tentative efforts to establish literacy programmes more closely linked to tackling some of the survival questions encountered great difficulties. There was no up-front resistance but neither the literacy staff nor the community members were able to free themselves of the weight of the formal system. Community education was always drawn back into the orbit of set programmes, the school year, the lessons in doses to be dispensed, exams and certificates as the "real" goal.

The fragile counter-movement of bottom up, participatory pedagogy was engulfed in a public service apparatus in crisis. Low-paid education workers were as vulnerable to the harsh economic climate as workers at CIM. Their need to take on additional jobs, to hustle in the informal sector, to be in the network of survival schemes and scams made it difficult for them to keep up the momentum in literacy.

At Manga itself, members of the core group of staff trainers were faced with these same economic difficulties. Professional up-grading was one way to earn a higher salary. Many of the most committed became full-time students in 1988, entering a three-year teacher training programmes in the newly opened Senior Pedagogical Institute in Beira. The Institute was designed for secondary school teachers and paid little attention to adult education. The Manga staff who had had the chance to debate literacy pedagogy internationally and had succeeded in promoting a remarkable change in pedagogy at their own centre were treated like the other entering students, empty heads to be filled by the Institute instructors.

Even more ironic, they were replaced by recent graduates from this course who had missed the educational revolution going on at Manga. These instructors took over the Manga classrooms and dismantled the structures that had so painstakingly been set up. Questions were interpreted as a sign of lack of respect and participation as indiscipline.

By 1990, the Ministry of Education itself was in disarray, with cuts in social sector spending resulting in minimally functioning education services across the boards. Teachers went on strike at the beginning of the school year in mid-February. Peaceful demonstrations in the national capital were met with riot police. A resentful education staff was back in the classrooms and literacy centres. Officials of the National Teachers' Organization spoke of an undeclared slowdown. The adult education department of the Ministry was in the process of being dismantled, with adult education sections now to be attached to the organization and pedagogy departments of the general education department. The Manga network saw this as a structural change that militated strongly against everything they had dreamed of building.

End of the "People's" Republic

Education Minister Graca Machel addressed an assembly of Ministry of Education workers in June 1985, on the tenth anniversary of independence, with the words, "The main thing we celebrate here is that we've survived -- and that Mozambique is still a people's republic." The years from 1985 to 1990 forced those in the Frelimo Party still committed to a popular project to make dramatic changes. By 1990 it was a "people's republic" no longer, a new constitution having been adopted in which "people's" was deleted from the country's name. Debate in the People's Assembly -- from which "people's" was also subsequently deleted -- were revealing. Deputy Teresa Veloso, still National Director of Adult Education at the time, spoke against dropping the name. She argued that the name when adopted in 1975 had nothing to do with "communism or socialism" but that it had "emotional implications" for Mozambicans and should be retained. Ministry of Security Mario Matsinhe argued that the original intention in calling Mozambique a "people's" republic was to signal a state controlled by workers and peasants. This excluded "certain parts" of Mozambican society and hence should be changed. In the end only three deputies voted to retain "people's" in the name. The "certain parts" hitherto excluded, most notably the private business sector, began to emerge even more strongly.

The 1990 constitution marked the culmination of five years of dramatic changes in Mozambique. Even by 1985, Mozambique was in severe crisis, with economic collapse added to the escalating war situation. Real production had fallen by a startling 37 percent between 1981 and 1985, amidst widespread shortages and inflation, acute foreign exchange problems and a government budget which could not be balanced. From 1982 on, virtually all foreign exchange earnings were spent in servicing Mozambique's foreign debt. By 1987, the debt stood at about $3.2 billion.

The Mozambican government unveiled an orthodox structural adjustment programme in early 1987, culminating four years of complex discussions with donor community members and the IMF/World Bank.[4] The shock tactics included a first devaluation from 40 MT to 200 MT to the U.S. dollar and subsequent devaluations up to the mid-1991 exchange rate of 1012 MT. Other features included liberalization of imports, privatization, cuts in public sector spending, active procurement of foreign investment and deregulation. Lip service was paid to social dimensions without effective programmes being established to cushion the impact. All of this took place in the context of the prolonged war of destabilization carried out by the apartheid regime.

Most Mozambicans found themselves cumulatively poorer as the first Economic Recovery Programme (PRE) unfolded from 1987-1989 and held little optimism for the Socio-Economic Recovery Programme initiated in 1990. The demoralization was the greater on hearing that first calculations of 1990 economic growth rate suggested about one percent after three years of four percent growth. Ordinary citizens were forced to contend with poverty, social degradation and a spiralling level of violence in home, community and workplace.

IMF financing was made dependent on Mozambican compliance with a series of conditions, from devaluations and deregulation to political pluralism and an adoption of a market economy.

> When it was announced, the PRE was depicted as simply a program "adjustment." Party leaders avoided discussing its political and ideological character.
>
> However, references to "the building of socialism" grew scarce, replaced by emphasis on the role of "economic agents" and the need to respect "market forces." Still, the political language was tactful and restrained, reflecting the natural discomfort with which a party professing to be Marxist-Leninist began to endorse capitalist concepts. This same government, after all, had once promoted the "dominant role" of the state sector and pressed for rigorous centralization. Now it was thrust into the position of exalting private initiative. Tact was needed to paper over tensions provoked by this process inside Frelimo and among its leaders.
> (Vasconcelos 1990:M5)

There was some debate externally in the late 1980s when the first structural adjustment programme was adopted about "strategic retreats" in the face of external pressures. The IMF/World Bank was understood as the economic arm of RENAMO, all part of the multi-facetted low-intensity war intent of destroying Mozambique's socialist project.

By the 1990s it had become clear how many senior leaders in party and state had themselves become convinced of the desirability of market forces. The debates in the Assembly of the Republic about privatization raised concerns about the economy falling into "the hands of foreign capital" rather than out of the hands of workers and peasants. Veteran Frelimo member and retired Major General Américo Mpfumo called for a "nationalist economic policy" and criticized the post-independence government for not promoting the emergence of a "national business class." (AIM 1991:3)

Certainly foreign pressure to adopt the neo-conservative economic agenda that is being promoted globally has been felt. In a moment of startling candour, President Joaquim Chissano spoke to delegates to a conference on "Rethinking Strategies for Mozambique and Southern Africa" of the pressures on Mozambique to change its political options.

> The U.S. said, "Open yourself to. . . the World Bank and IMF." What happened? . . .
> We are told now: "Marxism! You are devils. Change this policy." OK. Marxism is gone.
> "Open market economy." OK, Frelimo is trying to create capitalism. We have the task of building socialism and capitalism here.
> We went to Reagan and I said, "I want money for the private sector to boost people who want to develop a bourgeoisie." Answer: 10 million, then 15 million more, then another 15 million. You tell me to do away with Marxism, the Soviet Union and the GDR and give me [only] 40 million. OK, we have changed.
> Now they say, "If you don't go to a multi-party system don't expect help from us."
>
> (Post-conference briefing by President Joaquim Chissano to participants in "Rethinking Strategies for Mozambique and Southern Africa," held in Maputo, June 1990)

The strength of the internal Frelimo Party forces intent on building up this national business class -- and being members of it -- is not entirely clear. Even less clear is the strength of those still committed to some vision of "people's power" and participatory democracy.

Civil Society -- Cutting Both Ways

The shifting configuration of power and privilege in the latter half of the 1980s has clearly opened up new spaces of action for business and related interests. At the same time the situation for urban wage earners, peasant producers and those in the informal sector has deteriorated sharply. A return visit to CIM in August 1990 made this abundantly clear. Julieta Estevão, a single parent working as cleaner in the Electrical Department, spoke of a complete breakdown of the social fabric. Julieta had given up on passing her 3rd year. She talked about how impoverished workers now had to contend not only with rising food prices and new fees for health and education but also with survival scams of other workers like the notoriously low-paid primary school teachers. A return visit to CIM in August 1990 made this abundantly clear.

> It's hard to keep the children in school. There are fees of 6,000 meticais per semester. The books are not a difficulty. . . . The hard thing is the notes that come home with an amount written on them that the children must pay. . . . We the parents don't trust what is happening. What is this money being used for? But we pay it. If not, our children are prohibited from the classroom.
>
> (Interview with Julieta Estevão, August 1990)

By mid-1990, workers at CIM were spending half their pay on a food basket lasting only though half of the month. Alexandre Mondlane had worked for CIM for 12 years and still earned the minimum wage for loading sacks of flour onto delivery trucks for the city bakeries. Mondlane lived with his household of 11 on the city outskirts.

> The main problem is food -- food and clothing. A person eats badly, sleeps badly, dresses badly. In the house the blankets are poor, the beds are falling apart. With my 28,000 MT take-home I have to eat poorly to have money for clothes for the children. . . . The rations alone cost 15,000 MT. You can spend 10,500 on products and 2,600 on lunches at the factory. A person has to hustle. Women sell charcoal to have a sauce to go with the maize porridge. One sack of coal costs 10,000 MT. You have to scavenge outside the city. And outside the city there's war. Because of it we don't go to the farm any more. No cassava, no greens, no firewood, nothing.
>
> (Interview with Alexandre Mondlane, August 1990)

The word at popular level was that the structural adjustment programme had brought to the cities the suffering that RENAMO created in the rural areas. By the beginning of the 1990s, the huge disparities between privileged and impoverished so marked in the colonial era were once again in evidence. The Economic Recovery Programme, PRE, was seen to go hand in hand with what people ironically call the "PRI," the individual recovery programme. A small group of traders, larger farmers, private entrepreneurs and officials in state and military structures were visibly prospering. One Nampula trading family with new interests in Maputo and Inhambane provinces and a trucking fleet travelling regularly to Swaziland and South Africa indicated that they had earned more profit in the first two years of the PRE than in the entire previous decade.

In the cooperatives and literacy centres there were jokes about the frequent messages to "tighten your belts." Belt-tightening was all too real for urban workers -- there were complaints voiced at the OTM Congress that workers would break in two if they tightened their belts any more.

The riot threshold was crossed as the 1990s arrived. There was a wave of strike action throughout the country, with significant groups of workers out in all of the major cities, many of the strikes triggered by refusal of management to pay the customary 13th month wage. Workers at Tempo Magazine and at the steel rolling mill, CIFEL, were the first to strike. By the end of January, strikes had spread to the railways, the bus companies, Maputo Central Hospital, the Maputo City Council and APIE, the state housing authority. Workers in glass, tire and textile factories also went out on strike. By late January, health workers and construction workers in Beira, bus drivers in Nampula and coal miners in Moatize in northern Tete province had joined their southern colleagues. As the school year began in mid-February, school teachers also decided to strike for improved wages and working conditions.

As each group went out on strike, adding its particular demands to the general plea for higher wages, the weakness of management structures became more highly visible. Railway workers demanded back wages already two years in arrears. School teachers received only $30 per month and demanded full payment for teaching a second shift instead of the 60 percent on offer. Health workers demanded pay for over-time and week-end shifts. Workers complained that new pay scales linked to professional career categories and job classifications had not been implemented. They plaintively observed that while price or fee increases were implemented immediately, wage increases suffered indefinite delays.

The first wave of strikes was peaceful with two exceptions. Health workers shocked even fellow-workers with their disregard for maintaining vital services, resulting in deaths of intensive care patients. Riot police were sent in to attack a peaceful teachers' demonstration. Indeed the teachers were still bitter about this a year later and, like the health workers, had begun to operate on a virtual slowdown, albeit not formalized as a tactic. The National Teachers' Organization published an article and photos of riot police attacking teachers in their new journal, "so our provincial members really know what happened."

Manuel Golias, National Director of Education, spoke forthrightly of the deep resentment felt by the education workers. According to Golias, a typical teacher saw it this way. "We were forced to become teachers. We are poorly paid. We organized a peaceful demonstration. They beat us up. Only administrative responses. The lack of respect for us is total." Golias estimated that by 1991, most Maputo teachers would be earning five times more from private tutoring than from their monthly salaries, and even then would have difficulties paying food, rent, water and electricity bills.

Donor conditionalities around issues of governance in the late 1980s included the creation of an "enabling environment" for the newly espoused private sector and market economy. The conditionalities also included political pluralism, with multi-party elections placed firmly on the agenda. Autonomy was the watchword for business, labour, cooperatives, professional and women's organizations. New associations of all kinds emerged from development NGOs and housewives clubs to burial societies and a Rotary Club.

Ironically, these top-down pressures for political pluralism urged on by external dictate also created important new room for manoeuvre for organizations taking up the issues of the poor. Labour, cooperative, community and professional organizations found themselves in a situation of new-found autonomy at the same time that they were being pushed from below to take up more militant positions. Important new spaces also opened up for literacy and popular education.

The labour central, OTM, began to struggle to catch up with workers' demands. Its first official statement on the strikes affirmed the strikers' demands as "justified" and took immediate action to produce a manual on strike and grievance procedures. OTM General Secretary for Maputo city, Alberto Sebastião, gave a press-conference in January 1990 pinpointing the PRE as a central factor.

> At the start of the PRE, the workers were able to express their concerns in an organised way through the correct channels. . . but they received no satisfactory response from the relevant authorities. . . from this experience workers drew the conclusions that the methods recommended by the Frelimo Party "don't work and don't bring solutions."
>
> (AIM -- 16/1/90)

Government response to the strikes seems to have been one of surprise, although senior government officials have quickly made the link between the PRE and the PRI. Veteran Frelimo leader Sérgio Vieira, commented during a debate on spreading corruption at the People's Assembly, just before the strikes began:

> . . . when sacrifice and austerity are for everyone, then everyone is motivated -- that was our experience in the past. But when a handful of people grab benefits for themselves by illegal means, then we lose confidence and motivation.
>
> (AIM – 18/12/89)

Labour leader Sebastião, when interviewed half a year later, expressed enormous concern over the situation of workers and how weak the labour movement was, without budget or staff to service workers' needs even minimally. Strikes were ill-prepared, with no staff to work with locals to negotiate packages of demands with real substance. The wage and price study done by the OTM office in Maputo showed clearly the impossible economic conditions.

> Between the war and acceptance of the IMF, our people are living by begging. . . . There is widespread discontent and desperation. The strikes were not a political response but an economic response. The workers were fed up and needed an escape valve. Otherwise they would have exploded.
>
> (Interview with Alberto Sebastião, August 1990)

The final months of 1990 brought yet more strikes. Action by seasonal workers on sugar plantations near Beira resulted in both deaths and property damage. Other strikes included media workers, industrial workers at foreign-owned Tudor battery company and public employees in state construction and bus companies. State bus company workers in Nampula rampaged and destroyed furniture in reponse to a management decision to sack 126 of the 184 workers two months after resolution of a prolonged strike.

Other workers have resolved financial problems with direct action. Busworkers in Beira left without wages for four months took to pocketing fares without issuing tickets and refusing to provide change to entering passengers. Instructors at the teacher training college in Beira refused to release exam results until their foreign currency supplement was paid.

The CIM workers also went out on a brief strike. The reasons were not hard to find. Even Cardoso Muendane, Industrial Director at the time and soon after appointed General Director, readily acknowledged the impossibility of the workers' situation.

> I see workers who have been with us for years getting thin in front of my eyes. People here at CIM live with other worries, about how to get time for their farms, about food for their ducks and pigs. Even those without farms spend time and energy worrying about other things, with survival

> schemes that mean taking things from the factory, wood for a door here, something else there.
>
> (Interview with Cardoso Muendane, August 1990)

Why the CIM strike erupted exactly when it did is harder to ascertain. Some claim it was the general atmosphere. CIM trucks carrying workers back and forth to the factory were accosted by workers in other factories calling out "Haven't you gone out on strike yet?" "What's holding you back?" "If you don't strike you won't get anywhere."

Both management and workers at CIM mention agitators, although it is not clear whether they have the same people in mind. Some of the workers claimed that those in junior management positions were the ones urging strike action. One worker in the Accounts Department claimed that only the section heads had gained from the strike. They were the ones who had agitated for it. When the workers met with management, some workers indicated that there were others who had wanted to go on strike who weren't speaking up. "They can't say anything because they're part of management. So in the end, they're the only ones who gained anything because their salaries went up. They were behind the strike, agitating for it, but then they shut up." (Interview with João Machado, August 1990)

The strike was over quickly. Ordinary workers like Pedro Muhai in the Finished Products Warehouse did not feel it brought many results.

> Up to now there's no solution. They changed the 12 hour shifts to eight hours. We succeeded in getting the social security payment taken off our salaries and paid by management. We don't know what's happening up there at the top. Our hearts continue to pain.
>
> The OTM is in the hands of the management. . . OTM could work more for people here. We have workers who have been here for 30 years who rob one kilo of maize flour and get sacked. We talked about this during the strike. The OTM should defend these people. You shouldn't lose your job and your pension after working here for 25 years just for robbing one kilo of maize meal. . . . One result of the strike is that we now get ten loaves of bread every other day and twenty on Friday.
>
> (Interview with Pedro Muhai, Finished Products Warehouse)

Whether the OTM, after long years of subordination to party and state, can be revitalized is not clear. The second national OTM conference in November 1990 spent two full days debating the PRE. Clearly the emergence of autonomous trade unions added a new dimension to the situation. As Sebastião had indicated a few months earlier:

> It is now a moment of transformation. We [the OTM] emerged as part of the party. Now we have to speak with our own voice. Many of us are not ready. Now it is the market that dictates. Managers take decisions and do everything. The OTM was not prepared for this. . . . We need internal transformation within the organization.
>
> (Interview with Alberto Sebastião, August 1990)

Bottom-up Pressure from Peasants

By the late 1980s, there were bottom-up stirrings from peasants with revitalization of some of the already existing cooperatives and emergence of many new peasant associations. Stronger peasant voices opened up new spaces for literacy and popular education initiatives.

Cooperatives had been created from above in the late 1970s as part of a broader "socialize the countryside" policy. Few were able to withstand the difficult economic turns of the 1980s. Many existed in name only, grouping for sporadic distribution of inputs or visiting delegations from one of the multiple party/state structures to which they were subordinated.

The critique of agricultural policy made during the Fourth Congress in 1983 stated clearly that cooperatives and the family sector had been abandoned in favour of big agro-industrial projects. Despite the Congress decision to reverse this policy, combined pressures of war and scarce economic resources meant a de facto continuation of that neglect.

The real constraints on peasant producers went well beyond market prices. A coherent family agriculture policy was needed addressing broad issues from land, social organization and the gendered division of labour to technical questions of soils, seeds and storage.

Land has become the central point of contestation in the new economic context of privatization. Urban cooperative and family sector producers are being forced to fight hard to maintain their farms against the encroachment of an emerging urban business class. President Celina Cossa gave a strong warning at the 1990 Annual Assembly of the General Union of Agricultural and Livestock Cooperative of Maputo (UGCAPM) that anyone trying to steal land from the cooperatives in the Maputo Green Zones would have a struggle on their hands.

> Some people, arguing as ever that we are illiterate, incapable, ignorant and above all, almost all women, sum it up by saying that we don't know how to manage our property, our land. They say that with the PRE, what is important is private initiative. But there are many ways of developing private initiative. As poor people, we feel the need to unite and work together in cooperatives.
>
> (Mozambiquefile, No.165, April 1990, p.13)

While the urbanites have no demonstrated capacity to organize agricultural production, they do bring formidable "know-how" and "know-who" in making land claims. Cooperatives functioning under the, until recently, little defined cooperative legislation, have had to hire lawyers to secure their land. In the Maputo area, the UGCAPM has urged family sector producers to organize into peasant associations and affiliate with it as a way of defending their land.

The cooperative movement, then, has emerged as an important force. In Maputo, the UGCAPM alone has more than 200 cooperatives with a total of more than 10,000 members, more than 95 percent of them women. There are also construction material cooperatives in Maputo city and active agricultural cooperatives in rural districts like Marracuene.

In Nampula, the cooperatives have also taken on new life in recent years. The General Union of Agricultural Cooperatives now functions as an apex organization offering services and credit to its member cooperatives. It grew from about 30 member cooperatives in 1987 to more than 50 cooperatives and peasant associations by 1992. It offers family farmers access to inputs like seeds, fertilizers and boots, credit, tractor and transport services. It also services the general public after member needs have been met, an activity that provides a significant additional source of revenue for daily operational costs. It has become a modest but real producer-controlled market force, offering prices that compete favourably with those offered by private traders and the increasingly defunct state marketing board.

Women have now organized for independent membership and plot allocation within the cooperative movement and have proved a dynamic force. Peasant associations are forming in the city outskirts and seeking affiliation along with cooperatives still alive in Nampula's rural districts. President José Mussagy, indicated his own commitment to the cooperatives saying, "I never dreamed I could be part of an organization like this, fighting to build something with others like myself."

In both Maputo and Nampula, the growing strength of the cooperative movement has also breathed new life into literacy. In Maputo, the General Union has taken responsibility for literacy and adult education as in any other workplace but has stamped the programme with characteristics from the cooperative movement. In addition to programmes in individual cooperatives offering the basic literacy and post-literacy equivalent to lower primary level, the cooperatives run upper primary schools which they both staff and equip. These are schools that cater both to cooperative members and their older children, many of whom have had difficulty getting places in the city schools.

The literacy classes are not dramatically different in content or methodology from those in other literacy centres. The literacy programmes, however, form part of a larger programme of education and training in the cooperatives. The programme includes more technical courses on agriculture methods, raising chickens or rabbits, accounting, running small businesses and general leadership courses. The leadership course uses popular education methodology to deal with day to day issues of cooperative organization, including questions of leadership styles, participation and democratic practice. This course gives rank and file cooperative members a chance to reflect on the internal dynamics of their own cooperatives and often involves tense discussions about real abuses of power in the cooperatives. Women in the Maputo cooperative refer to the leadership course as the "xixinha" course, "xixinha" being a Ronga word for fear. In evaluating the cooperative movement, they have consistently singled out this course as the most useful. Clearly integration into the cooperative movement as a whole allows members to deal with some of the power, fear and knowledge questions in other contexts and enter the literacy class with a somewhat different agenda.

In Nampula also, the upsurge in cooperative activity since 1988 has brought with it renewed interest in literacy. Again language and speaking, reading and writing skills take on a different kind of resonance amidst the broader changes in the cooperatives. The General Union of Agricultural Cooperatives in Nampula now has a fortnightly general assembly in which all issues of the cooperatives, large and small, are tackled. Both Macua and Portuguese are fully accepted as languages for discussion. Peasants are encouraged to speak out and to develop skills of analysis and debate in order to participate actively in managing the cooperatives.

Each cooperative now has multiple contacts each week which demand language skills. There are a range of negotiations with the General Union staff to buy materials (seeds, rubber boots, pesticides), to contract services (tractors or transport), or to sell produce (kilos of rice or heads of lettuce). There are fortnightly visits by members to each other's cooperatives where peasants teach other peasants. There is attendance at courses, participation in planning meetings and hosting visitors. Many cooperative members from Nampula have now attended courses in Maputo or visited cooperatives in adjoining provinces and as far away as Zambia. The General Union publishes a regular bulletin in both Portuguese and Macua, another point where reading and writing skills take on relevance.

Prior to 1988, the cooperative members recount a history of silent compliance, with subordination to multiple powerful bodies. Everybody gave orders to the peasants in the cooperatives -- the ward secretary, the OMM, the Director of the Green Zones Office, the Director of Agriculture, the party. In recent years cooperative members have been encouraged to find their own voices -- and to talk to each other! In this context, literacy skills take on new importance. Three literacy centres have been set up in the Nampula Green Zones, with efforts to enrich the programme by adding activities to each unit of more immediate relevance to Nampula. Setting up courses for upper primary level is under discussion. There is also an attempt to have the literacy centres reinforce the promotion of the Macua language to be found in the cooperative movement as a whole.

These education activities run by the cooperatives are of particular interest in the face of the inability of the government schools to provide sufficient places for all children and its decreased attention to adult education. In 1990, a new policy was adopted to legalize privately run community schools. The assumption at popular level is that the newly emerging elite will now guarantee a good education for their children by establishing private schools with well-paid teachers, infrastructure and equipment while the poor will be left with not enough places in badly run state schools. Community schools organized by cooperatives or trade unions may point to interesting middle ground with some genuine local control and new possibilities for access, curriculum relevance and empowerment.

The churches are also playing more active roles as social change agents. This includes linking up with other citizen initiatives for community action such as the recently established development NGO, Progresso and the newly formed Community Development Foundation. The Foundation is committed to "national solidarity" to support poverty-stricken rural and urban communities improve their living standards. Headed by former Minister of Education, Graca Machel, the Foundation is also supported by other government leaders. At its opening seminar, Finance Minister Magid Osman admitted openly that the market economy towards which Mozambique was moving as a result of the PRE "does not guarantee harmonious economic and social development, much less social justice."

The churches are strong voices in support of the emerging civil society. Christian Council official Samuel Machava put it this way:

> The promotion of Mozambican organizations is very positive. They are needed for the socio-economic development of the country. But this socio-economic development cannot be directed from above, dictated. There needs to be a space for the creative initiative of various groups without the state giving directives. These groups are good. There will be links of mutual aid emerging without any party orientation.
>
> (Interview with Samuel Machava, August 1990)

There are important educational dimensions in the visions of the newly emerging community organizations and Mozambican NGOs promoting local development projects. Work with local communities on issues such as health, agriculture, water and environment immediately confronts the tensions between an approach based on empowerment and an approach based on a society of "experts." Are people basically poor because they are ignorant, and hence able to react to a transmission belt of useful knowledge on everything from potable water to animal husbandry. Or are people poor because they are exploited, made ignorant in a power relation in which others stand to benefit? If it is the latter, the starting point for change is not provision of knowledge but tackling social relations and empowerment.

Clearly structural adjustment and its "conditionalities" have brought about profound social and political changes. The PRE has created conditions for the emergence of new social forces within civil society. The most visible is the new class of businessmen with a coterie of bureaucrats, technocrats and consultants alongside. Yet, as we have seen, the PRE has also legitimized a multiplicity of new forces at workplace and community level. The IMF/World Bank's urgency to dismantle the role of the state is operative across the boards -- and has included the promotion of autonomy for labour, cooperatives and community organizations whose agendas are shaped by pressures from below.

The fact that "civil society" cuts both ways creates a difficult terrain for those committed to a genuine process of democratization in Mozambique. They are faced not only with huge organizational tasks on the ground. They also have to contend with the prevailing tendency to rewrite history. What was valuable in Mozambique's pre- and post-independence project of social justice and popular participation is being erased in conformity with a global script on the theme, "totalitarian regimes discover democracy."

This is not to side-step the fundamental weaknesses that did exist in Mozambique's earlier efforts of democratization as we have seen. There were always strong tensions between Frelimo's promotion of decentralized institutions and programmes, on the one hand, and the perpetuation of the command style of the armed struggle (with the mass organizations as cheer leaders) on the other. Democracy was premised on "collective" definitions -- "people's power" or a "worker-peasant alliance." But this remained a somewhat amorphous, at times even dangerous, group concept without a strong commitment to individual rights or political pluralism. The seemingly endless war of destabilization and economic collapse in the 1980s exacerbated the centralizing tendencies and command style even more.

A new context for democratic practice may now exist in Mozambique. The challenge of the 1990s for the most popularly rooted expressions of the new "civil society" is to find ways to operate effectively in this new context. How can they establish a genuinely democratic practice as they tackle the awesomely difficult problems of their workplace and community constituencies? How do they fight back against emerging interests whose constituencies are much more narrowly defined in terms of power and class privilege? And how will the politics of language and voice be played out in this phase?

Literacy: Litmus Test for Democratization

Reconstructing the history of openings and closures over the years in literacy offers some important lessons. Literacy in Mozambique, as elsewhere, takes us to the core of the larger project of participatory democracy. Democratic practice can be characterized by three inter-related principles, those of equality, participation and diversity. By the latter is meant respect for difference, viewing the multiple social locations shaped by gender, race, ethnicity, age, location, etc, as resources for building participatory democracy rather than categories through which the "figure in dominance" can silence and marginalize the "others."

Certainly one of the most vexing problems historically in socialist construction has been that of establishing the space for genuine democracy and "people's power" -- for popular initiatives that can engender a new vitality in local community and workplace. The signalling and defence of a space for genuine democracy includes discovery of new forms of governance, ones that encourage new forms for people to express their lives and concerns and new institutions for input and control of public policy from below.

Central to this practice of democracy and a revitalized civil society is a new respect for the importance of the local. One of the strongest mechanisms in the repertoire of forms used by the capitalist state for social control is the constant suppression of micro-level realities. Local experience, local languages, local voices are constantly made invisible. The construction of "national" and the "national interest" over against the suppression of what is merely "local" is a vital mechanism of state formation,[5] one through which a sense of powerless and lack of control are strongly maintained. Conversely genuine empowerment by definition includes espousal of a diversity of local experiences.

The repertoire of state forms and institutions to suppress local experience and flatten diversity into a collective subject make people lose sight of their own social history. Re-presentations of the past make invisible the specificity of the local. Devouring the "local" into a homogenized organization of parameters of time and space that constitute the nation are common, both in their liberal/paternal and authoritarian forms. Common also, however, are genuine yearnings for community that resist this process and find forms of expression, including a language and vocabulary to name and validate the local.

What are the characteristics of a literacy that validates the local and contributes towards building the progressive forces within civil society? For whom does this kind of literacy that validates the local hold promise or threat? Clearly literacy undertaken as a totalizing project for social control and the creation of "political subjects" will not view literacy for a "localite existence" as effective. But literacy committed to empowerment in a local community, cooperative or workplace, in which women and men are invited to "speak their lives, read the world and write history," might well view growing literacy skills put to immediate use, including literacy skills in a local language, as positive indeed.

As we have seen, questions of language and voice are absolutely central both to literacy and to participatory democracy. Literacy, historically, as we have seen, has often been used not to consolidate popular initiatives but as a stratification device. It has served as a means of social regulation that, while it defines some people in, also filters many people out. Different concepts of literacy and language are also different versions of politics.

"Social literacy" is an approach to literacy in which people develop a capacity to locate themselves in their local times and spaces, to legitimate their activities and inter-relatedness. People start to know their own way around, to give voice to their own experience, and recognize their own ways of seeing *and* saying as valid and communicable. Social literacy is thus a vital tool to build the principles of equality, participation and diversity in a vital civil society. As such, it is an integral feature for constructing participatory democracy.

Notes

1. In any case, the lessons from historical reconstruction of the long transition from feudalism to capitalism indicate a process measured not in decades but in centuries, with a jagged and uneven path within and between social formations at every point along the way. For an extremely thought-provoking reconstruction of that shift from feudalism to capitalism and the history of English state formation, see Corrigan and Sayer: 1985. Corrigan and Sayer argue strongly that the bourgeois revolution to create the institutions and agencies through which the English ruling class has organized its domination cannot be understood except as cultural revolution in which moral regulation, through state forms, plays a key role. All of this revolution has been played out in very jagged and uneven processes measured over centuries rather than in discrete events.

2. One of the most fascinating questions for future investigation in Mozambique is the period from 1975 to 1977 when the Dynamizing Groups were most active as expressions of "people's power." What caused that opening and those dynamic expressions of energy at the base to close down and formalize? The period saw an amazingly diverse set of forms emerge to express local power, with ordinary people coming forward to resolve local problems using the resources at hand. It was a very ragged and uneven process, with lots of ineffective actions and some abuses of power, but there was no doubt that it generated a high level of popular participation and ownership, effectively being the state, during this period when the new FRELIMO government was taking over the reigns of government.

While the historic reconstruction is still to be done, there is evidence that at least in education, the new state-sponsored programmes were experienced at the base in terms of power being taken away from the local communities. How much similar dynamics could be found around housing, health, cooperatives etc. is an open question. Equally vexing is the gap of information about the decision to phase out the Dynamizing Groups and begin to build up party cells of the newly established Marxist-Leninist party. Were there voices doubting the wisdom of this move, not out of a lack of sympathy with the politics it was meant to express so much as a fear of the potential for mystification and the distancing of people from their own political project that it represented? Ordinary people could identify with the political traditions of FRELIMO, Mondlane and Samora, and situate themselves within those traditions of struggle. It was harder to see how they placed their lives in the context of a Marxist-Leninist party and "socialism." Clearly the Frelimo Party recognized this and put political studies on the agenda in schools, training courses, study groups in the civil service etc. But who was to teach? A mixture of western Marxists and "diamat" experts used to teaching "dialectical materialism" in East Germany was invited to contribute. They caused ripples in high places by their opposing approaches, but for ordinary workers like those who were my colleagues in the Ministry of Education, it was simply a "confusion." Few felt capable of doing the political education component of literacy training courses; the initiatives to provide support texts around themes like "surplus value" or "historical materialism" resulted in memorization of these texts for tests and no illumination whatsoever about the daily realities of trying to construct socialism. For interesting studies of this period see Egero 1986,1987 and Saul (ed.) 1985.

3. My own involvement included setting up the trip to Latin America with the International Council for Adult Education and its Latin American affiliate CEAAL, as well as accompanying the group in a facilitator/support role.

4. Critical analysis of the structural adjustment programme in Mozambique raises disturbing questions about structural adjustment in a country at war and the social impact of structural adjustments. For fuller discussions see Julie Cliff. "The War on Women in Mozambique: Health Consequences of South African Destabilization, Economic Crisis and Structural Adjustment. Mimeo 1990; Joseph Hanlon. *Mozambique: Who Calls the Shots?* London: James Currey, 1991; Judith Marshall. "War Debt and Structural Adjustment in Mozambique: The social

impact." North South Institute, Ottawa, 1992; Marc Wuyts. "Economic Management and Adjustment Policies in Mozambique." Working Paper Series No. 52. Institute of Social Studies, The Hague, The Netherlands, 1989.

5. For an illuminating discussion on the construction of "difference" in everyday life over against the "figure-in-dominance," and all of this in relation to struggles to situate "difference" as a resource for empowerment, see Philip Corrigan, "Towards a Celebration of Difference(s)" in D. Robins. *Rethinking Social Inequality*. London: Gower Press, 1982.

Sources Consulted

1 PRIMARY SOURCES

1.1 Archival Sources

Companhia Industrial de Matola, Maputo, Mozambique

1.2 Unpublished Dissertations

Ashforth, Adam. 1987. *On the "Native Question": A Reading of the Grand Traditions of Commissions of Inquiry*. D. Phil. Dissertation. Oxford University.

Bowen, Merle L. 1986. *"Let's Build Agricultural Producer Cooperatives": Socialist Agricultural Development Strategy in Mozambique, 1975-1983*. Ph.D. Dissertation. University of Toronto.

Corrigan, Philip. 1977. *State Formation and Moral Regulation in Nineteenth-Century Britain: Sociological Investigations*. Ph.D. Dissertation. Durham University.

Harasim, Linda. 1984. *Literacy and National Reconstruction in Guinea Bissau: A Critique of the Freirean Literacy Campaign*. Ph.D. Dissertation. OISE.

Lind, Agenta. 1988. *Adult Literacy: Lessons and Promises. Mozambican Literacy Campaigns 1978-1982*. Ph.D. Dissertation. Institute of International Education, University of Stockholm.

Marshall, Judith. 1972. *The Two Kingdoms: The Political Economy of Dependency*. Masters' Thesis. Institute of Social Studies. The Hague, Holland.

Roesch, Otto. 1986. *Socialism and Rural Development in Mozambique. The Case of Aldeia Comunal 24 de Julho*. Ph.D. Dissertation. University of Toronto.

1.3 Interviews, Survey Results, etc.

During the course of my fieldwork from May 1985 to April 1986, I carried out extensive interviews and made detailed field notes. These were based on participant observation at Matola Industrial Company (CIM) and a four month study visit to Latin America with four provincial adult education instructors. I have also drawn on interview notes on women in factories in Mozambique by Stephanie Urdang which included interviews with women in CIM carried out in 1980. This material has been used with the author's permission.

2 SECONDARY SOURCES

2.1 Official Publications

CIM (Companhia Industrial de Matola). 1985a. "Intervenção do Director Geral da Companhia Industrial da Matola, António Almeida Matos, por Ocasião da Comemoração do 5 Aniversário do Intervencionamento pelo Estado." Maputo, July 20, 1985, Mimeo.

CIM (Companhia Industrial de Matola). 1985b. "Mensagem do Fenias Matsinhe, Secretário da Celula do Partido por Ocasião do 5 Aniversário do Intervencionamento da CIM pelo Estado." Matola, July 20, 1985.

Conselho Coordenador de Recenseamento. 1983. "1° Recenseamento Geral da População:" Informação Publica.

Council of Ministers, People's Republic of Mozambique. 1980. "Address to the Council of Ministers by the President of Mozambique, Samora M. Machel."

Council of Ministers, People's Republic of Mozambique. 1981. *Law 1/81*.

Fonseca, Rui. 1983. "Information on the Development of Literacy Programmes in Mozambique." Paper presented to an international seminar on Cooperating For Literacy, Berlin, October 1983, sponsored by the German Foundation for International Development.

FRELIMO (Inhambane Province). 1975. "Report to the National Seminar on Literacy in Ribáuè, April 1975."

FRELIMO (Manica and Sofala Province). 1975. "Report to the National Seminar on Literacy in Ribáuè, April 1975."

FRELIMO (Maputo Province) 1975. "Report to the National Seminar on Literacy in Ribáuè, April 1975."

FRELIMO (Nampula Province). 1975. "Report to the National Seminar on Literacy in Ribáuè, April, 1975."

FRELIMO (Tete Province) 1975. "Report to the National Seminar on Literacy in Ribáuè, April, 1975."

FRELIMO. 1976. "The match that lights the flame." Document submitted to UNESCO, January 1976. London: CFMAG, 1976.

Frelimo Party. 1977. "Como Age o Inimigo. Análise política da situação económica e social do país." Maputo: Imprensa do Partido.

Frelimo Party. 1983. "Out of Underdevelopment to Socialism." Maputo: INLD.

I.L.O. 1985. PARTICIPATORY RESEARCH IN NICARAGUA "Report on a Pilot Project." A document prepared by Malena de Montis for the Rural Employment Policies Branch, International Labour Organization, Geneva, May 1985.

Ministry of Education (INDE). 1983. "O processo de Alfabetização em Moçambique. O desenvolvimento das metodologias de Alfabetização." Maputo, Ministry of Education and Culture.

Ministry of Education (INDE). 1984. "The Problematic of Literacy in Mozambique." Study carried out by the National Institute for Education Development, Maputo.

Ministry of Education and Culture (DNAEA). 1978. "Basic orientations for speeches to open the 1st National Literacy Campaign."

Ministry of Education and Culture (DNEA). 1984. "A Experiência de Alfabetização e Educação de Adultos na República Popular de Moçambique." Document presented to the Seminar on Literacy and Adult Education for Portuguese-speaking Countries, São Tomé and Príncipe, June 22-July 3, 1984.

Ministry of Education and Culture (INDE). 1982. "Sistemas de Educação em Moçambique."

Ministry of Information, Mozambique. 1985. "Documentos da Gorongosa." Maputo, Mozambique: INLD.

National Planning Commission. 1984. "Economic Report."

Vieira, Sérgio. 1977. "The New Man is a Process." Address to the Second Conference of the Ministry of Education and Culture held in Maputo December, 1977.

2.2 Books, Journals and Unpublished Papers

Abrams, P. 1988. "Notes on the difficulty of studying the state." *Journal of Historical Sociology*. I, 1 (March): 58-89.

Aim (Mozambique Information Agency) Bulletin. Maputo, Mozambique.

Alonso, Ana Maria. 1988. "The Effects of Truth: Re-Presentations of the Past and the Imagining of Community." *Journal of Historical Sociology* I, 1 (March): 33-57.

Almond, Gabriel. 1960. *The Politics of the Developing Areas*. Princeton: Princeton University Press.

Anderson, C.A. & M.J. Bowman (eds.). 1965. *Education and Economic Development*. Chicago: Aldine Publishing Company.

Anderson, Perry. 1961/2. "Portugal and the End of Ultra-Colonialism." *New Left Review* 15 (May June): 83-102; 16 (July August): 88-123; 17 (Winter): 85-114.

Apter, David. 1965. *The Politics of Modernization*. Chicago: The University of Chicago Press.

Arnove, Robert F. (1986). *Education and Revolution in Nicaragua*. New York: Praeger.

Arnove, Robert F. and Harvey J. Graff (eds.). 1987. *National Literacy Campaigns in Historical and Comparative Perspective*. New York: Plenum Publishers.

Arrighi, Giovanni and John Saul. 1973. *Essays on the Political Economy of Africa*. New York: Monthly Review Press.

Arruda, Marcos. 1982. *Semeando a Democracia Participante: Educação Popular e Reforma Agrária na Nicaragua*. Rio de Janeiro: IBASE.

Azevedo, Mario. 1977. "A Century of Colonial Education in Mozambique" in Mugomba, A. & M. Nyaggah (eds.). 1980. *Independence Without Freedom*. International Conference of Colonial Education and Contemporary Conflict in Southern Africa, 1977. University of California, Santa Barbara.

Becker, Howard S. 1970. *Sociological Work*. Chicago: Aldine Publishing Company.

Bernstein, Basil. 1973. *Class, Codes and Control*, Volume I. London: Routledge and Kegan Paul.

Bernstein, Basil. 1977. *Class, Codes and Control*, Volume 3, 2nd edition. London: Routledge and Kegan Paul.

Bernstein, Henry and Philip Corrigan. 1984. "Neither market nor state: an alternative approach to development." *Third World Studies*. Block 5. Parts C-D. London: Open University Press.

Bhola, H. S. 1984. "Campaigning for Literacy". Report of a study submitted to UNESCO. Toronto: International Council for Adult Education.

Blaug, M. 1970. *An Introduction to the Economics of Education*. London: Allen Lane.

Brandão, Carlos Rodrigues (org.) 1987. *A questão política da educação popular*. São Paulo: Editora Brasiliense.

Brett, E.A. 1973. *Colonialism and Underdevelopment in East Africa*. New York: NOK Publishers, Ltd.

Carbonnier, George. 1969. *Conversations with Levi Strauss*.

Castillo, Afonso and Pablo Latapi. 1983. *Educacion no Formal de Adultos en América Latina*. Santiago, Chile: UNESCO Regional Office for Latin America and the Caribbean.

Cazden, C. and V. John and D. Hymes. 1972. *The Functions of Language in the Classroom*. New York: Teachers' College Press.

Chua, Beng-Huat. 1979. "Democracy as a Textual Accomplishment." *The Sociological Quarterly* 20 (August): 541-549.

Cipolla, C. 1969. *Literacy and Development in the West*. Harmondsworth: Penguin.

Clanchy, Michael. 1979. *From Memory to Written Record: England 1066-1307*. Boston: Harvard University Press.

Clanchy, Michael. 1981. "Literacy and illiteracy: hearing and seeing: England 1066-1307." Harvey J. Graff. *Literacy and Social Development in the West*. Cambridge: Cambridge University Press.

Cliff, Julie. 1990. "The War on Women in Mozambique: Health Consequences of South African Destabilization, Economic Crisis and Structural Adjustment. Mimeo.

Comaroff, Jean. 1985. *Body of Power, Spirit of Resistance*. Chicago: University of Chicago Press.

Comaroff, Jean and John Comaroff. 1988. "Through the looking glass: colonial encounters of the first kind." *Journal of Historical Sociology* I, 1 (March): 6-32.

Coraggio, José Luis. 1986. "Economics and Politics in the Transition to Socialism: Reflections on the Nicaraguan Experience." Fagen, Richard, Carmen Diana Deere and José Luis Coraggio. *Transition and Development*. New York: Monthly Review Press.

Correia, Sonia and Eduardo Homem. 1977. *Moçambique: Primeiras Machambas*. Rio de Janeiro: Margem Editora.

Corrigan, Philip (ed.) 1980. *Capitalism, State Formation and Marxist Theory*. London: Quartet Books.

Corrigan, Philip. 1982. "Towards a Celebration of Difference(s)." D. Robins. *Rethinking Social Inequality*. London: Gower Press.

Corrigan, Philip. 1983. "Into Textuality: timing our words." *Sociological Review*, 31(4) (November): 759-768.

Corrigan, Philip. 1986. "In/forming Schooling." David W. Livingstone and Contributors. *Critical Pedagogy and Cultural Power*. North Hadley, Massachussets: Bergin and Garvey.

Corrigan, Philip and Valerie Gillespie. 1978. *Class Struggle, Social Literacy and Idle Time*. Brighton: Noyce.

Corrigan, Philip and Harvie Ramsay and Derek Sayer. 1978. *Socialist Construction and Marxist Theory: Bolshevism and its Critique*. New York: Monthly Review Press.

Corrigan, Philip and Derek Sayer. 1981. "How the Law Rules: Variations on Some Themes in Karl Marx." Bob Fryer, Alan Hunt et al. (eds.). *Law, State and Society*. London: Croom Helm.

Corrigan, Philip and Derek Sayer. 1984. *Marxist Theory and Socialist Reconstruction in Historical Perspective*. Utafiti. Dar es Salaam, 6(2), (1984): 127-158.

Corrigan, Philip and Derek Sayer. 1985. *The Great Arch*. Oxford: Blackwell.

Corrigan, Philip and Derek Sayer. 1987. "Revolution Against the State: the context and significance of Marx's later writings." *Dialectical Anthropology* 12: 65-82.

Corrigan, Philip, Bruce Curtis and Robert Lanning. 1987. "The Political Space of Schooling." Witherspoon, Terry (ed.). *The Political Economy of Canadian Schooling*. Toronto: Methuen.

Cressy, David. 1980. *Literacy and the Social Order: Reading and Writing in Tudor England*. Cambridge: Cambridge University Press.

Dale, Roger. 1977. "The Hidden Curriculum for the Sociology of Teaching." Denis Gleeson (ed.). *Identity and Structure: Issues in the Sociology of Education*. Nafferton, Driffied: Nafferton Books.

Davidson, Basil. 1979. "The Revolution of People's Power: Notes on Mozambique 1979." *Race and Class* xxi 2: 127-143.

Davidson, Basil. 1992. "Africa: The Politics of Failure." Miliband, Ralph and Leo Panitch. *New World Order? Socialist Register*. London: The Merlin Press, 1992.

Davidson, Basil, J. Slovo and A.R. Wilkinson. 1976. *Southern Africa; The New Politics of Revolution*. Harmondsworth: Penguin.

de Brito, Luis. 1980. "Dependência Colonial e Integração Regional." *Estudos Moçambicanos*. Maputo, Mozambique 1: 23-32.

Dickenson, Margaret (ed). 1972. *When Bullets Begin to Flower*. Nairobi.

Draper, H. 1977,1978. *Karl Marx's Theory of Revolution*. New York: Monthly Review Press.

Duffy, James. 1959. *Portuguese Africa*. Cambridge, Harvard University Press.

Edwards, A.D. 1980. "Patterns of Power and Authority in Classroom Talk." Peter Woods (ed.). *Teacher Strategies*. London: Croom Helm.

Egero, Bertil. 1986. "People's Power. The Case of Mozambique." Barry Munslow (ed.). *Africa's Problems in the Transition to Socialism*. London: Zed Press.

Egero, Bertil. 1987. *Mozambique: A Dream Undone. The Political Economy of Democracy, 1975-1984*. Uppsala: Nordiska afrikainstitutet.

Eisenstein, Elizabeth. 1979. *The Printing Press as an Agent of Change*. Cambridge: Cambridge University Press.

Eisenstein, Elizabeth. 1981. "Some Conjectures About the Impact of Printing on Western Society and Thought: A Preliminary Report." *Journal of Modern History* 40: 7-29.

Elias, N. 1978. *The Civilizing Process, Volume I: The history of manners*. Oxford: Blackwell.

Fagen, Richard, Carmen Diana Deere and José Luis Coraggio. 1986. *Transition and Development*. New York: Monthly Review Press.

Fauvet, Paul. 1984. "Roots of Counter-Revolution: The Mozambique National Resistance." *Review of African Political Economy* 29: 108-121.

Fauvet, Paul and Alves Gomes. 1982. "The Mozambique National Resistance." *AIM Information Bulletin* (Supplement), No. 69.

Ferreira, Eduardo de Sousa. 1974. *Portuguese Colonialism in Africa: The End of an Era*. Paris: UNESCO Press.

First, Ruth. 1983. *Black Gold. The Mozambican Miner. Proletarian and Peasant*. Sussex: The Harvester Press.

Fitzgerald, Patrick. 1990. "Democracy and Civil Society in South Africa. A Response to Daryl Glaser." *ROAPE*. No. 49, 1990: 94-110.

Fordham, Paul (ed.). 1983. "Cooperating for Literacy." Report of an International Seminar held in Berlin, October 1983. International Council for Adult Education: Toronto.

Foucault, Michel. 1972, 1975. *Power/Knowledge: Selected Interviews and Other Writings 1972-1977*. New York: Pantheon Books.

Foucault, Michel. 1982. "The Subject and Power." *Critical Inquiry* No. 8, (Summer): 777-795.

Freire, Paulo. 1970. *Pedagogy of the Oppressed*. New York: Seabury Press.

Freire, Paulo. 1973. *Education for Critical Consciousness*. New York: Seabury Press.

Freire, Paulo. 1975. *Cultural Action for Freedom*. Harmondsworth: Penguin Books.

Freire, Paulo. 1985. *The Politics of Education*. Massachusetts: Bergin and Harvey Publishers, Inc.

Freire, Paulo and Donaldo Macedo. 1987a. *Literacy. Reading the Word and the World*. Massachusetts: Bergin and Harvey Publishers, Inc.

Freire, Paulo and Ira Shor. 1987b. *A Pedagogy for Liberation: Dialogues on Transforming Education*. Massachusetts: Bergin and Harvey Publishers, Inc.

Furet, Francois and Jacques Ozouf. 1977. "Three centuries of cross-fertilization: France." Harvey J. Graff (ed.). 1981. *Literacy and Social Development in the West: A Reader*. London: Cambridge University Press.

Giroux, Henry. 1980. "Teacher Education and the Ideology of Social Control." *Journal of Education*, Boston University, 162(1): 5-27.

Glaser, Barney G. and Anselm L. Strauss. 1967. *The Discovery of Grounded Theory: Strategies for Qualitative Research*. Chicago: Aldine Publishing Co.

Graff, Harvey. 1978/9. "Literacy Past and Present: Critical Approaches in the Literacy/Society Relationship." *Interchange*. Vol. 9, No. 2: 1-21.

Graff, Harvey. 1979. *The Literacy Myth*. New York: Academic Press.

Graff, Harvey (ed.) 1981. *Literacy and Social Development in the West*. Cambridge: Cambridge University Press.

Graff, Harvey. 1987a. *The Labyrinth of Literacy. Reflections on Literacy Past and Present*. London: Falmer Press.

Graff, Harvey. 1987b. *The Legacies of Literacy*. Bloomington: Indiana University Press.

Hammersley, M. 1977. "School Learning: the cultural resources required to answer a teacher's questions." P. Wood and M.Hammersley (eds.) *School Experience*. London: Croom Helm, 1977.

Hanlon, Joseph. 1984. *The Revolution Under Fire*. London: ZED.

Hanlon, Joseph. 1986. *Beggar Your Neighbours*. London: CIIR.

Hanlon, Joseph. 1991. *Mozambique: Who Calls the Shots?* London: James Currey Publications.

Harries, Patrick. 1982. "Kinship, ideology and the nature of pre-colonial labour migration: labour migration from the Delagoa Bay hinterland to south Africa, up to 1895." Marks, Shula and Richard Rathbone (eds.). 1982. *Industrialisation and Social Change in South Africa African Class Formation, Culture and Consciousness, 1870-1930*. London: Longman.

Heath, Shirley Brice. 1983. *Ways With Words: Language, Life and Work in Communities and Classrooms*. New York: Cambridge University Press.

Hedges, David. 1982. *Education, Missions and the Political Ideology of Assimilation, 1930-1960*. Maputo: Eduardo Mondlane University.

Hirshon, Sheryl L. with Judy Butler. 1983. *And Also Teach Them to Read*. Westport, Connecticut: Lawrence Hill & Company.

Hoyles, Martin (ed.). 1977. *The Politics of Literacy*. London: Writers and Readers Publishing Cooperative.

Illich, Ivan. 1981. *Shadow Work*. Boston. London: Marion Boyars.

Isaacman, Allan and Barbara Isaacman. 1983. *Mozambique from Colonialism to Revolution, 1900-1982*. Boulder, Colorado: Westview Press.

Jara, Oscar H. 1981. "Educação popular: a dimensão educativa da ação política." São Paulo: *CEPES Educação e Sociedade*, No.10.

Jessop, Bob. 1980. *The Capitalist State*. Oxford: Martin Robinson.

Johanssen, Egil. 1977. "The History of Literacy in Sweden." *Educational Reports Umea*. No.12: 2-42.

Johnston, Anton. 1989. *Study, Produce and Combat! Education and the Mozambican State*. Stockholm: Institute of International Education Akademi Press.

Judt, Tony. 1979. *Socialism in Provence 1871-1914*. Cambridge: Cambridge University Press.

Katzenellenbogen, Simon E. 1982. *South Africa and Southern Mozambique*. Manchester, Manchester University Press.

Lewis, Magda and Roger Simon. 1987. "A Discourse Not Intended for Her: Learning and Teaching Within Patriarchy." *Harvard Educational Review*. Vol. 56, No. 4, (November): 457-471.

Leys, Colin. 1975. *Underdevelopment in Kenya. The Political Economy of Neo-Colonialism*. Berkley: University of California Press.

Lind, Agneta. 1985. *O Desafio da Alfabetização*. Stockholm: Swedish International Development Authority (SIDA), Education division document No. 27 (December).

Lind, Agneta. 1988. *Adult Literacy Lessons and Promises: Mozambique Literacy Campaigns 1978-1982*. Stockholm: Institute of International Education Akademi Press.

Lockridge, K.A. 1974. *Literacy in Colonial New England*. New York: Norton.

Lofland, John. 1971. *Analyzing Social Settings*. Belmont, California: Wadsworth.

Machado de Graça, João and Maria Cremilda Messingue. 1990. "Mozambique and South Africa are bound by bitter past and shared destiny" *CUSO Journal*. July 1990:M5-M7.

Machel, Samora. 1974. "Educate Man to Win the War, Create a New Society and Develop Our Country," Speech at the Second Conference of the Department of Education and Culture, September 1970, quoted in Machel, Samora. *Mozambique Sowing the Seeds of Revolution*. London: CFMAG.

Machel, Samora. 1975. "The People's Republic of Mozambique: The Struggle Continues." Address at the Proclamation of Independence Ceremonies, June 25, 1975, in *Review of African Political Economy* 4 (November): 14-25.

Machel, Samora. 1975,1985. "Development of the People's Democratic Revolution in Mozambique." *National Liberation Struggles in the Portuguese African Colonies 1961-1973*. Moscow: Science, 1975. Quoted in Munslow, Barry (ed.) *Samora Machel: An African Revolutionary*. London: Zed Books Ltd., 1985.

Machel, Samora. 1976. "Notre tache principale: Batir une societe nouvelle. Interview with Samora Machel." *Afrique-Asie* 109 (May): 17-30.

Magaia, Lina. 1990. "Mother." *CUSO Journal*. Ottawa July 1990: M8-M11.

Marks, Shula and Anthony Atmore (eds.). 1980. *Economy and Society in Pre-Industrial South Africa*. London: Longman.

Marks, Shula and Richard Rathbone (eds.). 1982. *Industrialisation and Social Change in South Africa African Class Formation, Culture and Consciousness, 1870-1930*. London: Longman.

Marshall, Judith. 1976. "The State of Ambivalence: Right and Left Options in Ghana." *Review of African Political Economy*. No. 5: 49-62.

Marshall, Judith. 1984. *Reflexões sobre uma experiência de alfabetização no campo*. Ilha Josina Machel. Maputo, DNEA, August.

Marshall, Judith. 1985. "Making Education Revolutionary." John Saul. *A Difficult Road: The Transition to Socialism in Mozambique*. New York: Monthly Review Press.

Marshall, Judith and Susan McCord. 1987. "Pilot Project, Adult Education Staff Training in Mozambique, Phase Four Evaluation." National Directorate of Adult Education, October 1987.

Marshall, Judith. 1990a. "Gracias Nicaragua! Obrigado Brazil! South-South Exchanges as an Approach to Staff Training" in *Convergence*. Vol. XXIII, Number 1, 1990: 100-107.

Marshall, Judith. 1990b. "Literacy and People's Power in a Mozambican Factory" *Comparative Education Review*. Vol. 34, No. 1, February 1990: 61-84.

Marshall, Judith. 1990c. "Training for Empowerment: A Kit of Materials for Popular Literacy Workers Based on an Exchange Among Education from Mozambique, Nicaragua and Brazil." Toronto: Doris Marshall Institute.

Marshall, Judith. 1991. "Structural Adjustment in Mozambique: The Human Dimension." *Review of African Political Economy*. No. 47, 1991.

Marshall, Judith. 1992. *War, Debt and Structural Adjustment in Mozambique: The social impact*. Ottawa: North-South Institute, 1992.

Marx, Karl. 1845,1959. "Theses on Feuerbach," 1845 in Lewis S. Feuer (ed.). *Marx and Engels*. New York: Anchor Books.

Miller, Valerie. 1985 *Between Struggle and Hope: The Nicaraguan Literacy Crusade*. Boulder, Colorado: Westview Press.

Mondlane, Eduardo. 1969, 1983. *The Struggle for Mozambique*. Harmondsworth: Penguin Books Ltd. Reprint ed. London: Zed Press.

Mozambiquefile. No. 165. April 1990.

Munslow, Barry. 1983. *Mozambique: The Revolution and its Origins*. London: Longman.

Peixoto, Valentina. n.d. "O Seminário de Bagamoyo." Unpublished report from a meeting on literacy organized by the FRELIMO Department of Education and Culture in Bagamoyo, Tanzania, 1974.

Penvenne, Jeanne. 1979a. "The Streetcorner Press: Worker Intelligence Networks in Lourenco Marques, Mozambique, 1900-1962." Paper presented to the 22 Annual Meeting of the African Studies Association, Los Angeles, October/November 1979.

Penvenne, Jeanne. 1979b. "Attitudes Toward Race and Work in Mozambique Lourenco Marques, 1900-1974." Paper presented to the Second International Meeting on Modern Portugal, Durham, New Hampshire, June 1979.

Poulantzas, Nicolas. 1978. *State, Power, Socialism*. London: Verso.

Raikes, Philip. 1984. "Food Policy and Production in Mozambique Since Independence." *Review of African Political Economy* 29 (July): 95-107.

Robinson, William I. and Kent Norsworthy. 1985. "Nicaragua: The Strategy of Counter-revolution." *Monthly Review*. Vol. 37, No. 7 (December): 11-24.

Rockhill, Kathleen. 1987. "Gender, Language and the Politics of Literacy." *British Journal of Sociology in Education*. Vol. 8, No. 2: 153-168.

Roesch, Otto. 1987. *Rural Mozambique Since the FRELIMO Party Congress: The Situation in the Baixo Limpopo*. Toronto: York University. Mimeo.

Rostow, W. W. 1960. *The Stages of Economic Growth*. London: Cambridge University Press.

Sanderson, Michael. 1972. "Literacy and Social Mobility in the Industrial Revolution in England." *Past and Present*. No. 56 (August): 75-104.

Saul, John. 1973. "FRELIMO and the Mozambican Revolution." Giovanni Arrighi and John Saul (eds.) *Essays on the Political Economy of Africa*. New York: Monthly Review Press.

Saul, John. 1979. *The State and Revolution in Eastern Africa*. New York: Monthly Review Press.

Saul, John (ed.) 1985. *A Difficult Road: The Transition to Socialism in Mozambique*. New York: Monthly Review Press.

Sayer, Derek. 1987. *The Violence of Abstraction: Analytic Foundations of Historical Materialism*. London: Blackwell.

Schofield, R.S. 1973. "Dimensions of illiteracy, 1750-1850." *Explorations in Economic History* 10: 437-454.

Schofield, R.S. 1968. "The Measurement of Literacy in Pre-industrial England." J.R. Goody. *Literacy in Traditional Societies*. Cambridge: Cambridge University Press.

Searle, Chris. 1981. *We're Building the New School! Diary of a Teacher in Mozambique*. London: Zed Press.

Searle, Chris. 1984. *Words Unchained. Language and Revolution in Granada*. London: Zed Press.

Serra, Carlos & Eduardo Medeiros (eds.) 1983. *História de Moçambique, Volume 2, Agressão Imperialista (1886/1930)*. Maputo: Cadernos Tempo.

Simon, Roger I. 1987. "Empowerment as a Pedagogy of Possibility" in *Language Arts*. Vol. 64, No. 4 (April): 370-382.

Sketchley, Peter. 1985." The Struggle for New Social Relations of Production in Industry" in John Saul (ed.), *A Difficult Road: The Transition to Socialism in Mozambique*. New York: Monthly Review Press.

Smith, Dorothy. 1973. "Women, Family and Corporate Captalism." N.M Stevenson (ed.). *Women in Canada. Toronto: New Press.*

Smith, Dorothy. 1975. "The Social Construction of Documentary Reality." *Sociological Inquiry*. Vol. 44, No. 4: 257-268.

Smith, Dorothy. 1984. "Textually Mediated Social Organization." *International Social Science Journal*. Vol. xxxvi, No. 1 (September): 59-75.

Smith, Dorothy: 1987. *The Everyday World as Problematic. A Feminist Sociology*. Toronto: University of Toronto Press.

Spradley, James P. 1980. *Participant Observation*. New York: Holt, Rinehart & Winston.

Stoer, Stephen. 1981. "Democracy and socialism in education in Portugal." Roger Dale, Geoff Esland, Ross Fergusson and Madeleine MacDonald. *Schooling and the National Interest*. Sussex: The Falmer Press.

Stone, Lawrence. 1969. "Literacy and Education in England 1640-1900." *Past and Present*, No. 42: 76-83.

Sumner, C. 1981. *Crime, Justice and Underdevelopment*. London: Heinemann.

Terdiman, Richard. 1985. *Discourse-Counter-Discourse*. New York: Cornell University Press.

Thompson, E.P. 1963, 1968. *The Making of the English Working Class*. London: Victor Gollancz. Reprint ed. with revisions Harmondsworth: Penguin.

Torres, Carlos Alberto. 1983. "Adult Education Policy, Capitalist Development and the Class Alliance: Latin America and Mexico." *International Journal of Political Education*. Vol. 6. No. 2 (August): 157-173.

Torres, Rosa Maria. 1982. *De Alfabetizando a Maestro Popular: La Pos-Alfabetizacion en Nicaragua*. Managua: INIES.

Torres, Rosa Maria. 1985. *NICARAGUA. Revolucion Popular. Educacion Popular.* Managua: Editorial Linea.

Torres, Rosa Maria. 1986. *Los CEP: Educacion Popular e Democracia Participativa en Nicaragua.* Managua, CRIES, Cuadernos de Pensamiento Proprio.

Urdang, Stephanie. 1979. *Fighting Two Colonialisms: Women in Guinea-Bissau.* New York: Monthly Review Press.

Urdang, Stephanie. 1980. Unpublished interview notes.

Urdang, Stephanie. 1985. "The Last Transition? Women and Development." John S. Saul (ed.) *A Difficult Road: The Transition to Socialism in Mozambique.* New York: Monthly Review Press.

Urdang, Stephanie. 1988. *And Still They Dance.* New York: Monthly Review Press.

van Onselen, Charles. 1980. *Chibaro: African Mine Labour in Southern Rhodesia 1900-1933.* Johannesburg, Raven Press.

Vasconcelos, Leite. 1990. "Mozambique's Painful Transition" *CUSO Journal. July 1990: M2-M4.*

Vilas, Carlos M. 1986. *The Sandinista Revolution.* New York: Monthly Review Press.

"A Voz do Mineiro" in *Estudos Africanos* (1) 1980: 77-90.

Walsh, Catherine. 1987. "Language, Meaning, and Voice: Puerto Rican Students' Struggle for a Speaking Consciousness." *Language Arts.* Vol. 64, No. 2 (February): 196-206.

West, Gordon. 1987. ""Nicaragua is a School": A Progressive Educational Alternative for Latin American Youth in the Global Economic Crisis." Toronto: OISE, Department of Sociology in Education.

Winter, Gordon. 1981. *Inside Boss.* London: Penguin.

Witherspoon, Terry (ed.). 1987. *The Political Economy of Canadian Schooling.* Toronto: Methuen.

Wuyts, Marc. 1989. "Economic Management and Adjustment Policies in Mozambique." *Working Paper Series No.* 52. The Hague, The Netherlands: Institute of Social Studies, 1989.

About the Book

To pose questions about literacy is to pose questions about power and voice and whose experiences and language are validated in text. Whatever the dimensions of human liberation attached to literacy, literacy is also about governance and being governed. It is never just a question of reading and writing but also a question of the complex interplay of language meanings and practices, based as much on class, race, and gender as on grammar and syntax.

This critical, ethnographic study explores how women and men in a Mozambican factory in the mid-1980s made sense of literacy and the different ways they used it in their daily lives. The study explores the meanings factory workers brought to the literacy classroom of schooling and language, and what validity they attached to their own knowledge and to themselves as learners. These meanings were shaped by a history of Portuguese colonial domination in which education—and mastery of the Portuguese language—signalled the path from "savagery" and "indigenous" status to "civilization" and "assimilation" as Portuguese citizens. The meanings shifted dramatically at independence when the Frelimo government, which had won power through a decade of armed struggle, put Mozambique on a socialist development path. "People's power" in Mozambique included a commitment to mass literacy programs. The study probes the tensions between literacy as a tool for more active workers' voices and more grassroots democracy versus literacy as a tool for mobilizing at the base for top-down initiatives.

Linking micro- and macrolevels of analysis, the author examines the differentiated and changing meanings of literacy through an intense process of social change. The originality of the study lies in its ability to move from the intimacy of workers' lives in the microworld of the factory literacy classroom to the broadest questions of civil society, socialist construction, and participatory democracy.